OXFORD STUDIES I

OXFORD STUDIES IN METAPHYSICS

Editorial Advisory Board
David Chalmers (Australian National University)
Tamar Gendler (Syracuse University)
Sally Haslanger (MIT)
John Hawthorne (Rutgers University)
Kathrin Koslicki (Tufts University)
E. J. Lowe (University of Durham)
Brian McLaughlin (Rutgers University)
Kevin Mulligan (Université de Genève)
Theodore Sider (Rutgers University)
Timothy Williamson (Oxford University)

Managing Editor
Jason Turner (Rutgers University)

OXFORD STUDIES IN METAPHYSICS

Volume 2

Edited by
Dean W. Zimmerman

CLARENDON PRESS · OXFORD

OXFORD
UNIVERSITY PRESS

Great Clarendon Street, Oxford OX2 6DP

Oxford University Press is a department of the University of Oxford.
It furthers the University's objective of excellence in research, scholarship,
and education by publishing worldwide in

Oxford New York

Auckland Cape Town Dar es Salaam Hong Kong Karachi
Kuala Lumpur Madrid Melbourne Mexico City Nairobi
New Delhi Shanghai Taipei Toronto

With offices in

Argentina Austria Brazil Chile Czech Republic France Greece
Guatemala Hungary Italy Japan Poland Portugal Singapore
South Korea Switzerland Thailand Turkey Ukraine Vietnam

Oxford is a registered trade mark of Oxford University Press
in the UK and in certain other countries

Published in the United States
by Oxford University Press Inc., New York

© The Several Contributors 2006

The moral rights of the authors have been asserted
Database right Oxford University Press (maker)

First published 2006

All rights reserved. No part of this publication may be reproduced,
stored in a retrieval system, or transmitted, in any form or by any means,
without the prior permission in writing of Oxford University Press,
or as expressly permitted by law, or under terms agreed with the appropriate
reprographics rights organization. Enquiries concerning reproduction
outside the scope of the above should be sent to the Rights Department,
Oxford University Press, at the address above

You must not circulate this book in any other binding or cover
and you must impose the same condition on any acquirer

British Library Cataloguing in Publication Data

Data available

Library of Congress Cataloging in Publication Data

Data available

Typeset by SPI Publisher Services, Pondicherry, India
Printed in Great Britain
on acid-free paper by
Biddles Ltd. King's Lynn, Norfolk

ISBN 0-19-929058-X   978-0-19-929058-1
ISBN 0-19-929059-8 (Pbk.)   978-0-19-929059-8 (Pbk.)

1 3 5 7 9 10 8 6 4 2

PREFACE

Oxford Studies in Metaphysics is dedicated to the timely publication of new work in metaphysics, broadly construed. The subject is taken to include not only perennially central topics (e.g. modality, ontology, and mereology) but also metaphysical questions that emerge within other subfields (e.g. philosophy of mind, philosophy of science, and philosophy of religion). Each volume also contains that year's winner of the *Oxford Studies in Metaphysics* Younger Scholar Prize, described within.

D.W.Z

New Brunswick, NJ

CONTENTS

Oxford Studies in Metaphysics Younger Scholar
Prize Announcement ... ix

I. SYMPOSIUM: PROPERTY DUALISM

1. Max Black's Objection to Mind–Body Identity ... 3
   Ned Block
2. Mary and Max and Jack and Ned ... 79
   John Perry
3. A Posteriori Identities and the Requirements of Rationality ... 91
   Stephen L. White

II. THE OPEN FUTURE

4. Goodbye Growing Block ... 103
   Trenton Merricks
5. Rashi's View of the Open Future: Indeterminateness and Bivalence ... 111
   Eli Hirsch
6. General Facts, Physical Necessity, and the Metaphysics of Time ... 137
   Peter Forrest

III. ISSUES IN ONTOLOGY

7. Inexpressible Properties and Propositions ... 155
   Thomas Hofweber
8. Aristotle's Constituent Ontology ... 207
   Michael Loux
9. The Relation between General and Particular: Entailment vs. Supervenience ... 251
   Phillip Bricker

10. Epistemicism and Semantic Plasticity 289
    John Hawthorne

IV. METAPHYSICS AND THEISM

11. God and the Problem of Universals 325
    Brian Leftow
12. A Theistic Argument against Platonism
    (and in Support of Truthmakers and Divine Simplicity) 357
    Michael Bergmann and Jeffrey Brower
13. Beautiful Evils 387
    Hud Hudson

    Index 397

THE *OXFORD STUDIES IN METAPHYSICS* YOUNGER SCHOLAR PRIZE

Sponsored by the A. M. Monius Institute and administered by the editorial board of *Oxford Studies in Metaphysics*, the essay competition is open to scholars who are within ten years of receiving a Ph.D. or students who are currently enrolled in a graduate program. (Independent scholars should inquire of the editor to determine eligibility.) The award is $2,500. Winning essays will appear in *Oxford Studies in Metaphysics*, so submissions must not be under review elsewhere.

Essays should generally be no longer than 10,000 words; longer essays may be considered, but authors must seek prior approval by providing the editor with an abstract and word count by 1 November 2006. To be eligible for next year's prize, submissions mailed within the United States or from Canada must be postmarked by 15 January 2007. Authors mailing submissions from elsewhere should insure that they arrive before 20 January. Refereeing will be blind; authors should omit remarks and references that might disclose their identities, but enclose a cover letter with contact information. Receipt of submissions will be acknowledged by e-mail. The winner is determined by a committee of members of the editorial board of *Oxford Studies in Metaphysics*, and will be announced in late February 2007. At the author's request, the board will simultaneously consider entries in the prize competition as submissions for publication in *Oxford Studies in Metaphysics*, independently of the prize.

Previous winners of the Younger Scholar Prize are:

Thomas Hofweber, "Inexpressible Properties and Propositions", this volume;

Matthew McGrath, "Four-Dimensionalism and the Puzzles of Coincidence", forthcoming in Vol. 3.

Cody Gilmore, "Time Travel, Coinciding Objects, and Persistence", forthcoming in Vol. 3.

The A. M. Monius Institute is a non-profit organization dedicated to the revival of traditional metaphysics. Information about other activities of the A.M. Monius Institute may be found at *www.ammonius.org*.

Inquiries and submissions should be addressed to:

Dean Zimmerman, Editor
Oxford Studies in Metaphysics
Philosophy Department
Rutgers University
Davison Hall, Douglass Campus
New Brunswick, NJ 08903

Part I

SYMPOSIUM: PROPERTY DUALISM

1. Max Black's Objection to Mind–Body Identity

Ned Block

In his famous article advocating mind–body identity, J. J. C. Smart (1959) considered an objection (Objection 3) that he says he thought was first put to him by Max Black. He says "it is the most subtle of any of those I have considered, and the one which I am least confident of having satisfactorily met". This argument, the "Property Dualism Argument," as it is often called, turns on much the same issue as Frank Jackson's (1982, 1986) "Knowledge Argument", or so I will argue. This chapter is aimed at elaborating and rebutting the Property Dualism Argument (or rather a family of Property Dualism Arguments) and drawing some connections to the Knowledge Argument.[1] I will also be examining John Perry's (2001) book which discusses both Max Black's argument and the Knowledge Argument, and some arguments drawn from Stephen White's (1983) paper on the topic and some arguments inspired by unpublished papers by White.

I gratefully thank the following persons for commenting on a remote ancestor of this paper: Paul Horwich, Brian Loar, David Pitt, Stephen Schiffer, Susanna Siegel, Stephen White, and Dean Zimmerman; and my thanks to Tyler Burge, David Chalmers, and Stephen White for comments on a more recent version. I also thank students in my graduate seminar, participants in the NEH Santa Cruz Summer Institute of 2002, participants at an ANU Workshop ("Themes from Ned Block") in the summer of 2003, and the audience at the University of Houston for reactions to parts of the remote ancestor.

[1] Stephen White (1983, forthcoming *a*, *b*) has done more than anyone to elucidate the Property Dualism Argument. John Perry's (2001) book develops machinery that he uses against modal arguments for dualism, Jackson's Knowledge Argument and the Property Dualism Argument. Christopher Hill (1991, 1997), Joseph Levine (2001), and Colin McGinn (2001) have also put forward versions of the argument. Some of David Chalmers's (1996, 2004) arguments for dualism involve similar ideas. Brian Loar's (1990 and 1997) papers are also immersed in the territory of the argument, although not explicitly about it. Jerome Schaffer (1963) discusses the argument but in somewhat different terms than those used more recently. I will focus on a version of the Property Dualism Argument similar to the arguments given by Smart (though see n. 4), White, and Perry, and I will contrast my refutation with Perry's.

4 | Ned Block

I discovered rather late in writing this chapter (from Rozemond 1998[2]) that many of my arguments, especially those in the last third of the chapter, amount to a physicalistic adaptation of Arnauld's criticisms of Descartes. As I understand it, Arnauld criticized Descartes's idea that we have a complete intuition of the mental substance by arguing that nothing in our intuitive grasp of the mental rules out an objective "backside" to the mental whose objective description is out of reach of our intituitive grasp.

I will say a bit about what the basic idea of the Property Dualism Argument is and compare it with the Knowledge Argument. Then I will discuss Perry's view of both issues. Next, I will introduce an ambiguity in the notion of mode of presentation and use that to give a more precise statement and rebuttal of one version of the Property Dualism Argument. That is the first half of the chapter. In the second half, I will use this long set-up to exposit and rebut another version of the Property Dualism Argument and mention some related arguments. This chapter is long and detailed. Those who are very familiar with the issues will find it too long and detailed, but given the prevalence of confusion on these matters, I felt it was better to err on the side of explicitness.

I. WHAT IS THE PROPERTY DUALISM ARGUMENT?

Smart said "suppose we identify the Morning Star with the Evening Star. Then there must be some properties which logically imply that of being the Morning Star, and quite distinct properties which entail that of being the Evening Star." And he goes on to apply this moral to mind–body identity, concluding that "there must be some properties (for example, that of being a yellow flash) which are logically distinct from those in the physicalist story." (1959: 148) He later characterizes the objection to physicalism as "the objection that a sensation can be identified with a brain process only if it has some phenomenal property ... whereby one-half of the identification may be, so to speak, pinned down" (149), the suggestion apparently being that the problem of physicalism will arise for that phenomenal property even if the original mind–body identity is true. This concern motivated the "dual-aspect" theory, in which mental events are held to be identical to physical events even

[2] I am indebted to Tyler Burge for drawing the Rozemond book to my attention.

though those mental events are alleged to have irreducible mental properties. (See also Schaffer 1963.) Smart did not adequately distinguish between token events (e.g. this pain) and types of events (e.g. pain itself), or between token events and properties such as the property of being a pain, the property of being pain, or the property of being in pain—the first being a property of pains, the second being a property of a property, and the last being a property of persons. (For purposes of this chapter, I will take types of events to be properties—any of those just mentioned will do.) But later commentators have seen that the issue arises even if one starts with a mind–body property identity, even if the mind–body identity theory that is being challenged says that the property of being in pain (for example) is identical to a physical property. For the issue arises as to how that property is "pinned down", to use Smart's phrase. If the mind–body identity says that phenomenal property Q = brain property B_{52}, then the question raised by the argument is: is the property by which Q is pinned down non-physical or is something non-physical required by the way it is pinned down?[3]

John Perry (2001: 101) states the argument as follows: "even if we identify experiences with brain states, there is still the question of what makes the brain state an experience, and the experience it is; it seems like that must be an additional property the brain state has.... There must be a property that serves as our mode of presentation of the experience as an experience." Later in discussing Jackson's Knowledge Argument, Perry considers the future neuroscientist, Mary, who is raised in a black and white room (which Perry calls the Jackson Room) and learns all that anyone can learn about the scientific nature of the experience of red without ever seeing anything red. While in the room, Mary uses the term 'Q_R' for the sensation of red, a sensation whose neurological character she knows but has never herself had. Perry (ibid.) says:

If told the knowledge argument, Black might say, "But then isn't there something about Q_R that Mary didn't learn in the Jackson room, that explains the difference between 'Q_R is Q_R' which she already knew in the Jackson room, and (5) [Perry's (5) is: 'Q_R is this subjective character'], which she didn't?" There must be a new mode of presentation of that state to which "Q_R" refers, which is to say some additional and *apparently non-physical*

---

[3] White (1983, forthcoming a, b) runs the Property Dualism Argument against both token and type mind–body identities, but I am ignoring the issue of token identity.

aspect of that state, that she learned about only when she exited the room, that explains why (5) is *new* knowledge.[4]

On one way of understanding Perry, he uses 'mode of presentation' here, not in the usual Fregean sense of something cognitive or semantic about a representation, but rather for a property of the represented referent. It seems that he sees Black's problem as arising from the question of the physicality of the mode of presentation in that non-Fregean sense of the term. Smart speaks in the same spirit of a property that pins down one half of the identification.

The idea of the Property Dualism Argument, and, I will argue, the Knowledge Argument, is that the mind–body identity approach to phenomenality fails in regard to the phenomenality that is involved in a certain kind of subjective mode of presentation (in both the Fregean and non-Fregean senses mentioned) of a phenomenal state. Even if a mind–body identity claim is true, when we look at the mode of presentation of the mental side of the identity, we are forced to accept a "double aspect" account in which unreduced phenomenal properties remain. However, don't expect a full statement of the main version of the Property Dualism Argument until nearly the halfway point. The next items on the agenda are connections to the Knowledge Argument, then (section II) Perry's solutions to both problems. Then (section III) I will take up the question of the difference between and respective roles of the Fregean and non-Fregean notions of mode of presentation.

Consider a specific phenomenal property, Q, e.g. the property of feeling like the pain I am having right now. (If pain just is a type of feel, then Q is just pain.) The physicalist says, let us suppose, that Q = cortico-thalamic oscillation of such and such a kind. (I will drop the last six words.) This is an a posteriori claim. Thus the identity depends on

---

[4] Part of what Smart says is hard to interpret. I left out a crucial phrase in the Smart quotation that seems confused. What I left out is the italicized phrase in the following: "the objection that a sensation can be identified with a brain process only if it has some phenomenal property, *not possessed by brain processes*, whereby one-half of the identification may be, so to speak, pinned down". The italicized phrase is puzzling since Smart gives every indication of thinking that the threat from Max Black's objection is from a "double aspect" theory that says that token pains are token brain states, but that the token pains have irreducible *phenomenal properties*. The dualism is supposed to derive from the non-physicality of the phenomenal property, not a failure of the phenomenal property to apply to the brain processes. Perry explicitly avoids Smart's error when he says: "even if we identify experiences with brain states, there is still the question of what makes the brain state an experience, and the experience it is; it seems like that must be an additional property the brain state has".

the expressions on either side of the '=' expressing distinct concepts, that is, having distinct modes of presentation, for if the concepts and modes of presentation were the same, it is said, the identity would be a priori. (An ambiguity involved in this reasoning—involving (surprise!) the distinction between Fregean and non-Fregean modes of presentation—will be scrutinized in section IV.)

'Q' in my terminology is very different from 'Q_R' in Perry's terminology since 'Q_R' is a term that Mary understands in the black and white room. 'Q' by contrast is meant (by me even if not by Perry and Smart) as the verbal expression of a *phenomenal* concept. A phenomenal concept of the experience of red is what Mary lacked in the black and white room and what she gained when she went outside it. (She also lacked a phenomenal concept of the color red, but I will not depend on that.) Why do I insist that 'Q' express a phenomenal concept? Because the mind–body identity claim under consideration must be one in which the phenomenal property is referred to *under a phenomenal concept of it* for the Property Dualism Argument—in any of its forms—*even to get off the ground*. (The Knowledge Argument also depends on the use of a phenomenal concept in my sense.) Suppose that in the original identity claim we allowed *any old concept* of Q—e.g. 'the property whose onset of instantiation here was at 5 p.m.' or 'the property whose instantiation causes the noise "ouch" '. There is no special problem having to do with phenomenality for the physicalist about the cognitive significance of such properties or how such properties could pick out their referents. The modes of presentation of these properties raise no issues of the metaphysical status of phenomenality. If the original paradigm of mind–body identity were "the property whose onset of instantiation here was at 5 p.m. = cortico-thalamic oscillation", the property in virtue of which the left-hand term presents the referent would not be a special candidate for non-physicality. It would be the property of being instantiated here starting at 5 p.m. The Property Dualism Argument depends on an identity in which a *phenomenal concept* is involved on the mental side. To allow a non-phenomenal concept is to discuss an argument that has only a superficial resemblance to the Property Dualism Argument.

With all this emphasis on phenomenal concepts, you might wonder what they are supposed to be. A phenomenal concept is individuated with respect to fundamental uses that involve the *actual occurrence* of phenomenal properties. In these fundamental uses, an actually occurring experience is used to think about that very experience. No one could have a phenomenal concept if they could not in some way relate the concept to such fundamental uses in which the subject actually has an instance of the phenomenal quality.

That is what I mean by a phenomenal concept, but in the rest of this chapter, I will often adopt a simplification: the fundamental uses will be taken to be all the uses of the concepts. That is, I will assume that in the exercise of a phenomenal concept, the subject actually has to have an experience. Phenomenal concepts in this heavy duty sense do not really correspond to the kind of general ability that we take concepts to be individuated by. But since it is really these fundamental uses that figure in this chapter, it will make matters simpler if we simply talk about the concepts as if their only uses were the fundamental uses. The idea of these heavy duty phenomenal concepts is that an instantiation of a phenomenal property is used in the concept to pick out a phenomenal property (a type). Of course, the experience involved in the fundamental use need not be an *additional* experience, that is, additional to the referent. A single experience can be both the object of thought and part of the way of thinking about that object. Further, one does not *have* to have an experience of red in order to think about an experience of red. One can think about the experience of red using, for example a purely descriptional concept of it, e.g. "the color of ripe tomatoes".[5]

Perry (2001, 2004a, b) uses what may be a more relaxed notion of phenomenal concept, in which a phenomenal concept is a kind of mental folder that contains what he calls a "Humean idea" of the experience. He says (2004b: 221):

Thinking of having the experience of some kind in this way is not having the experience, but it is in some uncanny way like it. Usually the same kinds of emotions attach to the thinking as to the having, although in a milder form. It is usually pleasant to anticipate or imagine having pleasant experiences, and unpleasant to anticipate or imagine having unpleasant ones, for example.

Perry's notion of a phenomenal concept is vague on the crucial point. Sure, thinking of having the experience is not just having the experience. Dogs can have experiences but presumably they can't think about

---

[5] The heavy duty notion of phenomenal concepts has its origins in Brian Loar (1990, 1997); a version that is closer to what I have in mind is described briefly in Block (2002) and accounts that share the structure I am talking about appear in David Chalmers (2003), David Papineau (2002), and in an unpublished paper by Kati Balog.

them. The question is: does a phenomenal concept in Perry's sense require that the subject relate the concept to the fundamental uses I mentioned that involve an actual experience? Or, putting the point more clearly in terms of my simplified notion of a phenomenal concept, does the exercise of a phenomenal concept in Perry's sense involve an actual experience? As I shall argue in the section on Perry below, the problem for Perry's treatment hinges on whether phenomenal concepts in his sense are phenomenal enough to give the Knowledge Argument and the Property Dualism Argument a fighting chance.

It is time to turn to my claim that the Knowledge Argument hinges on the same requirement of a phenomenal concept in my sense as the Property Dualism Argument. Mary is reared in a colorless environment but learns all there is to know about the physical and functional nature of color and color vision. Yet she acquires new knowledge when she leaves the room for the first time and sees colored objects. Jackson concludes that there are facts about what it is like to see red that go beyond the physical and functional facts, and so dualism is true. From the outset, the following line of response has persuaded many critics.[6] Mary knew about the subjective experience of red via an objective concept from neuroscience. On leaving the room, she acquires a subjective concept of the same subjective experience. In learning what it is like to see red, she does not learn about a new property. She knew about that property in the room under an objective concept of it and what she learns is a new concept of that very property. One can acquire new knowledge about old properties by acquiring new concepts of them. I may know that there is water in the lake and learn that there is H_2O in the lake. In so doing, I do not learn of any new property instantiated, and in that sense I do not learn of any new fact. I acquire new knowledge that is based on a new concept of the property that I already knew to be instantiated in the lake. When Mary acquires the new subjective concept that enables her to have new knowledge, the new knowledge acquired does not show that there are any properties beyond the physical properties. Of course it does require that there are concepts that are not physicalistic concepts; however, that is not a form of dualism but only garden-variety conceptual pluralism: concepts of physics are also distinct from concepts of, say, economics and concepts of biology. The idea

---

[6] The articles by Paul Churchland, Brian Loar, William Lycan, and Robert van Gulick in Block, Flanagan, and Güzeldere (1997) all take something like this line, as do Horgan (1984) and Sturgeon (1994).

of the argument is to substitute a dualism of concepts for a dualism of properties and facts: there is a new concept but no new properties or facts in the relevant sense.

A natural rejoinder from the dualist is this. After seeing red for the first time, how does Mary "pin down" (to use Smart's obscure phrase) that old property? Or, to use an equally obscure phrase, what is Mary's "mode of presentation" of that old property?[7] When she acquires a subjective concept of the property that she used to have only an objective concept of, *a new unreduced subjective property* is required to pin down the old objective property. *This is the key stage in the dialectic about Mary, and this stage of the dialectic brings in the same considerations that are at play in the Property Dualism Argument.* Just to have a name for it, let us call this idea that the phenomenal concept that Mary acquires itself contains or else requires unreduced phenomenality the "metaphenomenal" move in the dialectic.[8]

The issue is sometimes put in terms of a distinction between two kinds of propositions. (See van Gulick 1993, 2005.) Coarse-grained propositions can be taken to be sets of possible worlds (or, alternatively, Russellian propositions that are n-tuples of objects and properties but contain no (Fregean) modes of presentation). The proposition (in this sense) that Harry Houdini escaped is the same coarse-grained proposition as the proposition that Erich Weiss escaped, in that the possible worlds in which Harry Houdini escaped are the same as the worlds in which Erich Weiss escaped, because Harry Houdini is Erich Weiss. (Alternatively, these are the same Russellian propositions because the proposition <Houdini, escaped> is the same proposition as <Weiss, escaped>.) Fine-grained propositions include (Fregean) modes of presentation, and so the different names determine different fine-grained propositions. When we say that Harry Houdini escaped, we express a

---

[7] Here, and in the rest of the discussion of Mary, unless otherwise stated, I intend both the Fregean and non-Fregean senses of "mode of presentation".

[8] I have the sense from a remark in Jackson (2004) that he might agree with this. On another issue: Jackson says that the matter should not be put in terms of whether there is a new fact involved in Mary's acquiring the subjective concept of the experience. When Mary closes her books and steps across the threshold, *everything* she does constitutes a new fact that was not described in her books. However, this would be motivation for a somewhat different way of setting up the Knowledge Argument in which Mary predicts everything that will happen to her in the first day of leaving the room *in physical terms*. So she does know about the fact of what she sees after leaving the room, albeit in physical terms. Using this device, one could then state the issue in terms of whether Mary learns any new facts.

different fine-grained proposition from the one we express when we say that Erich Weiss escaped. In these terms, the issue is: does Mary's new knowledge involve merely a new fine-grained proposition (in which case physicalism is unscathed because Mary's new knowledge does not eliminate any possibilities), or does it require a new coarse-grained proposition (as well)? *It is the phenomenal mode of presentation of Mary's new subjective concept of the property that she already had an objective concept of that motivates the idea that she gains new coarse-grained knowledge.* The metaphenomenal move is in play: the thought is that that phenomenal mode of presentation brings in something fundamentally ontological and not something on the order of (merely) a different description. The idea is that when something phenomenal is part of a mode of presentation, it will not do for the physicalist to say that that phenomenal item is unproblematically physical. Whether one agrees with this or not, if one does not recognize it, one misses a crucial step in the dialectic about Mary.

I said that the standard reply to Jackson's argument attempts to substitute a dualism of concepts for a dualism of properties and facts. But the dualist rejoinder that I have been describing—exploited in pretty much the same way by the Knowledge Argument and the Property Dualism Argument—is that the dualism of concepts *requires* a dualism of properties and facts.

I said that Mary acquires a subjective concept of the experience of red, whereas what she already had was an objective concept of it. However, it is a particular kind of subjective concept she acquires, namely a phenomenal concept of the experience of red. If it was an objective concept that she acquired, say the concept of the type of experience that occurred at 5 p.m., the argument would have no plausibility. But even some subjective concepts would not do, e.g. the concept of the type of experience that happened five minutes ago. This concept is subjective in that it involves the temporal location of the subject from the subject's point of view ("now"), but it is no more suitable for the Knowledge Argument than the objective concept just mentioned. What is required for the metaphenomenal move in the dialectic about the Knowledge Argument is that Mary acquires a mode of presentation that is either itself problematic for physicalism or that requires that the referent have a property that is problematic for physicalism. And in this, it is just like the Property Dualism Argument.

What Mary learns is sometimes put like this: "Oh, so *this* is what it is like to see red," where "what it is like to see red" is a phrase she understood in the black and white room, and the italicized 'this' is supposed to express a phenomenal concept. Since there is some doubt as to whether a demonstrative concept can really be a phenomenal concept (I'll explain the doubt below), we could put the point better by saying that what Mary learns is that P = the property of being an experience of red, where it is stipulated that 'P' expresses a phenomenal concept (of a phenomenal property) and "is an experience of red" is a term Mary understood in the black and white room. But there is nothing special about this item of knowledge in the articulation of the point of the Knowledge Argument as compared with other items of knowledge that use 'P'. In particular, one could imagine that one of the things that Mary learns is that P = the property of being cortico-thalamic oscillation. She already knew in the room that the experience of red = cortico-thalamic oscillation (where it is understood that 'the experience of red' is something she understood in the black and white room), but she learns that P = the property of being cortico-thalamic oscillation. The proposition that P = the property of being cortico-thalamic oscillation is supposed to be a new coarse-grained proposition, one that she did not know in the black and white room. This version of the Knowledge Argument makes the overlap with the Property Dualism Argument in the metaphenomenal move explicit: there is supposed to be something problematic about physicalism *if it is stated using a phenomenal concept*. That is, what is problematic is something about the "mode of presentation" of the phenomenal side of the identity. Both arguments can be put in the form: even if we take physicalism to be true, that supposition is undermined by the phenomenal "mode of presentation" in the knowledge or statement of it.[9]

[9] Although it would take me too far afield to go into the differences between the Knowledge Argument and the Property Dualism Argument, I should mention one: that the Knowledge Argument as usually stated concerns a supervenience form of physicalism (no mental difference without a physical difference) whereas the Property Dualism Argument is directed against mind–body identity. Indeed, Jackson is thinking of a really extreme form of physicalism which makes a commitment to all the facts following a priori from a set of base physical facts. Chalmers (1996) also regards this view as entailed by physicalism. On that view of physicalism, the Knowledge Argument is much more persuasive, since all that has to be shown is that what Mary learns does not follow a priori from what she already knows. On that form of physicalism, the move made here and in Perry's book of thinking of Mary as learning (or in Perry's case acquiring a sensitivity to) a new subjective concept of a property she already had an objective concept

I have used, more or less interchangeably, terms such as 'pin down', 'mode of presentation', 'concept', and 'way of thinking'. But there is an ambiguity (the ambiguity between Fregean and non-Fregean readings) that must be resolved in order to focus on a precise statement of these arguments. Before I turn to that topic, however, I will give a critique of Perry's approach to Max Black, the Knowledge Argument, and Modal arguments for dualism.

II. PERRY'S TREATMENT OF THE TWO ARGUMENTS

Perry's (2001, 2004a,b) approach to the Knowledge Argument is roughly along the lines mentioned above: that Mary does something like acquiring a new subjective concept of a property that she had an objective concept of already in the black and white room. But Perry gives that response two new twists with two ideas: that the new concept is part of what he calls a "reflexive content" and that Mary need not actually acquire the new concept so long as she is appropriately sensitive to it.

Here is a quotation from Perry (2001) that gives his response both to Max Black's problem and to the Knowledge Argument.

We can now, by way of review, see how Black's dilemma is to be avoided. Let's return to our imagined physicalist discovery, as thought by Mary, attending to her sensation of a red tomato:

"This$_i$ sensation = B_{52}" [where 'this$_i$' is an internal demonstrative and B_{52} is a brain property that she already identified in the black and white room—NB]

This is an informative identity; it involves two modes of presentation. One is the scientifically expressed property of being B_{52}, with whatever structural, locational, compositional and other scientific properties are encoded in the scientific term. This is not a neutral concept. The other is being a sensation that is attended to by Mary. This is a neutral concept; if the identity is true, it is the neutral concept of a physical property. Thus, according to the antecedent physicalist [who takes physicalism as the default view—NB], Mary knows the

---

of has little purchase. However, the Knowledge Argument can be discussed as it is here and in Perry's book from the perspective of a mind–body identity account of physicalism. The standard reply I have discussed is from that perspective, so even though some of the adherents of the Knowledge Argument are thinking of physicalism in a different way, that is irrelevant to the points made here.

brain state in two ways, as the scientifically described state and as the state that is playing a certain role in her life, the one she is having, and to which she is attending. The state has the properties that make it mental: there is something it is like to be in it and one can attend to it in the special way we have of attending to our own inner states. (2001: 205)

If Mary's concept were "being the sensation attended to by Mary" it could not be regarded as a topic-neutral concept unless the terms 'sensation' and 'attend' are themselves understood in a topic-neutral manner. (Ryle introduced the term "topic-neutral" for expressions that indicate nothing about the subject matter. Smart offered topic-neutral analyses of mental terms that were supposed neither to entail that the property is physical nor that it is non-physical. But it is clear that mentalistic terminology was supposed to be precluded, for otherwise no topic-neutral analyses would be needed—the terms would already have been topic-neutral.)

If Mary's concept is topic-neutral, it is not a phenomenal concept in the sense required by the Property Dualism Argument. Although Perry rejects the "deflationist" view that phenomenal concepts are analyzable a priori in non-phenomenal terms (as Smart advocated), his approach to arguments for dualism is to appeal to topic-neutral demonstrative/recognitional concepts as surrogates for phenomenal concepts. To explain what he has in mind, we need to introduce what he calls "reflexive content". Propositional attitudes have "subject matter" contents which are a matter of the properties and objects the attitudes are concerned with. The subject matter content of your belief that the morning star rises could be taken to be the Russellian proposition <Venus, rises>. But there are other contents that are concerned with the same subject matter and have the same truth condition: for example, that the heavenly object which you are now thinking of is in the extension of the property that is the object of your concept of rising. Before I mentioned it and brought it to your explicit attention, this might have been a reflexive content but not a subject matter content of your thought. ('Reflexive' is meant to indicate that what is being brought in has to do with the way thought and language fit onto the world or might fit onto the world.) The subject matter content of the claim that $this_i$ (where '$this_i$' is an internal demonstrative) = B_{52}, if physicalism is right, is the same as that $this_i$ = $this_i$ or that B_{52} = B_{52}. Perry's intriguing idea is that my belief can have reflexive contents, the concepts of which are not concepts that I actually have, or even if I have them, those concepts are not ones that I am exercising in using demonstrative or recognitional concepts that have those reflexive contents. However, he argues persuasively that these concepts may be psychologically relevant nonetheless if the subject is "attuned" to the concepts in reasoning and deciding. Attunement is a doxastic attitude that can have contents that are not contents of anything the subject believes or has concepts of. For example, I can be attuned to a difference in the world that makes a perceptual difference without conceptualizing the difference in the world. Perry's view is that our intuitions about contents are often a matter of reflexive contents that we are attuned to rather than to subject matter contents that we explicitly entertain.

Perry's solution to Max Black's problem and his reply to Jackson is to focus on a topic-neutral version of what Mary learns. I am not totally sure whether it is just the demonstrative/recognitional concept ('$this_i$') that is topic-neutral, or whether the reflexive content of it is also supposed to be topic-neutral. But both proposals evade the Max Black problem without solving it. In the passage quoted earlier, he says what Mary learns can be put in terms of '$This_i$ sensation is brain state B_{52}', where '$this_i$' is a topic-neutral internal demonstrative/recognitional concept. If the suggestion is that Mary acquires the belief that $this_i$ is brain state B_{52}, the problem is that the topic-neutral concept involved in this belief is not a phenomenal concept, so the real force of the Knowledge Argument (and Max Black's argument) is just ignored. However, it seems that Perry's suggestion is that Mary comes to be *attuned* to the relevant reflexive content instead of coming to believe it. He thinks that what Mary learns can be expressed in terms of something she is attuned to and Max Black's problem can be solved by appealing to attunement to the same content. That is, in using demonstrative and recognitional concepts in the thought "$This_i$ sensation = B_{52}", Mary becomes attuned to a reflexive content like "the sensation Mary is attending to is the scientifically described state" without explicitly exercising those concepts.

But does substituting attunement for belief avoid the problem of ignoring the real force of the argument? Does attunement help in formulating a response to the Mary and Max Black arguments that takes account of the metaphenomenal move in the Mary dialectic? I think not.

Distinguish between two versions of Jackson's "Mary". Sophisticated Mary acquires a genuine phenomenal concept when she sees red for the first time. Naive Mary is much less intellectual than Sophisticated

Mary. Naive Mary does not acquire a phenomenal concept when she sees red for the first time (just as a pigeon presumably would not acquire a new concept on seeing red for the first time), nor does she acquire an explicit topic-neutral concept, but she is nonetheless *attuned* to certain topic-neutral non-phenomenal content like that of "The sensation I am now attending to is the brain state I wrote my thesis on earlier." In addition, we might suppose (although Perry does not mention such a thing) that Naive Mary is also attuned to a genuine phenomenal concept of a color even though she does not actually acquire such a concept.

As I mentioned earlier, there is a well-known solution to the Mary problem that takes Mary as Sophisticated Mary. What Sophisticated Mary learns is a phenomenal concept of a physical property that she already had a physical concept of in the black and white room. Any solution to the Mary problem in terms of Naive Mary is easily countered by a Jacksonian opponent who shifts the thought-experiment from Naive to Sophisticated Mary. Consider this dialectic. Perry offers his solution. The Jacksonian opponent says "OK, maybe that avoids the problem of Naive Mary, but the argument for dualism is revived if we consider a version of the thought experiment involving Sophisticated Mary, that is a version of the thought-experiment in which Mary actually acquires the phenomenal concept instead of merely being attuned to it (or attuned to a topic-neutral surrogate of it). What Sophisticated Mary learns is a content that contains a genuine phenomenal concept. And that content was not available to her in the room. What she acquires is phenomenal knowledge (involving a phenomenal concept), knowledge that is not deducible from the physicalistic knowledge she had in the black and white room. So dualism is true." Indeed, it is this explicit phenomenal concept that makes it at least somewhat plausible that what Mary acquires is a new coarse-grained belief as well as a new fine-grained belief. Perry cannot reply to *this* version of the thought experiment (involving Sophisticated Mary) by appealing to the *other* one (that involves Naive Mary). And the thought experiment involving Sophisticated Mary is not avoided by appeal to attunement to a topic-neutral concept or even to a phenomenal concept.

As I indicated earlier, the crucial point in the dialectic about Mary is this: the dualist says "The concept that Mary acquires (or acquires an attunement to) has a mode of presentation that involves or requires unreduced phenomenality." If Perry appeals to the idea that the concept is topic-neutral or has a topic-neutral reflexive content, the dualist can reasonably say "But that isn't the concept I was talking about; I was talking about a genuinely phenomenal concept."[10]

Let us now turn to Perry's solution to the Max Black problem. Although the Max Black problem is mentioned a number of times in the book, Perry's solution is expressed briefly in what I quoted above. He clearly intends it to be a by-product of his solutions to the other problems. I take it that that solution is the same as the solution to the Mary problem, namely that the problem posed by the alleged non-physical nature of the mode of presentation of the phenomenal side of a mind–body identity or what is required by that mode of presentation can be avoided by thinking of what Mary learns in terms of a demonstrative/recognitional topic-neutral concept that—perhaps—has a topic-neutral reflexive content. The proponent of the Max Black argument (the Property Dualist) is concerned that in the mind-body identity claim 'P = B_{52}' where 'P' expresses a phenomenal concept, the phenomenal mode of presentation of 'P' undermines the reductionist claim that P = B_{52}. Someone who advocates this claim—and who, like Perry, rejects deflationist analyses of phenomenal concepts—is certainly not going to be satisfied by being told that the content that Mary is attuned to is topic-neutral. The Property Dualist will say "So what? My concern was that the mode of presentation of 'P' introduces an unreduced phenomenality; whether Perry's topic-neutral content is something we believe or are merely attuned to is not relevant." And even if what Mary is attuned to is a reflexive content that contains a genuine phenomenal concept, that also evades the issue without solving it, since the dualist can reasonably say that it is the actual phenomenal concept on which the argument for dualism is based.

Perry also applies his apparatus to the modal arguments for dualism such as Kripke's and Chalmers's. Why do we have the illusion that "$This_i$ sensation = B_{52}" is contingent, given that (according to physicalism) it is a metaphysically necessary truth? Perry's answer is that the

---

[10] Chalmers (2003) argues that phenomenal concepts cannot be demonstrative concepts. The main argument could be put as follows: for any demonstrative concept, say '$this_i$', $this_i$ has phenomenal property P would be news. But if the demonstrative concept was genuinely a phenomenal concept, there would be some claims of that form that are not news. I agree with the "not news" rule of thumb, though I would not go so far as to agree that it shows no demonstrative concept can be phenomenal. However, whether or not it shows that there can't be a concept that is both demonstrative and phenomenal, the demonstrative concepts that Perry is talking about are not phenomenal concepts in the sense required to motivate the Knowledge Argument and the Property Dualism Argument, the sense required to ground the metaphenomenal move.

necessary identity has some *contingent* reflexive contents such as: that the subjective character of red objects appears like so and so on an autocerebroscope, is called 'B_{52}', and is what I was referring to in my journal articles. The illusion of contingency comes from these reflexive contents. Here the metaphenomenal move I mentioned earlier has no role to play. I think Perry's point here has considerable force.

However, the dualist can respond to Perry by saying, "Look, I can identify the brain state by its *essential properties* and still wonder whether I could have that brain state (so identified) without *this$_i$* phenomenal property." A version of this argument, will be explored in section IV below.

Though I agree with Perry on many things about phenomenality, and find his book with its notion of attunement to reflexive concepts insightful and useful, there is one key item from which all our disagreements stem. He does not recognize the need for, or rather he is vague about the need for, a kind of phenomenal concept that itself requires fundamental uses that are actually experiential. When saying what it is that Mary learns, he says, "This new knowledge is a case of recognitional or identificational knowledge.... We cannot identify what is new about it with subject-matter contents; we can with reflexive contents" (2001: 147). The physicalist will agree that what Mary learns is not a *new* subject matter content (in the sense explained earlier). But the problem is that it is unclear whether the recognitional or identificational concepts that Perry has in mind have the phenomenality required to avoid begging the question against the advocate of Max Black's argument. When he proposes to explain away the intuitions that motivate the Max Black argument and the Knowledge Argument by appeal to a topic-neutral concept, he loses touch with what I called the metaphenomenal move and with it the intuitive basis of these arguments in phenomenal concepts, or so it seems to me.

The reader may have noticed that there has still not been an explicit statement of the Property Dualism Argument. I have postponed the really difficult and controversial part of the discussion, the explanation of an ambiguity in 'mode of presentation', a matter to which I now turn.

III. MODES OF PRESENTATION

The "mode of presentation" of a term is often supposed to be whatever it is on the basis of which the term picks out its referent. The phrase is also used to mean the cognitive significance of a term, which is often glossed as whatever it is about the terms involved that explain how true identities can be informative. (Why is it informative that Tony Curtis = Bernie Schwartz but not that Tony Curtis = Tony Curtis?) However, it is not plausible that these two functions converge on the same entity, as noted in Tyler Burge (1977) and Alex Byrne and Jim Pryor (forthcoming).[11]

I believe that these two functions or roles are not satisfied by the same entity, and so one could speak of an ambiguity in 'mode of presentation'. However, perhaps confusingly, the Property Dualism Argument depends on a quite different ambiguity in 'mode of presentation'.[12] I will distinguish between the cognitive mode of presentation (CMoP) and the metaphysical mode of presentation (MMoP). The CMoP is the Fregean mode of presentation mentioned earlier, a constellation of mental (cognitive or experiential) and semantic features of a term or mental representation that plays a role in determining its reference, or, alternatively but not equivalently, constitutes the basis of explanation of how true identities can be informative (and how rational disagreement is possible—I will take the task of explaining informativeness and rational disagreement to be the same, using 'cognitive significance' for both. I will also tend to simplify, using "cognitive" to describe the relevant constellation of features. Since semantic and experiential differences make a cognitive difference, they don't need to be mentioned separately). The importantly different, non-Fregean, and less familiar mode of presentation, the MMoP, is a property of the referent. There are different notions of MMoP corresponding to different notions of CMoP. Thus if the defining feature of the CMoP is taken to be its role in determining reference, then the MMoP is the property of the referent in virtue of which the CMoP plays this role in determining reference. If the defining feature of the CMoP is taken to be explaining cognitive significance, then the MMoP is the property of the referent in virtue of which cognitive significance is to be explained.

---

[11] Burge describes the two functions of Fregean sense as sense$_1$ and sense$_2$. (He also mentions a third function, sense$_3$, providing entities to be denoted in oblique contexts, which will not be discussed here. Byrne and Pryor talk of two different roles, the informativeness or cognitive significance role and the reference-determination role.

[12] A similar but not identical distinction is introduced in arguing for Property Dualism in two unpublished papers by Stephen White (White, unpublished *a*, *b*). These are my terms, not White's, and I do not agree with White about key features of the distinction. I will attribute very little specific content to White's unpublished papers, since those papers are in draft form as of the writing of this chapter.

For example, suppose, temporarily, that we accept a descriptional theory of the meaning of names. On this sort of view, the CMoP of 'Hesperus' might be taken to be cognitive features of 'the morning star'. 'The morning star' picks out its referent in virtue of the referent's property of rising in the morning rather than its property of being covered with clouds or having a surface temperature of 847 degrees Fahrenheit. The property of the referent of rising in the morning is the MMoP. (And this would be reasonable for both purposes: explaining cognitive significance and determining the referent.) The CMoP is much more in the ballpark of what philosophers have tended to take modes of presentation to be, and the various versions of what a CMoP might be are also as good candidates as any for what a concept might be. The MMoP is less often thought of as a mode of presentation—perhaps the most salient example is certain treatments of the causal theory of reference in which a causal relation to the referent is thought of as a mode of presentation. (Devitt 1981).

In the passage quoted earlier from Perry's statement of Max Black's argument, Perry seemed often to be talking about the MMoP. For example, he says: "even if we identify experiences with brain states, there is still the question of what makes the brain state an experience, and the experience it is; it seems like that must be an additional property the brain state has ... There must be a property that serves as our mode of presentation of the experience as an experience" (2001: 101, underlining added). Here he seems to be talking about the MMoP of the brain state (i.e. the experience if physicalism is right). When he says what Max Black would say about what Mary learns, he says: " 'But then isn't there something about Q_R that Mary didn't learn in the Jackson room, that explains the difference between 'Q_R is Q_R' which she already knew in the Jackson room, and (5) [(5) is: Q_R is this subjective character], which she didn't?" There must be a new mode of presentation of that state to which 'Q_R' refers, which is to say some additional and *apparently non-physical* aspect of that state, that she learned about only when she exited the room, that explains why (5) is *new* knowledge" (ibid., underlining added) Again, 'aspect' means property, a property of the state. So it looks like in Perry's rendition, a mode of presentation is an MMoP. However, his solution to Max Black's problem involves the idea that the concept that Mary acquires or acquires sensitivity to is topic-neutral, and that makes it look as if the issue in the Property Dualism Argument is centered on the CMoP. He says, speaking of a mind–body identity: "This is an informative identity; it involves two modes of presentation. One is the scientifically expressed property of being B_{52}, with whatever structural, locational, compositional and other scientific properties are encoded in the scientific term. This is not a neutral concept. The other is being a sensation that is attended to by Mary. This is a neutral concept; if the identity is true, it is the neutral concept of a physical property" (underlining added). The properties of being B_{52} and being a sensation that is attended to by Mary are said by Perry to be properties, but also concepts. The properties are modes of presentation in the metaphysical sense, but concepts are naturally taken to be or to involve modes of presentation in the cognitive sense. The view he actually argues for is: "We need instead the topic-neutrality of demonstrative/recognitional concepts" (205).

When I described the metaphenomenal move in the dialectic concerning the Knowledge Argument, I said the phenomenal concept that Mary acquires itself contains or else requires unreduced phenomenality. Why "contains or else requires"? In terms of the CMoP/MMoP distinction: if the CMoP that Mary acquires is partly constituted by an unreduced phenomenal element, then we could say that the concept contains unreduced phenomenality. If the MMoP that is paired with the CMoP involves unreduced phenomenality, one could say that the concept that Mary acquires *requires* an unreduced phenomenal property, as a property of the referent.

In the next section (IV) I will state a version of the Property Dualism Argument in terms of MMoPs. But as we shall see, that argument fails because of what amounts to equivocation: one premise is plausible only if modes of presentation are MMoPs, the other premise is plausible only if modes of presentation are CMoPs. A second version of the Property Dualism Argument (V) will also be couched initially in terms of MMoPs, but that treatment is tactical, and the argument will involve some degree of separate discussion of CMoPs and MMoPs.

I will pause briefly to say where I stand on the main issue. The Property Dualism Argument is concerned with a mind–body identity that says that phenomenal property Q = brain property B_{52}. The worry is that the mode of presentation of Q brings in a non-physical property. But mode of presentation in which sense? Start with the CMoP. Well, a phenomenal CMoP has a constituent that is phenomenal and is used to pick out something phenomenal. Let me explain.

If I think about the phenomenal feel of my pain *while I am having it*, I can do that in a number of different ways. I could think about it using the description "the phenomenal feel of this pain". Or I could think about it using the phenomenal feel of the occurring pain itself as part of the concept. But if a token phenomenal feel does double duty in this way (as a token of an aspect of both the pain and our way of thinking of the pain), no extra specter of dualism arises. If the phenomenal feel is a physical property, then it is a physical property even when it (or a token of it) does double duty. The double duty is not required by a phenomenal concept. One could in principle use one phenomenal feel in a CMoP to pick out a different phenomenal feel; e.g. the phenomenal feel of seeing green could be used to pick out the phenomenal feel of seeing red if the concept involves the description "complementary" in the appropriate way. But there is no reason to think that such a use brings in any new specter of dualism.

Move now to the MMoP. We can think about a color in different ways, using different properties of that color. I might think of a color via its property of being my favorite color or the only color I know of whose name starts with 'r'. Or, I may think about it via its phenomenal feel. And what holds of thinking about a color holds for thinking about the phenomenal feel itself. I can think of it as my favorite phenomenal feel or I can think about it phenomenally, for example, while looking at the color or imagining it. If the referent is a phenomenal property P, the MMoP might be taken to be the property of being (identical to) P. If P is physical, so is being P. So the MMoP sense generates no new issue of dualism. That is where I stand. The Property Dualist, by contrast, thinks that there are essential features of modes of presentation that preclude the line of thought that I expressed. That is what the argument is really about.[13]

---

[13] Although I am defending physicalism in this chapter, I do think there is a genuinely troubling argument for dualism, one that is completely different from Kripke's and Chalmers' modal arguments, the Knowledge Argument, and the Property Dualism Argument. What I have in mind is the multiple realization argument discussed in Block (2002): if there could be a creature whose phenomenology has a sufficiently different physical basis from ours, but whose phenomenology is similar to ours, then there would be a phenomenal similarity which is not explained by a physical similarity.

I spoke earlier of double duty. A phenomenal feel in a concept is used to pick out a phenomenal feel. But what I have just suggested amounts to "triple duty". A phenomenal feel in the CMoP serves to pick out a phenomenal feel as referent via a closely related phenomenal feel as MMoP. I don't want to make much of this "triple duty". The notions of CMoP and MMoP are artificial notions that make more intuitive sense in some cases than in others.

I have not given a detailed proposal for the nature of a phenomenal CMoP, since my case does not depend on these details. But for concreteness, it might help to have an example. We could take the form of a phenomenal CMoP to be "the experience: —", where the blank is filled by a phenomenal property, making it explicit how a CMoP might mix descriptional and non-descriptional elements.[14] If the property that fills the blank is phenomenal property P, the MMoP that is paired with this CMoP might be the property of *being P* and the referent might be P itself.

I will turn now to a bit more discussion of the CMoP/MMoP distinction and then move to stating and refuting the Property Dualism Argument.

Different versions of the Property Dualism Argument presuppose notions of CMoP and MMoP geared to different purposes. I have mentioned two purposes, fixing reference and accounting for cognitive significance. A third purpose—or rather a constraint on a purpose—is the idea that the MMoP is a priori accessible on the basis of the CMoP. And since one cannot assume that these three functions (cognitive significance, fixing reference, a priori accessibility) go together, one wonders how many different notions of CMoP and MMoP there are. Burge (1977) and Byrne and Pryor (forthcoming) give arguments that—although put in different terms—can be used to make it plausible that these three *raisons d'être* of modes of presentation do not generally go together. However, I will rebut the Property Dualism Argument without relying—except at one point—on any general claim that this or that function does not coincide with a different function. All of the versions of the CMoP that I will be considering share a notion of a CMoP as a cognitive entity, for example a mental representation. The MMoP, by contrast, is always a property of the referent. One way in which the different *raison/s d'être* matter is that for fixing reference, the MMoP must not only apply to the referent but uniquely pick it out—and further, have been in effect given a special authority in picking out the referent by the subject. But when it comes to cognitive significance, the MMoP need not even apply to the referent (as Byrne and Pryor note in somewhat different terms), so long as it seems to the subject to apply. However, I will not be making use of this difference.

---

[14] I take this formulation from Papineau (2002), although he does not use the CMoP/MMoP distinction. See also Block (2002) for a somewhat different formulation.

Physicalists say that everything is physical and thus they are committed to the claim that everything cognitive, linguistic, and semantic is physical. However, not all issues for physicalism can be discussed at once, and since the topic of this chapter is the difficulty for physicalism posed by phenomenality, I propose to assume that the cognitive, linguistic, and semantic features of CMoPs do not pose a problem for physicalism so long as they do not involve anything phenomenal.

I will argue that the key step in the Property Dualism Argument can be justified in a number of ways, assuming rather different ideas of what MMoPs and CMoPs are (so there is really a family of Property Dualism Arguments). There are many interesting and controversial issues about how to choose from various rather different ways of fleshing out notions of CMoP and MMoP. My strategy will be to try to avoid these interesting and controversial issues, sticking with the bare minimum needed to state and critique the Property Dualism Argument. In particular, I will confine the discussion to CMoPs and MMoPs of singular terms, since the mind–body identities I will be concerned with are all of the form of an '=' flanked by singular terms (usually denoting properties). I will not discuss belief contexts or other oblique contexts. The reader may wonder if all these different and underspecified notions of mode of presentation are really essential to any important argument. My view, which I hope this chapter vindicates, is that there is an interesting family of arguments for dualism involving a family of notions of mode of presentation and that this family of arguments is worth spelling out and rebutting.

Am I assuming the falsity of a Millian view, according to which modes of presentation do not figure in a proper understanding of concepts? Without modes of presentation, the Property Dualism Argument does not get off the ground, so if Millianism assumes that there are no modes of presentation involved in concepts, then I am assuming Millianism is false. However, the view of phenomenal concepts that I will be using has some affinities with a Millian view. In addition, I will be considering a version of the Property Dualism Argument (in the next section) in which metaphysical modes of presentation on both sides of the identity are assumed to be identical to the referent.

Modal arguments for dualism such as Kripke's and Chalmers's attempts to move from epistemic premises to metaphysical conclusions. (For example, the epistemic possibility of zombies is appealed to in order to justify a claimed metaphysical possibility of zombies.) A similar dynamic occurs with respect to the Property Dualism Argument. One way it becomes concrete in this context is via the issue of whether in an identity statement with different CMoPs there must be different MMoPs. That is, is the following principle true?

D(CMoP) → D(MMoP): A difference in CMoPs in an identity statement entails a difference in MMoPs

Prima facie, it seems that the D(CMoP) → D(MMoP) principle is false. Consider the identity 'the wet thing in the corner = the thing in the corner covered or soaked with H_2O'. Suppose the CMoP associated with the left-hand side of the identity statement to be the description 'the wet thing in the corner'. Take the corresponding MMoP to be the property of being the wet thing in the corner. Analogously for the right-hand side. But the property of being the wet thing in the corner = the property of being the thing in the corner covered or soaked with H_2O. $MMoP_1 = MMoP_2$, i.e. there is only one MMoP, even though here are two CMoPs.

Of course, a theorist who wishes to preserve the D(CMoP) → D(MMoP) principle, seeing MMoPs as shadows of CMoPs, can postulate different, more fine-grained quasi-linguistic-cognitive MMoPs that are individuated according to the CMoPs. There is no matter of fact here but only different notions of CMoP and MMoP geared to different purposes. In the discussion to follow, I will focus on the cognitive significance purpose of the CMoP/MMoP pair, since I think that rationale is the most favorable to the view I am arguing against, that we must—that we are forced to—individuate MMoPs according to CMoPs.[15]

Consider the familiar "Paderewski" example. Our subject starts out under the false impression that there were two Paderewskis of the turn of the twentieth century, a Polish politician and a Polish composer. Later, he has forgotten where he learned the two words and remembers nothing about one Paderewski that distinguishes him from the other.

---

[15] This (putative) example of the failure of the D(CMoP) → D(MMoP) principle is suboptimal in a number of ways. Something can be wet by being soaked with a liquid other than water and paint can be wet without being soaked at all. The words 'water' and 'H_2O' are different, and that might be said to provide a genuine metalinguistic difference in properties. Further, 'Water' is simple and 'H_2O' is compositional giving rise to another difference in properties. (Despite these flaws, I will use the example later in the chapter.) These flaws are corrected in a type of counterexample to come now. (See n. 29 as well.)

That is, he remembers only that both were famous Polish figures of the turn of the twentieth century. Prima facie, the cognitive properties of the two uses of 'Paderewski' are the same. For the referent is the same and every property associated by the subject with these terms is the same. We could give a name to the relevant cognitive difference by saying that the subject has two "mental files" corresponding to the two uses of 'Paderewski'. We could regard the difference in mental files as a semantic difference, or we could suppose that semantically the two uses of 'Paderewski' are the same, but that there is a need for something more than semantics—something cognitive but non-semantic—in individuating CMoPs. In either case, there are two CMoPs but only one MMoP, the MMoP being, say, the property of being a famous turn-of-the-twentieth-century Pole named 'Paderewski'. Thus "Paderewski = Paderewski" could be informative to this subject, despite identical MMoPs for the two terms.

As Loar (1988) notes, Paderewski-type situations can arise for general terms, even in situations where the subject associates the same description with the two uses of the general term. An English speaker learns the term 'chat' from a monolingual French speaker who exhibits cats, and then is taught the term 'chat' again by the same forgetful teacher exhibiting the same cats. The student tacitly supposes that there are two senses of 'chat' which refer to creatures that are different in some respect that the student has not noticed or perhaps some respect that the student could not have noticed, something biological beneath the surface that is not revealed in the way they look and act. We can imagine that the student retains two separate mental files for 'chat'. Each file has some way of specifying some observable properties of chats, for example that they are furry, purr, are aloof, are called 'chat', and most importantly, each of the files says that there are two kinds of creatures called 'chat': chats in the current sense are not the same as chats in the other sense. So if the student learns 'this chat = this chat' where the first 'chat' is linked to one file and the second is linked to the other, that will be informative. It is certainly plausible that there are different CMoPs, given that there are two mental files. But the MMoP associated with both CMoPs would seem to be the same—being furry, purring, being aloof, and being called 'chat'.[16]

---

[16] Schiffer (1990) has a similar example. Another case of two CMoPs but only one MMoP might be constructed from a variant of Austin's (1990) two tubes case. The subject

It may be objected that there cannot be only one MMoP since explaining cognitive significance requires postulating a difference somewhere—if not in the MMoP of the referent, perhaps there are two different MMoPs of that MMoP, or two different MMoPs of the MMoP of the MMoP of the referent.[17] But these higher-order MMoPs need not exist! The MMoP of chats in both senses of 'chat' is something like: being one of two kinds of furry, purring, aloof pet with a certain look, called 'chat'. There will not be any further MMoP of that MMoP unless the subject happens to have a thought about the first MMoP. What, then, explains the difference in cognitive significance between the two 'chat's? Answer: the difference in the CMoPs, the difference I have given a name to with the locution of different mental files. Objection: "But that difference in CMoP must correspond to a difference in MMoP!" To argue this way is simply to beg the question against the idea that there can be two CMoPs but only one MMoP.

Objection: "But the cognitive difference between the two CMoPs has to correspond to a difference in the world in order to be explanatory; e.g. the subject will think "The chat on my left is of a different kind from the chat on my right"." Answer: No, the example has been framed to rule out this kind of difference. The subject does not remember *any* differences between the two kinds of chat, not even differences in the situations in which he learned the terms.

It may seem that, wherever there is a difference in CMoP, there *has* to be *some* difference in MMoP of some kind, for otherwise how would the difference in CMoP ever arise? Thus, corresponding to the different CMoPs "covered with water" and "covered with H_2O" one might imagine that 'water' is learned or applied on the basis of properties such as, e.g. being a colorless, odorless, tasteless liquid coming out of the tap, and 'H_2O' is learned and applied on the basis of something learned in a chemistry class having to do with hydrogen and oxygen. Similarly,

looks through two fiber optic "tubes", one for each eye, and sees what he would describe as a red circular patch via each eye—with no differences between the patches. Further, the subject cannot tell which experience comes from the tube on the right and which from the tube on the left. A further wrinkle: unknown to the subject, the two fiber optic channels merge into one, so the object of the two experiences is exactly the same. From the subject's point of view, there are two experiences that may for all he knows be experiences of different things, so there are two CMoPs, but since they are in fact of the redness of one thing, there is only one MMoP.

[17] See the discussion of the "semantic premise" in section VII, The Relation between the Property Dualism Argument and Some Other Arguments for Dualism.

one might say that in the 'chat' case, there must be some difference between the property instantiated in the first and second introductions of the word 'chat' to the student. For example, perhaps the first one was introduced on a cloudy day and the second on a sunny day. Or at any rate, they were introduced at different times and so there is a difference in *temporal* MMoPs. For if there were no difference at all in the world, what would explain—that is explain as rational—why the subject thinks there are different referents?

But this reasoning is mistaken. Maybe there has to be some difference in properties in the world that explain the *arising* of the different CMoPs, but that difference can *fade away leaving no psychological trace*. After the student learns the word 'chat' twice, and tacitly assumes that it applies to different animals, the student may forget *all the specific facts* concerning the occasions of the learning of the two words, while still tacitly supposing that things that fit 'chat' in one sense do not fit it in the other. The *ongoing* use of two cognitive representations corresponding to the two uses of 'chat' do not require any *ongoing* difference in MMoPs to be completely legitimate and rational. Likewise for the 'Paderewski' example. To suppose otherwise is to *confuse ontogeny with metaphysics*.

The following reply would fit the view of many dualists such as Chalmers and White: "But doesn't there have to be a possible world, different from the actual world, that the subject rationally supposes he is in, in which the two CMoPs are CMoPs of different referents? For the subject who believes there are two different Paderewskis, a musician and a politician, the rationalizing world is a world that contains two persons named 'Paderewski', both born around the turn of the century, one famous as a politician, the other famous as a musician. Now in your version of the *chat* and Paderewski stories as you tell them, you have eliminated all differences in specific properties available to the subject. You have postulated that the subject does not believe that one is a politician and the other is a musician—but the same strategy can be followed all the same. The world that rationalizes the subject's view that there are two Paderewskis is a world in which there are two persons named Paderewski, both Europeans born around the turn of the century. The subject knows that there are bound to be many properties that distinguish them (if only their spatial locations) and he can single out two of them in his imagination, X and Y, such that one has property X but lacks Y, the other has property Y but lacks X. If the subject were

Max Black's Objection | 29

rationalizing his belief, he could appeal to X and Y, so they can constitute his different MMoPs. One of his MMoPs, call it, MMoP$_A$, is X; the other, MMoP$_B$, is Y. The fact that the subject does not know what X and Y are does not change the fundamental strategy of rationalizing the subject's error in which the cognitive difference, CMoP$_A$ vs. CMoP$_B$, requires a metaphysical difference, that between MMoP$_A$ and MMoP$_B$."

This territory will be familiar to those who have thought about modal arguments for dualism. The dualist supposes that the conceivability of zombies justifies the claim that there is a possible world in which there is a zombie, and that leads by a familiar route to dualism.[18] The physicalist resists the argument from epistemology to metaphysics in that case, and the physicalist should resist it here as well. We can explain the erroneous view that Paderewski is distinct from Paderewski by reference to *epistemic possibilities only*: The epistemically possible situation (not a genuine metaphysically possible world) in which, as one might say, Paderewski is not Paderewski. This is an epistemic situation in which Paderewski—who has property X but not Y (and, as we the theorists might say, is identical to the actual Paderewski) is distinct from Paderewski, who has property Y but not X (and who, as we the theorists might say is also identical to the actual Paderewski). Of course there is no such world, but this coherently describable epistemic situation accurately reflects the subject's epistemic state. We need only this coherently describable epistemic situation, not a genuine difference in properties in a genuinely possible world. (I follow the common convention of calling a genuinely possible situation a world and reserving 'situation' for something that may or may not be possible.) Likewise for the chat example. *The rationality of error can be explained epistemically with no need for metaphysics.* This is a basic premise of this chapter and it links the physicalist position on the Property Dualism Arguments to the physicalist position with regard to the Kripke–Chalmers modal arguments. Given this principle, I believe that the Property Dualism Argument, the Knowledge Argument, and the familiar modal arguments can be defanged, so the residual issue—not discussed here—is whether this principle is right. Chalmers and White argue that genuine

---

[18] The familiar point is put in a rather neat way in Perry's (2004a) rendition: If the putative zombie world contains cortico-thalamic oscillation, then according to the physicalist, it contains phenomenality and so is not a zombie world; but if the putative zombie world does not contain cortico-thalamic oscillation, then it does not fit the physical requirement of a zombie world. So physicalism cannot allow a zombie world.

worlds are needed to rationalize the subject's behavior, but I have not seen anything in which they argue against situations as rationalizers.

In my view, the issue I have been discussing is the key issue concerning all forms of the Property Dualism Argument (and some modal arguments for dualism as well). If the D(CMoP) → D(MMoP) principle does not come up in some form or other, the main issue has been skipped.

There is one reason for the view that a difference in CMoPs entails a difference in MMoPs that I have not yet mentioned and will not go into in detail until the end of the chapter in the "thin/thick" part of section VI: the view that MMoPs must be thin in the sense of having no hidden essence in order to account for their role in determining reference and explaining cognitive significance.

Of course, as before, those who prefer to see MMoPs as shadows of CMoPs can think of the property of being a chat—relative to the link to one mental file—as distinct from the property of being a chat—relative to the link to the other mental file. That is, the MMoP would be individuated according to the corresponding CMoP to preserve one–one correspondence.

What about the converse of the cases we have been talking about— one CMoP, two MMoPs? People often use one mental representation very differently in different circumstances without having any awareness of the difference. Aristotle famously used the Greek word we translate with 'velocity' ambiguously, to denote in some circumstances instantaneous velocity, and in other circumstances, average velocity. He did not appear to see the difference. And the Florentine "Experimenters" of the seventeenth century used a term translated as 'degree of heat' ambiguously to denote both heat and the very different magnitude of temperature. Some of their measuring procedures for detecting "degree of heat" measured heat and some measured temperature (Block and Dworkin 1974). For example, one test of the magnitude of "degree of heat" was whether a given object would melt paraffin. This test measured whether the temperature was above the melting point of paraffin. Another test was the amount of ice an object would melt. This measured amount of heat, a very different magnitude (Wiser and Carey 1983). One could treat these cases as one CMoP which refers via different MMoPs, depending on context. Alternatively, one could treat the difference in context determining the difference in CMoP, preserving the one–one correspondence. This strategy would postulate a CMoP difference that was *not available from the first-person point of view*, imposed on the basis of a difference in the world. That is, it would take a conceptual revolution for theorists of heat phenomena to see a significant difference between their two uses of "degree of heat", so the cognitive difference was not one that they could be aware of, given their conceptual scheme. A CMoP difference that is not available to the subject is not acceptable for purposes that emphasize the relevance of CMoP to the first person.

In what follows, I will assume independently individuated CMoPs and MMoPs. However, at one crucial point in the dialectic, I will examine whether individuating MMoPs according to CMoPs makes any difference to the argument, concluding that it does not. Why does it matter whether or not there is a one–one correspondence between CMoPs and MMoPs? I will now turn to a member of the family of Property Dualism Arguments that turns on this issue. The argument of the next section, or something much like it, has been termed the "property dualism argument" by McGinn (2001), though I think a somewhat different argument is more closely related to what Smart, Perry, and White have in mind, what I will call the "orthodox" property dualism argument in sections V and VI. The two arguments depend on nearly the same issues.

IV. E→ 2M VERSION OF THE PROPERTY DUALISM ARGUMENT

Saul Kripke (1980) argued for dualism as follows. Identities, if true, are necessarily true. But cases of mind without brain and brain without mind are possible, so mind–brain identity is not necessary, and therefore not true.[19] A standard physicalist response is that the mind–body relation is necessary, but appears, misleadingly, to be contingent: there is an "illusion of contingency". Most of the discussion of an illusion of contingency has focused on the mental side of the identity statement, but Richard Boyd (1980) noted that one way for a physicalist to explain the illusion of contingency of 'Q = cortico-thalamic oscillation' would be to exploit the gap between cortico-thalamic oscillation and its mode of presentation. When we appear to be conceiving of Q without the

[19] See n. 18.

appropriate cortico-thalamic oscillation (e.g. a disembodied mind or a version of spectrum inversion), all we are managing to conceive is Q in a situation in which we are misled by our mode of epistemic access to cortico-thalamic oscillation. What we are implicitly conceiving, perhaps, is a situation in which our functional magnetic resonance scanner is broken. So the physicalist is free to insist that cortico-thalamic oscillation is part of what one conceives in conceiving of Q, albeit not explicitly, and, conversely, Q is part of what one conceives in conceiving of cortico-thalamic oscillation.

But the sole reason for believing in *implicit* commitment to epistemic failure such as failing brain measurement devices in these thought experiments is that it avoids the non-physicalist conclusion, and that is not a very good reason. The conceivability of zombies, inverted spectra, disembodied minds, etc. does not seem *on the surface* to depend on implicit conceiving of malfunctioning apparatus. For example, it would seem that one could conceive of the brain and its cortico-thalamic oscillation "neat" (as in whiskey without ice or water), i.e. without conceiving of any particular apparatus for measuring cortico-thalamic oscillation.

However, the idea that one can conceive of cortico-thalamic oscillation "neat", is useful not just in combating Boyd's objection to Kripke's argument for dualism, but also in a distinct positive argument for dualism.[20]

Consider an empirical mind–body property identity claim in which *both* terms of the identity—not just the mental term—have MMoPs that are identical to the referent. (MMoPs are, of course, properties, and we are thinking of the referents of mind–body identity claims as properties as well.) McGinn (2001) claims—albeit in other terms—that this would be true for a standard physicalist mind–body identity claim. He says "it is quite clear that the way of thinking of C-fiber firing that is associated with 'C-fiber firing' is simply that of having the property of C-fiber firing... it connotes what it denotes" (294). Is cortico-thalamic oscillation or potassium ion flow across a membrane its own metaphysical

---

[20] I presented a version of the argument in a reply to David Chalmers at the Philadelphia APA in 1997, partly as a result of conversations with Brian Loar. There is an argument in Loar (1999b) that has some similarity to it. McGinn (2001) takes something of this sort to be the Property Dualism Argument, i.e. the one that Smart (1959) and White (1983) had in mind. I have heard unpublished versions of similar arguments by Martine Nida-Rümelin and John Hawthorne.

mode of presentation? That depends on what a metaphysical mode of presentation is supposed to be, and that depends on the purpose we have for them. I have mentioned a number of different conceptions of MMoPs, explaining cognitive significance, determining the referent, a priori graspability (on the basis of understanding the term it is the MMoP of).

Suppose we took explaining cognitive significance as primary. How can we explain why 'cortico-thalamic oscillation = cortico-thalamic oscillation' is less informative than 'Q = cortico-thalamic oscillation'? Do we need to appeal to an MMoP of *being cortico-thalamic oscillation* for 'cortico-thalamic oscillation'? First, if the identity is true, it is not clear that an MMoP of *being cortico-thalamic oscillation* is of any use. For if the MMoP of Q is *being Q*, then the MMoP of the left-hand side would be the same as for the right-hand side for both the trivial and the cognitively significant identity. Moreover, other MMoPs can explain the difference in cognitive significance. For example, a scientist might conceive of Q from the first-person point of view but think of cortico-thalamic oscillation in terms of the machinery required to detect it. A scientist might even think of it perceptually, in terms of the experience in the observer engendered by the apparatus, as radiologists often say they do in the case of CAT scans.

Suppose instead that we take the special reference-fixing authority as the *raison d'être* of the MMoP. This conception has the advantage that if we have given the special reference-fixing authority to an MMoP, then it is a priori graspable that the referent, if it exists, has that property (Byrne and Pryor, forthcoming). Again, it is not very plausible that the MMoP of 'cortico-thalamic oscillation' or 'potassium ion flow' is *being cortico-thalamic oscillation* or *being potassium ion flow*. What would be the point of giving the special reference-fixing authority for 'cortico-thalamic oscillation' to the property of *being cortico-thalamic oscillation*? (Recall that uniquely determining the referent is not enough for reference fixing—the subject must also have decided (even if implicitly) that that uniqueness property governs the term, as noted by Byrne and Pryor.)

But there is a kind of mind–body identity in which the right-hand term does more plausibly have an MMoP on both the cognitive significance and the reference-fixing sense that is identical to the referent (or at any rate has the relation of *being X* to X), namely a mental-functional identity claim. I will skip the cognitive significance rationale, focusing on determination of reference. What is our way of fixing reference to the property of being caused by A and B and causing C and D if not that property itself (or the property of having that property itself): that is, *being caused by A and B and causing C and D*? For many complex functional properties, it is hard to imagine any other reference-fixing property that could be taken very seriously, since it is hard to see how such functional properties could be singled out without singling out each of the causal relations. Further, the functional property would be plausibly a priori graspable on the basis of a typical concept of it. These considerations suggest that a mental-functional identity claim is a better candidate for the kind of identity claim being discussed here than the standard mental-physical identity claim.

Since the candidate identity claim has to be plausibly empirical, let us think of the physical side as a *psycho*functional property (see Block 1978, where this term was introduced), that is, a functional property that embeds detailed empirical information that can only be discovered empirically. For example, we can take the functional definition to include the Weber-Fechner Law (which dictates a logarithmic relation between stimulus intensity and perceptual intensity). To remind us that we are taking the right-hand side of the identity to be a psychofunctional property, let us represent it as 'PF'.

Let our sample mind–body identity be 'Q = PF', where as before, 'Q' denotes a phenomenal property. As before, let us use 'M' for the metaphysical mode of presentation of Q, and let us assume that M = *being Q*. *Ex hypothesi*, the metaphysical mode of presentation of PF is *being PF*. But since M = *being Q*, and the MMoP of PF = *being PF*, if the identity is true (Q = PF) it follows that the MMoPs of both sides are the same. (See Fig. 1.) But if the MMoPs of both sides are the same, then—supposedly—the identity cannot be a posteriori. Here I assume the principle that an empirical identity must have distinct MMoPs for the two sides of the identity. Call that Empirical → 2MMoP, or E → 2M for short. That would show that the original a posteriori identity claim—which embeds, you will recall, the Weber-Fechner Law and so cannot be supposed to be a priori—cannot be true: psychofunctionalism is refuted (or so it may seem).

The upshot would be that if we want a functionalist mind–body identity thesis, it can only be a priori (in which case deflationism–in the sense of conceptual reductionism about consciousness–holds). Or if we reject deflationism, the upshot is that functionalist mind–body

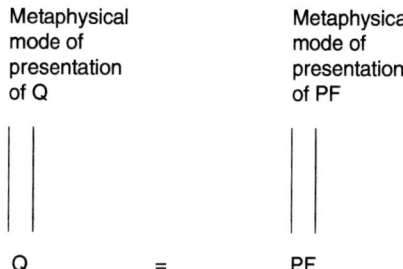

Figure 1: Empirical → 2MMoP Argument for Dualism.
MMoP (i.e. metaphysical mode of presentation) of Q = *being Q*, MMoP of PF = *being PF*, so if it is true that Q = PF, then the MMoP of PF = the MMoP of Q. But if the two MMoPs are the same, the identity is supposed to be a priori. However, since the identity is not a priori, the argument concludes, it is not true. The vertical '=' signs represent the relation between X and *being X*.

identity is false (i.e. the relevant form of dualism is true). So the conclusion is the same as that of the Property Dualism Argument, but restricted to functionalist mind–body identity claims: only dualism and deflationism are viable.

Why accept the E → 2M Principle? Suppose that different CMoPs entail different MMoPs (i.e. the D(CMoP) → D(MMoP) principle). An empirical identity requires different CMoPs, since, it may be said (but see below) if two of one's terms have the same cognitive significance, that fact is a priori available to the subject. An empirical identity requires different CMoPs, different CMoPs require different MMoPs, so an empirical identity requires different MMoPs. So it would follow that an empirical identity requires different MMoPs. This is one way of seeing why the considerations of the last section about the one–one correspondence between CMoPs and MMoPs matter for dualism.[21]

---

[21] A similar argument can be framed using Chalmers's and Jackson's primary intension/secondary intension apparatus (Chalmers 1996; Jackson 1998). The idea would be that for phenomenal and functional concepts, the primary intension is identical to the secondary intension. (Both views are endorsed by Chalmers (1996).) So if the secondary intension of a phenomenal/functional identity claim is true, so is the primary intension, and hence a phenomenal/psychofunctional identity claim is if true, a priori true. And since for reasons just given it is not a priori true, it is false. I will discuss the E → 2M Argument in this section, and then—in the Appendix—the variant using Chalmers's and Jackson's apparatus. So I will postpone saying what I take a primary intension to be until then.

You will not be surprised to learn that my objection to the argument is to the E → 2M Principle and the claim that different CMoPs require different MMoPs which engenders the E → 2M Principle. As I mentioned, a priority is better taken to be a matter of sameness of CMoPs, not a matter of sameness of MMoPs. In the example given above, before the subject learns that there is only one kind of creature called 'chat', he has two CMoPs but only one MMoP.[22]

The argument could be resuscitated if the CMoP of each side were identical to the referent. But at least on the right-hand side, this seems like a category mistake: our concept of a psychofunctional state (or something cognitive about it) is a poor candidate for identity with the psychofunctional state itself.

In comments on this chapter, David Chalmers suggested a variant of the E → 2M Argument. Instead of 'Q = PF', consider 'Q = P', where P is a physical property. Assume the E → 2M Principle—that an empirical identity must have distinct MMoPs for the two sides of the identity. If 'Q = P' is empirical, then it follows that the MMoP of Q is distinct from any MMoP of a physical property. For if the MMoP of Q were the MMoP of a physical property, PP, there would be an empirical identity claim (maybe a false one), Q = PP. If the MMoP of P = P, it follows that the MMoP of Q is distinct from any physical property, and so dualism is true.

My objections to this variant are, as before:

1. The argument assumes the E → 2M principle in the first step, in which it is argued that the MMoP of Q is distinct from any MMoP of any physical property, and as mentioned above, I reject the E → 2M principle.

2. The argument presupposes the view that it is reasonable to take the MMoP of a physical property, P, to be just P itself. (It would be better to take it to be being P, but I will ignore this glitch.) As I emphasized above, I find this doubtful for physical properties although more plausible for functional properties. So at most, the argument is an argument against empirical functionalism (psychofunctionalism) rather than against physicalism

---

[22] The point can be made with another more controversial type of example. Consider 'This property = this property' where the first demonstrative picks out the property of being water and the second picks out the property of being H$_2$O. (See Austin 1990). It could be said that each demonstrative picks out the property directly in the sense that the MMoP just is the property picked out. But if so, the form of the E → 2M Argument would give us a general argument against any empirical property identity!

V. BACK TO STATING THE ORTHODOX PROPERTY DUALISM ARGUMENT

The E → 2M Argument raises many of the same issues as the Smart, Perry, and White argument, to which I now turn, but is not quite the same.

To frame the orthodox Property Dualism Argument, we need to use a contrast between deflationism and phenomenal realism about consciousness.[23] In its strong form, deflationism is *conceptual reductionism* concerning concepts of consciousness. More generally, deflationism says that a priori or at least armchair analyses of consciousness (or at least armchair sufficient conditions) can be given in non-phenomenal terms, most prominently in terms of representation, thought, or function.[24] (If the analyses are physicalistic, then deflationism is a form of what Chalmers (1996) calls Type A physicalism.) The deflationist says phenomenal properties and states do exist, but that commitment is "deflated" by an armchair analysis that reduces the commitment. The conclusion of the orthodox Property Dualism Argument is that physicalism and phenomenal realism are incompatible: the phenomenal realist must be a dualist and the physicalist must be a deflationist.

In what follows, I will drop the term 'orthodox', referring to the argument I am spelling out simply as the 'Property Dualism Argument.'

The Property Dualism Argument in the form in which I will elaborate it depends on listing all the leading candidates for the nature of the MMoP of the mental side. My emphasis on the MMoP at the expense of the CMoP is artificial but has some dialectical advantages. The metaphenomenal move is what is really being explored, the view that with the statement of mind–body identity, either or both of the MMoP or the CMoP brings in unreduced phenomenality. Most of the issues that

---

[23] Deflationism with respect to truth is the view that the utility of the concept of truth can be explained disquotationally and that there can be no scientific reduction of truth (Horwich, 1990, 1998; Field, 1994). Deflationism with respect to consciousness in its most influential form is, confusingly, a kind of reductionism—albeit armchair reductionism rather than substantive scientific reductionism—and thus the terminology I am following can be misleading. I may have introduced this confusing terminology (in Block 1992, 1993), and though it is both confusing and misleading, it has already taken firm hold, and so I will use it here.

[24] Why "a priori or armchair"? Many philosophers adopt forms of functionalism, representationism, or cognitivism that, it would seem, could only be justified by conceptual analysis, while nonetheless rejecting a priority.

come up with respect to the MMoP could also have been discussed with respect to the CMoP. In rebutting the Property Dualism Argument, I will go back to the CMoP occasionally.

Recall that the phenomenal side (which I will always put on the left side of the sentence on the page) of the identity is 'Q'. Let the metaphysical, mode of presentation of Q be M (for *m*ental, *m*etaphysical, and *m*ode of presentation). The basic idea of the Property Dualism Argument is that even if Q is physical, there is a problem about the physicality of M. I will discuss five proposals for the nature of M. M might be (one or more of)

1. mental,
2. physical,
3. non-physical,
4. topic-neutral or
5. non-existent, i.e. the reference is "direct" in one sense of the term.

Here is a brief summary of the form of the argument. (1) is correct but useless in the sense that both the physicalist and the dualist will agree on it. The problem for the physicalist is to show how M can be both physical and mental. (2) is (supposed to be) ruled out by the arguments given below, which will be the main topic of the rest of this chapter. (5) changes the subject by stipulating a version of the original property identity 'Q = cortico-thalamic oscillation' in which Q is not picked out by a genuine phenomenal concept. So the remaining options are the dualist option (3), and the topic-neutral option (4). White (1983) argues that (4) is deflationist as follows: The topic-neutral properties that are relevant to the mind–body problem are functional properties. If M, the metaphysical mode of presentation of Q, is a topic-neutral and therefore—according to White—a functional property, then that could only be because the phenomenal concept has an a priori functional analysis; e.g. the concept of pain might be the concept of a state that is caused by tissue damage and that causes certain reactions including interactions with other mental states. But an a priori functional analysis is deflationist, by definition. The upshot is supposed to be that only (3) and (4) remain; (3) is dualist and (4) is deflationist. The conclusion of the Property Dualism Argument is that we must choose between dualism and deflationism: phenomenal realist physicalism is not tenable.

Of course the argument as I have presented it makes the title "Property Dualism Argument" look misguided. Anyone who does take the argument to argue for dualism would presumably want to add an argument against deflationism. However, Smart and Armstrong (and in a more convoluted version, David Lewis (1980)) use the argument the other way around: the threat of dualism was brought in to argue for deflationism. Their view is that 'pain' contingently picks out a physical state, for 'pain' is a non-rigid designator whose sense is *the item with such and such functional role*. But the view that stands behind this picture is that the nature of the mental is given a priori as functional. 'Pain' is a non-rigid designator, but what it is to have pain, that which cases of pain all share in virtue of which they are pains, is a certain functional property, and that functional property can be rigidly designated by, for example, the phrase 'having pain'.[25] So the view is a version of deflationism.

White (1983) adds an anti-dualist premise to the argument whose conclusion is *dualism or deflationism*, but in some papers in preparation (White (unpublished *a*, *b*)), he drops that premise, arguing instead for dualism. The point of view of the present chapter is phenomenal realist and physicalist, the very combination that the argument purports to rule out. (Though see Block 2002 for a different kind of doubt about this combination.) As we will see when I get to the critique of the Property Dualism Argument, the argument fares better as an argument for dualism than for deflationism, so the name of the argument is appropriate.

There are some well-known problems concerning the notion of a physical property.[26] But not all philosophy concerned with physicalism

---

[25] The rationale for the functionalist understanding of this point of view is spelled out in Block (1980) and in more streamlined form in Block (1994). Lewis (1980) adopts a more complex mixture of functionalism and physicalism.

[26] As Hempel (1969) noted, physicalism has a serious problem of obscurity. Physicalism about properties could be put as: all properties are physical. But what is a physical property? Hempel noted a dilemma (that has been further elaborated by Chomsky (2000); but see the critique by Stoljar (2001)): Horn 1 is: we tie physicalism to current physics, in which case physicalism is unfairly judged false, since there are no doubt physical entities and properties that are not countenanced by *current* physics. These entities and properties would be counted as non-physical by this criterion, even if the physics of next week will unproblematically acknowledge them. Horn 2 is: we define physicalism in terms of future physics. But what counts as physics? We cannot take physics as given in an inquiry about whether physicalism can be unproblematically defined. And we surely don't want to count as physics whatever is done in academic departments called 'Physics Departments'. For if theologians hijacked the name 'Physics', that would not make God physical.

can be about the problem of how to formulate physicalism. For some purposes, physicalism is clear enough.[27] In particular, the debate about the Property Dualism Argument seems relatively insensitive to issues about what exactly physicalism comes to. (If not, that is an objection to what follows.)

I will take the notions of physicalistic vocabulary and mentalistic vocabulary to be unproblematic. A physical property is a property canonically expressible in physicalistic vocabulary. (I won't try to explain 'canonically'.) For example, the property of being water is a physical property because that property = the property of being H_2O. The predicate '— is H_2O' is a predicate of physics (or anyway physical science), the property of being H_2O is expressed by that predicate, and so is the property of being water, since they are the same property. (Note that the relation of "expression" is distinct from referring.) A mentalistic property is a property canonically expressible in mentalistic vocabulary. '— is a pain' is a mentalistic predicate and thus expresses (or connotes) a mental property (that of being a pain). A non-physical property is a property that is not canonically expressible in physicalistic vocabulary. (So physicalism dictates that mental properties are canonically expressible in both physicalistic and mentalistic vocabularies.) I don't know if these notions can ultimately be spelled out in a satisfactory manner, but this is another of the cluster of issues involved in

---

[27] The big problem in defining physicalism is getting an acceptable notion of the physicalistically non-problematic without simply using the notion of the physical. One approach is to use a paradigm of the physicalistically unproblematic. I have suggested (1978) defining physicalism as the view that everything is decomposable into particles of the sort that make up inorganic matter. This definition uses "inorganic" as a way of specifying what is physicalistically unproblematic (following Feigl 1958, 1967), and so would get the wrong result if the inorganic turns out to be physicalistically problematic, e.g. if pan-psychism obtains (electrons are conscious). Thus it fails as a sufficient condition of physicalism. It does not capture the meaning of 'physicalism' (and it does not even try to define 'physical property'), but it does better as a necessary condition of physicalism. (See also Montero 1999.) Papineau (2002) takes the tack of specifying the physicalistically unproblematic by (in effect) a *list*. He suggests defining physicalism as the thesis that everything is identifiable non-mentally, that is, non-mental concepts can be used to pick out everything, including the mental. One problem with this way of proceeding is that "mental" has the same problem as "physical". We may one day acknowledge "mental" properties that we do not acknowledge today (much as Freudian unconscious mental properties are said not always to have been part of our conception of the mind). We can define the mental in terms of a list of currently acknowledged mental properties, which would be as problematic as defining the physical by a list. Or we could appeal to what will be recognized later as "mental", hitching our concept wrongly to the use of a term by future generations.

defining physicalism that not every paper concerning physicalism can be about.

Smart said that a topic-neutral analysis of a property term entails neither that the property is physical nor that it is non-physical. It would not do to say that a topic-neutral property is expressible in neither physicalistic nor non-physicalistic terms, since if physicalistic terms and non-physicalistic terms are all the terms there are, there are no such properties. The key kind of topic-neutral property for present purposes is a functional property, a second-order property that consists in the having of certain other properties that are related to one another (causally and otherwise) and to inputs and outputs, all specified non-mentalistically. One could say that a topic-neutral property is one that is expressible in terms of logic, causation, and non-mentalistically specified input–output language. The question may arise as to whether these terms are to be counted as part of physicalistic vocabulary or not. For purposes of this chapter, I will leave that issue undecided.

I will briefly sketch each of the proposals mentioned above for the nature of M (the metaphysical mode of presentation of Q, which you recall was introduced in the sample identity, 'Q = cortico-thalamic oscillation') from the point of view of the Property Dualism Argument, adding some critical comments at a few places. Then, after a section on phenomenal concepts, I will rebut the Property Dualism Argument.

Proposal 1: M is Mental

If M is mental, then the same issue of physicalism arises for M, the metaphysical mode of presentation of Q, which arises for Q itself. It isn't that this proposal is false, but rather that it presents a challenge to the physicalist of showing how it could be true.

Proposal 2: M is Physical

The heart of the Property Dualism Argument is the claim that M cannot be physical.[28] I will discuss three arguments for that claim. The first proceeds as follows. If M is physical, it will not serve to account for cognitive significance: specifically, the informativeness of identities and

---

[28] All three arguments are inspired by conversation with or published or unpublished papers by Stephen White. I doubt, however, that he would agree with my renditions or the conceptual apparatus they use.

the possibility of rational error. For example, suppose the subject rationally believes that Q is instantiated here and now but that cortico-thalamic oscillation is absent. He experiences Q, but also has evidence (misleading evidence, according to the physicalist) that cortico-thalamic oscillation is absent. We can explain rational error by appeal to two different MMoPs of the referent, only one of which is manifest. Let us take the metaphysical mode of presentation of the right-hand side of the mind–body identity 'Q = cortico-thalamic oscillation' to be a matter of the instrumentation that detects cortico-thalamic oscillation. We can think of this instrumentation as keyed to the oxygen uptake by neural activity. (Functional magnetic resonance is a form of brain imaging that detects brain activity via sensitivity to metabolism of the oxygen that feeds brain activity.)

The focus of this argument is on the left-hand side, the metaphysical mode of presentation of Q, namely M. According to the argument, if M is physical, it cannot serve the purpose of explaining rational error. For, to explain rational error, we require a metaphysical mode of presentation that makes rational sense of the subject's point of view. But the physical nature of M is not available to the subject. (The subject can be presumed to know nothing of the physical nature of M.) The problem could be solved if there was a mental mode of presentation of M itself, call it "M*". But this is the first step in a regress in which a physical metaphysical mode of presentation is itself presented by a mental metaphysical mode of presentation. For the same issue will arise all over again for M* that arose for M. Explaining rational error requires two modes of presentation, the manifestations of which are available to the first person at some level or other, so postulating a physical metaphysical mode of presentation just takes out an explanatory loan that has to be paid back at the level of modes of presentation of modes of presentation, etc. The upshot is that physical metaphysical modes of presentation do not pass the test imposed by one of the stipulated purposes of metaphysical modes of presentation.

There is also a related non-regress argument: if M is physical, a subject could believe he is experiencing Q, yet not believe he is in a state that has M. But there can be no epistemic gap of this sort between the metaphysical mode of presentation of a phenomenal property and the property itself.

Another argument that M cannot be physical is given by White (1983). He notes, plausibly enough, that "Since there is no physicalistic description that one could plausibly suppose is coreferential a priori with an expression like 'Smith's pain at t,' no physical property of a pain (i.e., a brain state of type X) could provide the route by which it was picked out by such an expression." (See ibid. 353, reprinted at Block, Flanagan, and Güzeldere 1997: 706). Or in the terms of this chapter, there is no physicalistic description that one could plausibly suppose is coreferential a priori with a mentalistic expression such as 'Q', so no physical property could provide the route by which it was picked out by such an expression. The property that provides the route by which Q is picked out by 'Q' is just the metaphysical mode of presentation (on one way of understanding that term) of Q, that is, M. So the upshot is supposed to be that M cannot be physical because there is no physicalistic description that is coreferential a priori with a phenomenal term.

A third argument that M cannot be physical is that MMoPs must be "thin". We can take a thin property to be one that has no hidden essence. "Thick" properties include Putnamian natural kinds such as water. According to the Property Dualist, the explanatory purpose of MMoPs precludes thick properties serving as modes of presentation. For, it might be said, it is not *all* of a thick property that explains rational error but only an *aspect* of it. The same conclusion can be reached if one stipulates that the MMoP is a priori available on the basis of the CMoP. Since hidden essences are never a priori available, hidden essences cannot be part of MMoPs. I will indicate later how the claim that MMoPs must be thin can be used to argue against the phenomenal realist physicalist position. This consideration can also be used to bolster the regress argument and the argument of the last paragraph.

I said earlier that the standard reply to Jackson's argument attempts to substitute a dualism of concepts for a dualism of properties and facts. And then I noted that the objection that is exploited by both the Knowledge Argument and the Property Dualism Argument is that the dualism of concepts is held to *require* a dualism of properties and facts. Thin MMoPs are in effect individuated according to the corresponding CMoPs. So the attempt to substitute a dualism of concepts for a dualism of properties and facts is opposed by the claim that properties and facts should be individuated according to concepts, and so if Mary acquires a new concept, she acquires a concept that involves new properties and facts.

Earlier I discussed the D(CMoP) → D(MMoP) principle, suggesting that there could be cases of two CMoPs with the same MMoP. One example was the identity 'the thing in the corner covered with water = the thing in the corner covered with H_2O'. The CMoP associated with the left-hand side is the description 'the thing in the corner covered with water', and the corresponding MMoP is the property of being the thing in the corner covered with water. Analogously for the right-hand side. But the property of being the thing in the corner covered with water = the property of being the thing in the corner covered with H_2O, so there is only one MMoP. But if MMoPs cannot be "thick", being covered with water cannot be an MMoP. The relevant MMoP would have to be some sort of stripped-down version of being covered with water that does not have a hidden essence.[29]

These three arguments are the heart of the orthodox Property Dualism Argument. I regard the three arguments as appealing to MMoPs in different senses of the term, and when I come to critiquing these three arguments later in the chapter, I will make that point more explicitly. In my critique, I will argue that two of the arguments do not stand on their own, but rather presuppose the third ("thick/thin") argument. Then I will examine that argument.

Proposal 3: M is Non-physical

If M is non-physical, dualism is true. So this proposal will not preserve the compatibility of phenomenal realism with physicalism and will not be considered further here.

Proposal 4: M is Topic-neutral

In effect, I covered this topic earlier, in my discussion of Perry. A genuinely phenomenal concept is required for getting the Property Dualism Argument (and the Mary argument) off the ground so a topic-neutral concept will not do.

---

[29] The second example I gave involving Loar's 'chat' case is, prima facie, not vulnerable to this objection. Or rather what it suggests is that the version of "thin property" needed by the property dualist is something more like "concept-individuated" rather than lacking a hidden essence. So the 'chat' MMoPs will be something like *being a furry purring aloof creature*—relative to mental file 1, and *being a furry purring aloof creature*—relative to mental file 2.

Proposal 5: There is no M: the Relation between 'Q' and its Referent is "Direct" in One Sense of the Term

A phenomenal concept is a phenomenal way of thinking of a phenomenal property. Phenomenal properties can be thought about using nonphenomenal concepts of them, for example, the concept of the property occurring at 5 p.m. As I keep mentioning, the Property Dualism Argument requires a phenomenal concept in my sense of the term, and so if the mind–body identity at issue does not make use of a phenomenal concept, the Property Dualist will simply substitute a mind–body identity that does make use of a phenomenal concept. Of course, if it could be shown that there could not be any phenomenal concepts, then the Property Dualism Argument will fail. But I believe in phenomenal concepts and so will not discuss this view further.

Phenomenal concepts are often said to refer "directly", but what this is often taken to mean in philosophy of mind discussions is not that there is no metaphysical mode of presentation, but rather that the metaphysical mode of presentation is a necessary property of the referent. Loar (1990) says:

> Given a normal background of cognitive capacities, certain recognitional or discriminative dispositions suffice for having specific recognitional concepts... A recognitional concept may involve the ability to class together, to discriminate, things that have a given objective property. Say that if a recognitional concept is related thus to a property, the property triggers applications of the concept. Then the property that triggers the concept is the semantic value or reference of the concept; the concept directly refers to the property, unmediated by a higher order reference-fixer.[30]

Consider the view that a phenomenal concept is simply a recognitional concept understood as Loar suggests whose object is a phenomenal property that is a physical property. I don't know if this would count as a concept that has no metaphysical mode of presentation at all, but certainly it has no phenomenal metaphysical mode of presentation, and so is not a phenomenal concept in the sense required for the Property

---

[30] The quotation is from the 1990 version of Loar's "Phenomenal States", 87. This picture is abandoned in the 1997 version of Loar's paper in which he retains talk of triggering and the direct reference terminology, but with a new meaning, namely: refers, but not via a contingent property of the referent. The view common to both the 1990 and 1997 paper is that a theoretical concept of e.g. neuroscience might pick out a neurological property "that triggers a given recognitional concept, and so the two concepts can converge in their reference despite their cognitive independence" (1990: 88).

Dualism Argument. For one can imagine a case of totally unconscious triggering of a concept by a stimulus or by a brain state. As Loar notes, there could be an analog of "blindsight" in which a self-directed recognitional concept is triggered blankly, without any phenomenal accompaniment. (Of course this *need* not be the case—the brain property doing the triggering could itself be phenomenal, or else the concept triggered could be phenomenal. In either case, phenomenality would have to be involved in the triggering of the concept.) And for this reason, Loar (1990: 98; 1997: 603) argues, a phenomenal concept is not merely a self-directed recognitional concept.

To sum up, the central idea of the Property Dualism Argument (and the Knowledge Argument) is the metaphenomenal move, the idea that in thinking about a phenomenal property, a further phenomenal property must be brought in as part of the CMoP or with the MMoP and that further phenomenal property poses a special problem for physicalism, because of its connection to a mode of presentation. There are three functions of modes of presentation on one or another conception of them that putatively lead to this resistance to physicalism, a function in explaining cognitive significance, of determining reference, and of a priori availability on the basis of understanding the term.

The Property Dualism Argument says that in the identity 'Q = cortico-thalamic oscillation', the metaphysical mode of presentation of Q (namely, M) must be either mental, physical, non-physical, topic-neutral, or "direct" (in which case there is no metaphysical mode of presentation). The mental proposal is supposed to be useless. The physical proposal is supposed to be ruled out because there is no a priori available physicalistic description of Q, because of supposed regress, and because the metaphysical mode must be "thin". The "direct reference" proposal appears to be ruled out by the fact that the concept of Q needed to get the argument off the ground is a phenomenal concept with a phenomenal metaphysical mode of presentation. So the only proposals for M that are left standing are the non-physical and topic-neutral proposals. The topic-neutral proposal involves a form of deflationism. So the ultimate metaphysical choice according to the Property Dualism Argument is between deflationism and dualism. The upshot is that the phenomenal realist cannot be a physicalist. The argument is a way of making the metaphenomenal move described earlier concrete: the statement of a mind–body identity claim is supposed to be self-defeating because the MMoP (or the CMoP—but I have focused on the MMoP) of the phenomenal term of the identity is supposed to bring in unreduced phenomenality. The only way to avoid that unreduced phenomenality is to give a deflationist analysis; the alternative is dualism.

Objections Concerning Phenomenal Concepts

I have been using a notion of phenomenal concept based on the observation that there is a fundamental exercise of it in which a token of a phenomenal property can serve in thought to represent a phenomenal property. In such a case, there is a phenomenal property that is part of the CMoP. There is a special case that I mentioned earlier in which a token of a phenomenal property can serve in thought to represent that very phenomenal property. In such a case, the phenomenal property does double duty: as part of the concept and also as the referent of that concept. Before I go on to rebutting the Property Dualism Argument, I will briefly consider two objections to this conception of a phenomenal concept.

Objection (put to me by Kirk Ludwig): I can truly think "I am not having an experience as of red now" using a phenomenal concept of that experience, but that would not be possible on your view of what phenomenal concepts are.

Reply: Ludwig is right that one can truly think "I am not having a red experience now" using a phenomenal concept of that experience. As I mentioned, a phenomenal concept has non-fundamental uses in which there is nothing phenomenal going on in exercising the concept. But even in one of the fundamental uses in which a token of an experience as of red is being used to represent that experience, it is possible to think a false thought to the effect that one is not having that experience. For example, one might set oneself to think something that is manifestly false, saying to oneself, "I am not having an experience as of red now", using a phenomenal concept—in my heavy-duty sense of phenomenal concept—of the experience.

Objection: On your view, a phenomenal property does double duty: as the referent but also as part of the mode of presentation of that referent. But if physicalism is true, cortico-thalamic oscillation would be part of its own mode of presentation. Does that really make sense?

Reply: The claim is not that the right-hand side of the identity 'Q = cortico-thalamic oscillation' has an associated mode of presentation (CMoP or MMoP) that involves cortico-thalamic oscillation. I have been supposing that the modes of presentation of the right-hand side have to do with the physical properties of oxygen metabolism that are revealed by scanning technology. Modes of presentation—both cognitive and metaphysical—are modes of presentation associated with *terms* or the concepts associated with the terms, and the identity involves *two* terms. There is no conflict with the indiscernibility of identicals if one keeps use and mention distinct. That is, cortico-thalamic oscillation is part of its own mode of presentation only as *picked out by the phenomenal concept of it*.[31]

---

[31] There is one outstanding issue involving phenomenal concepts that I will raise briefly without attempting to resolve. What makes it the case that a token phenomenal property in a phenomenal concept serves as a token of one phenomenal type or property rather than another? For example, suppose that a token of a mental image of red serves in a phenomenal concept to pick out an experience as of red. Why red rather than scarlet or colored? One answer is an appeal to dispositions. Suppose you are looking at chips in an ideal paint store that has a chip for every distinct color. (Robert Boynton estimates that there would be about a million such chips.) You are looking at $Green_{126,731}$, thinking that the experience as of that color is nice, using a phenomenal concept of that experience. But what experience is it that your phenomenal concept is of? The experience as of $Green_{126,731}$? The experience as of green? The answer on the dispositionalist view is that it depends on the subject's disposition to, for example, treat another experience as falling under the same concept. You are thinking that the experience is nice—but what will you count as another one of those? If only another experience as of $Green_{126,731}$ will count as an experience of the same type, the phenomenal concept is maximally specific; if any bluish-green experience will count as an experience of the same type, the concept is more abstract. If any experience of green will count as an experience of the same type, the concept is still more abstract. (Views of this general sort have been defended in conversation by Brian Loar and Kati Balog.)

This sort of view is similar to one interpretation of Berkeley's answer to the question of how an image of an isosceles triangle can be a concept of triangle, a concept that covers non-isosceles triangles as well as isosceles triangles. His answer (on this interpretation) was: because the image functions so as to apply to all types of triangles rather than just to isosceles triangles. There is a problem with Berkeley's answer that also applies to the view of phenomenal concepts I am talking about: namely, that it would seem that it is because one is *taking* the image of an isosceles triangle as a *triangle-image* rather than as an *isosceles-triangle-image* that it functions as it does, rather than the other way around. (This is not to impugn the functionalist idea that the role is what makes the concept the concept it is; rather, the point is that in some cases, there is something about the entity that has the role that makes it the case that it has that role.) Similarly, it is because one is taking the experience of a specific shade of green as a green-experience rather than as a $Green_{126,731}$ experience that makes it function as a concept of the experience of green rather than the concept of that highly specific shade of green. The dispositionalist view seems to get things backwards. However, no view of phenomenal concepts can sign on to the idea that an experience functions in a concept only under *another* phenomenal concept, since that would lead to a regress. My tentative thought is that there is a form of "taking" that does not amount to a further concept but is enough to explain the dispositions. But I cannot go into the matter further here.

VI. CRITIQUE OF THE PROPERTY DUALISM ARGUMENT

The Property Dualism Argument says that the metaphysical mode of presentation of Q, namely M, cannot be physical (using the identity 'Q = cortico-thalamic oscillation' as an example). I mentioned three (subsidiary) arguments to that effect, a regress argument, an argument concerning a priori availability, and an argument based on the thin/thick distinction. I also mentioned three different *raisons d'être* of modes of presentation, each of which could be used with respect to any of the three arguments, yielding in principle, nine distinct arguments—even eighteen if one counts the CMoP/MMoP dimension—making refutation potentially unmanageable. I will try to finesse this multiplicity by taking the strongest form of each argument, and bringing in the other *raisons d'être* as they are relevant. (I have already mentioned my focus on the MMoP in most of the argument at the expense of the CMoP.) The exposition of the argument has been long, but the critique will be much shorter. As we will see, the first two arguments do not really stand alone, but require the thin/thick argument. My critique of the thin/thick argument is aimed at depriving the conclusion of support rather than outright refutation.

Regress

The first argument mentioned earlier against the physical proposal is a regress argument. The idea is that if M is physical, it will not serve to account for cognitive significance (informativeness). For example, suppose the subject rationally believes that he has Q but not cortico-thalamic oscillation. As noted earlier, there can be rational error in supposing A is present without B when in fact A = B. That error can be explained if, at a minimum, there is a metaphysical mode of presentation of A, $MMoP_A$ and a metaphysical mode of presentation of B, $MMoP_B$, such that $MMoP_A$ is manifest and $MMoP_B$ is not.

Applied to the case at hand, the physicalist thesis that Q = cortico-thalamic oscillation, let us assume that the MMoP of 'cortico-thalamic oscillation' is the one mentioned earlier having to do with oxygen uptake by neural processes that affects a brain scanner. It is the other metaphysical mode of presentation that is problematic, namely M, the metaphysical mode of presentation of the left-hand side of the identity. The Property Dualist says that if M is physical, then M cannot serve to account for cognitive significance, since the subject need have no access to that physical description just in virtue of being the subject of that metaphysical mode of presentation. The problem could be solved if there was a *mental* mode of presentation *of M itself*, call it "M*". But this is the first step in a regress in which a metaphysical mode of presentation that is physical is itself presented by a metaphysical mode of presentation that is mental. For the same issue will arise all over again for M* that arose for M. Accounting for the different cognitive significances of the two sides of an identity statement requires two modes of presentation that are available to the first person at *some level or other*, so postulating a physical metaphysical mode of presentation just takes out an explanatory loan that has to be paid back at the level of modes of presentation of modes of presentation, etc.

This argument is question-begging. The argument supposes that if M is physical, it could not serve to account for cognitive significance, since accounting for cognitive significance requires a mental MMoP. But the physicalist thesis is that M is *both* mental and physical, so the physicalist will not be concerned by the argument.[32] Thus, the regress argument in the form I described is like the old objection to physicalism that says that brain states involve the instantiation of, e.g. electrochemical properties, but since pain does not involve the instantiation of such properties, pain can't be a brain state.

Of course if MMoPs must be thin, then M, which is an MMoP, cannot have a hidden physical nature, and so it cannot be both mental and physical. But if that is the claim, the regress argument depends on the "thick/thin" argument to be discussed below, and does not stand on its own.

I assumed that the MMoP of 'cortico-thalamic oscillation' is unproblematic, having to do, for example with oxygen metabolism as a result of brain activity. But the Property Dualist may say that this MMoP does not uniquely determine the referent and need not be a property to which the subject has given a special reference-fixing authority. (I will use the phrase 'fixes the referent' to mean uniquely determines the referent and has been given the special authority.) Why is this a reply to my point concerning the question-begging nature of the regress argument? The question arises: if the regress argument's appeal to cognitive significance

---

[32] I did say the mental option was "useless" in the sense that the dualist and the physicalist could agree on it. The mental option is useful, however, for the physicalist in avoiding the regress argument.

requires an MMoP for 'cortico-thalamic oscillation' that *does* fix the referent, what would that MMoP be? Someone could argue that that MMoP could only be the property *being cortico-thalamic oscillation itself*. And then it could be claimed that both sides of the identity statement are such that the MMoP of that side is identical with the referent. And this may be said to lead to dualism via the route canvassed earlier in the section on the E → 2M Argument. (If the MMoP of the right-hand side of an identity of the form X = Y is being Y; and the MMoP of the left-hand side is being X, then, if it is true that X = Y, it follows that being X = being Y, so the MMoPs of the two sides are the same. The E → 2M argument goes on to conclude that the identity must therefore be a priori if true, so therefore false.) I will not go into the matter again, except to note that it cannot be assumed that a property of the referent that accounts for cognitive significance also fixes the referent, and what counts in this argument is cognitive significance. As Burge (1977) and Byrne and Pryor (forthcoming) note, it is easy to see that properties of the referent that account for cognitive significance need not fix the referent. As Burge notes, the determination of reference depends on all sorts of non-conceptual contextual factors that "go beyond what the thinker 'grasps' in thought" (1977: 358). Byrne and Pryor give the example that *being a raspy-voiced singer* may give the cognitive significance for 'Bob Dylan', even though there are other raspy-voiced singers. And *being a raspy-voiced singer* need only be a property that the subject saliently associates with the referent, not a property to which the subject has given the special authority.[33] (This, incidentally, is the one point at which I appeal to general considerations about whether the three *raison/s d'être* for modes of presentation mentioned earlier go together.)

In sum, the regress argument depends on the "thin/thick" argument and does not stand alone.

---

[33] Perhaps it will be said that not any old "associated property" is enough to rationalize error. Let us use the notation RF['Dylan'] to mean the property to which the subject has given the special reference-fixing authority for using 'Dylan'. The view I expect to hear is that to rationalize error, we must ascribe to the subject a justified belief that RF['Bob Dylan'] is instantiated here, whereas, say RF['Robert Zimmerman'] is not. But this is a false picture of what it takes to rationalize error. If I have reason to believe that some abiding property, X, of Bob Dylan is instantiated here but that some abiding property, Y, of Robert Zimmerman is not, then other things equal, I have reason to think Dylan and Zimmerman are different people, no matter how unconnected X and Y are from reference-fixers.

52 | Ned Block

To avoid confusion, let me just briefly mention something the Property Dualism Argument is *not*. Someone might ask the question: in the identity 'A = B', how does one think of the metaphysical mode of presentation of A, $MMoP_A$? Doesn't one need a metaphysical mode of presentation of $MMoP_A$, which we could call $MMoP_A^*$? And another of that, $MMoP_A^{**}$? And the series won't end without some kind of "direct acquaintance" which does not require an MMoP (cf. Schiffer 1990: 255). Answer: One does not *need* to think about $MMoP_A$ in order to use $MMoP_A$ to think about A. However, if one does *happen* to want to think about $MMoP_A$, then one does need a concept of $MMoP_A$ with its own MMoP. "And don't we have to have a way of thinking of MMoPs that don't involve further MMoPs to avoid a regress?" Answer: No. To frame a thought about anything, we need a concept of it, including both a CMoP and an MMoP. To think about that CMoP, we need a further concept of it and to think about the MMoP we need a further concept of that. Every layer of thinking about a concept of a concept of... makes it harder and harder to do the mental gymnastics required to form the thought, and for most people, the ability to think these ever more complex thoughts will run out pretty quickly. So there is no regress—the mental gymnastics are voluntary. By contrast, the allegation of the Regress Argument that is part of the Property Dualism Argument, is that we *must* go up a level in order to explain cognitive significance at the preceding level. This is logically required and not just voluntary mental gymnastics.

A Priori Availability

The second argument presented above was that (to quote White 1983: 353), "Since there is no physicalistic description that one could plausibly suppose is coreferential a priori with an expression like 'Smith's pain at t,' no physical property of a pain (i.e. a brain state of type X) could provide the route by which it was picked out by such an expression." So the MMoP of the mental side of a mind–body identity claim could not be physical.

The first thing to notice about this argument is that if "Smith's pain at t" is taken to be the relevant mental concept in the Property Dualism Argument, it has the flaw of being purely linguistic and not a phenomenal concept of the sort I have argued is required for the argument. Still, it might seem that the argument goes through, for a genuinely phenomenal concept does not make a physical description of anything that could be called the route of reference any more available a priori than the description "Smith's pain at t".

Note that the *raison d'être* of modes of presentation assumed here is not the cognitive significance appealed to in the regress argument but rather: the property of the referent (i.e. MMoP) that provides "the route by which it is picked out". What is "the route by which it is picked out"? I think the right thing to mean by this phrase is what I have called fixing the referent, but I doubt that anything hangs on which of a number of candidates is chosen. Consider a case in which the subject conceives of the referent as being the local wet thing. Let us suppose that:

- The property of being the local wet thing is a priori available to the subject on the basis of understanding the term and therefore grasping its CMoP.
- The property of being the local wet thing uniquely determines the referent.
- The subject has given this property the special reference-fixing authority mentioned earlier.

My strategy is to concede all that could reasonably be said to be involved in reference fixing and to argue that nonetheless the argument does not work. For being wet = being at least partially covered or soaked with H_2O. But the subject whose metaphysical mode of presentation it is need not have a priori access to 'being at least partially covered or soaked with H_2O' or know a priori that this physical description is coreferential with the original description. The subject can give the property of being the local wet thing the special reference fixing authority and thus have that property a priori available from the first-person point of view, without ever having heard the description 'H_2O'. I hereby stipulate that the name 'Albert' is the name of the local wet thing. In virtue of my grasp of the term 'Albert", the property of Albert's being the local wet thing is a priori available to me. Also, I have stipulated that the property of being the local wet thing has the special reference-fixing authority. But I can do all that without knowing *all* descriptions of that property. That property *can be and is physical* even though I do not know, and therefore do not have a priori available, its physicalistic description.

Earlier, I considered the idea that MMoPs should be individuated according to CMoPs and thus that the property of being the local wet thing—considered as an MMoP-individuated-according-to-CMoP—is not identical to the property of being covered or soaked with H_2O because the *terms* 'water' and 'H_2O' are not identical. And of course this way of individuating the MMoP would provide an objection to the argument of the last paragraph.

However, the question then arises of what it is for such properties to be physical and what the physicalist's commitments are with respect to such properties. I believe that this question is best pursued not by inquiring about how to think of such strange entities as MMoPs-individuated-according-to-CMoPs but by focusing on the CMoPs themselves. And a further reason for turning the focus to CMoPs is that although the subject need have no a priori access to the physical descriptions of the physical properties that provide the metaphysical route of access, it may be thought that this is not so for CMoPs. After all, CMoPs are certainly good candidates for something to which we have a priori access!

Let us distinguish two things that might be meant by saying that a CMoP (or MMoP) is physical. First, one might have an *ontological* thesis in mind—that the CMoP (or MMoP) is identical to a physical entity or property or some conglomeration involving physical properties or entities. In this sense, a CMoP (or MMoP) can be physical whether or not the subject has a priori access to any physicalistic description of it. (The issue with which the Property Dualism Argument is concerned is whether phenomenal properties are, ontologically speaking, physical properties. I said at the outset that the issue of whether the cognitive apparatus involved in a CMoP is ontologically physical should be put to one side (except to the extent that that apparatus is phenomenal). My rationale, you will recall, is that although there is an important issue as to whether physicalism can handle cognitive (and semantic) entities or properties, in a discussion of whether *phenomenal* properties are physical, a good strategy is to suppose that non-phenomenal cognitive and semantic entities are not physically problematic.)

A second interpretation of the claim that a CMoP is physical is that it is *explicitly* physical or explicitly analyzable a priori in physical terms. In this chapter, I have been using 'physical*istic*' to mean explicitly physical. It is not obvious what it would mean to say that an MMoP is or is not physicalistic (since it is not a cognitive, linguistic, or semantic entity), but it does make sense to say that something that involves conceptual or linguistic or semantic apparatus is or is not physicalistic. For example, the CMoP 'being covered with water' is not physicalistic (at least if we restrict physics to microphysics), whereas 'being covered with H_2O' is physicalistic.

Is the CMoP of a phenomenal concept physical? Physicalistic? Recall, that according to me, a phenomenal concept uses a (token of a) phenomenal property to pick out a phenomenal property. Thus the CMoP of a phenomenal concept contains a non-descriptional element: a phenomenal property. And a phenomenal property is certainly not *explicitly* physical, i.e., physicalistic, that is, it does not contain conceptual apparatus or vocabulary of physics. A phenomenal property is not a bit of conceptual apparatus and it contains no conceptual apparatus. So, focusing on the 'physicalistic' sense of 'physical', the CMoP of a phenomenal concept is not physical. Must the physicalist therefore admit defeat? Hardly, for *physicalism is not the doctrine that everything is explicitly physical*. Physicalism does not say that all descriptions or conceptual apparatus are couched in physical vocabulary or analyzable a priori in physical vocabulary. Physicalists allow that there are domains of thought other than physics. Physicalists do not say that economics, history, and anthropology use physicalistic vocabulary or conceptual apparatus. This is an absurd form of conceptual or terminological reductionism that cannot be equated with physicalism.

Physicalism does not require that the CMoP of a phenomenal concept be physicalistic, but it does require that it is (ontologically) physical. Is it physical? That depends partly on whether all semantic and cognitive apparatus is physical, an issue that I am putting aside in this chapter. So the remaining issue is whether the phenomenal property that is part of the CMoP is physical. And that of course is the very issue of physicalism vs. dualism that this chapter is about. The Property Dualism Argument cannot *assume* that it is not physical—that is what the argument is supposed to show.

Where are we? Here is the dialectic: the Property Dualist says that in order for physicalism to be true, the physical description of the property that provides the route of reference (of the phenomenal term in a phenomenal-physical identity) has to be a priori available to the subject; it is not a priori available; so physicalism is false. I pointed out that even on very liberal assumptions about the role of the MMoP, a priori availability of a physical description of a physical property is an unreasonable requirement. But then I imagined a Property Dualist reply which said that I had failed to individuate the MMoP according to the CMoP. I then suggested that we eliminate the middleman, looking at the CMoP itself instead of considering the MMoP-individuated-according-to-the-CMoP. I pointed out that there is a sense of 'non-physical' (namely non-physicalistic) in which the CMoP of a phenomenal concept is indeed non-physical. I noted however that physicalists are not committed to all language or conceptual apparatus being physicalistic. Physicalists are committed to ontological physicalism, not conceptual reductionism. How does this apply to the MMoP-individuated-according-to-the-CMoP? It is true that if you individuate MMoPs according to CMoPs, then if there is no a priori available physical description, the MMoP is not "physical", and in this sense White's argument is correct. But all "physical" comes to here is *physicalistic*, and it is no part of physicalism to make any claim to the effect that phenomenal MMoPs or CMoPs are physicalistic. Thus the assumption of the second argument (namely, the topic of this section, the a priori availability argument) that the physicalist requires an a priori available description of the MMoP of the mental side of the mind–body identity is false.

If MMoPs have to be thin, then perhaps the distinction between an MMoP being ontologically physical and explicitly physical does not come to as much as would otherwise seem. Since a thin physical property has no hidden essence, it might be said to wear its physicality on its sleeve. However, if this is the only way to save the argument from a priori availability, that argument does not stand on its own but depends on the thin/thick argument, to which we now turn.

But first a brief reminder of what has been presupposed so far about the nature of MMoPs and CMoPs. In rebutting the regress argument, I assumed, along with the argument itself, that the *raison d'être* of MMoPs is to account for cognitive significance. The issue arose as to whether an MMoP defined according to its explanatory purpose must also fix reference or determine the referent. I noted that this cannot be assumed. The issue of the nature of CMoPs did not arise. In rebutting the second argument, I did not make any assumption about MMoPs or CMoPs that should be controversial, allowing a priori availability of the MMoP on the basis of the CMoP, reference-fixing authority and determination of the referent.

Thin/Thick

The third argument that the MMoP of a phenomenal concept cannot be physical involves the distinction mentioned between "thin" and "thick" properties. As we have seen above, the first two parts of the Property Dualism Argument fall flat on their own, but can be resuscitated using the thin/thick distinction. However, if it could be shown that MMoPs must be thin, these other arguments would be superfluous, since the claim that MMoPs must be thin leads to dualism by a shorter route, as I will explain shortly.

First, I must air an issue as to what exactly the thick/thin distinction is. I have been taking it that whether a property is thick or thin is a matter of whether it has a hidden essence. On this view, the primary bearer of thickness is a property, and a thick concept would be a concept that purports to be a concept of a thick property. However, this definition will be wrong if fundamental physical properties are thin. For since being water = being H_2O, if being H_2O is thin and being water is thick, whether a property is thick or thin is relative to what concept one has of that property. (Of course, being H_2O is not a candidate for a fundamental physical property—I used that description as a surrogate since I don't know how to describe water in terms of electrons, quarks, etc.) On the picture of the thick/thin distinction in which whether a property is thin is concept-relative, one could define a thin concept as follows: the extension of the concept in a possible world does not depend on its extension in the actual world. (In terms of Chalmers's apparatus, the primary intension is the same as the secondary intension.) And thin properties would be defined in terms of their relation to thin concepts.[34]

Are fundamental physical properties thin? Or, to put the matter from the other perspective, are fundamental physical concepts concepts of thin properties? We could approach the issue via the question of whether there could be a "twin earth" case for fundamental physical concepts. In my view, the answer is yes. I gave an example long ago (Block 1978) in terms of matter and antimatter. The idea is that there is a counterfactual situation in which people who are relevantly like us—functionally like us—use the term 'electron' to refer to anti-electrons. That is, the counterfactual situation is one in which our doppelgängers inhabit a universe or a place in our universe in which antimatter plays the role played here by matter. And as a result, their Ramsey sentence for fundamental physics is the same as ours.[35] Which suggests that the functional role of a concept inside the head is not enough to determine

---

[34] Another reason for taking thinness to be a matter of the relation between concepts and properties—say, properties individuated according to concepts—is given in n. 29.
[35] Ramsey sentences are defined in the text connected with n. 37.

its full nature, since the concept of an electron is not the same as the concept of an anti-electron.

But what if science can delve further into the matter/antimatter distinction, coming up with structure that explains the distinction and that will make a difference between the functional role of our concept and the doppelgängers' concept? The problem is that what we regard as fundamental physics is full of symmetries that can ground further examples, the idea being that there is more to physical reality than can be cashed out in a Ramsey sentence.

Of course, I don't think this mere suggestion settles the matter. Rather, I take the upshot to be that the issue of whether fundamental physical properties are thin cannot be settled here. Another argument in favor of that view is the point (Block 2003) that it is compatible with much of modern physics that for each level there is a still more fundamental level, the upshot being that there is something defective about the notion of a "fundamental" level in physics.

Ideally, I would consider the issues concerning the thick/thin distinction using both approaches, thin properties defined in terms of thin concepts and the other way around. However, this chapter is already much too long, so I will simply make a choice based on ease of discussion: taking properties as basic. I don't think any issues will depend on this choice.

Whether a property is thick or thin, then, will be considered here to be a matter of whether it has a hidden essence. For example, water or the property of being water is thick, since whether something is water goes beyond superficial manifestations of it. Examples of thin properties are mathematical properties, at least some functional properties, and phenomenal properties if dualism is true. (The last point about dualism could be challenged—see Nagel (2002)—but I will put the issue aside.) Artifact properties such as being a telephone might also be taken by some to be thin. As I mentioned, fundamental properties of physics might be alleged to be thin.

Note that it is not necessary for the Property Dualist to claim that *all* MMoPs are thin properties; it would be enough if this were true only for the MMoPs of phenomenal concepts. I do not have a blanket argument against all attempts to show that MMoPs for phenomenal concepts must be thin, but I do have arguments for a number of specific attempts.

Why believe that MMoPs must be thin? I will start with two arguments.

1. The A Priori Argument, which appeals to the idea mentioned earlier that the MMoP is a priori available on the basis of the CMoP.
2. The Aspect Argument, according to which, the cognitive significance role of MMoPs precludes thick properties serving as modes of presentation. For, as mentioned earlier, the Property Dualist may say that it is not *all* of a thick property that explains rational error but only an *aspect* of it, the thin aspect.

These two arguments for MMoPs (at least for phenomenal concepts) being thin appeal to different features of MMoPs and their relations to CMoPs. Although I have registered doubt as to whether the same entities can serve both functions, I will put that doubt aside.

The A Priori Argument for Thin MMoPs

Let us assume that the MMoP of a concept is a priori available on the basis of the CMoP. For example, if one grasps the term 'Hesperus', and if its CMoP is the meaning or other mental features of 'the morning star', then the MMoP of rising in the morning is supposed to be a priori available in virtue of one's grasp of the term and its CMoP. This constraint might be taken to rule out thick MMoPs, for it might be said that I do not know a priori whether I am on Earth or Twin Earth (McKinsey 1991). A thick MMoP might vary as between Earth and Twin Earth, which would be incompatible with a priori availability on the basis of the CMoP which is shared between me and my twin on Twin Earth.

I will give a fuller treatment of such arguments in the next section, but for now I will reply for the special case of phenomenal concepts, using the points made earlier about a phenomenal property doing "double duty".

I mentioned that a phenomenal property might be part of a CMoP, but also be brought in by the MMoP. For example, the CMoP might be taken to be the meaning or other mental features of: "the experience: ___ ", where the blank is filled by phenomenal property P. And the MMoP might be the property of *being P*. Such a relation between the CMoP and the MMoP allows for the MMoP to be a priori available on the basis of the CMoP, even if the property P is a thick property with a hidden essence. That is, the property of *being P* is a priori available on the basis of grasp of a CMoP that has property P as a constituent whether or not P is thick.

Although the a priori relation in itself does not appear to pose an obstacle to thickness of the MMoP, it might be thought to pose a problem combined with another argument, to which we now turn.

The Aspect Argument

As mentioned, the idea of the Aspect Argument is that it is not *all* of a thick property that explains cognitive significance in general and rational error in particular, but only an aspect of it, the aspect that is available a priori on the basis of the CMoP. But on the face of it, *that aspect can itself be thick*. Recall the example of Albert, which I pick out on the basis of its being the local wet thing. Albert's property of being the local wet thing fixes reference, uniquely determines the referent, is a *priori available and also thick*.

The Property Dualist may say that the property that would serve in explanations of error is not that it is wet but that it *looks* wet. However, consider a non-perceptual case: I infer using inductive principles that something in the corner is wet, and pick it out via its property of being wet. In this case, the substitution of *looks wet* for *wet* is unmotivated. The MMoP just does not seem perceptual. Nor artifactual, nor, more generally, functional. On the face of it, the MMoP is a thick property, the property of being wet, i.e. (roughly) at least partially covered or soaked with water (which is thick because being covered or soaked with water is being covered or soaked with H_2O).

But perhaps this rebuttal misses the significance of aspects to the first-person point of view. Perhaps the Property Dualist will say something like this: "If phenomenal property Q is a physical property, then it can be picked out by a physical—say neurological—concept that identifies it in neurological terms. But those neurological identifications are irrelevant to first-person phenomenal identifications, showing that the first-person phenomenal identification depends on *one aspect* of the phenomenal property—its 'feel'—rather than *another aspect*—its neurologically identifying parameters. You have suggested that 'cortico-thalamic oscillation' picks out its referent via the effect of cortico-thalamic oscillation on instruments that monitor oxygen uptake from blood vessels in the brain. But this effect is not part of the first-person route by which we pick out Q, so it follows that not every aspect of the physical property is relevant to the first-person route. Therefore the identity 'Q = cortico-thalamic oscillation' is supposed to be one in which the terms pick out a single referent via different properties of it, different MMoPs. And so the Property Dualism Argument has not been avoided."

I agree that the two terms of the identity 'Q = cortico-thalamic oscillation' pick out the referents via different aspects of that referent, different MMoPs. And I also agree that the aspect used by the mental term of the identity is available to the first-person whereas the aspect used by the physical term is not. But it does not follow that the aspect used by the mental term is thin. It is true that no neurological property is explicitly part of the first-person route, but that does not show that it is not part of the first-person route, albeit ontologically rather than explicitly. The MMoP of 'Q' is stipulated to be phenomenal, and may be taken to be the property of *being Q*. But being identical to Q, on the physicalist view, is *both* a thick property, and available to the first person. Being identical to Q is a physical property (being identical to cortico-thalamic oscillation) but is nonetheless distinct from the MMoP I have been supposing for 'cortico-thalamic oscillation', which has to do with the oxygen uptake that fMRI scanners use to identify it. On the physicalist view, the feel and the neurological state are not different aspects of one thing: they are literally identical. If they are aspects, they are identical aspects. But the MMoP of the right-hand term of the identity is still different from the MMoP of the left-hand term.

As mentioned earlier, some will say that oxygen uptake cannot provide the MMoP for the term 'cortico-thalamic oscillation', which should be taken to be cortico-thalamic oscillation itself, or perhaps being identical to cortico-thalamic oscillation. In this supposition, there is a germ of a different argument for dualism, the E → 2M Argument discussed earlier.

I say that the aspect of a property that accounts for cognitive significance can itself be thick, appealing to examples. But the Property Dualist may suppose that if we attend to the mental contents that are doing the explaining, we can see that they are *narrow* contents, contents that are shared by Putnamian twins, people who are the same in physical properties inside the skin that are not individuated by relations to things outside the skin. If the relevant explanatory contents are narrow contents, then the corresponding explanatory properties—MMoPs—will be thin.

Here is the argument, the Narrow → Thin Argument, in more detail, offered in the voice of the Property Dualist:

N → T Argument: Suppose my CMoP is "the wet thing in the corner" (in a non-perceptual case) and my twin on Putnam's twin earth would put his CMoP in the same words. Still, the difference between what he means by 'wet' and what I mean by 'wet' *cannot matter to the rationalizing explanatory force* of the CMoPs. And since CMoPs are to be individuated entirely by rationalizing explanatory force, my twin and I have the same CMoPs: namely, the CMoPs are narrow. But since the MMoP is a priori available to anyone who grasps the CMoP, the twins must have the same MMoP as well as the same CMoP, so the MMoP must be thin. Narrow CMoP, therefore thin MMoP.

The N → T Argument presupposes the familiar but controversial idea that only narrow content can serve in intentional explanations. However, on the face of it, my 'water'-concept can be used in an explanation of my drinking water ("I wanted water, I saw water, so I drank water") but would not explain my drinking twin-water.[36] The idea that only narrow contents can serve in a rationalizing explanation is certainly controversial. I will not enter into this familiar dispute here, since there is another less familiar problem with the reasoning.

The inference from narrow content/narrow CMoP to thin MMoP has some initial plausibility, but it is actually question-begging. I agree with the premise of the N → T Argument that phenomenal CMoPs are narrow. (I won't go into the possibility that there is a descriptive part of the CMoP that is wide.) However, it does not follow that the MMoP is thin. The physicalist says that since phenomenality supervenes on the physical, Putnamian doppelgängers will share CMoPs: CMoPs are narrow. For example, a phenomenal CMoP containing phenomenal property P for one twin will also contain phenomenal property P for the other twin. The MMoP, *being P*, will also be the same for both twins, but that MMoP can nonetheless be thick. In short, the phenomenal part of a CMoP and the corresponding phenomenal MMoP will in general be narrow in virtue of being necessarily shared by doppelgängers, but will nonetheless be thick on the physicalist view. That is, what the doppelgängers necessarily share will be a property with a scientific essence.

The point can be approached by looking at the anomalous nature of phenomenal kinds. Phenomenal concepts of the sort that I have

---

[36] This dialectic appears in Fodor (1982) and Burge's (1982) reply. See also Burge (1986, 1989, 1995).

described here are natural kind concepts in that they purport to pick out objective kinds, and if the physicalist is right, those kinds have scientific natures whose scientific descriptions cannot be grasped a priori simply on the basis of having the concept. But they differ from most natural kind concepts in that the Twin Earth mode of thought experiment does not apply. The Twin Earth mode of thought experiment involves a pair of people who are the same in physical properties inside the skin (that are not individuated by relations to things outside the skin) but with a crucial physical difference. In Putnam's classic version (1975), twins who are relevantly the same in physical properties inside the skin pick out substances using the term 'water' that have physically different natures, so (it is claimed), the meanings of their 'water' terms and 'water'-thought contents differ. They are (relevantly) physically the same, but different in 'water'-meaning and 'water'-content.

But how is the Twin Earth thought experiment supposed to be applied to phenomenality? If physicalism is true, the twins cannot be the same in physical properties inside the skin (that are not individuated by relations to things outside the skin) and also differ in the physical natures of their phenomenal states! (That's why I say the N → T Argument begs the question against physicalism.) So there is no straightforward way to apply the Putnamian Twin Earth thought experiment to phenomenal concepts. (The issue concerning Burgean thought experiments is more complex, since it hinges on the ways in which our terms express phenomenal concepts. I can't go into the matter here.)

But perhaps only a superficial analysis of Twin Earth thought experiments require that the twins be the same in physical properties inside the skin (that are not individuated by relations to things outside the skin). One way to think of Twin Earth cases is that what is important is that they be *mentally* alike in ways that don't involve relations to things outside the skin. (Thus, for some purposes, functional alikeness might seem more relevant than microphysical alikeness. This line of thought was what I used in my earlier discussion of whether fundamental physical properties are thin.) But phenomenality is certainly part of mentality, so if twins are to be the same in phenomenal CMoPs, there had better not be any physical difference between them that makes a phenomenal difference. However, from the physicalist point of view, the shared phenomenality of the twins' CMoPs has to be explained by a shared physical basis of it. So the shared narrow CMoP is compatible with a shared thick MMoP.

The upshot is that phenomenal concepts are an *anomaly*—at least from the physicalist point of view. They are natural kind concepts in that they allow for objective scientific natures that are "hidden" (the scientific descriptions are not a priori available on the basis of merely having the concept). But they are different from other natural kind concepts in that no reasonable facsimile of a Putnamian Twin Earth scenario is possible.

So even if the inference from narrow CMoP to thin MMoP applies in a variety of other cases, it should not be surprising that it fails to apply in this anomalous case. The CMoPs for phenomenal concepts can be narrow even though the corresponding MMoPs are thick. Indeed, the CMoPs themselves can be both narrow *and* thick. Narrow because non-relational, thick because they involve a phenomenal element that has a hidden scientific nature.

I have rebutted the Aspect and A Priority Arguments and a subsidiary argument, the N → T Argument, which all push for the conclusion that MMoPs of phenomenal concepts must be thin. But one can also look at the thesis itself independently of the arguments for it. Here are two considerations about the thesis itself.

Issues about the Claim of Thin MMoPs for Phenomenal Concepts

First, the assumption of thin MMoPs is perhaps sufficient for the conclusion of the Property Dualism Argument *all by itself*. For what are the candidates for a thin MMoP for a phenomenal concept? Artifact properties such as being a telephone (even assuming that they are thin) and purely mathematical properties are non-starters. Some kind terms that are not natural kind terms, e.g. 'dirt', may yield thin properties. But phenomenal MMoPs are not artifactual or mathematical and they are or purport to be natural kinds as just pointed out. It is not clear whether there are any natural kind terms that express thin properties. Even if there are fundamental physical properties that are thin, the Property Dualist can hardly suggest fundamental physical properties as candidates for MMoPs for phenomenal concepts, since that has no independent plausibility and in any case would be incompatible with the conclusion of the Property Dualist's argument. So it would seem that the only remotely plausible candidates for thin MMoPs by which phenomenal concepts refer are (1) purely functional properties, in which case deflationism would be true, and (2) phenomenal properties that are non-physical, in which case dualism is true. The conclusion would be the same as the conclusion of the Property Dualism Argument itself: that phenomenal realist physicalism is untenable.

The upshot is that much of the argumentation surrounding the Property Dualism Argument can be dispensed with if the arguments of this chapter are correct. The most obvious arguments that MMoPs of phenomenal concepts cannot be physical (the Regress Argument and the A Priori Availability Argument, presented earlier) do not stand alone but rather depend on the Thin/Thick Argument. I have not shown that there is no good argument for the claim that MMoPs of phenomenal concepts are thin, but I have rebutted some obvious candidates, and it is hard to see how the Regress and A Priori Availability Arguments could be used to justify the thinness claim since they presuppose it. So if my arguments are right, the burden of proof is on the Property Dualist to come up with a new argument for the claim that MMoPs of phenomenal concepts are thin.

Here is the second point. So far, I have argued that the assumption of thin MMoPs leads directly to dualism or deflationism, putting a heavy burden of proof on the Property Dualist to justify that assumption. But actually I doubt that deflationism really is an option. Let me explain. The functionalist characterizes functional properties in terms of the Ramsey sentence for a theory. Supposing that 'yellow teeth' is an "observation term", the Ramsey sentence for the theory that smoking causes both cancer and yellow teeth is $\exists F_1 \exists F_2 [F_1$ causes both F_2 and yellow teeth], i.e. the Ramsey sentence says that there are two properties one of which causes the other and also yellow teeth. Focusing on psychological theories, where the "observation terms" (or "old" terms in Lewis's parlance) are terms for inputs and outputs, the Ramsey sentence could be put as follow: $\exists F_1 \ldots \exists F_n$ $[T(F_1 \ldots F_n, i_1 \ldots i_m, o_1 \ldots o_p)]$. The 'i' terms are input terms and the 'o' terms are output terms. Functional properties of the sort that can be defined in terms of the Ramsey sentence are properties that consist in having certain other properties that have certain causal relations to inputs, outputs, and other properties.[37] The inputs and outputs can be characterized in many ways. For example, an output might be characterized neurally, or in terms of movements of a hand or leg, or distally, in terms of e.g. water in the distance, or distally

---

[37] More specifically the functional definitions work as follows. If 'F_{17}' is the variable that replaced 'pain', 'pain' could be defined as follows: pain = the property of being an x such that $\exists F_1 \ldots \exists F_n [T(F_1 \ldots F_n, i_1 \ldots i_m, o_1 \ldots o_p)$ and x has $F_{17}]$.

and mentalistically in terms of drinking water. *But all these characterizations are plausibly thick, not thin.* Perhaps you will think that some of them are *themselves* to be cashed functionally, but then the issue I am raising would arise for the input and output specification of *those* functional properties. Since the problem I am raising depends on the thickness of the input and output properties, I put those terms for those properties, ('i_1'... 'i_m', 'o_1'... 'o_p'), in bold in the Ramsey sentence earlier. The only functional properties I know of that are plausibly thin are *purely formal* functional properties that abstract from the specific nature of inputs and outputs, the kind of functional property that could be shared by a person and an economy. (See Block 1978.) For example, in the case of the theory that smoking causes cancer and yellow teeth, a purely formal Ramsey property would be: being an x such that $\exists F_1 \exists F_2 \exists F_3([F_1$ causes F_2 and $F_3]$ and x has $F_1)$. This is the property of having a property which causes two other properties. Such a property could be shared by a person and an economy. Since not even a deflationist should agree that the metaphysical modes of presentation of our phenomenal states are *purely* formal, the only remaining option is dualism. So the assumption of thin properties plausibly leads right to dualism.

To sum up the points about the thin/thick argument: The "aspect" rationale for MMoPs being thin seems doubtful because the aspect can itself be thick. And the rationale for thin MMoPs in terms of the supposed a priori relation between CMoP and MMoP is problematic because the key phenomenal feature of the MMoP can also be present in the CMoP, when the relevant concept is phenomenal. At least this is so on one plausible notion of phenomenal concepts, which the Property Dualist would have to challenge. Narrow CMoPs can be used to argue for thin MMoPs, but this reasoning begs the question against the physicalist. I explained at the outset that the emphasis on MMoPs at the expense of CMoPs was tactical: the metaphenomenal move—that says that modes of presentation bring in unreduced phenomenality—can be discussed equally with respect to either mode of presentation. This was the place in the argument where the artificiality is most apparent—CMoPs must be discussed explicitly.

Moving to the thesis itself independently of arguments for it, the assumption of thin MMoPs amounts to much the same thing as the Property Dualism Argument itself. Further, the only remotely plausible candidates for thin MMoPs are purely formal properties that we do not have ordinary concepts of and phenomenal properties, dualistically conceived. The purely formal properties, though more plausible than some other candidates, are not very plausible, even from a deflationist point of view. Deflationist functionalism is based on analyses of mentality in terms of sensory input and behavioral output. Purely formal properties do not adequately capture such analyses, and cannot without thick input and output terms. The upshot is that the assumption of thin MMoPs for phenomenal concepts adds up to dualism itself. To assume thin MMoPs begs the question against the physicalist.

Of course, I have not shown that there cannot be an argument for thin phenomenal MMoPs, but I hope I have shown that a number of candidates do not succeed.

VII. THE RELATION BETWEEN THE PROPERTY DUALISM ARGUMENT AND SOME OTHER ARGUMENTS FOR DUALISM

Loar (1997) locates the flaw in Jackson's "Mary" argument and Kripke's modal argument in a certain principle: the "semantic premise".[38] The semantic premise (on one understanding of it) says that if a statement of property identity is a posteriori, then at least one of the MMoPs must be contingently associated with the referent. The idea behind the principle is that if the two concepts pick out a property non-contingently, it must be possible for a thinker who grasps the concepts to see, a priori, that they pick out the same property. Again the issue arises as to what notion of MMoP is at stake. Consider, for example, the reference-fixing notion of MMoP. In this sense, the "semantic premise" is plainly false. Note that the person formed by a certain sperm = the person formed by a certain egg. This identity is a posteriori, yet both terms pick out their referents via essential and therefore necessary properties of it, assuming that Kripke is right about the necessity of origins. Call the sperm and egg that formed George W. Bush 'Gamete-Herbert' and 'Gamete-Barbara' respectively. The person formed from Gamete-Herbert = the person formed from Gamete-Barbara. "The person formed from Gamete-Herbert" does not pick out George W. contingently, nor does

---

[38] Loar (1999a) extends this analysis to Chalmers's and Jackson's modal arguments. White (forthcoming b), argues for a weakened version of the semantic premise and for its relevance to the Property Dualism Argument.

"The person formed from Gamete-Barbara". My example is put in terms of individuals but it is easy to see how to frame a version of it in terms of properties. Even if Kripke is wrong about the necessity of origins, the logic of the example remains. One thing can have more than one necessary but insufficient property, both of which can be used to pick it out, neither of which a priori entails the other. Thus the terms in a true a posteriori identity can pick out that thing, each term referring by a different necessary property as the MMoP.

Of course there is some contingency in the vicinity. Gamete-Herbert might have joined with an egg other than Gamete-Barbara or Gamete-Barbara might have joined with a sperm other than Gamete-Herbert. And this might suggest a modification of the principle (one that White (forthcoming $_b$) suggests in response to an earlier version of this chapter), namely, if a statement of property identity is a posteriori, then it is not the case that both terms refer via MMoPs that are necessary and sufficient conditions for the property that is the referent. Or, more minimally, if a property identity is a posteriori, then it is not the case that one term refers via a sufficient property of it and the other refers via a necessary property of it. But a modification of my example (contributed by John Hawthorne) suggests that neither of these will quite do. Let the identity be: the *actual* person formed from Gamete-Herbert = the *actual* person formed from Gamete-Barbara. Arguably, each designator refers via a property that is both necessary and sufficient for the referent. So the revised version of the semantic premise is also false.

The reference of the terms 'Gamete-Herbert' and 'Gamete-Barbara' need not be fixed via properties that involve George Bush. The gametes can be identified independently, for example before George Bush was conceived. But perhaps the names will pick them out via some contingent reference-fixing property, e.g. a perceptual demonstrative ("that egg") or by description. And that motivates White (ibid.) to suggest a beefed up form of the semantic premise that says that there must be contingency either in the relation between MMoPs and referent or in the relation between MMoPs and the MMoPs of those MMoPs, or... I reject the beefed-up semantic premise for the reason given earlier: I don't think these further MMoPs need exist. That is, in the identity 'a = b', there will be MMoPs associated with both sides. But there will be no MMoPs of those MMoPs unless the subject happens to refer to the first level MMoPs in another voluntary cognitive act.

VIII. CONCLUSION

The Property Dualism Argument attempts to exploit the idea that the mind–body identity approach to phenomenality fails when it comes to the mode of presentation of a phenomenal state. The argument is a way of making concrete what I called the metaphenomenal move: the idea that in a phenomenal mind–body identity claim, the CMoP is partly constituted by something with unreduced phenomenality or the MMoP is an unreduced phenomenal property.

My response has been to argue that phenomenality in modes of presentation is no different from phenomenality elsewhere. I tried to dissolve apparent impediments to the phenomenal element in the CMoP and the MMoP being physical. My way out involves a notion of a phenomenal concept that has some affinities with the "directness" story in which there is no metaphysical mode of presentation at all, since my phenomenal MMoPs are not very different from the referent itself. I considered a family of arguments based on the idea that MMoPs must be thin, arguing that appeal to narrow content does nothing to establish thinness. According to me, phenomenal concepts are both narrow and thick, which is why the phenomenality in the CMoP can be physical. I also considered a different version of the Property Dualism Argument that assumes that an empirical identity must have different MMoPs, so that if the MMoPs of the two terms of an identity are the same, then the identity is a priori. I argued that whereas sameness of CMoP makes for a priority of the identity, sameness of the MMoP does not.

Much of the argumentation involved the principle that a difference in CMoP requires a difference in MMoP (D(CMoP) → D(MMoP)). I argued that nothing forces us to adopt notions of CMoP and MMoP on which this principle is true. However, at a key point in the dialectic I considered a notion of MMoP individuated with respect to CMoP, which I argued did not rescue the Property Dualism Argument.

Although I expressed skepticism about whether any one thing can explain rational error, fix reference, and be relevantly a priori available, I have not claimed that these *raisons d'être* fail to coincide except at one point at which I noted that an explanatory MMoP need not fix the referent. The other rebuttals were keyed to one or another specific version of MMoPs and CMoPs and their relation. My strategy was to avoid multiplying arguments based on different notions of CMoP/

MMoP by choosing what seemed to me the strongest argument of each type. In the end, everything hinges on the claim that MMoPs of phenomenal concepts are thin, and I attempted to remove the most straightforward motivations for that view.

I have pursued a divide-and-conquer strategy, distinguishing among different senses of 'mode of presentation' and further dividing those by the *raisons d'être* of modes of presentation in those senses. My claim is that once we do that, the Property Dualism Argument dribbles away. I have not claimed to refute these arguments conclusively but I believe that the ball is in the Property Dualist's court.

Appendix on a Variant of the E → 2M Argument Using Primary Intensions Instead of MMoPs

I mentioned that there is a version of the E → 2M Argument using the notion of a primary intension instead of the notion of an MMoP. The primary intension of 'water' is the function from worlds considered as actual (as actual world candidates in Davies and Humberstone's (1980) sense) to what water turns out to be in that world. (Or so I will understand the term. Chalmers uses various different ways of specifying what a primary intension is but since this is a very brief discussion, I will just pick that one.) Thus the primary intension of 'water' picks out water in the actual world and XYZ ("twin-water") on Putnam's Twin Earth. Since Putnam's Twin Earth could have both XYZ and H_2O in it, the primary intension is a function from "centered" worlds—worlds with a privileged point—to referents. What makes the primary intension of 'water' pick out the XYZ in Putnam's Twin Earth is that the center of that world has the relevant relation to XYZ rather than H_2O. (For example, the center might be surrounded by XYZ whereas there might be only a few molecules of H_2O that are light years away. If there are people on twin earth, we can suppose causal commerce of the relevant sort between XYZ (but not H_2O) and uses of the term 'water' that have some appropriate relation to the center.)

I read Chalmers (1996) as stipulating that the primary intension captures the a priori component of content, and on this reading the primary intension would be more like a CMoP than an MMoP. Given this stipulation, my complaint that MMoPs are not what is relevant to a priority would fall away, the pressure instead being on the issue of whether primary intensions in the sense in which they are stipulated to capture the a priori aspect of content are indeed the same as secondary intensions. That is, the analog of the E → 2M principle, the "E → 2 PI principle", would be a stipulation, but the other premise of the argument—that the phenomenal and functional primary intensions are identical to the secondary intensions—would then take the heat. The secondary intension of 'water' is the function from worlds to what 'water' denotes in those, worlds, namely, water, if there is any. The worlds are considered "as counterfactual" (as familiar from Kripke): we take reference of 'water' in the actual world as fixed, and given that fixed reference, the function picks out what is identical to the actual referent in each counterfactual world, namely H_2O if there is any (assuming the usual philosophical myth that 'water' refers to H_2O in the actual world). So the doubtful premise—according to me—would be whether primary intensions stipulated to capture the a priori component of content are the same as secondary intensions for both the phenomenal and the psychofunctional term. Of course, there is no plausibility of the primary intension being identical to the secondary intension for 'water'. Twin Earth is a counterexample since the primary intension picks out XYZ whereas the secondary intension picks out H_2O. To the extent that the right-hand side of mind–body identity claims are natural kind terms like 'water', the version of the Property Dualism Argument presented in this Appendix has no plausibility whatsoever. You can see why one might be doubtful about this by noting that since primary intensions in this incarnation correspond to my CMoPs—which are also stipulated to capture the a priori aspect of content. As noted in the text, there is no plausibility at all that the CMoP of, say a functional term, is identical to the referent. Consider a very simple functional term, 'solubility'. The CMoP of 'solubility' is something like a meaning, but the referent is a property of sugar and salt. Why should we suppose that the solubility of sugar and salt is a kind of *meaning*? This seems like a category error.

In many of his writings, Chalmers has one notion—primary intension—corresponding to the two notions of my apparatus—CMoP and MMoP. But in Chalmers (forthcoming), he considers dividing the primary intension into two notions. As I understand it, the *epistemic* intension of 'water'—which is stipulated to capture the a priori aspect of content—is a function from situations (situations, not worlds) to what turns out to be water in those situations. The primary intension—which, on this version is not stipulated to capture the a priori aspect of content—is a function from worlds to what turns out to be water in those worlds. So on this scheme, epistemic intensions roughly correspond to my CMoPs, whereas primary intensions roughly correspond to MMoPs. On this new notion of a primary intension, it becomes a substantive question whether primary intensions capture an a priori component of content. If it turns out that they do for phenomenal terms and psychofunctional terms, then the Property Dualism Argument of this section would avoid the first of the two objections I mentioned above to the E → 2M analog for primary intensions. So it is worth taking a closer look at the prospects for the substantive—as opposed to stipulated—claim that primary intensions capture an a priori component of content.

I will start with a criticism of the notion of a primary intension as stipulated to capture an a priori component of content (see Block 1991, Block and Stalnaker 1999, and Chalmers (forthcoming: s. 5.8) for a response) Take the value of the primary intension of 'water' to be what turns out to be water in a world considered as actual. How do we know what turns out to be water in a world considered as actual? By consulting our intuitions about what one should say about various worlds considered as actual. We ask ourselves what we should say if, for example, we became convinced we were living on Putnam's Twin Earth. In my view, these intuitions are not just the epistemic basis of the primary intension—they are also its metaphysical basis. I won't try to justify this claim here.

Now ask yourself about another of Putnam's (1970) thought experiments, which we could put like this. Suppose we discover that cats are actually robots controlled from Mars that were put on earth 100 million years ago to spy on the intelligent beings they predicted would evolve. There never were any naturally evolving cat-like creatures, since the robot cats killed off anything that had a chance of becoming one. When intelligent primates finally evolved, the robot cats made themselves appealing to people and came to develop the close relation to people portrayed in *Garfield*. We are wrong about many of the properties we take cats to have. The robot cats pretend to be aloof but are actually very interested in us and love us. They would like nothing better than to act more like dogs, but their orders are to act aloof. They do not actually purr but use mind-control to make us think so.

I think the story is intelligible and I hope you think so too. But notice that other stories would have been equally intelligible in which cats fail to have other properties that we ordinarily think they have. The world I mentioned is a world considered as actual in which cats are not cute aloof purring animals. But there are other worlds considered as actual in which they lack other properties that we ordinarily think they have. Perhaps all the properties we ascribe to cats—or at least the ones that distinguish them from, say dogs—are in this sense dispensable. Some may want to retreat to *seeming* to have such properties, but in this direction lies the phenomenalism of C. I. Lewis. If the primary intension of 'cat' is determined by such intuitions and captures the a priori component of content, it looks as if there is very little to the a priori component of content. Maybe one can't imagine a world considered as actual in which cats are not moving middle-sized physical entities—but that will not distinguish a putative a priori component of 'cat' from that of 'dog'. A more serious problem is: How do we know whether in having these intuitions, we have correctly changed the meaning of 'cat'?

The problem would be avoided if one had some other notion of the a priori component of content that could be used in defining primary intensions, for example an account along the lines of the suggestion from Kripke that some words can be defined metalinguistically or Katz's more orthodox definitions. The primary intension of 'cat' would be the function from worlds considered as actual to what is picked out in that world by the proposed definition. But then we would not need the primary intension as an account of the a priori component of content because we would already have such an account: the definition.

Note that the problem is not one of indeterminacy in our intuitions or of cases decided by our intuitions—of course there are cases our intuitions do not decide. The problem is with cases that our intuitions *do* decide, like the robot cat case. Our intuitions are a function of the simplest overall account, and as Quineans have long said, *there is no guarantee that anything putatively a priori will be preserved in the simplest account.* If one believes in determinate a priori intensions, the thing to say is that our intuitions present us with situations in which we find it natural to change those a priori intensions. That is, in considering the Putnam robot cat world, we tacitly change our meaning of 'cat' (Katz 1972, 1975).

So there is a dilemma for the advocate of primary intensions as stipulated to capture an a priori component of content. If our advocate goes with Katzian or metalinguistic definitions, then there is no need for the notion of a primary intension. However, if our advocate rejects those definitions, then it is not clear why we should believe in any interesting a priori aspect of content or the primary intensions that are stipulated to capture it. Of course, primary intensions are just functions, and so the primary intension of 'cat' can be said to exist trivially. Yes, but that function may include inputs in which the word 'cat' is used in a different sense from the normal one and so could not be said to capture anything semantic. (See the coumarone example in Block and Stalnaker 1999.) The question is: why should we believe in a primary intension that *does* capture an a priori aspect of content? *Given the unreliability of the intuitions about cases as a pipeline to an a priori notion of content, primary intensions which are stipulated to capture an a priori notion of content become highly doubtful theoretical entities.* The upshot for the E → 2M form of the Property Dualism Argument is this. If an intension—primary or epistemic—is simply stipulated to capture an a priori aspect of content, then it is in doubt for the reasons just given. If we put this doubt aside, accepting the analog of the E → 2M principle, the identity of those intensions with secondary intensions is in doubt—that is, the other premise of the argument is in doubt. What if the intension is not stipulated to have this a priori significance, but it is claimed to have it nonetheless? The Putnamian considerations I raised cast doubt on that claim, but putting that doubt aside, my view is that to the extent we can show an intension to capture an a priori aspect of content, it will be doubtful that that intension can be identified with a secondary intension, so the two premises of the E → 2M argument will never be satisfied together.

New York University

REFERENCES

Austin, D. F. (1990) *What's the Meaning of "This"*? (Ithaca, NY: Cornell University Press).

Block, Ned (1978) "Troubles with Functionalism", *Minnesota Studies in the Philosophy of Science 9*, ed. C. W. Savage. (Minneapolis: University of Minnesota Press); 261–325. Reprinted in N. Block (ed.), *Readings in Philosophy of Psychology*, Vol. 1, Cambridge, Mass.: Harvard University Press, 1980). Reprinted (shortened version) in W. Lycan (ed.), *Mind and Cognition*, (Oxford: B. H. Blackwell, 1990), 444–69. Reprinted (shortened version) in D. M. Rosenthal (ed.), *The Nature of Mind* (Oxford: Oxford University Press, 1991), 211–29. Reprinted (somewhat longer shortened version) in David Chalmers (ed.), *Philosophy of Mind: Classical and Contemporary Readings* Oxford: Oxford University Press, 2002).

—— (1980) "What is Functionalism?" in *Readings in Philosophy of Psychology* (Cambridge, Mass.: Harvard University Press), 171–84.
—— (1991) "What Narrow Content is Not", in B. Loewer and G. Rey (eds.), *Meaning and Mind: Fodor and his Critics* (Oxford: Blackwell).
—— (1992) "Begging the Question Against Phenomenal Consciousness", *The Behavioral and Brain Sciences* 15/2, repr. in Block, Flanagan, and Güzeldere (1997: 177).
—— (1993) review of Daniel Dennett, *Consciousness Explained*, in *The Journal of Philosophy* 90/4: 181–93.
—— (1994) "Functionalism", in S. Guttenplan (ed.), *Blackwell's Companion to Philosophy of Mind* Oxford: Blackwell.
—— (2002) "The Harder Problem of Consciousness", *Journal of Philosophy* 49/8 (August), 1–35. A longer version is in *Disputatio* 15 (November 2003).
—— (2003) "Do Causal Powers Drain Away?" *Philosophy and Phenomenological Research* 67/1 (July 2003), 110–27.
—— and Dworkin, G. (1974) "IQ, Heritability and Inequality. Part I", *Philosophy and Public Affairs*, 3/4: 331–409.
—— and Stalnaker, Robert (1999) "Conceptual Analysis, Dualism and the Explanatory Gap", *Philosophical Review*, 108 (January), 1–46.
—— and Flanagan, O., Güzeldere, G. (1997) *The Nature of Consciousness: Philosophical Debates* (Cambridge, Mass.: MIT).
Boyd, Richard (1980) "Materialism without Reductionism: What Physicalism Does Not Entail", in Block (1980: 67–106).
Burge, Tyler (1977) "Belief *De Re*", *Journal of Philosophy* 74/6: 338–62.
—— (1982) "Two Thought Experiments Reviewed," *Notre Dame Journal of Formal Logic* 23: 284–93.
—— (1986) "Individualism and Psychology", *Philosophical Review* 95: 3–45.
—— (1989) "Individuation and Causation in Psychology", *Pacific Philosophical Quarterly* 707: 303–22.
—— (1995) "Intentional Properties and Causation", in C. Macdonald and G. Macdonald (eds.), *Philosophy of Psychology: Debates about Psychological Explanation* (Oxford: Blackwell).
Byrne, Alex, and Pryor, James (forthcoming), "Bad Intensions", in Manuel Garcia-Carpintero and Josep Macia (eds.), *The Two-Dimensionalist Framework: Foundations and Applications*.
Chalmers, David (1996) *The Conscious Mind* (New York: Oxford University Press).
—— (2003) "The Content and Epistemology of Phenomenal Belief", in A Jokic and Q. Smith (eds.), *Consciousness—New Philosophical Perspectives* (Oxford: Oxford University Press).
—— (2004) "Phenomenal Concepts and the Knowledge Argument", in Peter Ludlow, Yujin Nagasawa, and Daniel Stoljar (eds.), *There's Something About Mary* (Cambridge, Mass.: MIT).

Chalmers, David (forthcoming) "The Foundations of 2D Semantics", in M. Garcia-Carpintero and J. Macia (eds.), *Two-Dimensional Semantics: Foundations and Applications* (Oxford: Oxford University Press). An abridged version, "Epistemic Two-Dimensional Semantics", is in *Philosophical Studies* 118/1–2 (2004), 153–226.

Chomsky, N. (2000) *New Horizons in the Study of Language and Mind* (Cambridge: Cambridge University Press).

Davies, Martin, and Humberstone, Lloyd (1980) "Two Notions of Necessity", *Philosophical Studies*, 38: 1–30.

Devitt, Michael (1981) *Designation* (New York: Columbia University Press).

Feigl, Herbert (1958, 1967) *The "Mental" and the "Physical": The Essay and a Postscript* (Minneapolis: University of Minnesota Press). Originally published in 1958 in *Minnesota Studies in the Philosophy of Science*.

Field, Hartry (1994) "Deflationist Views of Meaning and Content", *Mind* 103: 249–285

Fodor, Jerry (1982) "Cognitive Science and the Twin-Earth Problem", *Notre Dame Journal of Formal Logic* 23: 98–119.

Hempel, Carl G. (1969) "Reduction: Ontological and Linguistic Facets", in S. Morgenbesser, P. Suppes, and M. White (eds.), *Philosophy, Science, and Method: Essays in Honor of Ernest Nagel* (New York: St Martin's Press), 179-99.

Hill, Christopher (1991), *Sensations: A Defense of Type Materialism* (New York: Cambridge University Press), 98–101.

—— (1997) "Imaginability, Conceivability, Possibility and the Mind–Body Problem", *Philosophical Studies* 87.

Horgan, Terrence (1984) "Jackson on Physical Information", *Philosophical Quarterly* 34: 147–83.

—— and Tienson, John (2001) "Deconstructing New Wave Materialism," in Carl Gillett and Barry Loewer (eds.), *Physicalism and Its Discontents* (New York: Cambridge University Press).

Horwich, Paul (1990, 1998) *Truth* (Oxford: Blackwell. Second edn. 1998 (Oxford: Oxford University Press).

Jackson, Frank (1982) "Epiphenomenal Qualia", *American Philosophical Quarterly* 32: 127–36.

—— (1986). "What Mary Didn't Know", *Journal of Philosophy* 83: 291–5.

—— (1998) *From Metaphysics to Ethics: A Defense of Conceptual Analysis* (Oxford: Oxford University Press).

—— (2004). Review of Perry (2001) in *Mind* 113/449 (January), 207–10.

Katz, Jerrold (1972) *Semantic Theory* New York: Harper & Row.

—— (1975) "Logic and Language: An Examination of Recent Criticisms of Intentionalism", in *Minnesota Studies in the Philosophy of Science 7*, ed. K. Gunderson (Minneapolis: University of Minnesota Press).

Kripke, Saul (1980), *Naming and Necessity* (Cambridge, Mass. Harvard University Press).
Levine, Joseph (1993) "On Leaving Out What It's Like," in M. Davies and G. Humphreys (eds.), *Consciousness* (Oxford: Blackwell), 137–49. Reprinted in Block, Flanagan, and Güzeldere (1997: 543–55).
—— (2001), *Purple Haze: The Puzzle of Consciousness* (Oxford: Oxford University Press).
Lewis, David (1980) "Mad Pain and Martian Pain", in N. Block (ed.), *Readings in the Philosophy of Psychology*, (Cambridge, Mass.: Harvard University Press), 216–22.
—— (1988) "What Experience Teaches", *Proceedings of the Russellian Society*, Sydney, Australia. Reprinted in Lycan 1990*a*.
—— (1990) "What Experience Teaches", in Lycan (1990*a*).
Loar, B. (1988) "Social Content and Psychological Content", in R. Grimm and P. Merrill (eds.), *Contents of Thoughts* (Tucson: University of Arizona Press).
—— (1990) "Phenomenal states", in J. Tomberlin (ed.), *Philosophical Perspectives*, iv. *Action Theory* (Northridge, Calif.: Ridgeview).
—— (1997). *Phenomenal states* (2nd version), in Block, Flanagan, and Güzeldere (eds.).
—— (1999*a*) "David Chalmers' *The Conscious Mind*". *Philosophy and Phenomenological Research* 59: 464–71.
—— (1999*b*) "Should the Explanatory Gap Perplex Us?", in T. Rockmore (ed.), *Proceedings of the Twentieth World Congress in Philosophy* (Charlottesville, Va.: Philosophy Documentation Center), ii. 99–104.
McGinn, Colin (2001) "How Not to Solve the Mind–Body Problem", in Carl Gillett and Barry Loewer (eds.), *Physicalism and Its Discontents* (New York: Cambridge University Press).
McKinsey, Michael (1991) "Anti-individualism and Privileged Access", *Analysis* 51: 9–16.
Montero, Barbara (1999) "The Body Problem", *Noûs* 33/3: 183–200.
Nagel, Thomas (2002) "The Psychophysical Nexus", *Concealment and Exposure and Other Essays* (New York, Oxford University Press, 2002), ch. 18. An earlier version appeared in Paul Boghossian and Christopher Peacocke (eds.), *New Essays on the A Priori*, (Oxford, Clarendon 2000).
Nemirow, L. (1980), Review of Thomas Nagel, Mortal Questions. *Philosophical Review* 89/3: 473–7.
Papineau, David (2002) *Thinking about Consciousness* (Oxford: Oxford University Press).
Perry, John (1979) "The Problem of the Essential Indexical", *Noûs* 13/1.
—— (2001) *Knowledge, Possibility and Consciousness* (Cambridge Mass.: MIT).

Perry, John (2004a) "Précis of *Knowledge, Possibility and Consciousness*", *Philosophy and Phenomenological Research* 68/1 (January), 172–82.

—— (2004b) Replies, *Philosophy and Phenomenological Research* 68/1 (January), 207–29.

Putnam, Hilary (1970) "Is Semantics Possible?", in H. Kiefer and M. Munitz (eds.), *Language, Belief, and Metaphysics*, (Albany, NY: State University of New York Press), 50–63. Reprinted in Putnam, *Mind, Language and Reality*, (Cambridge: Cambridge University Press), 139–52.

—— (1975) 'The Meaning of "Meaning" ', in K. Gunderson (ed.), *Language, Mind, and Knowledge* (Minneapolis: University of Minnesota Press).

Rozemond, Marleen (1998) *Descartes's Dualism* (Cambridge Mass.: Harvard University Press).

Schaffer, Jerome (1963) "Mental Events and the Brain", *The Journal of Philosophy* 60/ 6: 160–6

Schiffer, Stephen (1990) "The Mode-of-Presentation Problem", in C. A. Anderson and J. Owens, (eds.), *Propositional Attitudes* (Stanford: CSLI), 249–68.

Smart, J. J. C. (1959) "Sensations and Brain Processes", *Philosophical Review* 68: 141–56.

Stoljar, Daniel (2001) "Physicalism", *The Stanford Encyclopedia of Philosophy* (Spring) ed. Edward N. Zalta, <http://plato.stanford.edu/archives/spr2001/entries/physicalism/>, accessed 4 July 2005.

Sturgeon, Scott (1994) "The Epistemic View of Subjectivity", *Journal of Philosophy* 91/5.

van Gulick, Robert (1993) "Understanding the Phenomenal Mind: Are We All Just Armadillos?" in M. Davies and G. Humphrey (eds.), *Consciousness* (Oxford: Blackwell).

—— (2005) "Jackson's Change of Mind: Representationalism, *A Priorism* and the Knowledge Argument", in Ian Ravenscroft.

White, Stephen (1983) "The Curse of the Qualia", in Block, Flanagan, and Güzeldere, 695–718.

—— (forthcoming a) "Why the Property Dualism Argument Won't Go Away", at <http://www.nyu.edu/gsas/dept/philo/courses/consciousness/papers/White.pdf>, accessed 4 July 2005.

—— (forthcoming b) "The Argument for the Semantic Premise", ed. Torin Alter and Sven Walters.

Wiser, M., and Carey, S. (1983) "When Heat and Temperature Were One", in D. Gentner and A. Stevens (eds.), *Mental Models* (Hillsdale, NJ: Lawrence Erlbaum).

2. Mary and Max and Jack and Ned

John Perry

INTRODUCTION

There is more in Ned Block's rich chapter than I can discuss with the allotments of time, space, and, especially, wit and acumen, that various higher authorities have allotted me. I confine myself to replying to some of his criticisms of my treatment of the knowledge argument in *Knowledge, Possibility and Consciousness* (Perry 2001), mainly by restating my view in ways that connect with at least some of his reservations.

Pace Block, the knowledge argument is about knowledge. In Frank Jackson's classic statement it is a simple and gripping three-step argument. Mary has *new* knowledge when she steps out of the black and white room and sees a red fire hydrant. But while in the black and white room she knew *all* the physical facts relevant to color vision. Conclusion: her new knowledge is of a non-physical fact. It is Mary's new knowledge that is the crucial step. Some physicalists deny that she has new knowledge. I do not deny this. Instead, I offer an account of Mary's new knowledge that is consistent with the identity of qualia and physical brain states. There is no more direct way to confront the knowledge argument.

MARY

Mary thinks something like this: "The type of *this$_i$* color experience is what it is like (for me now) to see the color of *that* fire hydrant; that fire hydrant is red; I am normal and conditions are normal, so this type of experience is what it is like (for people with normal vision in normal conditions) to see red; that is, the type of *this$_i$* color experience is Quale$_{RED}$."[1] It is the relation between types of color experiences and

---

[1] Ordinarily we feel free to report knowledge that a subject would express with indexicals in indirect discourse. I will, however, use quotation marks around a sentence that Mary

colors that is crucial, at least in the original form of the argument, for this is what Mary, it seems, could have already known in the black and white room, if qualia were physical states of the brain.[2]

Block wants us to concentrate on what Mary knows when she is actually having the experience; in Perry (2001) I gave an account that also covered the knowledge Mary retains after having had the experience, but I'm happy to set that aside.

Mary could have known "The type of *this$_i$* color experience is what it is like (for me, in these conditions) to see the color of *that* fire hydrant"; even if her belief that the color of *that* fire hydrant is red was false, perhaps because some trickster had painted all the local fire hydrants green. She believes that there is nothing special about her color vision at the present moment, that there is nothing special about the light and other relevant conditions, that her color vision is normal, and that the fire hydrant she is seeing, like virtually all fire hydrants, is red. It is only the basic new knowledge that needs to be explained, that would be intact if all these beliefs were false, that is philosophically problematic. This knowledge, though philosophically problematic, is relatively trivial, but not completely so. There might not be a fire hydrant; she might not be seeing anything at all, while people play brain games with her in a completely dark room.

There are then four things involved in the truth of Mary's thought: her color experience, the type of color experience it is, the fire hydrant, and its color.

Consider Mary's phenomenology, as she studies the fire hydrant. I will use the term "experience" so that Mary's visual experience is a complex experience, and she can distinguish between the experiences that are parts of the complex. The color experience she has when she has an experience of the fire hydrant is different than the experience she has of the yellow dandelion next to it, and different than the experience she has of the fire engine. The experiences of the colors of the fire engine

could naturally use to express the knowledge, sometimes inserting a gratuitous "that" because it sounds better, as any indirect discourse formulation raises a number of questions about attitude reports that aren't essential to the points I make and on which almost no two philosophers agree. Although this way of formulating things might suggest it, I do not believe we need indexicals and demonstratives to think the thoughts we naturally express with them.

[2] Or, for that matter, if they were objective states, in some sense of that word, of any kind. See Perry (2001).

and the fire hydrant are of the same type, and different in type from that of the dandelion.

Mary knows that colors are properties that material objects have that are detectable by normally sighted people in favorable light, and that the color is seen at the surface of the object, and can be either uniform or varied. She knows that the visual experience of the color of an object involves the part of the visual field enclosed by the visually perceived boundaries of the object. She has had similar experiences before, but only of black and white and, I suppose, various shades of grey, the fillings for parts of her visual field delineated by the boundaries of objects while she was in the black and white room. She takes it that she is seeing a color, and having, for the first time, the ordinary experience one has when one does so. She knows that the object does not cease to be colored when she closes her eyes and her color experience ceases. So she knows that there are two types of things involved: the fire hydrant, with its color, and her color experience, which is of a certain type.

We can use "mode of presentation" both for the way that things are perceived and the way things are thought about. In the former sense, we would usually have in mind the particular way the object was presented to the subject. So Mary's mode of presentation of the fire hydrant has to do with the type of impressions, in Hume's sense, that it gives rise to, which will in turn depend on her position, the light, and so forth. In this sense, there are no modes of presentation of one's own experiences. One doesn't perceive them; they are not presented to one as the cause of experiences.

However, to *think* about her particular experience, Mary does need a mode of presentation of it. How does Mary *think of* her present experience as she has it? She thinks of it as playing a certain role in her life, as the present color experience she is having, occupying a certain part of her visual field, and due to the object that is determining what goes on in that part of her visual field. To think of something as playing a role in one's life in this sense, one does not need to have the concepts to articulate the role; it suffices to be attuned to the facts. Naive Mary would exhibit attunement to these facts in a variety of ways: by closing her eyes if she doesn't like it; by getting closer to the fire hydrant if she does like it; by focusing her attention on it if something about it interests her; by thinking the sort of thoughts I am getting at with the locution "this$_i$ experience is so and so", and so on. Sophisticated Mary will not only be attuned to such facts, but be able to think and talk explicitly about them.[3]

To form an idea or concept of a kind or a type of thing, it usually suffices to have an exemplar and a similarity relation. Mary has both for the type of color experience. She has the experience to which she is attending. She contrasts that experience with other experiences that she has had in the past and is having now: the experience she remembers having when she saw objects in the black and white room, the experience she has when she diverts her attention to the dandelion next to the fire hydrant (not similar), the experience she has when she diverts her attention to the fire engine (similar), and so forth. She knows that by playing with her brain, or lights, or some combination, her captors could give her similar experiences when the material objects seen were not of the same color, or when there were not material objects seen at all. Even if she is super-cautious, she can think: "this$_i$ type of color experience, whether it be Quale$_{RED}$ or Quale$_{GREEN}$ or whatever, is the type of experience I have, at least right now, when I see that color, whether it be red or green or some other color". In so thinking, she would be employing what seems to me to be a good candidate for what Block calls a "phenomenal concept".

How do the truth-conditions of Mary's doxastic states change, and why, when she acquires this new knowledge? In particular, the most basic new acquisition, that she would express as:

The type of *this$_i$* color experience is what it is like for me to see the color of *that* fire hydrant.

What is required for Mary's new belief to be true? It depends on what we take as given. Given only that Mary's thought is appropriately expressed by the quoted English words, "*This$_i$* type of color experience is what it is like (for me in these conditions) to see the color of *that* fire hydrant," what is required is that there be some fire hydrant, and some type of color experience, so that Mary is seeing and attending to the fire

---

[3] Block describes my view in terms of "being attuned to concepts". But this isn't a phrase I use in this situation, nor do I quite understand what Block has in mind. If Mary refers to the fire hydrant as part of a speech act, this might require her to be attuned to facts about the concepts of other people. To use demonstratives effectively in speech one needs to be attuned to facts about what other people see and don't see; this is the sort of situation in which I would talk abut being attuned to concepts, i.e. being sensitive to who has what concepts without having the concepts to articulate that to which one is sensitive.

hydrant, and is having and attending to an experience of that type, and the color experience is caused in the appropriate way by the color of the object and the conditions she is in. So the conditions of truth involve all four things, the experience, the type, the fire hydrant, and its color.

Given, in addition, that the type of her color experience is Quale$_{RED}$ and the color of the fire hydrant is red, and she is a normal person, her thought will be true iff

Quale$_{RED}$ is the type of experience normal people have when they see red in normal conditions;

and this is something she already knew in the black and white room. So the truth-conditions of her thought *given* those facts does not get at the new knowledge.

So, if we think Mary has new knowledge, but that she could have known in the black and white room which types of color experience go with which colors, we must find the new knowledge, the conditions that the truth of her new belief imposes on the world, in abstraction from those facts.

The natural answer to this is the one we all learned from Frege. Although the objects (the type of experience, the color) are old, the modes of presentation are new. She has thought of red many times, but never as the color of which she is having a normal experience. She has thought of Quale$_{RED}$ many times, but never as the type of an experience she is having and to which she is attending.

Frege's idea that one object can have numerous properties that individuate it, each of which, or at least many of which, can serve as modes of presentation, which he introduces in the first long paragraph of *Über Sinn und Bedeutung*, needs to be kept distinct from his theory of *Sinne*, as it is developed in the rest of that essay. According to this theory, when one thinks of an object, via a mode of presentation, as meeting a certain condition, that mode of presentation is a constituent of the *Gedanke*, the proposition that corresponds to one's thought that the object meets the condition. The proposition that is the object of one's thought, in turn, is the *Sinne* of the complement sentences of true reports of the thought. Jumping from the plausibility of Frege's insight about modes of presentation, to the validity of his theory of *Gendanken* and *Sinne*, is a little like jumping from the distinction between up and down, to Newton's theory of absolute space.

Indexicals and demonstratives make this pretty clear, for the need for distinguishing modes of presentation is vivid, but the rest of the theory of *Sinne* has to give somewhere. I see Ned Block and believe, on the basis of what I observe, "that man is suave and debonair". My perceptual mode of presentation of Block is something like: *the man I am looking at and attending to*. I am attuned to facts about occupants of this role; I use demonstratives reliably for such objects; I am sensitive to the difference between objects I am looking at and attending to and those I am not; I know how to pick up information about such objects.

But my perceptual mode of presentation does not seem to be part of *what I think*. I avert my gaze, in order not to be overly charmed; I continue to think the same thing, but via a new mode of presentation, my memory of the man I saw.[4] You can truly report my belief by pointing at Ned Block and saying, "Perry believes he is suave and debonair." Your mode of presentation of Block is as the man *you* are seeing, attending to, and calling attention to. I believe the same thing, while I am looking at Block and remembering him; but my modes of presentation differ; your report is correct, although your mode of presentation is not mine.

One of the identities of Frege's theory needs to be gainsaid, that between modes of presentation and constituents of *Gedanken*, or that between *Gedanken* and what is thought, or that between what is thought and the *Gedanken* that correspond to the complement sentences of true reports of the thoughts. My approach is (roughly) to hold to the second and the third, and give up the first. Other responses to the data provided by indexical and demonstratives are certainly possible; Stalnaker and Lewis can be thought of, ignoring subtleties and differences, as holding the first and second and giving up the third.[5]

If we accept all three identities, then if Mary has new knowledge, there has to be a new proposition *P*, so that we can truly report "Mary knows that *P*" and not just a new way of knowing a proposition already known. While not all advocates of the knowledge arguments are Fregeans, something like the Fregean identities are always lurking.

Give up the identities and it does not follow from the fact that Mary has a new belief, a new opportunity to be wrong or right about things, new conditions on the truth of her mental states, that there is a new fact

---

[4] See Perry (1980, 1997) for an exploration of such issues.
[5] See Stalnaker (1981) and Lewis (1979).

known, about a new property of experiences, that wasn't any of the properties she knew about in the black and white room. Her new belief puts the same conditions on colors and types of experiences as one of her old ones, but it puts new conditions on other things, the things that are parts of the modes of presentation and not of the subject matter. For the new belief to be true Mary has to be having an experience of Quale$_{RED}$, but this experience isn't part of the subject matter of her new belief or her old belief, but has to do with the modes of presentation of her new belief.

Perhaps Mary is so intelligent that she predicted that she would see a red fire hydrant and have Quale$_{RED}$ when she steps out of the room. She can predict this as an existential generalization: "there is a unique fire hydrant and a unique time when I am to be released, and there will be an experience caused by the fire hydrant at that time, and the hydrant will be red at that time and the experience an instance of Quale$_{RED}$..." She could existentially instantiate and assign names: Call the fire hydrant A and the experience E and the time T. She then could formulate her prediction, using the tenseless 'be': "The type of E be what it's like to see the color A be at T; the type of E be Quale$_{RED}$; the color of A be red." That thought, uttered at any time, will have the same subject matter truth-conditions as her thought, at the time of the experience, "The type of *this$_i$* color experience is what it's like to see the color that *hydrant* is *now*; the type of *this$_i$* color experience is Quale$_{RED}$; the color of *that hydrant* is red". But the modes of presentation will be different—in the theory reflexive truth-conditions of these thoughts will be different. However confident Mary was of her prediction, the equations "*this$_i$* color experience = E" and "*that fire hydrant = A*" and "$T = now$" still contain new information, because the modes of presentation are different. Super-intelligent Mary provides a more complex knowledge argument, but no new issues of principle.

NED

Block thinks my account leaves out phenomenal concepts. Whether Mary acquires a phenomenal concept depends on what we mean by this phrase. At one point Blocks says "A phenomenal concept of the experience of red is what Mary lacked in the black and white room and what she gained when she went outside it." By having the experience of seeing red, she gained a new way of thinking of Quale$_{RED}$, as the type of an experience she was having and attending to. This way of thinking of the quale of red did not require that she realize that it was the quale of red, the one she called "Quale$_{RED}$" even while in the black and white room. She could consider the possibilities that if there were a trickster, or her vision was not as normal as she assumed, that it was Quale$_{GREEN}$ or Quale$_{YELLOW}$ and so forth.

Blocks also says,

> With all this emphasis on phenomenal concepts, you might wonder what they are supposed to be. A phenomenal concept is individuated with respect to fundamental uses that involve the *actual occurrence* of phenomenal properties. In these fundamental uses, an actually occurring experience is used to think about that very experience. No one could have a phenomenal concept if they could not in some way relate the concept to such fundamental uses in which the subject actually has an instance of the phenomenal quality.

Again, I see no problem, although the word "individuation" almost always sends shivers up my philosophical spine when it is used with respect to concepts. Mary is having an experience, and using that experience to think about the type to which it belongs. She uses the concept to bring various other experiences in her total visual experience under it, the ones she deems to be similar, and contrast them with others she is having and remembers from her days in the black and white room.

Or consider this:

> Consider a specific phenomenal property, Q, e.g. the property of feeling like the pain I am having right now. (If pain just is a type of feel, then Q is just pain.) The physicalist says, let us suppose, that Q = cortico-thalamic oscillation... This is an a posteriori claim. Thus the identity depends on the expressions on either side of the '=' expressing distinct concepts, that is, having distinct modes of presentation, for if the concepts and modes of presentation were the same, it is said, the identity would be a priori.

No problem again. As we have seen, Mary can have the phenomenal concept, without knowing which quale it is of and so, should qualia be physical states, without knowing which physical state it is of.

But then problems develop:

> 'Q' in my terminology is very different from 'Q$_R$' in Perry's terminology since 'Q$_R$' is a term that Mary understands in the black and white room. 'Q' by contrast is meant (by me even if not by Perry and Smart) as the verbal expression of a *phenomenal* concept. A phenomenal concept of the experience

of red is what Mary lacked in the black and white room and what she gained when she went outside it.

There is nothing mysterious about "Q_R"; it's just short for "the quale caused in normal people by seeing red objects in normal light". There is no reason Mary shouldn't understand that term in the black and white room.

But what is Block's "Q"? What *is* this term that Mary couldn't understand until she had the experience? Since it is the verbal expression of a phenomenal concept, it looks like it should just be "the quale I am having now, as I attend to the color of the fire hydrant" or "the property of being the sort of sensation I am having now, as I attend to the color of the fire hydrant". What reason is there to suppose that Mary couldn't understand such terms in the black and white room? Indeed, there may have been black or white or grey fire hydrants in her room, or visible from her room, or on the black and white videos she was allowed to see in the room. She would have known "the property of being the sort of sensation I am having how, as I attend to the color of the fire hydrant, is not Quale$_{RED}$, since I am confined to a black and white room".

These words would have expressed a *different* concept than they do after she is allowed outside the room—just as "being the size of *that* man" could express different concepts at different times as one attended to different men. Maybe there is some superior way of expressing Mary's new phenomenal concept, using terms that she couldn't understand in the black and white room. Could be... but what would these terms be? I assume Block's "Q" is supposed to be shorthand for the verbal expression of a phenomenal concept, but we are never given the longhand version of it, so how are we to be sure that Mary couldn't understand this term in the black and white room?

Block continues:

Why do I insist that 'Q' express a phenomenal concept? Because the mind–body identity claim under consideration must be one in which the phenomenal property is referred to *under a phenomenal concept of it* for the Property Dualism Argument—in any of its forms—*even to get off the ground*. (The Knowledge Argument also depends on the use of a phenomenal concept in my sense.)... If the original paradigm of mind–body identity were "the property whose onset of instantiation here was at 5 p.m. = cortico-thalamic oscillation", the property in virtue of which the left-hand term presents the referent would not be a special candidate for non-physicality. It would be the property of being instantiated here starting at 5 p.m. The Property Dualism Argument depends on an identity in which a *phenomenal concept* is involved on the mental side. To allow a non-phenomenal concept is to discuss an argument that has only a superficial resemblance to the Property Dualism Argument.

I don't see much here to disagree with; I think Mary acquires a phenomenal concept; it is quite different from the sorts that Block mentions as not interesting; it is different because it is exactly the concept that Mary would have, the one she would naturally express with "This experience" or other words to that effect.

Block also says this (n. 10):

> Chalmers (2003) argues that phenomenal concepts cannot be demonstrative concepts. The main argument could be put as follows: for any demonstrative concept, say 'this$_i$', this$_i$ has phenomenal property P would be news. But if the demonstrative concept was genuinely a phenomenal concept, there would be some claims of that form that are not news. I agree with the "not news" rule of thumb, though I would not go so far as to agree that it shows no demonstrative concept can be phenomenal. However, whether or not it shows that there can't be a concept that is both demonstrative and phenomenal, the demonstrative concepts that Perry is talking about are not phenomenal concepts in the sense required to motivate the Knowledge Argument and the Property Dualism Argument, the sense required to ground the metaphenomenal move.

This leaves me perplexed. As we saw, demonstrative phrases can be used to express different concepts in different situations. As Mary turns her attention from the fire hydrant to the lawn next to it, she might use the phrase "this$_i$ color experience" for different concepts; the two concepts might be part of the same thought: "this$_i$ color experience is much more soothing than [turning her head back to look at the fire hydrant] this$_i$ color experience". But how exactly is it news to Mary, as she looks at the fire hydrant, that "this$_i$ color experience has phenomenal property P", if phenomenal property P is exactly the property she has never experienced until now, and is now experiencing, and attending to, and referring to with "this$_i$ color experience"?

CONCLUSION

As I said, Block's paper is rich and interesting—and long. I don't claim to have digested all that he has to say, and have not tried here to discuss all of it. I hope to return to the issue of Black's argument and the variety of modes of presentation at a later time, after having enlisted the help of seminar students in coming to grips with more of it.

Stanford University

REFERENCES

Frege, Gottlob (1892) *Über Sinn und Bedeutung* (repr. Göttlingen: Vandenhoeck & Ruprecht, 1994).

Lewis, David (1979) "Attitudes 'De Dicto' and 'De Se' ", *Philosophical Review* 88: 513–43.

Perry, John (1980) "A Problem about Continued Belief", in Jerome Dokic (ed.), *Pacific Philosophical Quarterly* 61/4: 317–22.

—— (1997) "Rip Van Winkle and Other Characters", in Jerome Dokic (ed.), *European Review of Philosophy*, ii. *Cognitive Dynamics* (Stanford, Calif.: CSLI), 13–39.

—— (2001) *Knowledge, Possibility and Consciousness* (Cambridge, Mass.: MIT).

Stalnaker, Robert (1981) "Indexical Belief", *Synthese* 49: 129–51.

3. A Posteriori Identities and the Requirements of Rationality

Stephen L. White

I. PROLOGUE

Imagine that a medical team and submarine have been miniaturized and injected into the brain of a conscious subject to correct an otherwise irreparable condition. As leader of the team carrying out this procedure, your greatest fear is that the subject, who is unaware of his situation, will take aspirin in response to the extensive c-fiber firing that you are apprehensively watching develop. For, as you know, in the subject's compromised condition, aspirin would cause nerve impulses and thus electrical activity in the brain that would completely destroy normal cognition. What you don't know is that the brain you are trying to repair is your own—that the nerve impulses from your body (minus the brain) produce the inputs (via a wireless connection) to the very brain whose activities you are witnessing. As a result, and because of the stress of the situation, you reach for the bottle of aspirin...

II. THE CHALLENGE TO THE IDENTITY THEORIST

Ned Block's chapter is a model of clarity and care, and the impossibility of an adequately detailed reply is a matter of genuine regret. What I propose is to concentrate on the challenge that the Property Dualism Argument poses for a certain form of the mind–body identity theory and on Block's positive response. The challenge is to the theorist who identifies pain with some physical phenomenon (call it c-fiber firing) and for whom the identification is a posteriori. And it is a challenge to explain how it is that one could be perfectly rational in believing, for example, what one would naturally express by saying "I am in pain but my c-fibers are not firing." I shall argue that Block has provided neither an explanation nor the grounds to suppose that one exists. I shall then summarize the points on which we disagree.

This challenge to the identity theorist is appropriate because if the identification is to be made a posteriori, there must be a coherently characterizable possibility—a possibility that makes rational disbelief of, or lack of belief in, that identity possible. The question, then, is what this entails. And the answer is that if the identity is true, then the subject who doubts it must apparently have two different modes of presentation of the same token event which is both the pain and the c-fiber firing. The obvious analogy (and one that the identity theorist insists upon) is with the possibility of one's believing, for example, what one would express by saying 'Hesperus is inhabited and Phosphorus is not'. And what makes this possible is the existence of two modes of presentation of Venus such that one believes of Venus under one mode of presentation that it is inhabited and under the other that it is not. Thus Block is correct in assuming that the relevant conception of mode of presentation is one that serves to explain the differences in cognitive significance of coreferring expressions.

What, though, is a mode of presentation? If we follow the model of Phosphorus and Hesperus, we will distinguish cognitive modes of presentation (CMoPs) and metaphysical modes of presentation (MMoPs). Let us imagine a rational subject S who believes of Venus that it is and is not inhabited because S associates the description 'the last heavenly body visible in the morning' with 'Phosphorus' and the description 'the first heavenly body visible in the evening' with 'Hesperus'. Such descriptions belong on the representational side of the line that divides representations and/or content from the world. Thus, as used by S, 'Phosphorus' and 'Hesperus' refer to Venus in virtue of the two distinct cognitive modes of presentation that are the two descriptions.

But why do these two cognitive modes of presentation pick out *Venus*? They do so, of course, in virtue of two real (and, apparently, distinct) properties of the planet—the property of being the last heavenly body visible in the morning and the property of being the first heavenly body visible in the evening. These are the metaphysical modes of presentation corresponding to the cognitive modes—they belong on the nonrepresentational side of the line that divides representations and/or content from the world. And this notion of correspondence, it seems, will make for a very tight connection—indeed an a priori connection—between cognitive modes of presentation and their metaphysical counterparts. After all, it is in virtue of the property of being the last heavenly body visible in the morning that Venus is picked out for S by 'Phosphorus' and in virtue of its being the first heavenly body visible in the evening that it is picked out for S by 'Hesperus'—*and not vice versa*.

Furthermore, it seems that it is in virtue of the fact that the expression 'being the last heavenly body visible in the morning' expresses the property of being the last heavenly body visible in the morning that it has the meaning (in the sense of cognitive significance) that it has. Similarly for 'being the first heavenly body visible in the evening'. (The proposal that this could be a matter of inferential role alone is not an option. I shall discuss this below.) If so, then the fact that the predicate expressions (embedded in the definite descriptions) express the properties they do explains why the sentence to which S assents—'Hesperus is inhabited and Phosphorus is not'—has as its content (in the relevant sense) a coherently characterizable possibility. It is simply the possibility that the properties of being the last heavenly body visible in the morning and being the first heavenly body visible in the evening were instantiated by different objects, only the second of which was inhabited. And the identity theorist who believes that the identity is a posteriori is committed to providing a coherent account of what the world would be like if the belief of the uninformed subject S were not mistaken.

The move from a difference in cognitive significance to the existence of two metaphysical modes of presentation presupposes that we individuate properties very thinly. But suppose it is objected that the property of being the last heavenly body visible in the morning might well be *identical* with the property of being the first heavenly body visible in the evening. This does, after all, seem *possible*. We can imagine that scientists determine that, given all the physically possible trajectories of "heavenly bodies", these two properties coincide as a matter of physical necessity. And we can suppose that they determine that because they have the same extension at all physically possible worlds they are the same property. Certainly nothing prevents our individuating properties in this coarse-grained way for some explanatory purposes. But there are other explanatory purposes besides those of theoretical science, and doing justice to the rationality of the subject who believes of Venus that it is and is not inhabited is one such purpose.

We are, then, if we identify the property of being the last heavenly body visible in the morning and the first one visible in the evening, committed to recognizing *other* properties to provide a rationalizing explanation of S's belief. For example, we might recognize different aspects or second-order properties of the property of being the last heavenly body visible in the morning (= the property of being the first heavenly body visible in the evening). Or we might recognize modal properties, such as the property a body might have in virtue of there being a logically or conceptually (but not physically) possible world at which it was the last heavenly body visible in the morning and not the first heavenly body visible in the evening. Could we identify even the second-order or modal properties? Quite possibly the answer is yes. But this is not to the point. For to do so in the absence of *other* distinct properties in virtue of which Venus figures twice in S's thought without his knowing it is to leave unrealized an explanatory project to which the identity theorist is committed.

III. BLOCK'S RESPONSE

Block disputes this. According to Block we can have two distinct cognitive modes of presentation, each of which picks out the object in question in virtue of the *same* metaphysical mode of presentation. Block's argument relies on his Paderewski example.

Our subject starts out under the false impression that there were two Paderewskis of the turn of the twentieth century, a Polish politician and a Polish composer. Later, he has forgotten where he learned the two words and remembers nothing about one Paderewski that distinguishes him from the other. That is, he remembers only that both were famous Polish figures of the turn of the twentieth century.

With regard to the example Block claims: "there are two CMoPs but only one MMop, the MMoP being, say, the property of being a famous turn-of-the-twentieth-century Pole named 'Paderewski'. Thus "Paderewski = Paderewski" could be informative to this subject, despite identical MMoPs for the two terms."
But, far from being informative,

(1) Paderewski = Paderewski

seems to express a proposition that the subject cannot even entertain. What the subject can entertain, of course, are *quantified* propositions ("There was exactly one famous Polish Paderewski at the turn of

A Posteriori Identities and Rationality | 95

the twentieth century", "There were none", "There were two", etc.). But the ability to entertain such quantified propositions is not the ability to entertain a proposition such as the one expressed by (1) that involves genuine singular reference. Certainly Block's subject can wonder whether there were two Paderewskis or one. And he can even wonder whether, for example, Paderewski ever wrote to Paderewski (in the sense that he can wonder whether one Paderewski ever wrote to the other). But he cannot wonder, for example, whether Paderewski ever wrote to Paderewski *or vice versa*, since he cannot distinguish the propositional contents of the two disjuncts. Thus we do not have a case in which there are two distinct cognitive modes of presentation of a single referent, and indeed there is no possibility of singular reference at all. And there is no such possibility precisely because there is no cognitive mode of presentation of the kind that would be required to pick out a particular object of reference. Thus we do not have the kind of case Block wants.

In light of these facts, why does Block insist that there are two CMoPs of Paderewski? Presumably he is not imagining that the subject produces two orthographically different terms for Paderewski by stipulation—say by introducing subscripts. For how would S suppose that 'Paderewski$_1$' came to pick out one rather than "the other"? Block's reference to S's "separate files" suggests that what he has in mind in talking about different cognitive modes of presentation are not different things at the personal level, but at the level of subpersonal causal mechanisms. After all, even if S cannot distinguish between different tokens of 'Paderewski' in his own usage, it could have been the case that some were caused by one person and some by another. Does this give Block what he needs?

The answer is no. And the reason is that subpersonal causal chains, by themselves, don't provide rationalizing explanations of subjects' beliefs. Suppose that S thinks that he dimly remembers that Paderewski was a musician (overlooking momentarily his belief that there are two Paderewskis whom he has apparently no way of distinguishing in thought). Later he thinks he dimly remembers that Paderewski was a politician (again momentarily overlooking his belief in "the two Paderewskis"). And because he remembers his earlier thought that he would have expressed by saying "Paderewski was a musician" he concludes that Paderewski was both a musician and a politician. This is clearly irrational, and irrational by S's own lights. But of course, in fact, the causal chains that produce the two thoughts and the two tokens of 'Paderewski' originate in the same person. Clearly, though, this doesn't get S off the hook—the inference is still irrational, subpersonal facts notwithstanding. Even putting this point aside, however, it is difficult to see how the reference to different files could help Block. If there are two distinct files, there are two causal chains, and the property of being the source of one is different from the property of being the source of the other. Hence there seems to be no example in which we have two CMoPs and only one MMoP.

We can now see the problem for Block's view. Complications aside, Block holds that our normal mode of access to our pains is via phenomenal concepts—descriptions in connection with which an instance of the pain itself occurs. That is, the pain is given in such a way that we stand in a demonstrative relation to it. Thus our mode of access to the qualitative character of our pains is direct in the sense that the physical property that is identical with the feeling of pain is its own mode of presentation. But this is to confuse directness in Russell's sense—acquaintance (in which sense-data are given directly and *are* their own modes of presentation)—with ordinary demonstrative access. And as the demonstrative versions of Frege's problem show, even in such cases, ordinary objects are not their own modes of presentation. In Evans's example, one points out of a window at a ship and says, "That ship was built in Japan." And one points out of another window and says, "That ship was not", without realizing that one has pointed to the same ship twice.[1] It seems clear, then, that even in demonstrative cases, ordinary objects are picked out in virtue of some but not others of their properties.

IV. EPILOGUE

The example in the prologue is simply a demonstrative version of Frege's problem for pains and c-fiber firings. Thus Block's positive account in terms of demonstrative access neither provides the two CMoPs and their corresponding MMoPs necessary to rationalize the subject, nor does it absolve us of the responsibility of doing so. But now consider: for any physical property that we might try to identify with the qualitative character of pain, we can imagine such a demonstrative version of

[1] Gareth Evans, *The Varieties of Reference* (Oxford: Clarendon, 1982), 84.

Frege's problem. Thus until we postulate a mentalistic property of (or suitably related to) the pain (= the c-fiber firing), our commitment to doing justice to the rationality of the subject who (intuitively speaking) fails to believe one of the relevant identities remains undischarged.

V. CONCLUSION

Having reviewed in synoptic form the challenge that the Property Dualism Argument poses for the physicalist identity theorist and my reasons for thinking that Block's positive account fails, I shall conclude with ten basic points on which I think Block and I disagree.

1. We need two CMoPs to deal with the various versions of Frege's problem. But why couldn't the object be given once under a mode of presentation and once "directly"? Consider, however, that the only model the physicalist identity theorist has of our being given something directly is the way in which something is given when we stand in a demonstrative relation to it. (Russell's notion of acquaintance, for example, is not available to the physicalist.) Even in such a case, however, the object is given under a cognitive mode of presentation, as is shown by the existence of the demonstrative versions of Frege's problem.
2. The cognitive modes of presentation must be available to the subject at the personal level. That is, they must be consciously available and characterizable from the first-person point of view. To suppose that CMoPs don't have to be described from the subjective point of view and given at the personal level is to forget their role in providing a rationalizing explanation for the subject.
3. We need two corresponding metaphysical modes of presentation. These are required for a number of explanatory purposes:
   (a) We must explain what features the object has in virtue of which it is picked out by the two distinct CMoPs.
   (b) We must explain what the difference in the meaning (cognitive significance) of the two CMoPs consists in. And it cannot be merely orthographic. We can have two orthographically distinct names that we use completely interchangeably precisely because we associate exactly the same cognitive modes of presentation with them. Nor can it be solely a matter of

linguistic descriptive content, since we must explain how the words in the descriptions come to have their meanings, and we cannot have an infinite regress of descriptions. Similarly it must be more than a matter of inferential role if this is understood solely in terms of language-to-language connections. (To suppose otherwise would be to suppose that language was merely an uninterpreted formal calculus.) Furthermore, the explanation cannot be a matter of either subpersonal functional states or external causal chains that are unavailable to the subject, either alone or in connection with descriptive content. This means that differences in the cognitive modes of presentation must be more than merely a matter of orthography, syntax, or causation. And as the demonstrative versions of Frege's problem show, even in demonstrative cases we pick out objects in virtue of some of their properties and not others. Thus we have to explain how language is grounded in the world, subject to the constraints imposed by Frege's problem. This is why there must be thin properties and, in the case of predicates embedded in descriptions, properties that correspond to them a priori.

(c) We must explain what coherent possibility allows a perfectly rational subject to doubt the identity in question. And thin properties that are related a priori to the subject's CMoPs and which could (without contradiction) have been instantiated by different objects provide the appropriate explanation.

4. The distinction between, on the one hand, a rationalizing explanation of a subject and, on the other, a causal explanation of a subject who is simply assumed (without explanation) to be rational cannot be ignored. To ignore the requirement that we rationalize subjects is to take a *locally eliminativist* view of the intentional states (in this case the belief states) in question. This is because (minimal) rationality is required by the ascription of intentional states and by the constraints of radical interpretation. So to ignore the constraint in a certain class of contexts is to forego the intelligibility of belief ascriptions in those contexts, and so the idea that there *are* beliefs in those contexts. And local eliminativism is unstable. If we treat beliefs in this way whenever the alternative presents difficulties, we are not committed to rationality (in belief ascriptions)

and so should simply count ourselves as eliminativists across the board where *intentional* states are concerned.
5. Problems with the description theory of reference do not warrant abandoning the idea that CMoPs must be available to the subject at the personal level. What we need is to know—to put it somewhat metaphorically—how the object gets into the subject's thought (at the personal level). And there is nothing in the commitment to this being in virtue of two CMoPs at the personal level (in the relevant examples) that requires that they be descriptions. Even in demonstrative cases (at least some of which could not be a matter of descriptive access if demonstrative access is to ground language), the same arguments for the existence of two CMoPs available to the subject apply.
6. Ordinary objects cannot be their own modes of presentation. Again contemporary "direct reference" views might tempt us to think otherwise. But the project of providing the referents of the singular terms of a language of a community, of saying what is expressed for the community by the predicates, and of providing the truth conditions of the sentences (e.g. as the output of a compositional theory) cannot be assumed to be the same as the project of explaining differences in the cognitive significance of the linguistic expressions of a speaker.
7. We cannot, then, in general take current semantic theories as unproblematic in this context. Nor can we assume that semantics, apart from issues directly connected with qualia, is unproblematic for physicalism. To suppose that a theory of cognitive significance must be physicalistic and then to reject what would otherwise seem to be necessary constraints on such a theory would clearly beg the question.
8. We cannot avoid the issue of narrow content. Theories of narrow content have been motivated both by issues of supervenience and by issues of cognitive significance, but increasingly the emphasis has been on the latter.[2] Thus the discussion of issues of narrow content is not an optional extra in this context.

---

[2] See my "Partial Character and the Language of Thought", *Pacific Philosophical Quarterly* 63 (1982), 347–65, repr. in *The Unity of the Self* (Cambridge, Mass.: MIT Press/Bradford Books, 1991), 27–49, and "Narrow Content", in *The MIT Encyclopedia of the Cognitive Sciences*, ed. Robert Wilson and Frank Keil (Cambridge, Mass.: MIT Press/Bradford Books, 1999), 581–3.

9. We cannot avoid fine-grained properties by looking at a subset of the logically or conceptually possible worlds. Though, as we have seen, two properties might have the same extensions at all physically possible worlds (and so be deemed the same property), such coarse-grained properties are not in general adequate for the rationalizing project to which the identity theorist is committed.
10. We cannot avoid questions of ontological commitment by adopting a question-begging criterion. If we are committed to the rationality of subjects and to the existence of qualitative states such as pain and intentional states such as belief, then we are committed to the things we need to postulate to make coherent sense of these things. That the upshot is Cartesian is by no means a foregone conclusion—in part because of the apparent alternative of treating pain as an intentional state.[3] But even if this proves to be possible, my view certainly involves a distinction similar to that between *verstehen* and causal explanation. And this is not a consequence that I find unwelcome.

Tufts University

---

[3] See Michael Tye, *Consciousness and Persons: Unity and Identity* (Cambridge, Mass.: MIT Press/Bradford Books, 2003), 48–62.

Part II

THE OPEN FUTURE

4. Goodbye Growing Block
Trenton Merricks

I. THREE THEORIES

Eternalism says that all times are equally real. Objects existing at past times and objects existing at future times are just as real as objects existing at the present. Properties had at past times and properties had at future times are had just as much as properties had at the present. Indeed, there is no metaphysical difference at all between past, present, and future. They differ only as a result of one's perspective, akin to the way "right here" differs from "over there". And so the eternalist takes 'the present' to be an indexical, like 'here' or 'this place'. With all this in mind, let's say that the eternalist believes in a *subjective present*.

Presentism says that only the present time is real. Every object that exists, exists at the present time. Objects that exist only at other times—like objects that exist only in fiction or objects that exist only in other "possible worlds"—simply do not exist at all. Moreover, an object has only those properties it has at the present time. The difference between past, present, and future is metaphysical, not perspectival. With all this in mind, let's say that the presentist believes in an *objective present*.

The *growing block universe* theory of time says that the past is real. In this much, growing block agrees with eternalism. But, according to growing block, the future is not real. In this much, growing block agrees with presentism. As time passes, according to growing block, the sum total of being increases. And the "growing edge" of being is the present.

These are not the only logically possible views of time. Someone might, for instance, defend a "shrinking block universe", according to which only the future and present exist, the present being the "shrinking edge" of being. But eternalism, presentism, and growing block are typically regarded as the only live options.[1] Of the three, growing block has the fewest defenders. I shall argue that it should have none.

---

[1] Eternalists include Lewis (1986), Quine (1960), and Sider (2001). Presentists include Bigelow (1996), Markosian (2003), Merricks (1999), and Zimmerman (1998). Growing

II. GROWING BLOCK AND 'THE PRESENT'

Growing blockers agree with eternalists about the nature of the past. They believe that past times are just as real as the present time. Thus they believe that just as you are sitting in the present reading this chapter, so—for example—Nero is sitting in the past watching a gladiator bout. And just as you think to yourself "I am sitting here at the present time," so Nero thinks to himself "I am sitting here at the present time."

To further clarify this point, let's consider some remarks by a prominent growing blocker, C. D. Broad. Broad claims that as something goes from being present to being past, nothing intrinsic to it changes. The only change is relational. Thus Broad:

> It will be observed that such a theory as this accepts the reality of the present and the past, but holds that the future is simply nothing at all. *Nothing has happened to the present by becoming past except that fresh slices of existence have been added to the total history of the world.* The past is thus as real as the present. On the other hand, the essence of a present event is, not that it precedes future events, but that there is quite literally *nothing* to which it has the relation of precedence. (1923: 66; first emphasis added)

And:

> When Queen Anne's death [first came into existence], it came into relations with all that had already [come into existence], and to nothing else, because there was nothing else for it to be related to. All these relations it retains henceforth and forever. As more events [come into existence] it acquires further relations, which it did not have, and could not have had while those events were non-existent. *This is all that ever happens to the event in question.* (1923: 82; emphasis added)

Suppose Broad is right about the nature of time. Then, when Nero's thoughts are present, no event exists that is later than them. When Nero's thoughts are past, they are related to later events. But the

---

blockers include Broad (1923) and Tooley (1997). Perhaps my "live options" should include a fourth view, one that endorses the reality of past, present, and future (like eternalism) but adds that there is an objective present, moving from past to future. (Broad (1923: 59) described this as the "policeman's bull's-eye" view of the present.) I suspect there is no coherent story to be told about what, according to this view, *being present* amounts to. Moreover, I think this chapter's argument against growing block can easily be adapted to undermine the policeman's bull's-eye view of the present.

intrinsic nature of those thoughts never changes. So *what it is like* to be Nero sitting in the Colosseum is the same whether that sitting is present or past. This is a result of any view that agrees with the eternalist about the nature of the past. And so it's a result of every version of growing block.

Given growing block, *what it is like* to be Nero sitting in the Colosseum is the same whether that sitting is present or past. Of course, Nero is not (any longer) on the growing edge of being. So what are we to make of Nero's thoughts like "I am sitting here at the present time"? The most obvious reply is that Nero is—and forevermore will be—thinking *false* thoughts, *falsely* thinking that he sits at the growing edge of being.

I think this most obvious reply is uncharitable to growing block. For consider that you think "I am reading this chapter at the present time." If 'the present time' refers to the growing edge of being, you ought to conclude that your own thought is false. After all, given growing block, once you have a thought, you continue to have that thought forever. That thought is on the growing edge of being for just the briefest moment and is thereafter and forever not on the growing edge.[2] As a result, the probability that your thought is on the growing edge is vanishingly small. Thus if Nero is wrong, then so—almost certainly—are you (cf. Braddon-Mitchell 2004). That is an unwelcome result.

Happily, there is a more charitable reply to be made on behalf of the growing blocker, a reply that does not imply that each and every thought explicitly about the present is virtually always—and so almost certainly—false. This reply invokes the above distinction between the *objective* present and the *subjective* present. Growing blockers should say that Nero's thoughts like "I am sitting here at the present time" are always about the *subjective present*. Such thoughts can be true even though Nero is not at the growing edge of being. Similarly, growing blockers should also say that nearly all of everyone else's thoughts about "the present" are about the subjective present too.

None of this should be too surprising. After all, the growing blocker shares some of the eternalist's views, specifically, those about the nature of the past. And the idea of a merely subjective present—the idea that

---

[2] Suppose the growing edge has no temporal extent. Suppose a thought about the present cannot occur instantaneously. Then the growing blocker might have to concede that thoughts about the present are never—not even for an instant—on the growing edge of being.

'the present' is an indexical—is part and parcel of eternalism. Thus it is not a big surprise to see this idea pop up in a view such as growing block, which has other areas of agreement with eternalism.

Of course, the eternalist says that the subjective present is the only present. But the growing blocker cannot say this. She thinks that there is also an *objective present*: the growing edge of being. (Whenever growing blockers explain their view, they use 'the present' to refer to this growing edge (Broad 1923: ch. 2; Tooley 1997).) As a result, even though we typically and nearly always mean the subjective present by 'the present', there is at least one context—that of elucidating the growing block—when it is used to refer to the objective present.

The growing block theory of time has two results. First, there are *two notions* of the present—objective and subjective—and 'the present' is correspondingly ambiguous (cf. Sider, 2001: 21–5). Second, 'the present' typically means the subjective present. 'The present' means the growing edge of being rarely, perhaps only when the growing block theory itself is being discussed.

III. MOTIVATION BY CONFLATION

The growing blocker must distinguish the subjective present from the objective present. A corollary of this is that she must distinguish the *subjective future* from the *objective future*. The subjective future follows the subjective present. (Some of the subjective future almost certainly exists; some of it does not yet exist.) The objective future is not yet part of being. Relatedly, the growing blocker must distinguish the *subjective past*, which precedes the subjective present, from the *objective past*, which precedes the objective present.

Given growing block, our typical thoughts about the present are about the subjective present. Likewise, given growing block, our typical thoughts about the future are about the subjective future. For you are surely right when you say: "My death is in the future." But then—given growing block—you had better be talking about the subjective future. After all, for all you know your death (like Nero's) is in the objective past. Indeed, that your death is thus like Nero's is the safe bet. For, given growing block, you shall be saying "my death is in the future" for an eternity, but during that eternity your death will be in the objective future for the mere passing flicker of a human life.

Typically, our thoughts about the future are about the subjective future. Indeed, given growing block, it seems we have thoughts about the objective future only when we are thinking about the growing block theory itself. It is only philosophers of time, while they are discussing growing block, who use 'the present' to mean the growing edge. Similarly, it is only they who use 'the future' to mean only the non-being that is yet-to-be. Given the growing block theory of time, all of us most of the time, and most of us all of the time, use 'the future' to mean the subjective future.

Suppose the growing block view is true. Then the "ordinary" present is the subjective present. The "ordinary" future is the subjective future. And—presumably—the "ordinary" past is the subjective past. The objective past, objective present, and objective future are, in contrast, technical devices for spelling out the growing block theory. I suppose that 'past', 'present', and 'future' are bad names for these technical devices, names likely to encourage a conflation of those devices and everyday life's past, present, and future.

This conflation is not merely hypothetical. Tooley opens his defense of growing block with: "The view of time according to which the past and the present are real, but the future is not, is a very natural one" (1997: 1). But there is nothing natural at all about Tooley's theory, since the everyday notions of *past, present,* and *future*—which are subjective according to growing block—are not those in terms of which Tooley's theory is defined. Tooley's theory appears natural only given the conflation just noted.

Broad also proceeds as if the growing block view is intuitively attractive and quite natural. But—once we distinguish the subjective present from the objective present—we should find his way of proceeding misguided. To take just one example, consider Broad's discussion of "tomorrow":

> If we ask what fact judgments ostensibly about the future refer to, we must answer that there is no such fact. If I judge to-day that to-morrow will be wet, the only fact which this judgment can refer to, in our sense of the word, is the fact which renders it true or false. Now it is obvious that this fact is the wetness or fineness of to-morrow when to-morrow comes. To-day, when I make the judgment, there is no such fact as the wetness of to-morrow and there is no such fact as the fineness of to-morrow. (Broad 1923, 73)

Broad assumes that growing block delivers the unreality of tomorrow. But growing block cannot guarantee the unreality of tomorrow any more than it can guarantee the unreality of your death.

I can see why one might desire a theory of time that guarantees that one's death and a week from Thursday are unreal, but provides for the reality of one's most recent birthday and the present. But such a theory is not to be had. For a theory tailored to satisfy these and similar desiderata would be nothing other than the growing block. But—I have argued—the growing block fails to satisfy them. The desire for a theory of time that makes the past real but not the future is like the desire to eat one's cake but also have it. It is understandable and incoherent.

IV. UGH

Consider the *unmotivated growing hunk* universe theory of time ('UGH' for short). According to UGH, the past and present are real. But UGH adds that a small part—and only that part—of the future is real too: the next ten years. Thus UGH seems to differ from growing block only with regard to the objective present's relation to the growing edge of being. UGH places the objective present ten years behind the growing edge, while growing block identifies it with the edge itself.

But this seeming difference is no difference at all. For UGH and the growing block agree that the growing edge of being is the growing edge of being. And they also agree that what trails the growing edge by ten years trails the growing edge by ten years. Any further disagreement is merely a difference in what is stipulated about the words 'the objective present' and not a disagreement about the nature of time. (Growing block stipulates that 'the objective present' means the growing edge; UGH stipulates that 'the objective present' means the slice of being ten years behind the edge.) Insofar as it is a theory about time—as opposed to a convention about how to use 'the objective present'—the growing block is UGH.[3]

The growing block is UGH. It is also UGH_{11}, the view according to which reality encompasses all and only the past, the present, and the first eleven years of the future. And it is UGH_{12}, and UGH_{13}, and so on. And so it is no more or less misleading to say that, according to this

---

[3] That is, the growing block is UGH if the past is infinite. They might differ if the past is finite, since UGH—unlike standard growing block—suggests that time started off with ten years of being. But even if the past is finite, there is no difference at all between UGH and non-standard growing block, according to which time first came into existence with ten past years.

view, the present is the growing edge of being than it is to say that, according to this view, the present trails the growing edge by ten years. As a result, I conclude that growing block/UGH/UGH$_{11}$ is not intuitively natural or attractive. It is wholly unmotivated. Growing block/UGH/UGH$_{11}$ is like "shrinking block". It is logically consistent but should not be a live option.

V. FRYING PAN TO FIRE

Growing blockers might object that their claim that the objective present is right at the growing edge differs substantively from UGH's claim that it is ten years behind. The disagreement between growing block and UGH—they might insist—is not over merely what is stipulated regarding 'the objective present'.

This objection makes sense only if we have some intuitive grasp of the objective present. It makes sense only if the objective present is something more than a technical device. Presumably, this objection presupposes that the objective present is our ordinary, pre-theoretical, intuitive notion of the present, the notion learned at our mother's knee.

Growing blockers who insist that the objective present is the mother's-knee present can differentiate growing block from UGH. More generally, they can resist most of my objections above to growing block. After all, those objections assume that—given growing block—our ordinary notion of the present (along with that of the past and the future) is the subjective.

But these growing blockers thereby return to the aforementioned "uncharitable" interpretation of their view. They must concede that the far and away most probable conclusion is that you believe an out-and-out falsehood when you believe "I am reading this chapter at the present time." Similarly they must concede that in all likelihood the mother's-knee past—which they should identify with the objective past—includes your death, tomorrow, and even the human outposts on Mars settled early in the fourth millennium.[4] Indeed, they must

---

[4] Growing blockers might claim that our mother's-knee notion of the present is a mix of subjective present and the growing edge of being. This is the worst of both worlds. For it implies that there is some truth both to the charge that growing block is no better than UGH and also to the charge that growing block makes it overwhelmingly probable that tomorrow is in the past.

concede that any event in one's *subjective* future—no matter how many thousands of years it is after today—is in all probability in the *objective* past. For that event will enjoy an eternity in the objective past but only finitely many years in one's objective future.

As I said earlier, the growing blocker should find such results unwelcome. They are also ironic. For this way of "saving" the growing block goes counter to the ideas typically advanced in its favor. In saying this, I do not deny that this way guarantees that—given the growing block— the future does not yet exist though the past and present do. However, this way of saving the growing block does not guarantee the non-existence of your death or tomorrow or outposts on Mars a thousand years hence. Indeed, this way of saving the growing block implies that, in all probability, your death and tomorrow and the Martian outposts are in the past. Nothing could be further from the spirit that animated growing block in the first place. And so even if we "save" growing block by distinguishing it from UGH, growing block is still wholly unmotivated. It is still like "shrinking block". Again, it should not be a live option.

REFERENCES

Bigelow, John (1996) "Presentism and Properties", in J. Tomberlin (ed.), *Philosophical Perspectives*, x. *Metaphysics* (Cambridge, Mass.: Blackwell).
Braddon-Mitchell, David (2004) "How Do We Know it is Now Now", *Analysis* 64: 199–203.
Broad, C. D. (1923) *Scientific Thought* (London: Routledge & Kegan Paul).
Lewis, David (1986) *On the Plurality of Worlds* (Oxford: Basil Blackwell).
Markosian, Ned (2003) "A Defense of Presentism", in Zimmerman (ed.), *Oxford Studies in Metaphysics* (Oxford: Clarendon Press), i.
Merricks, Trenton (1999) "Persistence, Parts, and Presentism", *Noûs* 33: 421–38.
Quine, W. V. O. (1960) *Word and Object* (Cambridge, Mass.: MIT).
Sider, Theodore (2001) *Four-Dimensionalism* (Oxford: Clarendon).
Tooley, Michael (1997) *Time, Tense, and Causation* (Oxford: Clarendon).
Zimmerman, Dean (1998) "Temporary Intrinsics and Presentism", in P. van Inwagen and D. W. Zimmerman (eds.), *Metaphysics: The Big Questions* (Cambridge, Mass.: Blackwell).

5. Rashi's View of the Open Future: Indeterminateness and Bivalence[1]

Eli Hirsch

The notion of indeterminateness has figured in three familiar contexts: the open future, vagueness, and quantum physics. Typical philosophical treatments of indeterminateness involve denying some principles of straight logic. In this chapter I explore a position of Rashi in which a belief in indeterminateness is combined with adherence to all of straight logic, including the principle of bivalence.

1. RASHI'S VIEW

Rashi holds that when someone makes a choice we cannot know whether it had previously been true that that choice was going to be made. This position is presented in the context of various issues of Talmudic law. As a simplified illustration, suppose a property owner has the two houses A and B for sale, and someone pays her a sum of money to buy one of the houses, specifying it as follows: "the house my son will choose next week". We are imagining that both the buyer and seller intend that the transaction—that is, the change of ownership—take place immediately. A week passes and the buyer's son has now chosen house A. Is it retrospectively revealed that A had been purchased

---

I was helped significantly in writing this chapter by comments from Michael Lockwood, David Spring, Timothy Williamson, and Palle Yourgrau.

[1] Rashi (Rabbi Shlomo ben Yitzchak, 1040–1105) was a preeminent medieval Talmudist. His position on the open future is implicit in his Talmudic commentary on the topic of "*breira*", especially in *Giṭṭin* 25a and 74a and '*Eruvin* 37b. Throughout this chapter I assume the interpretation of Rashi given in my "Talmudic Destiny" (manuscript available from *philosophia@Brandeis.edu*). Strictly speaking (as Mark Steiner showed me), what I am here calling Rashi's position is the Talmudic position of "*en breira*" as explained by Rashi; however, this position is the one that stands as the Talmudic verdict (modulo various complications). In any case, I hope it will be clear that the position I am attributing to Rashi is of philosophical interest, whether or not one accepts the attribution.

last week? Rashi holds that we cannot know whether the proposition "*A* will be chosen" was true last week; hence we cannot know whether the expression "the house that will be chosen" referred to—was true of—*A* last week. The legal consequence is that we are left with an unresolved question as to whether *A* was purchased last week.

Rashi's position is different from any approach found in the standard philosophical literature on the open future. Aristotelians, who hold that there are no truths about future contingencies, would claim that the proposition "*A* will be chosen" was definitely not true last week; hence the expression "the house that will be chosen" definitely did not refer to *A* last week.[2] The legal consequence of this position would seem to be that *A* was definitely not purchased last week. Anti-Aristotelians, including certain Ockhamists, would claim that we now know that the proposition just mentioned was true last week, and that the related expression did therefore refer to *A* last week. A possible legal consequence of this position is that *A* was purchased last week. In contrast to both of these standard positions Rashi neither affirms nor denies that "*A* will be chosen" was true last week, but holds that this remains an open question.

One might be tempted to suggest that Rashi's question is simply whether or not the Aristotelians are right. But that cannot be. For Rashi does not merely hold that it remains a question whether house *A* had been purchased. He holds that it also remains a question whether house *B* had been purchased! Even though house *A* has now been chosen it remains a question whether the proposition "House *B* will be chosen" was true last week. There is nothing in the standard positions that can make any sense out of this question.

We can understand Rashi's position as deriving from two commitments. First there is the commitment to straight logic (including straight meta-logic). "If I forget thee, O straight logic, let my tongue cleave to the roof of my mouth"—that was Rashi's attitude, as I imagine it. The second commitment is to its being in some deep sense indeterminate what choices people are going to make. A cautious formulation

---

[2] I assume the second interpretation given in J. L. Ackrill, *Aristotle's Categories and De Interpretatione* (Oxford University Press, London, 1963), 140–2. A helpful exposition of Aristotle's position is presented in Palle Yourgrau, *Godel Meets Einstein* (Open Court, Chicago, Ill., 1999), 126–9. I take it for granted that the clearest (but not necessarily the only) example of a "future contingency" is a "future choice", leaving it open exactly how to interpret these expressions.

of a principle of indeterminateness might be this: When a choice is made we cannot thereby conclude that it had previously been true that that choice was going to be made. Rashi accepts indeterminateness in that sense, as does Aristotle. It follows that from the fact that *A* rather than *B* has now been chosen we cannot conclude that it was true last week that *A* rather than *B* was going to be chosen. Hence, we cannot conclude that the proposition "*B* will not be chosen" was true last week. But, given straight logic, to say that "*B* will not be chosen" was true last week is equivalent to saying that "*B* will be chosen" was not true last week.[3] Since the indeterminateness of the future forbids us from saying the first thing it also forbids us from saying the second. Hence, even though we now see that *A* rather than B has been chosen, we cannot conclude that "*B* will be chosen" was not true last week.

Rashi's position will seem completely unintelligible if one supposes that, though *A* has now been chosen, we are left with some ordinary kind of factual ignorance as to whether the proposition "*B* will be chosen" was true last week. That cannot be what Rashi means. His point is rather that the indeterminateness of the future forces us to remain silent—and in that sense to leave it a "question"—what the truth was last week about which house was going to be chosen. We cannot say that "*B* will be chosen" was not true last week, for logic would then force us to say—contrary to our commitment to the indeterminateness of the future—that "*B* will not be chosen" was true last week. So we must remain silent about what the truth-value was last week of "*B* will be chosen". For Rashi the phenomenon of indeterminateness is characterized by a special kind of silence about the truth, a silence that stems not from ordinary ignorance but from the demands of logic and metaphysics.

Aristotle avoids this result by denying straight meta-logic, in particular the principle of bivalence, which says that either a proposition or its negation must be true. Aristotle would have said that last week neither "*A* will be chosen" nor "*B* will be chosen" nor the negation of either of these propositions was true. Anyone who has gone through Timothy Williamson's book *Vagueness* will have a vivid sense of how difficult it is to sustain Aristotle's logic.[4] The argument that follows is an adaptation

---

[3] The argument here depends on the natural assumption that "*B* will not be chosen" is understood in the sense in which it is the negation of "*B* will be chosen" (i.e. in the sense in which "not" has wider scope than "will"), so that it is equivalent to "*B* will never be chosen."

[4] Timothy Williamson, *Vagueness* (Routledge, New York, 1994).

114 | Eli Hirsch

of Williamson's discussion (pp. 162–3, 187–90). Williamson is not the first philosopher to present this general form of argument, but I suspect that his is the clearest and most persuasive formulation of it and the one most likely to influence future discussion. Moreover, he develops the argument in a certain direction that has a special bearing on Rashi's position, as I will explain in section 3.

The most fundamental problem is that, if we are committed to the basic principles of straight object-level logic, as Aristotle was, then denying the principle of bivalence requires the denial also of the most intuitive forms of the disquotation principle. The bare bones of the argument can be formulated simply as follows.

(1) Either p or not-p (by the law of excluded middle).
(2) p is true iff p, and not-p is true iff not-p.
(3) Therefore, ether p is true or not-p is true (from 1 and 2 by straight object-level logic).

To flesh this out and apply it to Aristotle's position, let us imagine that we are back last week at the time of the transaction. By the law of excluded middle, which Aristotle accepts, either A will be chosen or A will not be chosen. One highly intuitive form of a "disquotation" principle for the truth of propositions is this: "The proposition p is true if and only if p." (Strictly speaking, a disquotation principle applies to a quoted expression, but we can speak analogically of a disquotation principle for propositions.) This principle itself can be derived from three assumptions that seem on the face of it undeniable: "The proposition p is true if and only if it is true that p," "It is true that p if and only if it is the case that p;" and "It is the case that p if and only if p." If this principle is accepted then it follows that the proposition that A will be chosen is true if and only if A will be chosen, and the proposition that A will not be chosen is true if and only if A will not be chosen. It then follows from the law of excluded middle, together with some other elementary principles of straight object-level logic accepted by Aristotle, that either the proposition that A will be chosen is true or the proposition that A will not be chosen is true. It is clear, and certainly not denied by Aristotle, that the sentence "A will be chosen" expresses the proposition that A will be chosen, and the sentence "A will not be chosen" expresses the proposition that A will not be chosen. It immediately follows that either the proposition expressed by the first sentence is true or the proposition expressed by the second sentence is true. But

Aristotle holds that neither sentence is true, which surely implies that neither of the propositions expressed by the sentences is true. He must therefore block this argument by denying the principle, "The proposition p is true if and only if p." (In our specific example he must deny either "The proposition that A will be chosen is true if and only if it is true that A will be chosen," or "It is true that A will be chosen if and only if it is the case that A will be chosen," or "It is the case that A will be chosen if and only if A will be chosen.") It is not hard to understand why Rashi might not want to go along with this.[5]

Let me emphasize that it is not my aim in this chapter to defend the argument from disquotation to bivalence. The literature on this argument is extensive, and I have nothing original to add to it.[6] The standard argument against bivalence, however, is that it is incompatible with indeterminateness, and my aim here is to try to explain an apparently new position, coming out of Rashi, that reconciles bivalence with indeterminateness.

Aristotle seems to imply that, given that A has now been chosen, the proposition "A will be chosen", which was not true last week, has in some sense "become true".[7] This idea is easier to understand if we shift to a proposition of the "will have been" form. According to Aristotle, "A will have been chosen" was not true last week but is true now. The corresponding point, for Rashi, is that, whereas it is indeterminate

---

[5] Since Aristotle accepts the law of excluded middle he is not treating "neither true nor false" in the manner of a three-valued logic (cf. the description of Lukasiewiz's account in Williamson, *Vagueness*, 102–3). I want to confine myself in this chapter to philosophical positions that at least accept the law of excluded middle.

[6] An early formulation of the argument is found in William and Martha Kneale, *The Development of Logic* (Oxford University Press, New York, 1962), 46–7. A kind of compromise position is suggested in Bas van Fraassan, "Singular Terms, Truth-Value Gaps, and Free Logic", *Journal of Philosophy*, 63/17 (1966), 481–95, at 493–5. Van Fraassan suggests that the inference from "p" to "It is true that p" is valid, but bivalence fails because the material conditional "If p then it is true that p" is not valid (that is, we cannot affirm "Not: both p and it is not true that p"). Williamson's response to this position—that it does not capture the intuition behind the disquotation principle—is given in *Vagueness*, 162–3. A model-theoretic treatment of Aristotle's position is presented in Richmond Thomason, "Indeterminist Time and Truth-Value Gaps", *Theoria* (1970), 36: 264–81. Thomason's interesting and widely cited paper suffers, however, from an internal contradiction: At first he defends van Fraassan's position (p. 273), but then he develops a disquotational formulation (principle (8.1) on p. 278) without apparently realizing that it entails "If p then it is true that p." (Thomason has offered in correspondence an emended formulation in terms of double indexes; hopefully this will be presented elsewhere.)

[7] See Ackrill, *Aristotle's Categories and De Interpretatione*, 140.

whether the proposition "*A* will have been chosen" was true last week, it is determinate that the proposition is true now.

The two positions agree that it is not now determinate that the proposition "*A* will have been chosen" was true last week, and obviously not determinate that the proposition was false last week. Only Rashi's position, however, draws the consequence, required by the principle of bivalence, that it is neither determinate that the proposition was not true last week nor determinate that it was not false last week. It must be indeterminate whether the proposition was true or false last week. It might be asked why bivalence could not be sustained by holding that, although it was indeterminate last week whether the proposition was then true or false, it is now determinate that the proposition was true last week. I think it immediately seems dubious that something about last week, which was then indeterminate, can be determinate now. If the proposition had no determinate truth-value last week, how can it now be determinate what its truth-value was last week? But I will address this question more directly in section 4.

A paradoxical consequence of Rashi's position is that, even after we find out that *A* has been chosen, the conjunctive proposition "*A* will have been chosen, and '*A* will not have been chosen' was true last week" is regarded as having no determinate truth-value rather than as being determinately false. This follows from the (I think) evident principle that, if it is determinate that p and indeterminate whether q, then it is indeterminate whether both p and q. A comparable paradox for the Aristotelian position is that the conjunctive proposition "*A* will have been chosen, and '*A* will have been chosen' was not true last week" is regarded as determinately true rather than as determinately false. It seems that if we accept the idea of the indeterminateness of the future then paradox follows one way or the other. Certainly it is not my role in this chapter to defend the indeterminateness of the future (an idea to which I am in fact not committed), and I will not try to say which paradox is worse, Aristotle's or Rashi's. I have tried to explain the central theoretical motivation for Rashi's position. As regards the paradoxical proposition "*A* will have been chosen, and '*A* will not have been chosen' was true last week", one should note, first of all, that the claim that the proposition's truth-value is indeterminate certainly does not threaten either bivalence or disquotation. It is clear that we do not have an "intertemporal" disquotation principle of the form "p if and only if 'p' was true at time t in the past", since this would trivially run afoul of such examples as, "*A* has now been chosen if and only if '*A* has now been chosen' was true last week." (Perhaps a "tenseless intertemporal" disquotational principle might be defended by philosophers who "don't take tenses seriously"—who reject McTaggart's "A-series"—but it seems obvious that philosophers who accept the indeterminateness of the future generally do take tenses seriously, and cannot therefore have an "intertemporal" disquotational principle.) Moreover, the paradoxical proposition can be regarded in Rashi's position as a metaphysical contradiction in the sense that it necessarily cannot be determinately true. It is not, however, a metaphysical contradiction in the stronger sense of necessarily being determinately false. If we have been sufficiently impressed by the basic idea that no proposition about a future choice can have a determinate truth-value, then I think we will be able to tolerate—as merely a surprising corollary of the basic idea—that the paradoxical proposition cannot be assigned a determinate truth-value.[8]

2. BIVALENCE AND VAGUENESS

What distinguishes Rashi's position from the standard philosophical approaches, then, is a combined commitment to both bivalence and indeterminateness. I have not come across any philosophical discussion of this position in connection with the open future. Williamson, however, does discuss—and argue against—a corresponding position with respect to vagueness.

In the area of vagueness the counterpart of Aristotle's position is supervaluationism, which accepts the law of excluded middle and rejects the principle of bivalence. A sentence is true if and only if it is true on every admissible precisification of the language. If Jones is a borderline case of "bald", so that it is indeterminate whether Jones is bald, then the sentence "Jones is bald" is true on some precisifications but false on others; hence the sentence is neither true nor false.

The counterpart of Rashi's position is a modified version of supervaluationism. The central idea of supervaluationism is accepted, namely,

---

[8] As I try to show in "Talmudic Destiny", Rashi explicitly embraces the paradox. A close to literal rendering of Rashi's Hebrew formulations would yield something like this: "It cannot be ruled out that what has actually happened is different from what was (going) to happen." I take this to mean that, given what has actually happened, it remains indeterminate what (the truth was about what) was going to happen.

that a sentence is vague because we are semantically undecided between different ways of making it precise, so that in using the sentence we are in some sense straddling all the admissible precisifications. It follows as in the standard supervaluationist position that a sentence can be *known* to be true only if it can be known to be true on every precisification. We can also say, as in the standard position, that a sufficient condition for a sentence to be true is that it is true on every precisification. What we cannot say is that this condition is necessary for the truth of a sentence, for that would lead to the abandonment of bivalence. If it is indeterminate whether Jones is bald, then it is also indeterminate whether "Jones is bald" is true. By the principle of bivalence the sentence is either true or false, but we can say nothing more than that. Here again we have what I called in connection with Rashi's position the silence of indeterminateness.[9]

I began this chapter with a legal application of the disagreement between Aristotle and Rashi. It is easy to construct an example in which the disagreement between the standard and modified supervaluationist positions might plausibly have a legal consequence. Imagine that a fruit vendor has his apples arranged in a sorites series going from green to red. Someone pays him for an apple that is specified as "the first red one (whichever one that may be)". Suppose it is indeterminate whether apple a is the first red one. On the standard supervaluationist position it is determinate that "a is the first red one" is not true; hence it is determinate that "the first red one" does not refer to a. The legal consequence would seem to be that a has not been purchased. On the modified position, however, since it is indeterminate whether "the first red one" refers to a, the legal consequence might be that we have an unresolved question whether a was purchased.

One seems to find it said in some supervaluationist writings that it is indeterminate whether a vague term refers to a borderline case, so that it would be indeterminate whether "the first red one" refers to a, and indeterminate whether "bald" refers to Jones (who is borderline bald). I must take this to be merely a sloppy formulation. Since on the standard supervaluationist position "Jones is bald" is not true, it surely seems to follow that "bald" is not true of Jones, which means that "bald" does not refer to Jones. Indeed, since it is determinate that

---

[9] Silence may figure in vagueness in still another way; see Williamson's account of "Chrysippan silence" in *Vagueness*, 12–22. A version of the modified position is defended in Vann McGee and Brian McLaughlin, "Distinctions Without a Difference", *Southern Journal of Philosophy* 33, suppl. (1994) 203–51.

neither "Jones is bald" nor "Jones is not bald" is true, it is determinate that neither "bald" nor "(thing that is) not bald" refers to Jones. There is no indeterminateness here at all. (Another sloppy formulation found in the literature is when supervaluationists often say that, if it's indeterminate whether Jones is bald, then the sentence "Jones is bald" is indeterminate in truth-value; what they really mean is that it's determinate that the sentence has no truth-value.) It is only on the modified position, in which it is indeterminate whether "Jones is bald" is true, that it is also indeterminate whether "bald" refers to Jones.[10]

---

[10] The editors of the *Journal of Philosophy* objected as follows: "What [Hirsch] calls 'standard supervaluationism' is not properly presented. For example, if it is indeterminate whether apple *a* is the first red one (in a sorites series), then supervaluationally the statement '*a* is the first red apple' is not true, but this is not to say that it is determinate that 'the first red apple' does not refer to *a*. On the contrary, supervaluationally it is indeterminate whether it refers to *a*. [Hirsch] considers this, but says that this would merely be a 'sloppy formulation.' Why so? Since [Gareth] Evans's argument ['Can There Be Vague Objects', *Analysis* 38 (1978)], a lot has been said about this sort of indeterminate reference, and [David] Lewis's paper ['Vague Identity: Evans Misunderstood', *Analysis* 48 (1988), 128–30)] explains why a supervaluationist can and must say that it is indeterminate whether vague terms refer to borderline cases." (Correspondence from the *Journal of Philosophy*, January 2001.)

It is important to see why these objections are off the mark. The editors evidently understand supervaluationism to involve the idea that truth and reference need not be logically connected in the normally expected ways. On this version of supervaluationism, whereas truth is not disquotational, reference ("truth of") is. The idea must be that "the first red apple" refers to *a* if and only if *a* is the first red apple (this amounts to disquotation for reference); hence, since it's indeterminate whether *a* is the first red apple, it is also indeterminate whether "the first red apple" refers to *a*. According to the editors' version of supervaluationism, therefore, the following conjunction cannot be determinately ruled out: The expression "the first red apple" refers to *a*, and "*a* is the first red apple" is not true. (The conjunction cannot be determinately ruled out because, according to the editors' position, the second conjunct is true and the first is neither true nor false.) It is not surprising that the best-known supervaluationist literature contains no mention (let alone defense) of any such anomalous connection between truth and reference.

The editors state, however, that "Lewis's paper ... explains why supervaluationists can and must say that it is indeterminate whether vague terms refer to borderline cases." This seems to be patently wrong. Lewis does not appeal at all to indeterminateness of reference. He explains clearly that it can be indeterminate whether *a* is identical with *b* if different precisifications of the term "*a*" yield different referents. In this case we cannot make a valid inference from "It's indeterminate whether *a* is identical with *b*" to "*a* is something *x* such that it's indeterminate whether *x* is identical with *b*." Blocking that inference is the key to understanding why Evans's argument at the level of variables does not carry over to the level of identity statements. Lewis certainly does not imply that it can be indeterminate whether a given thing is the referent of a vague term. On the contrary, if some precisifications of a vague term yield *x* as a referent and some do not, there is every reason to suppose that, according to Lewis's supervaluationism, the vague (unprecisified) term determinately

If we allow higher-order vagueness then there will indeed be examples in which, on the standard view, it's indeterminate whether a sentence is true and also indeterminate whether a term refers to something. If Smith is on the border between being determinately bald and being borderline bald, then it is indeterminate whether "Smith is bald" is true, and indeterminate whether "bald" refers to Smith. The basic points made above remain: Truth and reference go together, and only on the modified position can it be indeterminate whether a vague term refers to a (determinately) borderline case.

The distinction between the standard and modified supervaluationist positions has a bearing on the issue whether the indeterminateness of vagueness is an objective phenomenon in the world or merely a feature of language. This issue has often been discussed in connection with special problems involved in indeterminate identity, but I am interested here in a more general question.[11] Suppose we want to say, as supervaluationists, that the indeterminateness of Jones's baldness is a linguistic phenomenon, in contrast to the objective indeterminateness that may be found in quantum physics or with regard to the open future. What could we mean by this? Of course our semantic indecision with regard to the vague word "bald" is a matter of language, but it doesn't immediately follow that the indeterminateness described using this word is itself a matter of language.

I think that the answer to this question implicit in much of the supervaluationist literature is that objective indeterminateness pertains to *propositions* (or *facts*), whereas the indeterminateness of vagueness pertains only to *sentences*. Consider objective indeterminateness with respect to the open future: A sentence about the future, such as "*A* will be chosen," determinately expresses a certain proposition *p*, and if we say that it is indeterminate whether *A* will be chosen, we are saying that is not determinate that *p* and not determinate that not-*p*. When we say that it is indeterminate whether Jones is bald, however, this is because

---

fails to refer to *x*. The editors have evidently confused Lewis's statement that a vague singular term has multiple precisifications with the claim that it is indeterminate what the term's reference is. This is no different from confusing the standard supervaluationists' statement that a vague sentence has multiple precisifications with the claim, which they deny, that it is indeterminate what the sentence's truth-value is.

[11] The typical supervaluationist treatment of indeterminate identity is given by Evans and Lewis in the papers cited in the previous note, and is explained in Williamson, *Vagueness*, 253–4. A different supervaluationist treatment is attempted in my "The Vagueness of Identity", *Philosophical Topics* 26 (1999).

we are semantically undecided as to which proposition to express with the sentence "Jones is bald." Any proposition that might be expressed by the sentence is either determinately true or determinately false. Indeterminateness in this case, therefore, attaches only to the vague sentence, not to a proposition.

Now it is extremely tempting—and I think that supervaluationists have often indulged the temptation—to elaborate the above explanation by imagining that there are a number of propositions, some true and some false, and, because of our semantic indecision, it is indeterminate which of these is expressed by "Jones is bald." But it would be a mistake for standard supervaluationists to say this, a mistake akin to saying that it is indeterminate whether a vague term refers to a borderline case. Surely a sentence (relative to a certain context of utterance) is true if it expresses a true proposition and false if it expresses a false proposition. If there is a true proposition p such that it is indeterminate whether the sentence "Jones is bald" expresses p, then it cannot be determinate that the sentence is not true, as claimed by the standard supervaluationist. Only the modified supervaluationist position can hold that it is indeterminate which proposition is expressed by the sentence, and hence indeterminate whether the sentence is true. The standard position must hold that, since different precisifications of the sentence express different propositions, it is determinate that the vague (unprecisified) sentence expresses no proposition.[12]

We saw in the last section that Aristotelians, who deny bivalence both for sentences and propositions, are therefore forced to deny the highly intuitive principle that a proposition p is true if and only if p. The standard supervaluationists can accept this principle and accept bivalence at the level of propositions, and they can try to explain why bivalence fails at the level of sentences by appealing to the fact that these sentences do not express any propositions.

---

[12] Might it be suggested instead that the vague sentence expresses all the propositions that could be expressed by its precisifications? This seems untenable, first, because if a vague sentence could somehow express both a true and a false proposition, standard supervaluationists ought to say, not that the sentence is both not true and not false, but that it is both true and false. Furthermore, the suggestion seems incoherent. Throughout this chapter when I talk about a sentence I presuppose a relevant context of utterance. Of course a sentence may express different propositions in different contexts, but in a given context it expresses at most one proposition—the proposition that is asserted (stated, said) by the utterance of the sentence in that context. (The suggestion certainly cannot be that a vague sentence expresses the conjunction of true and false propositions expressed by its precisifications, since that conjunction is determinately false.)

The obvious difficulty, however, is that, if vague sentences do not express any propositions, why aren't they simply meaningless? Even vague sentences that are determinately true will not express any propositions on this view. If it is determinate that Brown is bald, since the sentence "Brown is bald" has many precisifications, it cannot express any specific proposition. How, it must be asked, can a sentence that "says nothing" be true?

The standard supervaluationists must try to answer that vague sentences have the kind of vague meanings that they are required to have. They have just the kind of vague meanings that sentences must have when we are semantically undecided about what precisely to mean by them. And because the vague sentences have this kind of vague meanings, their truth-values must be evaluated supervaluationally.

The modified supervaluationist position seems to do better. By holding that a vague sentence does express a proposition, though it is indeterminate which one, this position is less vulnerable to the complaint that vagueness is a form of meaninglessness.

There is, however, a major problem faced by this position, brought out by Trenton Merricks.[13] If we are modified supervaluationists then we hold that, for some sentence x and some proposition p, it is indeterminate whether x expresses p. If this indeterminateness is itself to be treated in the manner of supervaluationists, it follows that we are semantically undecided whether to include in the reference of "expresses" the pair consisting of x and p. But what can be the nature of this semantic indecision? What relevant choices are we faced with as to what to mean by "expresses"? This baffling question evidently applies to other semantic notions. As modified supervaluationists we hold that it's indeterminate whether certain words refer to certain things (e.g. whether "bald" refers to Jones). We must be undecided, therefore, whether to apply the word "refers" to a pair consisting of a certain word and a certain thing. What indecision about the meaning of "refers" could yield this result?

It may seem that there is another problem here. In formulating our semantic indecision about an expression we must make use of semantic vocabulary. We say that we are undecided as to which things "bald" should refer to, and which proposition "Jones is bald" should express.

---

[13] Trenton Merricks, "Varieties of Vagueness", *Philosophy and Phenomenological Research* 62/1 (2001), 145–57. Merricks does not distinguish between standard and modified supervaluationism, but the issue he raises seems to me to bear most critically on the latter position.

If our indecision extends to semantic words such as "refers" and "expresses", we will have to use these very words to formulate our indecision about them. Isn't this circular? But I think this is not really a problem—or, at least, it is not a problem specific to this kind of example. We often have to explain the vagueness of expressions using those very expressions (or equivalent ones). As an obvious example, consider the expressions "expression" and "indecision". These are surely vague, and to formulate our indecision about these expressions we have to use them.

As regards Merricks's question, I think the answer we have to give, as modified supervaluationists, is that our commitment to various disquotation principles, combined with our indecision about non-semantic expressions, automatically generate a certain kind of indecision about the semantic expressions.[14] The following obviously idealized picture may provide a sense of how this works. Because of our indecision about "bald" we are undecided about which proposition to express with the sentence "Jones is bald." Imagine that there are n propositions, $p1$, $p2, \ldots, pn$, such that we are undecided which of these to express with the sentence. We are, however, committed to asserting, "The sentence 'Jones is bald' expresses the proposition that Jones is bald." We are therefore committed to treating the term "expresses" as referring to the pair consisting of the sentence and the proposition that Jones is bald. Since we are undecided which of the n propositions to count as "the proposition that Jones is bald", we are undecided whether to use the word "expresses" to refer to the pair consisting of the sentence and $p1$, or to the pair consisting of the sentence and $p2$, and so on, for all of the n propositions. In this manner our indecision about "bald" and other non-semantic expressions generates a derivative indecision about which pairs of sentences and propositions are to qualify as cases of "expresses". The same account applies to other semantic expressions.

To appreciate the force of Merricks's question one has to bear in mind that when we say that it is indeterminate which proposition is expressed by the sentence "Jones is bald" we are talking about the sentence as it stands, that is, in its vague unprecisified form. We are not merely saying that if we were to decide to precisify the sentence so that it expresses a certain proposition, then we would use "expresses" to refer to the pair consisting of the sentence and that proposition. In order for the answer

---

[14] Compare with Kit Fine's treatment of disquotational truth in "Vagueness, Truth, and Logic", *Synthese* 30 (1975), 265–300, at 296; and see Williamson's discussion in *Vagueness*, 163.

in the last paragraph to work it must make sense to say that our commitment to disquotation somehow generates a kind of indecision as to how to apply the semantic vocabulary to vague language. I am not confident that the answer does work.

It may seem that Merricks's problem will arise even for the standard supervaluationists, once we bring in higher-order vagueness (and the vagueness of vagueness), but I think this is not really the case.[15] If Smith is on the border between being determinately bald and being borderline bald, then, on the standard view, it's indeterminate whether "bald" refers to Smith. Hence "refers" must be vague even on this view. But the explanation for this is that, on the standard view, "refers" ("expresses", "true") is equivalent to "refers" ("expresses", "true") on every precisification. Our indecision about "refers" stems from our indecision as to where to draw the boundaries of what counts as an "admissible precisification", which is in turn related to our indecision about what to count as "(a sufficient degree of) indecision about the correct use of language".[16] No doubt there are serious problems in understanding these forms of indecision, but not the specific and especially baffling problem of understanding what sort of indecision we can have about "refers" if, on the modified view, it is not equivalent to "refers on every precisification".

The modified view has in common with Rashi's position the attempt to combine bivalence with indeterminateness. The problem that I have just gone over, however, has to do with vagueness and semantic indecision, and therefore represents no threat to Rashi's view about the objective indeterminateness of the future. Williamson's main objection to the modified position, however, to which I now turn, does apply just as much to Rashi's position.

3. QUANTUM PHYSICS AND THE EXPLANATORY ROLE OF INDETERMINATENESS

Williamson's most basic objection to the modified position is less an argument than a straightforward challenge to the very intelligibility of

---

[15] Higher-order vagueness will not yield examples in which, on the standard view, it's indeterminate whether a sentence expresses a proposition, but such examples can arise if it's indeterminate whether a sentence is vague. In what follows I will use an example of the indeterminateness of reference.

[16] Compare with Williamson, *Vagueness*, 158–61.

the position. "If we cannot grasp the concept of [determinateness] in terms of the concept of truth [as in the standard supervaluationist position], can we grasp it at all? No illuminating analysis of ['determinately'] is in prospect. Even if we grasp the concept as primitive, why suppose it to be philosophically significant?"[17] On the standard supervaluationist position "indeterminateness" is defined as "no truth one way or the other". If that explanation is ruled out by our commitment to the principle of bivalence, and we are therefore led to the modified position, then we are left with no way of explaining what indeterminateness means. If Jones is borderline bald then, on the modified position, we hold that the statement "Jones is bald" is either true or false, but we cannot say which. How can this amount to anything different than our being simply ignorant whether Jones is bald? What sense can we make of the purported difference between what I have been calling the silence of indeterminateness and the familiar silence of plain ignorance?

I certainly have no decisive answer to Williamson's challenge. I think that we must indeed accept indeterminateness as essentially a primitive notion if we are to make sense of the modified supervaluationist position or Rashi's view on the open future.[18] However, I am less sceptical than Williamson appears to be about the prospects for understanding this notion and appreciating its importance. What I am inclined to say in part is that Williamson is perhaps not being sufficiently theoretical in this matter. We may be justified in accepting indeterminateness as a primitive notion because that notion plays an important theoretical-explanatory role in various areas of discourse. Whether this justification can really suffice to overcome Williamson's kind of skepticism is a matter of judgment.

Wherever we invoke indeterminateness it is in order to try to explain something. In the case of vagueness we are trying to explain why we

[17] Ibid. 164 (Williamson has "definite" where I have put "determinate"). See his related comments, ibid. 194–5, and his further discussion in "Definiteness and Knowability", *Southern Journal of Philosophy* 33, suppl. (1994), 172–91.
[18] McGee and McLaughlin ("Distinctions Without a Difference", 214–17 and 245–6 n. 16) imply that we can explain what it means for a sentence that is either true or false to have no determinate truth-value by saying that neither the sentence nor its negation corresponds to a fact. The immediate problem is that "corresponds to a fact" must here be understood to mean "determinately corresponds to a determinate fact" (cf. Williamson, "Definiteness and Knowability", 178). To explain the notion of determinate truth by appealing to determinate correspondence to a determinate fact seems tantamount to treating the notion as primitive.

cannot know things that it seems we ought to be able to know. Having counted every hair on Jones's head, what stops us from knowing whether he is bald? The supervaluationist answer is that, because of our semantic indecision, it is indeterminate whether Jones is bald, and it makes no sense to know whether p if it is indeterminate whether p. If we are committed to straight meta-logic we will develop this idea along the lines of the modified position and say that, since it is indeterminate whether Jones is bald, it is also indeterminate whether "Jones is bald" is true. Williamson's explanation is that we cannot know whether Jones is bald because we lack the capacity to make sufficiently fine-grained discriminations between what we actually mean by the word "bald" and what we might have meant.[19] On his epistemic view our not knowing whether Jones is bald is a special case of ignorance. I am not passing judgment here on which of these explanations seems most plausible. My point is only that there does seem to be an intuitive difference between the explanations. Even if we are committed to straight logic, including bivalence, the distinction between indeterminateness and ignorance seems to make sense within the framework of the different total explanatory stories they enter into.

In the issue of the open future the central thing I think we are trying to explain is why, if a choice (or some other "contingency") occurred at a certain time, then prior to that time it was still in some sense possible for the choice not to have been made, but once that time passes there no longer is that possibility. The explanation that appeals to indeterminateness says that the future is open in the sense that it is indeterminate what is going to happen, whereas it is determinate what already has happened. If we are committed to bivalence we will develop this explanation along the lines of Rashi's position and say that it is indeterminate which propositions about the future are true. This explanation seems to differ intuitively from one in which it is held that we are merely ignorant as to which propositions about the future are true.

It is in quantum physics, however, that the explanatory role of indeterminateness seems most prominently on display. Even the most limited knowledge of quantum physics—which is all that I personally possess—seems to reveal that this is one area where the notion of indeterminateness has been posited for explicitly explanatory reasons. This fact presents, I think, a serious difficulty for Williamson's point of

[19] Williamson, *Vagueness*, chs. 7 and 8.

view. There are a number of possible interpretations of quantum indeterminateness—including "quantum logic"—but I am now concerned with only two of these, the one that corresponds to the Aristotle/standard-supervaluationist position and the one that corresponds to the Rashi/modified-supervaluationist position. The essential question again concerns the principle of bivalence, for I want to assume in accordance with these two positions that the law of excluded middle and other basic principle of straight object-level logic are accepted. If it is indeterminate whether a certain electron is spin-up, the positions agree that the electron is either spin-up or not spin-up. (I'll make the further assumption that, if the electron is not spin-up, it is spin-down, so that it is either spin-up or spin-down.) On the first position it is determinate that the proposition "The electron is spin-up" is not true, whereas on the second position it is indeterminate whether the proposition is true.

The position in quantum physics that roughly corresponds to Williamson's position on vagueness is Einstein's rejection of quantum indeterminateness. (Einstein needs "hidden variables" in his version of quantum physics and Williamson needs "hidden boundaries" in his version of vagueness.) Williamson's skepticism would seem to imply, however, that once we assume all of straight logic (including bivalence) then the difference between talking about indeterminateness, as many physicists do, and talking about ignorance, as Einstein does, vanishes into unintelligibility. But I think that is an exaggeration.

The issue in quantum physics of ignorance versus indeterminateness is often presented against the background of two critical experiments, the EPR (Einstein-Podolski-Rosen) experiment and Bell's experiment. I want to give a rough sketch of what I understand to be the explanatory role of indeterminateness with respect to these experiments (assuming the "orthodox" model of quantum indeterminateness roughly associated with Heisenberg and Bohr).[20] In one version of the EPR experiment a pair of electrons are generated in a manner that guarantees that their spin orientations will be opposite when measured in any direction. We know, therefore, that, with respect to any direction, the following disjunction is true: "Either the first electron is spin-up and the second is spin-down or the first is spin-down and the second is spin-up."

---

[20] A helpful discussion is found in Peter Kosso, *Appearance and Reality: An Introduction to the Philosophy of Physics* (Oxford University Press, New York, 1908). The paradoxical implications of Bell's experiment are brought out in N. David Merman, "Quantum Mysteries for Anyone", *Journal of Philosophy* 78 (1981), 397–408.

Quantum theory implies that it is impossible to predict which disjunct will turn out to be true when we perform a measurement. Einstein wanted to interpret this as simply a matter of our being necessarily ignorant as to which disjunct is true. The interpretation in terms of quantum indeterminateness holds that there is in a sense nothing for us to be ignorant about, since prior to making a measurement neither disjunct is determinately true, although the disjunction as a whole is determinately true. Measuring an electron's spin orientation brings about a "collapse of the wave" whereby the electron's spin orientation changes from being indeterminate to being either determinately up or determinately down.

Bell's idea was to measure the pair of electrons in different directions. In one version of his experiment we have three directions 1, 2, and 3 at certain specified angles from each other, so that we initially know that the following disjunction is true: "Either the first electron is 1-up and 2-up and 3-up and the second is 1-down and 2-down and 3-down, or the first is 1-up and 2-up and 3-down and the second is 1-down and 2-down and 3-up, or..." Bell was able to show, by what appears to be a completely simple and incontrovertible computation, that, given any one of these disjuncts, there is a certain probability of observing matching spin-orientations when a pair of electrons is measured along a randomly chosen pair of different directions. This computed probability diverges significantly from the accepted fact (based both on theory and experiments) of how the observed spin-orientations correlate. The explanation in terms of quantum indeterminateness is that, since the electrons have no determinate spin-orientations prior to being measured, there can be a probabilistic law governing how the spin-orientations will statistically correlate when they become determinate. The divergent computed probability, which takes a disjunct as given, is irrelevant because none of the disjuncts is determinately true prior to making a measurement.

On both the ignorance view and the indeterminateness view Bell's experiment proves that measuring the first electron has a probabilistic effect on the second electron, but the question is what the nature of this effect is. On the ignorance view the effect must be that the electron's spin changes (either from up to down or from down to up). On the indeterminateness view the effect is a change from having no determinate spin-orientation to having a determinate spin oriented in one of the two ways. This latter change (from indeterminate to determinate) is not a determinate change in the electron's physical state (at least in the classical sense of "physical state"); it is something different, something peculiar to quantum physics. Whether this difference constitutes an important theoretical advantage for the indeterminateness view is a matter of controversy. (Those who think it is an advantage will often speak of the unique "quantum holism" exhibited by the behavior of the particles in the EPR experiment and Bell's experiment.) What seems clear, however, is that most physicists regard the distinction between the ignorance view and the indeterminateness view as at least intelligible, and as potentially having an explanatory bearing on the experiments. Moreover, its intelligibility does not seem to depend on accepting an Aristotelian anti-bivalence interpretation of quantum indeterminateness. In fact, I tacitly presented the experiments in terms of a straight-logic interpretation, for I implied that, if it is indeterminate whether the electron is spin-up, then it is indeterminate whether "The electron is spin-up" is true.

There are (at least) three major camps in quantum theory. First, there are those physicists (David Bohm, for example) who follow Einstein in rejecting quantum indeterminateness, and who attempt to construct physical laws that can explain Bell's results within a framework of determinateness. Second, there is the "collapse view", according to which the states of particles are often indeterminate and this indeterminateness sometimes collapses and gives way to determinateness. On the "orthodox" version of this view—which is what I was assuming in my previous discussion of the experiments—the collapse is somehow brought about by measuring or observing the particles, whereas more recent versions of the view try to explain the collapse in other ways.[21] Finally, there is the "many worlds view". Members of this third camp hold that the only proper way to explain the EPR experiment and Bell's experiment is by positing indeterminateness that never collapses into determinateness and that pervades even the measurements and observations.[22] I am not remotely qualified to assess the relative merits of

---

[21] A helpful discussion of different versions of the collapse view is presented in David Albert and Barry Loewer, "Tails of Schrodenger's Cat", in R. Clifton (ed.), *Perspectives on Quantum Reality* (Kluwer Academic, Boston, 1996).

[22] A far-ranging philosophical treatment of the "many worlds view" is presented in Michael Lockwood, *Mind, Brain, and the Quantum* (Blackwell, Oxford, 1989). See also the symposium articles on Lockwood's book in *British Journal for the Philosophy of Science* 47 (1996), 159–258, and Lockwood's "Replies", 446–61.

these different approaches. The critical point for my argument is that members of the second and third camps—certainly these include some of the most eminent physicists in the world—hold that indeterminateness figures in the best explanations available in physics. If Williamson's philosophical position implies that these physicists are being incoherent, then this seems to set philosophy against physics in a way in which I am confident Williamson himself would not welcome.[23]

4. INDETERMINATENESS AND IGNORANCE

Even if indeterminateness has to be accepted as essentially a primitive notion there may be ways of representing or picturing it that helps us to gain an intuitive sense of what it involves. I'll mention one such representation in what follows. I'll then suggest that, on Rashi's position, there is a general characterization of the difference between indeterminateness and ignorance.

Physicists talk about quantum indeterminateness in terms of "superpositions". If it is indeterminate whether an electron is spin-up, the electron is said to be in a superposition of spin-up and not spin-up. Assuming the law of excluded middle, it is given that the electron is either spin-up or not spin-up. Its being in a superposition of those contradictory states is therefore not a third state that excludes each of them, but is rather a state that makes it senseless to ask which of the contradictory states the electron is in. Of course to understand what this means is to understand indeterminateness, so in a sense we are merely going in a circle. Nevertheless, such conceptual circles, when embedded within our theoretical explanations, may provide a kind of intelligibility.

[23] Williamson has tentatively suggested in correspondence that "indeterminateness" in physics may not mean what it does in philosophy, so that his attack on the philosophical notion may have no bearing on what physicists are talking about. Although I can see no immediate force to this suggestion with respect to the "collapse view", it may be quite plausible with respect to the "many worlds view", since the latter typically contains claims that seem to make little intuitive sense in terms of the philosophical notion of indeterminateness. For instance, on Lockwood's view, it can easily happen that there is a superposition in one component of which I am now thinkinq about quantum physics and in another component of which I am now comatose, so that it is indeterminate whether I am now conscious (or indeterminate whether I am now making this judgment). (Lockwood has stated in correspondence that quantum indeterminateness, on his interpretation, may indeed have little in common with the traditional philosophical notion of indeterminateness.) Certainly Williamson's suggestion needs to be explored further.

The idiom of superpositions can be adapted to the principle of bivalence, as well as the law of excluded middle. If we want to maintain bivalence we can say that the proposition "The electron is spin-up" is either true or false and that, furthermore, the proposition is in a superposition of truth and falsity. We might also say—taking "facts" as equivalent to "true propositions"—that there is a superposition of the fact that the electron is spin-up and the fact that it is not spin-up. (Insofar as facts can be viewed as states of the world, a superposition of facts is a special kind of superposition of states.)

The idiom of superpositions seems especially congenial to the perspective of Rashi's position. On Rashi's view there is at any moment a superposition of contradictory future-tense facts, for instance, the fact that A will be chosen and the fact that A will not be chosen.

A representation of indeterminateness that is similar to superpositions is Thomason's "non-linear" model of time.[24] On this model there is at each time a number of "alternative futures", which are not merely epistemic possibilities but are built into "the ontological structure of time". The truth-value of a future-tense proposition at a time depends supervaluationally on its truth-value relative to each of the alternative futures. Thomason develops this idea along Aristotelian lines (but see n. 6, above), but it can serve Rashi's position just as well. On Rashi's position a future-tense proposition is determinately true (false) at a time if it is true (false) relative to every alternative future. If the proposition is true relative to some alternative future and false relative to another, then it is indeterminate what its truth-value is.

Although the idiom of superpositions might be generalized innocuously to apply to linguistic vagueness, it is best reserved, I think, as a kind of picture of objective indeterminateness.

Let me now suggest that one essential difference between ignorance and indeterminateness has to do with their changeability. If we were merely ignorant last week as to whether a certain electron was then spin-up, we may no longer be ignorant now; we may know now that the electron was then spin-up. Notice that I am not merely saying that we may know now that the electron is now spin-up; the point is that we may know now that the electron was then spin-up. But if what we are saying is that it was indeterminate last week whether the electron was then spin-up, it would make no sense to say that it has now

[24] Thomason, "Indeterminist time and Truth-Value Gaps". See especially 265, 270–1.

become determinate that the electron was then spin-up (though it may of course be determinate now that the electron is now spin-up). Someone who does not accept this point is, I think, simply not getting the intuitive distinction between ignorance and indeterminateness. The point is made more vivid when recast in terms of superpositions. If the electron was in a superposition of spin-up and not spin-up last week then nothing can happen to eradicate that superposition retroactively. Evidently, we must continue to say that the electron was in a superposition state last week. Therefore, we must continue to say that it is indeterminate whether the electron was spin-up last week.

If indeterminateness is attached to truth, as in Rashi's position, the difference between the changeability of ignorance and indeterminateness might be stated in general terms as follows: Whereas our ignorance at time t whether proposition p is true at t can give way to knowledge at a later time that p was true at t, it is impossible for it to be indeterminate at t whether p is true at t but determinate at a later time that p was true at t (although it may of course be indeterminate at t whether p is true at t and determinate at a later time that p is true at that later time). This point is central to Rashi's position. If we hold that we were merely ignorant last week about whether the proposition "House A will be chosen" was true, then we would surely say that, now that we see that A has been chosen, our ignorance has lifted; we now know that the proposition was true last week. But if we are saying that it was indeterminate last week whether the proposition was then true, we must continue to say that it is indeterminate whether the proposition was then true. It helps again to recast this point in terms of superpositions. On Rashi's view there is at any moment a superposition of contradictory future-tense facts. Looking back at last week we see that there was then a superposition of the fact that A was going to be chosen and the fact that A was not going to be chosen. Since we are asserting that there was a superposition of these facts last week, we cannot also assert, with respect to one of them, that it but not the other obtained. It must therefore remain indeterminate what the truth was last week as to whether house A was going to be chosen.

What I have just said about house A holds as well for house B: It remains indeterminate what the truth was last week as to whether B was going to be chosen. Rashi draws the legal consequence that there was a superposition last week of A's being purchased and B's being purchased. Viewed in this light it seems that Rashi is acutely right in his startling claim that, even after house A has been chosen, we cannot rule out that house B was purchased.[25]

The *principle of the permanence of indeterminateness*, as I will call it, says that if it is indeterminate at time t whether a proposition p is true at t, then it is always indeterminate whether p is true at t. In terms of facts, the principle says that if it is indeterminate at time t whether a certain fact obtains at t, then it is always indeterminate whether that fact obtains at t.

In the context of Rashi's position the principle implies the following: If t is prior to t', and p is the proposition that a certain choice occurs (shall have occurred) at t', then it is permanently indeterminate whether p is true at t, and it is indeterminate prior to t' whether p is true at t'. The basic rationale is that at any time prior to the occurrence of a choice there is a superposition of the fact that the choice is going to occur and the fact that the choice is not going to occur.

The principle of the permanence of indeterminateness must be applied carefully. Suppose that u is a time at which JFK was eating his final breakfast. It is obviously a determinate fact now that JFK was eating his final breakfast at u, although it was not determinate at u that he was then eating his final breakfast (since it was not determinate that he would not have future breakfasts). This does not violate the permanence of indeterminateness, because it remains indeterminate now, just as it was indeterminate at u, what the truth-value was at u of the proposition that JFK was eating his final breakfast at u. In saying that it is now a determinate fact that JFK was eating his final breakfast at u we do not imply that it is now determinate that it was a fact at u that JFK was then eating his final breakfast.

The general point is that in applying the principle of the permanence of indeterminateness one has to take account of the distinction Ockhamists draw between "hard" and "soft" facts.[26] Although it has proven difficult in the literature to make this distinction rigorous, its intuitive import seems clear. A fact about time t is hard only if it does not depend on any facts that obtain after t. It is a hard fact that JFK was eating

---

[25] There are, however, various Talmudic/legal objections to Rashi's position that are not related to the present discussion; cf. "Talmudic Destiny".

[26] See Marilyn Adams, "Is the Existence of God a 'Hard' Fact?" *The Philosophical Review* 76 (1967), 492–503; John Fisher, "Ockhamism", *The Philosophical Review* 94 (1985), 81–100, and "Hard-Type Soft Facts", *The Philosophical Review* 95 (1986), 591–601.

breakfast at time u, but a soft fact that this was his final breakfast. If it is determinate now that a certain hard fact holds about a past time, it must also be determinate now that the fact held at that past time. If it is now a determinate fact that JFK was eating breakfast at time u, then it must have been a fact at u that JFK was then eating breakfast. On the other hand, the principle of the permanence of indeterminateness is not contravened by saying that, although it is now determinate that a certain soft fact holds about a past time, it was not then determinate (and is not now determinate) whether the fact held at that time.

Up to a point Rashi's position is similar to that of the Ockhamists. Last week, before house A was chosen, the Ockhamists would say, "It's either a fact now that A will be chosen, or it's a fact now that A will not be chosen, but it's unsettled (unfixed) what the fact is." They would say, further, that it's because the fact is unsettled that it does not interfere with the future choice. Rashi might say all this, too, except that, in my formulation of his position, the word "unsettled" is replaced by the word "indeterminate". What is the difference? The critical difference comes out a week later, after A has been chosen. The Ockhamists say, "It's now settled that it was a fact last week that A was going to be chosen." For Rashi this is never settled.

5. CONCLUSION

In Rashi's position on the open future we find the notion of indeterminateness operating within a framework in which both the law of excluded middle and the principle of bivalence are accepted. I have considered how analogous positions might apply in the areas of vagueness and quantum physics. I hope it is obvious that I have not meant to suggest that someone who accepts indeterminateness in one of these areas ought to accept it in the others. In general, the substantive issues in these different areas are unrelated. I do think it plausible to suppose, however, that the general logic of the notion of indeterminateness might carry over from one area to another. I also hope it is obvious that I have not been suggesting that the notion of indeterminateness—with or without bivalence—is easy to understand. It is in fact a baffling notion, as I think everyone agrees. Indeed, it may well be that in the final analysis Williamson's skepticism about the notion is correct. What I have tried to suggest is that a version of the notion that includes bivalence does seem to have some intuitive intelligibility within the wider context of explanatory theory, especially when supplemented with the picture of superpositions, and with the principle (implicit in Rashi's position) of the permanence of indeterminateness. My main aim in this chapter has been to introduce Rashi's position into the dialectical mix and to suggest that, if we are going to accept the notion of indeterminateness, then it is arguably best to do so without abandoning bivalence.[27]

[27] Given my own predilections in favor of "common-sense philosophy", what I would be looking for is a position on indeterminateness that, all things considered, is as charitable as possible to the judgments of ordinary people. I will leave for another place a discussion of whether that position might be Rashi's, Aristotle's, Ockham's, or something else.

6. General Facts, Physical Necessity, and the Metaphysics of Time

Peter Forrest

In this chapter I assume that we accept, perhaps reluctantly, *general facts*, that is states of affairs corresponding to universal generalizations. I then argue that, without any addition, this ontology provides us with physical necessities, and moreover with various grades of physical necessity, including the strongest grade, which I call absolute physical necessity. In addition there are consequences for our understanding of time. For this account, which I call the Mortmain Theory, provides a defence of No Futurism against an otherwise serious objection due to David Armstrong. In addition the Mortmain theory enables me to argue against the "Parmenidean" or Block Universe position that future and past are both real.

1. A THEORY OF TRUTH-MAKERS

This is not the place to provide a detailed truth-making theory. The seminal papers in the area are: "Truth-makers" (Mulligan, Simons, and Smith 1984) and "Truthmaker" (Fox 1987). For some recent work, readers are referred to Armstrong (2004), *Truth and Truthmakers*, and to a special edition of *Logique et Analyse* (Forrest and Khlentzos 2000). There are, however, some phrases—including "making true" itself—which could be confusing unless a truth-making theory is sketched.

Definition of sufficient truth-making:
Item x is said to be a *sufficient truth-maker* for *truth-bearer* p just in case necessarily if x exists then p is true.

I am indebted to Kevin Mulligan and to Dean Zimmerman for their perceptive comments on an earlier version of this chapter.

Note 1: I take truth-bearers to be speech acts—adjust what I say if you take them to be beliefs or propositions.

Note 2: Truth-maker theory is a theory of *truths*. As such it might but does not have to be used as part of a theory of *truth*. Following David Lewis (2001) we could replace the above definition by:

Item x is said to be a *sufficient truth-maker* for p just in case, necessarily, if x exists then p.

In that case there is no mention of truth on the right-hand side of the definition and the hyphenated word "truth-maker" does not demand analysis into its constituents.

Note 3: There is no commitment to an irreducible predicate "exists". If you can paraphrase "x exists" as "There is something of type X", then by all means do so.[1]

The Truth-maker Principle is that every truth has a sufficient truth-maker. Hence, I take it, the sum of all sufficient truth-makers, known as "Donald", is a universal truth-maker.[2] If we posit that as the only truth-maker we have trivialized the theory. But trivialization can occur in other ways too. Consider the truth that the Earth revolves around the Sun. The solar system as it actually is would be a sufficient truth-maker for this truth, but truth-maker theorists would prefer something less substantial, such as the state of affairs that the Earth revolves around the Sun. But what do we mean by "the state of affairs that the Earth revolves around the Sun"? If we mean whatever turns out to be the *minimal* sufficient truth-maker for "The Earth revolves around the Sun", then that might turn out to be Donald again, because there is no smaller truth-maker.[3]

There is, then, some difficulty in making it clear what we mean when we say, as I shall, that for suitable predicates F and G there are states of affairs corresponding to the generalization that all Fs are Gs. Are we merely saying that "All Fs are Gs" has a truth-maker, which might turn out to be Donald? Or what? Here is my proposal, inspired by Barry

---

[1] I am using quotation marks both in their ordinary senses and as Quinean corner quotes.

[2] I was informed of this usage by Barry Smith. The sum of all truth-makers probably owes its name to Davidson's "slingshot argument", which would seem to imply that all truths correspond to the same fact.

[3] I call the threat that, for any contingent truth the smallest truth-maker might turn out to be Donald, the *Entanglement Problem* (Forrest, 2000).

Smith and Berit Brogaard (2000). A truth-bearer *S corresponds* to *X* just in case "*S*-ing", the nominalization of *S*, refers to *X*. So if *S* is "space is curved" then "*S*-ing" is "space's being curved" and if there is something corresponding to "space is curved" then it is *space's being curved*.

Not all truths correspond to something. But I also assume that there is a relation of analytic entailment between some truth-bearers. Hence I am able to state:

Revised Truth-maker Principle
In a sufficiently expressive language every truth is analytically entailed by some truths that correspond to some things.

The things corresponding to truths analytically entailing *S* may be said to be the *truth-makers* for *S*. Hence, although not every truth corresponds to something, every truth has truth-makers. Just what kinds of thing can be truth-makers need not here concern us. I shall stipulate that any thing of the appropriate kind to be a truth-maker will be called a state of affairs (or a fact) unless it is an object.[4] An object presumably corresponds to a rather complicated set of truths that completely describe the essential characteristics of the object and hence make true all essential truths about the object.

The qualification "in a sufficiently expressive language" is required because we might have a truth *S* in a language *L* analytically entailed by a truth *T* in a more comprehensive language *L**. In that case it might turn out that *T* corresponds to some thing but there is no truth in *L* corresponding to any thing. For instance we might hold, following Armstrong, that truth-makers are composed of universals and particulars and that there are no vague universals. Then the language *L** in which there are truths corresponding to things would contain precise predicates, while every predicate in *L* might be vague.

2. TRUTH-MAKERS FOR GENERALIZATIONS

I propose that we follow Russell and grant that for some predicates *F* and *G* there are general facts, that is items which are not objects and which correspond to generalizations. So there are states of affairs:

---

[4] I am here using the term "object" to cover enduring 3D objects, instantaneous 3D stages or 4D spatio-temporal object-analogues, whichever is appropriate.

The fact that all Fs are Gs,
The fact that no Fs are Gs;
The fact that some F is a G.

Given the above characterization of correspondence this is equivalent to asserting that:

For some F and G, "All Fs being Gs" refers;
For some F and G, "No Fs being G" refers;
For some F and G, "Some Fs being G" refers.
And these nominalized sentences refer to things that are not objects.

Among the facts that all Fs are Gs we shall, I regret to say, have to include ones with disjunctive G, for instance the fact that a stable hydrogen nucleus has either no neutron or just one neutron. I also regret to say that we must allow various relational predicates. Indeed, as far as truth-maker theory goes, there might, for all I know, be states of affairs corresponding to *any* sentences expressible in a regimented language with a restricted range of predicates.[5] For example, suppose R and S are non-adjacent regions of space-time. Then I say that the disjunction "Either there being an electron in region R or one in region S" is the right kind of phrase to refer. If we deny that it and similar disjunctive expressions do refer that should be because of a commitment to determinacy, and the resulting rejection of indeterminacy interpretations of quantum theory. It should not follow from the truth-maker theory by itself that there are no indeterminate states of affairs.

3. COST-FREE BUT TRIVIAL NECESSITY

Time-dependent necessity was a topic investigated by medieval thinkers such as William of Ockham, and more recently by Arthur Prior. The idea is not controversial so much as apparently trivial. For example, the truth-maker for "Bob Hawke in 1957 incorrectly predicted that he would be Prime Minister of Australia in 1977" also makes it *now necessary* that Bob Hawke in 1957 incorrectly predicted that he would be Prime Minister in 1977. Many would say that this was *true* back in 1957, although this truth

---

[5] This regimented language might well be based upon the Sentential Calculus with an operator *nom* forming names out of propositions, so $nom(p)$ is the nominalization of p. And the predicates might all be precise ones.

was not *necessary* until 1977. This difference between truth and necessity, if it is a genuine one, lies in the rules governing the ascription of past truths rather than in any metaphysics. Time-dependent necessity may thus seem a rather trivial matter, truth under another guise. Note, however, that it is cost-free. Truth-makers for non-modal truths are also truth-makers for time-dependent necessities.

Need it be trivial? If the state of affairs that Bob Hawke in 1957 incorrectly predicted that he would be Prime Minister of Australia in 1977 had existed in 1957, then we would say that it was predestined, or fated, in 1957 that he would not be Prime Minister by 1977. Of course we have no reason to believe that such a state of affairs could have come to exist before 1977, so the non-trivial cases might seem quite fanciful. They do, however, show us how non-trivial necessities can arise, namely by states of affairs pre-existing the particulars they are intuitively about.

Realists about past and future, whom I refer to as Parmenideans, might wonder how being in the past could have modal consequences lacked by being in the future. What difference could it make? There are three possible responses to this. First we might grant that past states of affairs do confer modal status, argue that future ones—if there were any—would likewise do so, draw the fatalist conclusion and take that as a *reductio ad absurdum* of the Parmenidean position. The second is to say that time-dependent necessity is tied conceptually to causation, in that nothing is necessary at time *t* if it is the effect of causes that were still contingent at time *t*. Then the difference between past and future concerning modal status derives from a supposed impossibility of backwards causation. The third is to offer a deflationary account of time-dependent necessity, and hence, it will turn out, a quasi-Humean account of physical necessity. We would be told that the folk have this idea that the future is not real, and so have a concept of necessity based upon that "benighted" idea.

4. PHYSICAL NECESSITIES

Suppose that there has always existed the state of affairs that no horse is a horned animal. Then it would always have been necessary that there never were nor ever will be any unicorns. In this way we would have a necessity, which is far from trivial. It would be, I submit, a physical necessity. As far as I can see there is no reason why evolution might not have resulted in unicorns, so this example is implausible. Suppose, more plausibly, that it is a true universal generalization that the conservation of mass-energy has no exceptions. Then I hypothesize a truth-maker corresponding to that generalization, namely the state of affairs that energy is always conserved. When did that truth-maker come into existence? Suppose it came into existence a million years ago. Then it has been necessary for a million years that mass-energy is conserved but before then it was an accidental generalization. (Think of God retaining the power to break this "law" until a million years ago and then deciding to abdicate that power.) If however it is a physical necessity that energy is always conserved, then I am proposing that is because the corresponding general fact is as old as our universe.

My name for the proposed account of physical necessity is the Mortmain theory: the dead hand of the past is constraining the future. It replaces an earlier theory of mine, which was based upon realism about possibilities and the principle that with the passage of time fewer things are still possible (Forrest 1996.) Although I still hold that principle I now reject my previous commitment to a reality that *shrinks* with the passage of time. It is much more intuitive to say that reality *grows* because more things, including more states of affairs, come to exist.[6]

At no extra ontological cost the Mortmain theory gives us some highly non-trivial necessities. How was the trick worked? Simply by dating the state of affairs before the things it was intuitively about. This might seem peculiar. But if it is peculiar it is a peculiarity we already have accepted in giving a Russellian truth-maker theory. For whatever makes it true that there were no flying animals before the Carboniferous is intuitively about flying animals, so it is about what did not at the time exist. Again, suppose there was an accurate All Earth Census in 1900, and consider the truth-maker for "No human being alive in 1900 travelled to the Moon." It is not just about the billions of human beings who were listed in the All Earth Census. It also entails the indicative conditional, "if there are any other human beings living in 1900 not listed in the All Earth Census, none of them travelled to the Moon either" which is not about anyone who exists because, we are supposing, they all were in fact listed.

---

[6] I hold a similar objection to Storrs McCall's (1994) theory of falling branches of the tree of being.

5. GRADES OF NECESSITY

You do not just get one necessity free when you purchase the complete collection of truth-makers; you get, at no extra cost whatever, grades of necessity.

Some laws of nature might well hold only for our domain or sub-universe. The laws of chemistry might well be like this depending as they do on some quite exquisite fine-tuning of constants. In other domains maybe there is no chemistry, but neither any high-school students to rejoice in its absence. Now we have to posit, I submit, general facts involving relational predicates. We need them anyway as truth-makers. So, suitably ancient general facts involving relational predicates provide us with local laws. For example, suppose there are faraway regions of the universe in which chemistry is different from ours and there is a stable compound, helium oxide. Then consider the general fact that no helium oxide molecule occurs in the forward light cone from D, where D is a domain existing in the early universe at time k after the Big Bang. If this general fact came into existence at time k then it constrains the chemistry in the forward light cone from D, but not at other times and places. So if the visible universe is all in the forward light cone from D we have the genuine but spatio-temporally restricted necessity that there is no such compound as helium oxide in the visible universe.

At the other extreme if there is a time before our universe began we can distinguish a stronger than usual grade of necessity, namely that due to general facts that have always existed. For then there is a distinction between a state of affairs that has always existed and one that has existed for as long as our universe. Call this stronger grade *absolute physical necessity*. I distinguish it from an even stronger grade of necessity, *ontological necessity*, which I characterize as entailment by the correct analytic ontology, whatever that may be, and in whatever detail is appropriate. For example, if there are universals but no tropes then this truth is not merely an absolute physical necessity but an ontological necessity. My proposal then is to treat what is often called metaphysical necessity as ambiguous between ontological necessity and absolute physical necessity.

Why might we want yet another grade of necessity between ordinary physical necessity and the ontological? We might hypothesize that mental and physical properties are not identical but necessarily correlated in all actual universes, not just ours. If they were identical then indeed the correlation of the mental with the physical would be a matter of ontological necessity. But otherwise the strongest available necessity is absolute physical necessity, which has held in all universes at all times even perhaps before our universe existed.

6. DATING STATES OF AFFAIRS

It is now true that Constantinople fell in 1453. It is not obvious that there is anything *corresponding* to that truth, in the sense of correspondence defined in section 1. But for the sake of exposition let us suppose there is some corresponding state of affairs. Then it is not any *stage* of that city, which would also make true irrelevancies such as the colour of the city walls. So we may assume there is a state of affairs of *Constantinople's falling in 1453*, which makes it now true that Constantinople fell in 1453. This state of affairs might be taken by some as itself atemporal, but my account of necessities commits me to dating such states of affairs. There are three or four positions to choose between depending on the answers to two questions:

> Is the state of affairs of Constantinople's falling in 1453 located wholly in 1453 or does it persist forever?
>
> If it does persist, does it endure as the numerically identical state of affairs or is there a whole series of states of affairs: Constantinople's falling now; its falling yesterday; its falling last year, etc?.

I hold that the state of Constantinople falling in 1453 is located wholly in the past. My reasons for dating such states of affairs as now over are that: (1) I hold states of affairs depend on objects and (2) I would analyse an event as a state of affairs. Thus the event of Constantinople falling is the state of affairs of Constantinople falling at some time or other.

The account I have given of physical necessity does not, however, require any one theory of the dates of states of affairs, provided they are not atemporal, dateless entities. Here are three arguments in favour of dating states of affairs. The first is that parsimony should prevent us having a category of events as well as states of affairs. So the event of Constantinople falling in 1453 is the same as the state of affairs of

Constantinople falling in 1453. So such states of affairs, being events, must have dates.[7]

The second is that many states of affairs have temporal constituents and so are themselves temporal. Thus it is highly counter-intuitive to suggest that the state of affairs of Constantinople falling (or having fallen or being such as will fall) in 1453 could predate the city Byzantium-Constantinople-Istanbul, which is a constituent of that state of affairs.

The third argument that states of affairs are temporal is that they are not just truth-makers, they are causes and effects. Causes bring things into existence or change things. Hence the idea of a timeless effect is of doubtful coherence, and in any case an extravagant addition to metaphysics, unless we need it elsewhere. The only excuses for a timeless effects that I can think of are theological, concerning either the relations in the Trinity on a certain interpretation, or Descartes's thesis that even necessary truths depend on God's will, which might suggest that God timelessly causes numbers.

Incidentally, this attention to when states of affairs come into existence answers David Lewis's objection that the state of affairs that there are no unicorns would exert some strange power preventing unicorns existing. The answer is that if the state of affairs that there are no unicorns prior to time t comes into existence at some earlier time u, then it does indeed exercise a strange power, from u to t, as in my account of non-trivial necessities. But if it comes into existence at time t, then it is too late for it to get in the way of the unicorns in question.

7. A MORE PARSIMONIOUS ACCOUNT?

As I understand it Armstrong's most recent account of the truth-maker of the generalization that all Fs are Gs is the sum of the state of affairs that a is G, the state of affairs that b is G, etc. and the state of affairs that k *totalizes* the Fs, where k is the sum of a, b, etc., where in fact a, b, etc. are all the Fs (Armstrong 2004: 141–6.) This totalizing relation holds just in case every F is part of k. To be sure, we might find it unduly mysterious, but I shall not press that point. Instead I note that

---

[7] On a variant the event is the coming into existence of the corresponding state of affairs, which persists when the event has ceased occurring. This variant still leads to the dating of states of affairs.

Armstrong's totalizing relation account does not cohere with the Mortmain theory. For it is not plausible that a state of affairs could exist before its constituents. So, as Dean Zimmerman (1997: 77–8) has argued, the claim that the state of affairs that all *F*s are *G*s has always existed is only plausible if its constituents are the universals *F*-ness and *G*-ness and other ancient things rather than particular *F*s and *G*s that must extend in time to the very last *F* and *G*

Against Armstrong's account, I shall argue that we require truth-makers that involve the universals without any role for the particulars that instantiate them. I argue for this by considering states of affairs corresponding to existential generalizations. If we grant this then simplicity requires that we reject Armstrong's account and also grant that there are states of affairs corresponding to universal generalizations. Now Armstrong rejects states of affairs corresponding to existential generalizations because the state of affairs that *Fb&Gb* is a sufficient truth-maker for "Some *F*s are *G*s". In reply I provide two arguments.

My first argument concerns relational properties. The Earth has the relational property of being within 200 million kilometres of a star, and we might well be interested in that very relational property, which for an Earth-like planet might be a necessary condition for complex life forms to evolve. To be sure the Earth also has the relational property of being within 200 million kilometres of Sol where "Sol" names our local star. Nonetheless we might well consider the former relational property to be a genuine universal, in which case there is a state of affairs formed from it, namely that the Earth is within 200 million kilometres of a star. But that is the very same state of affairs as that there exists a star of which the Earth is within 200 million kilometres, a state of affairs that has existential form.

Another example of a relational property involving an existential quantifier is *being a hydrogen atom which is part of a methane molecule*, or if you prefer: *being a hydrogen atom which is bonded to some carbon atom itself bonded to three other hydrogen atoms*. Now consider the state of affairs that this hydrogen atom is part of a methane molecule, or, if you prefer, that this region of space-time is occupied by a hydrogen atom which is part of a methane molecule. There are alternative analyses of the state of affairs in question but they are all existential in form.

My other argument concerns the analysis of causation. In retrospect we say that this very person, quite unique, was caused to exist by parental sex, but we may also say that parental sex caused there to be a human being of such-and-such genetic composition. Thus we may distinguish the causation of the particular from the causation of the general. Question: "Is causation of the particular to be analysed in terms of the causation of the general, or vice versa?" Parsimony would suggest that one or other of the answers is always correct, but all I need for this argument is that sometimes causation of the particular is to be analysed in terms of causation of the general. For then there must be general facts.

The same distinction may be made at the microscopic level. For example the cause might be that this region of space-time contains a gamma ray and the effect might be that in some contiguous region there is an electron-positron pair. That would be causation of the general. In this case the causation of the particular would specify, I take it, precise trajectories for the electron and the positron. Hence in this case causation of particulars carries with it a commitment to precise trajectories. That might be unwelcome either because you hold a Whiteheadian position, according to which such trajectories are constructs out of thinner and thinner regions, or because you hold that an electron with a precise trajectory has a precise position and momentum, which might conflict with your interpretation of quantum theory. Or if you say that in this case the particular involved is a particle and not a region of space-time, then I would commend to you a causal account of what distinguishes individual objects, but that in turn, to avoid circularity, requires that the causation be of general rather than particular effects.

In addition, there is a case for existential states of affairs based upon probabilistic causation. To avoid controversial details let us start with a fanciful example. Suppose a magician, a real magician, has to make a living pretending to pretend to be a magician. That is easy enough. One of the magician's tricks is to take five dice each with playing card images on the faces—thirty faces in all—shake them in a cup, put the cup upside down on a board, take the cup off the board to reveal four of a kind. Of course she pretends she is palming the dice. But actually the magic words cause five dice to arrange themselves as required. But there is nothing in the magic ensuring that there are four Jacks rather than four Aces. Because the magic words cause the five dice to appear with four of a kind and because they have no further causal influence, the probability is one sixth that, say, there are four Jacks. That explanation of the probability requires us to say that in this case the causation of the particular depends on the causation of the general. For the explanation given went thus: the magic words cause the five dice to appear with four of a kind. And that is a general effect. I now challenge those who reject general facts to paraphrase this in such a way as to preserve the explanatory power of symmetry but without involving the causation of the general.

This will apply not merely to the real magician pretending to be a stage magician but to any situation in which the cause causes some effect of a given kind, but where just which effect occurs is not determined by the cause but instead the probabilities are constrained by symmetry. Perhaps the cause is the mixing of two chemicals and the effect is either one version of a crystal or the mirror image version. If both are equally likely why not explain this by appeal to symmetry together with the effect that there is some such crystal? Why propose as more fundamental that there is a 50 per cent probability of bringing about a particular effect and 50 per cent of bringing about the mirror image effect, thus hypothesizing what could be explained by symmetry?

A further argument for treating causation of the general as at least sometimes more fundamental than causation of the particular concerns the case in which the effect is negative. Suppose there is a last living organism, and that it dies of radiation. The radiation causes the end of life. Should we analyse this as the end of these life-forms or the end of life, period; as the end of life in this universe or the end of life, period? For what it is worth my intuition concerning such doom is that the radiation causes a general albeit negative state of affairs. That provides a case for Russellian negative facts and hence a precedent for other Russellian general facts. For the generalization that all Fs are Gs may be thought of as the double negative: no Fs are non-Gs.

There is a case then for holding that effects are sometimes to be analysed as general facts. When added to the argument that existential properties, such as *being within 200,000,000 kilometres of* a lead to existential facts, this gives us reason to prefer Russellian general facts over Armstrong's account.

Thus I have defended the Mortmain theory, and I conclude that an honest truth-maker theory, one that posits enough states of affairs to provide sufficient truth-makers for all truths, supplies at no extra cost various grades of physical necessity.

8. IMPLICATIONS FOR THEORIES OF TIME

But there is more! The Mortmain theory has implications for theories of time. First we can defend No Futurism from the criticism that whatever its other merits it coheres poorly with truth-maker theory. Armstrong (2004) makes this claim in his book on truth-makers. There are some truths about the future, we are invited to concede, and their truth-makers will be future entities, contrary to No Futurism. One response might be that states of affairs are atemporal, but clearly that is not one I can make. My response instead is that the only truths about the future are ones that have truth-makers that are already in the past. Thus if we suppose that it is true that the universe will exist for at least another hour, then I say that is because its continued existence is now necessary. No Futurism may be defended, then, against any supposed incoherence with truth-maker theory precisely by using the Mortmain theory of necessity.

Presentists may say something similar *provided* they adopt the expedient of saying that once states of affairs come into existence they endure forever as the very same states of affairs. In that case presentists should not think of states of affairs as tensed, with each as it were dying while giving birth to its successor. For if they do then they need causal connections between time slices of perduring states of affairs and hence they have to say that the real was caused by the unreal. It is better for presentists to follow John Bigelow (1996) and Dean Zimmerman (1997) and stick with enduring states of affairs and incorporate the tense in the truth-making relation.[8]

This proviso is open, however, to an objection, which we should examine. States of affairs are, I submit, *abstract* in the sense of having to depend for their existence on some object. Thus the state of affairs of the Earth revolving around the Sun depends for its existence on the solar system or at least on part of the solar system. From the abstract character of states of affairs we may conclude that presentists should not hold that there are states of affairs that outlast the objects they depend on. For the existent cannot depend on the non-existent, whether causally or otherwise. Hence the proviso required if presentists are to meet the objection from the truth-makers of past truths is itself open to

---

[8] Bigelow (1996: 42) is, however, considering the Stoic "lekta", translated as 'true propositions' rather than "states of affairs".

objection as counter-intuitive. Nor may presentists hypothesize that God is the sustaining cause of states of affairs, for that would make the truth of history depend on God's willing to continue sustaining the states of affairs. Bigelow (1996: 46) suggests that the states of affairs could be constituted by the World's having various properties, where the World is the sum total of things. But is the World an object?

My mention of causal dependence might make some suspicious. Perhaps the abstract nature of states of affairs is a general difficulty for the Mortmain theory. On what, and how, does the general fact that, say, mass energy is conserved depend? Not on the many events governed by that law. For that would make it an accidental generalization, as well as being incompatible with the No Futurism that I am defending. The only plausible answer is that the general fact in question has a cause, which might be taken either as God or time, or both.[9] In that case the general fact F depends for its existence on the further state of affairs that C causes F, where C is God or time or both together. In the case of causation it is plausible that the effect depends on the causal state of affairs, which in turn depends on the cause. Either we take dependence to be transitive, in which case F depends on C, or we do not, in which case we amend the principle that states of affairs always depend on something concrete, allowing them to depend on something else abstract provided eventually the abstract depends on the concrete.

Not merely does the Mortmain theory provide a defence of No Futurism, it also provides an argument against the "Parmenidean" position, the position that the past and the future are real. This argument concerns the supposed peculiarity of Russellian general facts, something I am supposing that we truth-maker theorists are driven to. This peculiarity is worth investigating further. For on reflection it is only Parmenideans who should find Russellian general facts peculiar. The phenomenological difference between past and future is that the past is complete, but the future is not. Suppose, for instance, there is a genuine vacuum occurring in a laboratory in 1987. We cannot now cause a little mini-universe, with its own beginning and end all within six months, to occur in that vacuum. And that is not just due to our lack of power. Not even God could do it. There has to be some feature of the

---

[9] Perhaps agency is always negative, always the exercise of a veto power. In that case time might spontaneously tend to cause anything still possible at random, but agents, including God, could direct affairs by restricting what happens to only some of these possibilities. As my New Age friends would say, I am comfortable with that.

past that implies this completeness, and Russellian general facts perform that role. Thus the negative fact that there is no mini-universe occupying a small region on the Earth in 1987, a negative fact that exists at the end of 1987, serves to prevent any further addition to 1987. If you ask what causes this general fact to exist the simplest answer is that the passage of time—the ending of 1987—is the cause.

No futurists should, then, welcome Russellian general facts. But for Parmenideans they should be puzzling. For they somehow exercise control only after a certain time, the time they come into existence. (Otherwise we are stuck with Lewis's objection that there being no unicorns exercises a strange causal-seeming power, annihilating potential unicorns before they could exist.) If the power that Russellian general facts exercise was an ordinary causal power then this would not be surprising, it would just be a further instance of there being no backwards causation. But it is a non-causal necessitation, and why should that be restricted to acting in a forward direction? Because, I say, until they come to exist temporally they do not exist in any sense. But Parmenideans deny this.

In addition, then, to undermining Armstrong's argument against No Futurism and Presentism, Russellian general facts provides us with an argument against the Parmenidean position, namely that that general facts cohere much better with the thesis that the past but not the future is complete.

I anticipate the objection that backward causation *is* possible. Indeed if the universe is otherwise deterministic in character we might brazenly appeal to backwards causation to defend the libertarian position (Forrest 1985). If there is backwards causation then the distinction between past and future is not that the former is complete and the latter not. The distinction would instead be one of comparative completeness. This could be made more precise by considering world histories and supposing that at each time t there is a set S_t of histories that are still possible at time t. Then there is more completeness at a later time v than at any earlier time u in that S_v is a proper subset of S_u. S_t consists of histories compatible with all the states of affairs that exist at or before t, so the more states of affairs that have come to exist the smaller the set of still possible worlds. For example, suppose it was indeterminate whether or not there were an odd or even number of (radioactive) Strontium 90 atoms in Aphra Behn's sternum at 7 p.m., 20 September 1670 (time u) but this becomes determinately even one second later (time v). Then the state of affairs that there was an even number of them at time u is a state of affairs that only came into existence at the later time v. So at times between u and v it was neither true nor false that at time u Aphra had an even number of Strontium 90 atoms in her sternum but this became true at time v. In this way the Mortmain theory may be adapted to cover the case of backwards causation.

University of New England

REFERENCES

Armstrong, David (2004) *Truth and Truthmakers* (Cambridge: Cambridge University Press).

Bigelow, John (1996) "Presentism and Properties", in James Tomberlin, (ed.), *Philosophical Perspectives* x. *Metaphysics* (Oxford: Blackwell), 35–52.

Forrest, Peter (1985) "Backward Causation in Defence of Free Will", *Mind* 94: 210–17.

—— "Physical Necessity and the Passage of Time", in Peter Riggs, (ed.), *Natural Kinds, Laws of Nature and Scientific Methodology* (Kluwer: Dordrecht), 49–62.

—— (2000) "The Entanglement of Truth-Makers", *Logique et Analyse*: 185–94.

—— and Khlentzos, Drew (2000) (eds.), *Logique et Analyse*: 169–70.

Fox, John (1987) "Truthmaker", *Australasian Journal of Philosophy*: 188–207.

Lewis, David (2001) "Forget about the 'Correspondence Theory of Truth'", *Analysis* 69: 275–80

McCall, Storrs (1994) *A Model of the Universe: Space-Time, Probability, and Decision* (Oxford: Clarendon).

Mulligan, Kevin; Simons, Peter; and Smith, Barry (1984) "Truth-Makers", *Philosophy and Phenomenological Research*: 287–321.

Smith, Barry, and Brogaard, Berit (2000) "A Unified Theory of Truth and Reference", *Logique et Analyse*: 49–94.

Zimmerman, Dean (1997), "Chisholm and the Essences of Events", in Lewis Hahn (ed.), *The Philosophy of Roderick M. Chisholm*, Library of Living Philosophers 25 (Chicago: Open Court), 73–100.

Part III

ISSUES IN ONTOLOGY

7. Inexpressible Properties and Propositions

Thomas Hofweber

1. THE RELEVANCE OF INEXPRESSIBLE PROPERTIES FOR THE LARGE-SCALE DEBATE ABOUT (TALK ABOUT) PROPERTIES

Everyone working on metaphysical questions about properties or propositions knows the reaction that many non-philosophers, even non-metaphysicians, have to such questions. Even though they agree that Fido is a dog and thus has the property (or feature or characteristic) of being a dog, it seems weird, suspicious, or confused to them to now ask what that thing, the property of being a dog, is. The same reservations do not carry over to asking what this thing, Fido, is. There is a substantial and legitimate project to find out more about Fido, but is there a similar substantial and legitimate project to find out more about the property of being a dog? Metaphysicians know that there is a straightforward way to motivate such a project, and much of the contemporary debate in the metaphysics of properties is in the ballpark of carrying it out. If we agree that Fido has the property of being a dog, then there is something that is a property and that Fido has. Thus we can ask about what this thing is that he has. How does it relate to Fido? Is it concrete or abstract? Is it fully present in each object that has it? And so on and so forth. Maybe the non-philosophers are merely not used to asking such questions about unusual entities such as properties, but they are equally legitimate for them as they are for any other thing. However, even metaphysicians sometimes have the nagging feeling that something has gone wrong in the metaphysics of properties, and that a substantial metaphysical investigation into their

Thanks to John Perry, Sol Feferman, John Etchemendy, Johan van Benthem, Mark Richard, Kent Bach, Rich Thomason, Allan Gibbard, Jim Joyce, Eric Lormand, Adam Morton, Jessica Wilson, Peter Railton, and Ted Sider for their help. The beginnings of this chapter date back to the author's attending ESSLLI 97 in Aix-en-Provence with support from Johan van Benthem's Spinoza Grant, which is hereby gratefully acknowledged.

nature is somehow based on a confusion. This is not based on a rejection of metaphysics in general, but concerns the metaphysics of properties in particular. One obvious way to defend that such investigations are based on a confusion is either to reject talk about properties as being based on a mistake of some kind, or to accept such talk, but hold that it is not literally true. If property talk is not to be taken literally, then no wonder that an investigation into the nature of properties is not on a par with an investigation into the nature of Fido. But these two options are not very attractive. Property talk can't just be rejected without paying a stiff price, and construing it as fictional can only work if the fictional goes way down to the basics of our ordinary discourse, a conclusion not many are willing to accept.[1] But there might be other options.

Let's call a *minimalist approach to the theory of properties* a philosophical theory that explains why substantial metaphysical projects into the nature of properties are mistaken, while at the same time accepting talk about properties, and construing such talk as literal and often literally true. This can be contrasted with a *substantial approach to the theory of properties*, which holds that substantial metaphysical investigations into the nature of properties are not confused, but merely unusual and maybe difficult. Basically all the work done these days in the theory of properties is in the ballpark of a substantial approach to the theory of properties, whereas a minimalist approach would be congenial to the non-philosopher's judgments. The hard question, however, is how one could possibly defend such a minimalist approach. It would have to explain what is wrong with the simple and straightforward motivation of a substantial metaphysical theory of properties outlined above. But what could possibly be mistaken about asking what things these properties really are, given that one holds that there are properties? In this chapter we will outline some ways in which one can hold on to a minimalist approach, both for properties and for propositions as well. These minimalist approaches, however, will be threatened by considerations about expressibility that rely on inexpressible properties and propositions. Formulating such minimalist approaches and rejecting the concerns about expressibility will be the main goals of this chapter.

To get a first idea about how a minimalist approach to the theory of properties could go, we can note that talk about properties has something in common with talk about truth, and this feature of talk about truth is central for motivating minimalist theories of truth. To see this we merely

---

[1] For someone who does accept it, see Yablo (2000).

have to look at what would happen if we gave up talk about properties. A substantial investigation into the nature of properties would be mistaken if there are no properties at all, and if thus talk about properties should be stopped. Not many people have actually endorsed this view, but there are some who played with it. Quine, in "On What There Is" was one of them.[2] In a well-known passage Quine discusses a view that accepts that even though there are red houses, red sunsets, and red roses, there is nothing they have in common. To accept that there is something they have in common would involve accepting quantification over properties or universals. But to deny such quantification would allow for the view that there are no properties such as redness, even though there are red things. According to this view, quantification over properties should be avoided in serious scientific talk, and should be understood as merely a loose and popular way of speaking. Quine seemed to have thought that such a rejection of quantification over properties was a feasible option, one that would avoid the usual metaphysical quarrels. But quantification over properties can't be rejected without paying a stiff price. Quantification over properties is not just something that we need when we formulate metaphysical theories. It is something we need in ordinary, everyday communication. Quantification over properties increases our expressive power in a way that we rely on in everyday life, not just metaphysics. This is quite analogous to the need we have for talk about truth in everyday life, outside of metaphysical debates about the nature of truth. If we think that what Jones said during the trial is nothing but the truth, but we can't recall what precisely he said we can only communicate our belief about Jones's trial performance by saying

(1) Everything Jones said during the trial is true.

If we knew what Jones said we could just restate it, case by case, and say that Jones said it, and that this is all he said. But if we can't remember we need a truth predicate to communicate this. Similarly for quantification over properties. Sometimes we need to use quantification over properties to communicate what we want to communicate in everyday situations that have nothing to do with metaphysical debates. I might know that

(2) There is a property Clinton and Reagan share, but Nixon doesn't have,

but not know what it is. If I knew I could just tell you what it is. I could simply say

[2] See Quine (1980).

(3) Both Clinton and Reagan like sushi, but Nixon doesn't.

But without knowing what it is I have to use quantification over properties to say what I want to say. Quantification over properties, just like a truth predicate, fulfills an expressive need we have quite independently of debates in metaphysics. We need it in everyday life. Even though talk about properties has a function in ordinary communication, it is not so clear what we do when we engage in it. In particular, it is not so clear if one can't accept quantification over properties but still reject the substantial metaphysical questions about properties as being based on a mistake. To make this clearer, we should distinguish two general large-scale views about what we do when we quantify over, and more generally talk about, properties. The first is that talk about properties is talk about some mind and language independent domain of objects (or entities). These entities are out there, part of reality, independently of our expressing them with predicates. When I say that there is a property such that Φ then I say that there exists a certain entity which is a property such that Φ. Let's call this view about talk about properties the *externalist view*. The externalist view takes properties to be independent of and external to the language used to talk about them. Properties are out there, waiting to be expressed by predicates, grouping things together independently of any mind or language.

The second way of looking at talk about properties is that it is not talk about some language-independent domain of objects, and maybe even not talk about some domain of objects at all. Rather properties are mere *shadows of predicates*, as the metaphor goes, and quantification over them is a device that increases our expressive power in a certain purely logical or metaphysically thin way: quantification over properties is nothing but a generalization over the instances. According to this view such quantified statements will be truth-conditionally equivalent to infinite disjunctions or conjunctions of the instances. The expressive power we get from adding quantification over properties to our language is thus equivalent to a certain infinitary expansion of our language. Thus when I say that there is a property such that Φ then what I say is truth-conditionally equivalent to the infinite disjunction over all the instances in my language. For example, when I utter (2) then my utterance will be truth-conditionally equivalent to something like

(4) Clinton and Reagan are tall, but Nixon isn't, or Clinton and Reagan are slim, but Nixon isn't, or...

where for every predicate in my language there is a disjunct involving that predicate.[3] In particular, I am not talking about a language-independent domain of properties as objects (or entities). The function that such talk has in ordinary communication is supposed to come from the metaphysically thin and purely logical increased expressive power alone. Let's call this view of talk about properties the *internalist view*. The internalist view is understood broadly here, to include both the view that properties are not entities at all, and thus talk about properties is not talk about some domain of entities (call this the *strict internalist view*), and the view that talk about properties is talk about entities, though these entities are not mind-and language-independent (call this the *loose internalist view*). Both views hold that quantification over properties is equivalent to disjunctions and conjunctions over all the instances in our language. The difference between loose and strict internalist will be apparent in their different understanding of quantifier-free talk about properties. A loose internalist will believe that in a sentence such as

(5) Redness is a color,

the phrase "redness" refers to or denotes some entity. A strict internalist will believe that this phrase is not a denoting expression. I would like to sideline the differences between loose and strict internalists for now, and focus on the question whether or not quantification over properties could be truth-conditionally equivalent to infinite disjunctions and conjunctions over all the instances in one's own language. The difference between these two versions of internalism will reappear later.[4] So far the characterization of internalism is only a simplistic first approximation. In the next section we will spell out more of the details, including the relationship between predicates, nominalized predicates, and quantification over properties.

---

[3] This is, of course, only a simplistic first step. The details of this will have to be spelled out by the defender of such a view. In the next section we will see more about how such an assignment of truth-conditions can go that has this result.

[4] Internalist views have surfaced in the literature as the view that quantification over properties is substitutional quantification. See Schiffer (1987), for example, where he discusses an internalist view of properties and propositions, though not under that name. Schiffer (288 n. 6) briefly discusses inexpressible properties and propositions and suggests that some quantifiers over propositions are neither objectual nor substitutional. See also his more recent (1994, 1996).

If strict internalism is the correct view about talk about properties then a minimalist approach to the theory of properties follows. Strict internalism does not reject talk about properties, and it accepts such talk as being literally true. However, no substantial theory into the nature of properties is legitimate. Talk about properties is not talk about any entities at all. Thus no substantial investigation into the nature of these entities makes sense. Even though it is true that there is a property that Fido has, there is nothing to be said about what this entity is that Fido has, since there is no entity that he has. We will see more details on how internalism can maintain this, but for now we can say that if internalism were true then a minimalist approach to the theory of properties would be the natural conclusion to draw. Whether or not internalism is true thus seems of great interest for the question whether or not substantial theories of properties are ultimately based on a mistake.

To decide whether or not the internalist or externalist view is correct might seem to be a substantial and difficult issue. It might seem to be quite parallel to the debate about minimalist theories of truth. Is the function of talk about truth captured by this increased expressive strength, and is truth thus more a logical than a metaphysical notion? Or is the increased expressive strength we get from talk about truth merely a side effect of some metaphysically more heavy-duty main function it has? This is a difficult issue that has been widely discussed. And similarly, it might seem that to settle the difference between internalist and externalist views about talk about properties one will have to look at a number of difficult and substantial issues. It seems that one has to look at the semantic function of quantifier phrases in certain uses, issues about the relationship between quantification and ontology, the function of talk about properties in ordinary communication, the role of properties in metaphysics, or at some other similarly complex issue. However, internalism can apparently be rejected for a much more direct and simple reason. There is a simple argument that seems to show that internalism is false, and that externalism is the only viable option. This argument has nothing to do with the semantics of quantifier phrases, the function of talk about properties, or the role of properties in metaphysics. It is simply the argument that the internalist view makes a too close connection between predicates and properties. The internalist view seems to be committed to the claim that every property is expressible by a predicate in our language. But that doesn't seem to be right. There are properties that are not expressible in our language, and this is sometimes required for what we say to be true. Sometimes we say that there is a property such that Φ, but the only properties that are Φ are properties that are not expressible in present-day English. Therefore the truth-conditions of such statements can't be equivalent to infinite disjunctions or conjunctions of sentences of present-day English where a predicate has to be a witness for such a property. Therefore the internalist view is wrong. The externalist view, however, has no such problems. According to it, properties are language-independent entities. Some of them might not be expressed by any predicate in present-day English. It seems that the externalist view is the only viable option.

I will argue that considerations about inexpressible properties do not refute internalism, but they do show something important about how internalism should be understood more precisely. And once this is made clear we will see that inexpressible properties are compatible with the internalist view of talk about properties. In the first part of this chapter I will show that this is so. I will show how it is consistent that there are inexpressible properties and that quantification over properties is expressively equivalent to an infinitary expansion of our language without such quantification (without any additions to the language). If I'm right then internalism is not refuted by there being inexpressible properties. After that I will argue that internalism also is not refuted by certain other, more technical, arguments. This will make internalism a viable option in the debate about the metaphysics of properties, and in the debate about the function of our talk about properties. To decide between internalism and externalism is harder than it might initially seem. Whether or not there are inexpressible properties is also an important end-game consideration in a number of contemporary debates, like the debate about minimalist theories of truth. The relevance of the present consideration to this debate will be discussed after a more refined version of internalism has been formulated. Finally, we will look at how, why and in what sense different languages differ in their expressive strength. Our discussion so far will suggest a hypothesis about this, which we will formulate and discuss.

2. THE FORMULATION OF INTERNALISM

In the above section we have roughly characterized internalism and its rival externalism. For the following it will be necessary to give some more details about how internalism is supposed to be understood more precisely. In this section we will thus briefly discuss two important issues about internalism that will clarify the position and contrast it with externalism more clearly than we did above: what view about quantification it is based on and how certain quantified statements are associated with infinitary disjunctions and conjunctions.[5]

2.1. Quantification

If internalism is true then quantification over properties is equivalent to infinitary conjunctions or disjunctions with the disjuncts or conjuncts formed within one's own language. This might seem like not much of a substantial claim since it is often the case that quantified statements are truth-conditionally equivalent to infinite disjunctions or conjunctions formed within one's own language. Take quantification over natural numbers. When I say

(6) There is a natural number larger than 100,

then this is in fact equivalent to

(7) Either 1 is larger than 100 or 2 is larger than 100 or 3 is...

That such an equivalence obtains can be agreed upon by all sides in a philosophical debate about numbers. What can be controversial, though, is whether the equivalence obtains *de facto* or *de jure*. On the one side of this distinction is the view that it just happens to be the case for natural numbers that we have a term in our language for each one of them. So, as it happens, a quantifier over natural numbers is equivalent to a disjunction or conjunction, *de facto*. This, though has nothing to do with quantification over numbers as such. Such quantifiers range over a domain of entities, and it happens to be the case that we have a term for each of them. On the other side is the view that quantification over natural numbers has the function to generalize over the instances. It is thus no accident that such quantifiers are equivalent to disjunctions and conjunctions over the instances. That is their semantic function, and such an equivalence thus holds *de jure*.

The same options apply to quantification over properties. The internalist view is that such an equivalence does not merely hold as a matter of

---

[5] I am indebted to Ted Sider and Dean Zimmerman for pressing me to make this clearer.

fact, but that the function of quantification over properties is such that this equivalence is guaranteed. It holds *de jure*, not merely *de facto*. How this can be so will need to be explained, and it will require some story about quantification. One rather implausible option that an internalist has is to claim that all quantification is *de jure* connected to infinitary conjunctions and disjunctions. This would be so, for example, if all quantification is substitutional quantification. But this is not a very plausible view about quantification in general. Some uses of quantifiers clearly seem to have the function to make a claim about a domain of objects out there, no matter how they relate to the terms we have in our language to describe these objects. Some uses of quantifiers are not equivalent to conjunctions and disjunctions formed within our own language (such as quantification over real numbers, and many ordinary everyday uses of quantifiers), some are equivalent to such conjunctions and disjunctions *de facto* (such as quantification over natural numbers, according to widely held views in the philosophy of mathematics, which we will not challenge here), but according to the internalist, some such equivalences hold *de jure*. But how can that be? How could it be that quantifiers sometimes have a function such that this equivalence is guaranteed, and sometimes apparently have a different function? An internalist view about (talk about) properties or any other domain will have to rely on a view about quantification that explains how this can be so.

This chapter is not the place to discuss quantification in any detail, and it is also not the place to provide a positive defense of internalism. In this chapter we focus on whether or not internalism is refuted by considerations about expressibility. I would like to briefly outline a view about quantification that I believe to be true, and that I have defended in Hofweber (2000 and 2005). This view about quantification provides exactly what is required for internalism, about any domain, to get off the ground. It does not guarantee that internalism about any domain is true, but a brief look at it will be helpful for some of the discussion below.

Many expressions in natural languages are semantically underspecified. That is to say, the language does not fully determine what contribution an utterance of that expression makes to the truth-conditions of an utterance of a sentence of which it is a part. There is a variety of different kinds of such underspecification, from simple indexicals to subtle structural underspecification. A good example of this is polysemy.

The verb "run", for example, makes different contributions to the truth-conditions to standard utterances of

(8) He ran the company well

and

(9) He ran the race well.

These different uses of "run" are not cases of ambiguity. We do not have two different words that happen to be pronounced the same way. Rather, it is the same word that can make different contributions to the truth-conditions. These two uses of "run" are not unrelated, and it is no accident that one and the same word is used in these two ways.

In Hofweber (2005 and 2000) I argue that ordinary natural language quantifiers are semantically underspecified as well. One and the same quantifier can make different contributions to the truth-conditions, and we can see from general needs we have for quantifiers in ordinary, everyday communication that this is so and what these truth-conditions are. Natural language quantifiers have at least two readings, corresponding to two general needs we have for them, and two functions that they have. One is the *domain conditions reading*. When quantifiers are used in this reading they make a claim about a domain of objects, whatever it may be. The contribution to the truth-conditions that quantifiers make in this reading corresponds to the usual model theoretic semantics for quantifiers. We will also call this reading the *external reading*. In addition quantifiers are used for their inferential role, in their *inferential role reading*. In this reading they make a contribution to the truth-conditions that gives them a certain inferential role. In the case of the particular quantifier, for example, it would simply be the inferential role that 'F(t)' implies 'Something is F'. This reading we will also call the *internal reading*. That we have a need for quantifiers in their internal reading, and that the internal and external reading of the quantifiers do not coincide in truth-conditions is argued for in the two papers mentioned. I'd like to add that the argument for an internal reading of quantifiers is made not on metaphysical or ontological grounds, but on the basis of general communicative needs in ordinary, everyday communication. I will not repeat these arguments here.

The truth-conditions of quantified statements with the quantifier used in its internal reading has to be such that a certain inferential role results. The most direct way this is so is for the statement to be equivalent to an infinitary conjunction or disjunction, formed within one's own language. Thus quantifiers in their internal reading are the kind of quantifiers that an internalist about a certain domain will have to rely on in their formulation of the internalist view. Using this view of quantification one can state an internalist view, for example, that quantifiers over properties are used in their internal reading. This will, of course, have to be defended. How it is to be decided, even granting the view about quantifiers outlined, whether or not ordinary uses of quantifiers over properties, say, are in the internal or external reading is quite another issue. The view about quantification outlined is, however, quite relevant for our present discussion.

If it is true that quantifiers are sometimes used in an internal, inferential role reading, and sometimes in an external, domain-conditions reading then this has two consequences that are of philosophical importance. First, internal quantifiers will in certain respects mirror Meinongian quantifiers, without the ontology of non-existent objects. This point is discussed in some length in Hofweber (2000). For example, a negative existential statement such as

(10) The Fountain of Youth does not exist

will imply a quantified statement, with the quantifier used in its internal reading, namely,

(11) Something does not exist, namely the Fountain of Youth.

So, in a sense we get quantification over non-existent objects, but we do not get a domain of non-existent objects over which these quantifiers range, as the Meinongians want to have it. The latter would only be so if (11) were true with the quantifier used in its domain-conditions reading. But with the quantifier used internally (11) can be literally true without there being a domain of non-existent objects that the quantifier ranges over.

A second consequence of the two readings of the quantifiers is a version of Carnap's internal–external distinction about ontological questions. I discuss this aspect in Hofweber (2005). If quantifiers are semantically underspecified then there is more than one question that can be asked with the words

(12) Are there properties?

According to the view about quantifiers outlined above, there are at least two such questions, and this has a number of things in common with the position set out in Carnap's (1956) essay "Empiricism, Semantics, and Ontology". Just as Carnap thought, there will really be two questions that can be asked with these words, and one of them is trivial, and the other one is the one that is of interest to metaphysicians. But contrary to Carnap, the questions that interest the metaphysicians are not meaningless. We will thus get a version of a neo-Carnapian approach to ontology that affirms ontology as a meaningful discipline, but holds on to a distinction between internal and external questions about what there is.

A defense of internalism about properties and propositions is a task that is much beyond the scope of this chapter. Here I attempt only to investigate whether internalism about properties and propositions can be easily refuted by considerations about expressibility. I hope to establish at the end that this is not so, and to do so it will be useful to have some idea about what an internalist view will look like. There are a variety of different ways one can spell out the background necessary to formulate more precisely an internalist view, and I have outlined only one of them, the one I prefer. Some of this background will be of use later in our discussion, as will a better understanding how we assign infinitary conjunctions and disjunctions to ordinary quantified statements, which we will now turn to.

2.2. The Internalist Truth-Conditions

The internalist holds that quantification over properties and propositions is merely a logical device for increased expressive power that is metaphysically innocent. Such quantification is supposed merely to generalize over the instances, but not to range over a language-independent domain of entities. And as we outlined above, this can be understood as such quantification being truth-conditionally equivalent to infinitary conjunctions or disjunctions. How quantified statements get assigned these conjunctions or disjunctions has not been discussed so far, and we will briefly do this here, as required for our discussion below.

To give a precise semantics for a fragment of a natural language is a substantial and difficult task. It involves assigning expressions in that fragment systematically to counterparts in a formal language with clearly specified formal semantics. Such an assignment has to meet certain conditions, such as preserving inferential relations. We will not attempt to do this here for talk about properties and propositions, nor do most other philosophical discussions of properties or propositions do this. There are a number of difficult obstacles that need to be overcome in doing this, no matter what ultimately one's philosophical views are. For propositions there is obviously the semantics of propositional attitudes, but the difficulties in no way end there. To mention one example, both properties and propositions exhibit the so-called substitution failure. There is a clear difference between

(13) Lance feared that Jan will attack,

and

(14) Lance feared the proposition that Jan will attack,

as well as

(15) Being a philosopher is fun,

and

(16) The property of being a philosopher is fun.

How can we explain this if "being a philosopher" just stands for the property of being a philosopher?[6] We will not attempt to solve any of the hard problems in this section, but merely outline how quantification over properties and propositions can be assigned infinite disjunctions or conjunctions as their truth-conditions.

Let's look at the simpler case of propositions first. We will take recourse to the notion of a (grammatical) instantiation of a quantified statement. So, for a statement such as

(17) He fears something I believe,

an instantiation is

(18) He fears that p and I believe that p.

To make this notion precise one will have to address a number of issues, for example about the scope of quantifiers, a task not unique to the internalist. Secondly, we take recourse to the notion of a (grammatical) sentence. Finally, we assign to a quantified statement infinitary sentences as follows:[7] Suppose that 'S[something]' is a statement with a particular

---

[6] See Bach (1997) and King (2002) for discussions of such examples for the case of propositions.

[7] I will describe only the case of the particular quantifier. The universal quantifier is analogous. I will not discuss in this chapter how to extend it to a treatment of generalized

quantifier over propositions, and 'S[that p]' is an instantiation of the former. Let 'V_p S[that p]' stand for the disjunction over all instances of 'S[that p]', whereby for every sentence of our language there is one instance of 'S[that p]', replacing 'p' with that sentence. Equivalently, for present purposes, bind 'p' with a (particular) substitutional quantifier with the substitution class being all the sentences in our language.

The case of quantification over properties is a little more complicated since quantification over properties can apparently occur in subject as well as in predicate position, and there is an issue about higher-order predication. Whether or not there ever is quantification into a predicate position is controversial. Possible examples are sentences such as

(19) He is something I am not (namely rich).

It is not clear whether this is quantification into predicate position since the 'is' of the predicate is still present. In any case, an internalist can specify the truth-conditions of such utterances quite directly, again by taking recourse to the notion of an instantiation of such a quantifier, and that of a predicate of our language. In this case an instance will be something like

(20) He is F and I am not F.

The truth-conditions of the quantified statement are then simply the disjunction over all the instances formed with predicates in our own language. Thus in this case it would be 'V_P (He is P and I am not P)'.[8]

Quantification over properties, however, often is not of this kind. Often the instances of quantifiers over properties do not directly involve predicates, but expressions such "the property of being F" or "being F". One example would be

(21) There is a mental property which is not a physical property (namely the property of feeling pain).

Here the instances would be something like

---

quantifiers. This brings in further issues that are not central for our main discussion, in particular the role of formal models in semantics.

[8] Here the notation is an adoption of the above one we used for propositions above. 'P' here is a predicate, whereas above 'p' was a sentence. The other changes for the case of properties are analogous.

(22) Being F is a mental property and being F is not a physical property.

We will have to expand our account to include such cases of quantification over properties as well. This can be done quite directly by exploiting the connection between a predicate, such as 'is F' and its nominalization 'being F' or 'the property of being F'. In cases where a quantifier over properties is a quantifier into a subject position we still form a conjunction (or disjunction) where there is a conjunct corresponding to each predicate, but now the predicate appears in its nominalized form. Let '$[_{nom}F]$' stand for the nominalization of the predicate 'F'. Then the infinitary disjunction assigned to a quantified statement that quantifies into subject position is the disjunction of all the instances such that there is an instance for every predicate in its nominalized form. In the case of 'Some property is G' it is the disjunction '$\vee_P([_{nom}P]$ is G)'.

One final issue to address briefly before we can return to our main discussion is the issue of higher-order predication. Since properties themselves can have properties there is a well-known division in the theory of properties between those who take a typed and those who take a type-free approach. For the former, all properties implicitly come with a type, and every quantifier over properties only ranges over some type of properties or other. In cases of higher-order predication properties of higher type are predicated of properties of lower type. There are many options one has in spelling this out in some more detail, and we will not get into them here. For a type-free approach one denies that properties come in types and claims that quantifiers over properties range over all of them. In predication properties can be applied to all others, even to themselves, in principle. To do this the predicate occurs nominalized in the subject position, and regularly in the predicate position, as in

(23) Being a property is a property.

In our notation we can write self-application as

(24) $[_{nom}P]$ is P,

or

(25) P ($[_{nom}P]$).

We will discuss this topic again later in the chapter, in connection with the paradoxes. An internalist has both of these options available as well, and the hard work that needs to be done in a typed approach, like assigning types to particular occurrences of quantifiers, can be carried over to a typed internalist approach as well. Instead of types being assigned to properties directly they will be assigned to predicates, and disjunctions and conjunctions will be formed involving only predicates of the appropriate type. In a type-free version this will not be necessary. We will return to this later.

With the internalist truth-conditions outlined above we can now see in outline how an internalist would assign infinite disjunctions and conjunctions to a large variety of quantified statements. For example,

(26) There is something we have in common

will by the above account be equivalent to the disjunction over the instances formed within our language.[9] In this case it is quantification into subject position, and thus we get

(27) V_P (we have $[_{nom}P]$ in common),

which is equivalent to

(28) V_P (you have $[_{nom}P]$ and I have $[_{nom}P]$),

which in turn, granting the equivalence between 'x has the property of being P' and 'x is P', is equivalent to

(29) V_P (you are P and I am P).

Whether or not a predicate occurs nominalized or regular in a disjunction is determined by the grammar of the sentences in which it occurs. To avoid confusion, but at the price of extra notation, we will make this explicit in the following, using the above notation.

Now it is time to return to our main discussion: is internalism easily refuted by considerations about inexpressible properties? Since an internalist claims that all such disjunctions are formed using predicates from our own language, it would seem that internalism is refuted by there being inexpressible properties. We will now look at this in detail.

---

[9] One further issue that will have to be addressed is quantifier domain restriction. I dare say here that both the internalist and the externalist have the same or at least analogous options available, whether or not quantifier domain restriction is properly understood as a semantic phenomenon. A discussion of this and a survey of the options would take us too far off course, however, so we will not attempt to do this here.

Inexpressible Properties, Propositions | 171

3. INTERNALISM AND THE INDUCTIVE ARGUMENT

3.1. Inexpressible Properties and the Inductive Argument

I take it that we all believe that there are properties inexpressible in English. It is, however, not so clear why we accept it. After all:

1. For a property to be inexpressible in a language means that no predicate (however complex) expresses it. Simply because there is no single word in a certain language for a certain property doesn't mean it isn't expressible in that language.
2. We can't be persuaded that there are properties inexpressible in English by example. One can't say in English without contradiction that the property of being Φ isn't expressible in English.

So, why again do we believe that there are inexpressible properties?

There are a number of different arguments for there being inexpressible properties. We will look at several of them in this chapter. The simplest and most important argument is the following:

> Even though we can't give an example of a property inexpressible in English, we can give examples of properties not expressible in older, apparently weaker languages. For example, the property of tasting better than Diet Pepsi is not expressible in Ancient Greek. So, there are properties expressible in English, but not in Ancient Greek. In addition, we have no reason to believe that English is the final word when it comes to expressing properties. We can expect that future languages will have the same relation to English that English has to Ancient Greek. Thus, we can expect that there are properties inexpressible in English, but expressible in future languages. In short, there are properties not expressible in present-day English.

Let's call this argument for inexpressible properties *the inductive argument*. It is a powerful argument. The main task for the next few pages will be to see whether or not the inductive argument refutes internalism about talk about properties.

Internalism seems to be committed to a view that might be called *expressive chauvinism*, the view that our present language is somehow better than other languages when it comes to what can be expressed. Our present language can express everything there is to express, whereas other languages can't express everything. But expressive chauvinism has to be rejected. Whatever reason we have to believe that our language is expressively better than other languages, it will make it plausible that some other (possibly future) language will be better in that respect than our present language. Internalism has to free itself from expressive chauvinism if it wants to be a contender in the debate about properties.

3.2. Some Distinctions

What does it mean for a property to be expressible in English? Well, that there is a predicate of English that expresses it. But that could mean at least two things. On the one hand, it could mean that there is a predicate of English that expresses this property in the language English. On the other hand, it could mean that there is a predicate of English such that a speaker of English expresses this property with an utterance of that predicate. Which one of these we take will make a difference for the issue under discussion. To illustrate the difference, consider:

(30) being that guy's brother

This predicate does not express a property *simpliciter*, it only expresses one on a particular occasion of an utterance of it, that is, in a particular context. In different contexts of utterance it will express different properties. However,

(31) being Fred's brother

expresses a property independent of particular utterances, or better, expresses the same one in each utterance.[10] If "that guy" in an utterance of (30) refers to Fred then this utterance of (30) will express the same property as any utterance of (31) will. However, there might be contexts in which an utterance of (30) will express a property that can't be expressed by an "eternal" predicate such as (31).

So, when we ask whether or not a property P is expressible in a language L we could either ask

1. whether or not there is a predicate Φ (of L) such that in every context C, an utterance of Φ (by a speaker of L) in C expresses P, or

---

[10] I assume that "Fred" and "brother" are disambiguated, i.e. with respect to whether we talk about a monk or a sibling, and whether it's Fred Dretske, Fred Astaire, Fred Flintstone, or any other Fred.

2. whether or not there is a predicate Φ (of L) and a context C such that an utterance of Φ (by a speaker of L) in C expresses P.

Let's call expressible in the first sense *language expressible* and expressible in the second sense *loosely speaker expressible*. The latter is called *loosely* speaker expressible because it only requires for there to be a context such that an utterance of Φ in that context by a speaker of L would express P. Any context is allowed here, whether or not speakers of that language actually ever are in such contexts. We can distinguish this from what is *factually speaker expressible*. Here we allow only contexts that speakers of that language actually are in.[11] Let me illustrate.

Ancient Greek does not allow for the expression of the property

(32) tasting better than Diet Pepsi

in the sense of being language expressible. We can assume that. However, it seems that it is expressible in Ancient Greek in the sense of being loosely speaker expressible. In the context where there is Diet Pepsi right in front of a speaker of Ancient Greek he could simply utter the Ancient Greek equivalent of

(33) tasting better than this

while demonstratively referring to Diet Pepsi. But since there was no Diet Pepsi around during the time when Ancient Greek was a living language, this context is not allowed when considering the question whether or not this property is factually speaker expressible. In this case, it seems that the property is not factually speaker expressible in Ancient Greek, just as it is not language expressible in Ancient Greek.

Being language expressible implies being factually speaker expressible, which implies being loosely speaker expressible, and none of these implications can be reversed (or so we can concede for now).

What all this shows is that both the inductive argument and the above account of the internalist view of talk about properties was too simplistic. In the latter it was simply assumed that contextual contributions to

---

[11] To simplify, we consider someone only as a speaker of their native language. This is also implicitly assumed in the inductive argument. We can also ignore complicated issues about identities of languages over time. For present purposes it does not matter what the details are about how long and under what conditions a language continues to be the same. Intermediate notions between factually speaker expressible and loosely speaker expressible can also be formulated depending on how strictly one takes "actually". This is of no consequence for our discussion, though.

content do not occur and that the truth-conditions of talk about properties can simply be given by infinite disjunctions and conjunctions of eternal sentences of the language in question. But that's not always so. Sometimes predicates express properties in some contexts that can't be expressed with eternal predicates. To say this is not to deny that properties are shadows of predicates, just that they are shadows of eternal predicates. Let's call a version of internalism about talk about properties *extreme internalism* if it claims that quantification over properties is equivalent to infinite disjunctions and conjunctions formed with eternal predicates. And let's call a form of internalism *moderate internalism* if it accommodates contextual contributions to content. What we have seen so far is that extreme internalism can't be right. An internalist will have to endorse moderate internalism. But how is this form of internalism supposed to be understood? How can internalists accommodate contextual contributions to what is expressed by a predicate while at the same time holding that quantification over properties is merely a logical device for increased expressive power?

3.3. The Problem

Here is the problem: even if an utterance of a sentence with demonstratives in Ancient Greek in the right context would express the property of tasting better than Diet Pepsi, it is quite a different story to extend this to an internalist account of the truth-conditions of quantification over properties. In fact, it seems that this can't be done.

Let's suppose, for the sake of the argument, that the only property of beer that interests Fred is that it tastes better than Diet Pepsi. So

(34) There is a property of beer that interests Fred.

An internalist account of quantification over properties has to get this to come out true. But it seems that this requires that there is a disjunct in the infinite disjunction that corresponds to

(35) tasting better than Diet Pepsi

This is no problem for our language, English. But if the disjunctions have to be formed in Ancient Greek then it doesn't seem to work. To be sure, and as we have seen above, the property of tasting better than Diet Pepsi is loosely speaker expressible in Ancient Greek. But how can this be used in the infinite disjunction? After all, merely having

(36) tasting better than this

as part of one of the disjunctions won't do unless the demonstrative refers to Diet Pepsi. But how could it? The referent of a demonstrative is fixed at least partly by the intentions of the speaker using it. And in an utterance of (34) there are no such intentions that could back this up. For one, one can utter (34) while having no idea what property it is that interests Fred. And secondly, speakers of Ancient Greek will have no idea what Diet Pepsi is, nor will they have any around to refer to demonstratively. So, there is no way such speakers can fix the referent of such a demonstrative to be Diet Pepsi. Thus the truth-conditions of quantified statements can't be equivalent to infinite disjunctions and conjunctions over the instances, even if the instances may contain demonstratives. Thus it seems that internalism is refuted, after all, even given the above distinctions.

3.4. The Solution

An internalist claims that quantification over properties is equivalent to infinite disjunctions and conjunctions formulated using only the basic vocabulary of the language on which the quantification occurs, plus possibly extra logical tools. This would make quantification over properties merely a generalization over the instances. And it contrasts internalism with externalism, which claims that such quantification ranges over some mind-and language-independent domain of entities. The above considerations suggest that extreme internalism should be rejected. Extreme internalism is in trouble since not every object is referred to with an eternal term, and thus what properties can be expressed with eternal predicates is strictly less than what properties are expressed with context sensitive predicates, namely in cases where a demonstrative refers to an object that isn't the referent of an eternal term. These considerations show that what objects there are matters for what properties and propositions there are, not merely what objects are referred to with eternal terms. The case of demonstrative reference to an object that isn't the referent of any eternal term illustrates this. We should not, however, give demonstrative reference too central a role in this. What objects there are matters, not what objects can be referred to, even with a demonstrative. So, if there are any objects that can't be referred to with a demonstrative, for whatever reason, these objects would nonetheless be relevant to what properties there are. We thus have to take 'speaker expressible' liberally here. Any object has to be able to be contributed in a context. Context-sensitive expressions can have terms in them that in a context can stand for an object. Demonstrative reference is one way in which this can happen, but we will more liberally consider the notion of a context contributing any object as the value of a 'demonstrative' or context-dependent singular term. Thus 'loosely speaker expressible' has to be understood as expressible with a predicate where context may contribute any object whatsoever as the value of a 'demonstrative' or otherwise context-sensitive singular term. This will properly accommodate the above insight that what objects there are matters for what properties and propositions there are. So, an internalist will have to claim that quantification over properties is a generalization over all the instances of context-sensitive predicates, with demonstratives being allowed to stand for any objects whatsoever, but without requiring referential intentions or the like on the part of the speakers. Let's look at this more closely and clarify the situation with the help of artificial languages.

Let's assume that the truth-conditions of a fragment of a natural language without quantification over properties is correctly modeled with a certain formal language L. Adding quantification over properties to that language should give us an infinitary expansion of L, according to the internalist. Now, to accommodate demonstratives, we can do the following. Add infinitely many new variables to L, which model the demonstratives. Build up formulas as usual, but don't allow ordinary quantifiers to bind these new variables. To accommodate talk about properties, we represent the truth-conditions of quantification over properties with an infinite disjunction or conjunction as before, with one difference. Whenever we form an infinite disjunction or conjunction we also existentially or universally (respectively) bind all these new variables. Thus, now we do not simply represent "there is a property such that Φ" as the infinite disjunction over all the instances "$\Phi([_{nom}P])$", i.e. as "$V_P\Phi([_{nom}P])$". Now we take this disjunction and add existential quantification on the outside binding all the new variables. So, we now represent "there is a property such that Φ" as "$\exists v_1, v_2 \ldots V_P\Phi([_{nom}P])$".

The new free variables play the role of the demonstratives in this account, and the quantifier binding them plays the role of the arbitrary contexts that we allow in loosely speaker expressibility. For example, the disjunction that spells out the truth-conditions of (34) will contain a disjunct corresponding to

(37) tasting better than v_i.

Now there will be an existential quantifier that binds v_i from the outside. Since it will range over Diet Pepsis this disjunct will be true, and thus the disjunction will be true. And this will be so independently of there being a referring expression that refers to Diet Pepsi in the language in question

However, there is no finite upper bound on how many of these new variables will occur in these disjunctions. Since we allow, and have to allow, every predicate to occur in the disjunction, we can't give a finite upper bound on how many variables can occur in these predicates. So, in the infinite disjunction there will be infinitely many variables that have to be bound, all at once, from the outside. But this can be done. We just have to go to a higher infinitary logic. Not only do we need infinite disjunctions and conjunctions, we need quantification over infinitely many variables. Before we only used a small fragment of what is called $\mathcal{L}_{\omega_1,\omega}$, now we use a small fragment of $\mathcal{L}_{\omega_1,\omega_1}$. This latter logic also allows for quantification over countably many variables.[12] In both cases we expand our original base language by only logical notions and no other non-logical vocabulary.

Given this new model of talk about properties we have the following:

- Properties are shadows of predicates, but not shadows of eternal predicates.
- Talk about properties gives rise to an infinitary expansion of the original language, but not just to a small fragment of $\mathcal{L}_{\omega_1,\omega}$, but to a small fragment of $\mathcal{L}_{\omega_1,\omega_1}$.

So, the property of tasting better than Diet Pepsi is not expressible in Ancient Greek in the sense of language expressible nor in the sense of

---

[12] $\mathcal{L}_{\omega_1,\omega}$ is an infinitary logic that allows conjunctions and disjunctions over countable sets of formulas, but only quantification over finite sets of variables (as in regular first-or higher-order logic). $\mathcal{L}_{\omega_1,\omega_1}$ allows for both conjunctions and disjunctions over countable sets of formulas, plus quantification over countable sets of variables. The basic language is usually the one of first-order logic, but one can define infinitary expansions of other languages just as well. See Keisler (1971) and Barwise (1975) for much more on this. In our case here we use only very small fragments of these logics. All these fragments will be finitely representable, for example, and smaller than the smallest fragments studied in Barwise (1975) or Keisler (1971).

factually speaker expressible. It is however, expressible in Ancient Greek in the sense of loosely speaker expressible. And by the inductive argument we get that we have reason to believe that there are properties that are not expressible in English, but we get that only when 'expressible' is understood in the sense of either language expressible or factually speaker expressible. However, according to the present version of internalism, quantification over properties has to be understood as being based on what is loosely speaker expressible with predicates. Therefore it will be true that

(38) There are properties that are not expressible in English,

if expressible is understood as being language expressible or factually speaker expressible, but false, according to the internalist, if it is understood as being loosely speaker expressible.

Internalism is not easily refuted with the inductive argument. Once we distinguish between extreme and moderate internalism, and between different notions of expressibility, we can see that moderate internalism is not refuted by the inductive argument. A moderate internalist should endorse the inductive argument as showing something interesting and important about a difference in what is language or factually speaker expressible in different languages. We will see more about this in section 6 below. But before that we will have to have a closer look at whether or not other arguments using considerations about expressibility refute internalism. We can grant that extreme internalism is refuted by the inductive argument, though I have argued that moderate internalism isn't refuted by it. We will now have to see whether or not moderate internalism can be refuted as well, and thus 'internalism' will mean 'moderate internalism' from now on.

4. FURTHER ARGUMENTS AGAINST INTERNALISM USING EXPRESSIBILITY CONSIDERATIONS

We have looked at the inductive argument above, and seen that endorsing it poses no threat to internalism about talk about properties, rightly understood. The inductive argument, however, is not the only argument that tries to refute internalism using inexpressible properties. In this section we will look at several other arguments for this conclusion, and we will see that they are no problem for internalism either. To be sure, I can't claim to deal with all possible such arguments, but once we see that the arguments discussed in the present section are no problem for internalism it should be plausible that internalism is in fact not threatened by issues about inexpressible properties. After that we will look at some positive and more large-scale issues.

I will divide the further arguments against internalism from inexpressible properties into several groups: First, arguments that are modifications of the inductive argument. Secondly, arguments that try to establish that there are strictly more properties than expressible properties. These arguments thus try to establish that the cardinality of the set of properties is larger than the cardinality of the set of expressible properties. Thirdly, we will look at arguments that internalism is in conflict with some lessons that have to be drawn from the semantic paradoxes. After that we will look at an argument trying to establish that we can "diagonalize out" of the expressible properties. Finally, we will look at arguments that take recourse to modal considerations.

4.1. Modified Inductive Arguments

We have to see what reason one might have for believing that there are properties that aren't loosely speaker expressible. And, since this again can't be motivated by giving an example of such a property, one way to go will be a version of the inductive argument, but this time an inductive argument for there being properties that are not loosely speaker expressible. And to start such an argument we have to point to a property that is loosely speaker expressible in English, but not loosely speaker expressible in, say, Ancient Greek. What could that be? The best candidates for such properties are ones that relate to an area where there is a substantial difference between Ancient Greece and us, such as scientific understanding of the world. A tricky example is

(39) being a quark.

It might seem that it isn't even loosely speaker expressible in Ancient Greek. Whatever one's prima facie intuitions about this are, we should note that since this property is (language) expressible in present-day English, but presumably not in English of AD 1600 something must have happened in the recent history of English that allowed for the language expressibility of this property. So, how did we come to be able to express it? That certainly is a hard question, related to some difficult issues in the philosophy of science. Two possibilities come to mind, though, namely:

- "being a quark" is a theoretical predicate of physics. It is at least in part implicitly defined by the physical theory that uses it. Thus we can express it because we have the theory.
- We can express the property of being a quark because we have been in contact with observable phenomena that are caused by quarks, such as effects they have on some measuring instrument.

If either one of these is the correct account then there is no problem for the internalist. The reason is simply the following. If the first is correct then the problem of expressing the property of being a quark reduces to expressing the theory that implicitly defines "being a quark", plus making the implicit definition explicit. Simply put, the property of being a quark is the property of being such that the theory truly describes you. Thus the problem is pushed back to the properties used in the implicit definition of "being a quark", that is in the formulation of the theory that implicitly defines it. In general, though, if the apparent increased expressive power of new theoretical concepts comes from their implicit definition in scientific theories (or from mixing those with the above second point) then internalism is not in trouble.

If the second possibility is the right one then the increased expressive power does come from being in contact with more objects. If we introduced "being a quark" as

(40) being the kind of thing that causes these effects on the measuring instrument,

or something along this line then being a quark is loosely speaker expressible in older languages, though not language expressible. This case thus essentially reduces to the case of the (standard) inductive argument.

To be sure, these are only rough outlines of how this can work. How such predicates work in general is very difficult to say. We should, however, keep the fact in mind that something must have happened in the last few hundred years that made the change from speakers of English not being able to (language) express this property (at least not with a simple predicate) to their being able to (language) express it with just a few words. One easy explanation of how this might have happened is that speakers were able to express the property before, after all, either with a complex eternal predicate, or with some non-eternal predicate in the right context. If this is so then there is no puzzle how we can now express it with a few simple words: we just introduced a word to stand for a property that we could express already, though only with a complex predicate, or only in special circumstances. But if this isn't so, what might have happened that made the difference? One answer is holism, and it is hard to see what another answer might be. We will get more into the details of this issue at the end of this chapter.

4.2. Cardinality Considerations

The second strategy to argue against internalism using considerations about inexpressible properties takes recourse to cardinality considerations. Such arguments try to establish that the set of all properties is strictly larger than the set of all expressible properties. I would like to divide these arguments into two groups. The first group takes recourse to a principle that connects how many objects there are with how many properties there are, and argues that since there are a certain number of objects there are more properties than expressible properties. The second group of arguments takes recourse to "closure" principles. These arguments are based on that what properties there are is closed under some general principle. Using such principles, the argument continues, we can see that there are more properties then there are expressible properties.[13] Let's look at these in turn.

4.2.1 Arguments from Objects

Here is a paradigmatic argument from objects against internalism:

Our language has only a finite base vocabulary, and only finite combinations of it are allowed to form predicates that express

---

[13] Arguments from closure principle don't necessarily attempt to reach the conclusion that the cardinality of the set of expressible properties is smaller than the cardinality of the set of properties. Some of them might try to establish only that the set of expressible properties is a proper subset of the set of all properties. In the relevant section below we will mainly discuss closure principles that, if they were true, would lead to a cardinality argument. Thus arguments using closure principles are dealt with under the heading of cardinality arguments here. In section 4.4 below we will discuss additional arguments that the expressible properties form a proper subset of all the properties that are not cardinality arguments.

properties. Thus overall we can form countably many predicates. But there are uncountably many properties. There are, for example, uncountably many real numbers. And for every real number there is the property of being larger than that real number, or other properties of this kind. Thus there are uncountably many properties. So, internalism has to be false.

This is prima facie a very plausible argument. But once we take into account the distinctions that were drawn above we can quite easily see that it is flawed. The argument would work against extreme internalism, which holds that properties are shadows of eternal predicates. But, of course, this is not the form of internalism we are discussing now. Internalism has to be understood as moderate internalism, which holds that properties are shadows of predicates, though not of eternal predicates.[14] The truth-conditions of quantification over properties are understood as being modeled by infinitary disjunctions as well as infinitary first-order quantification. In particular, what is in the domain of the first-order quantifiers will matter for the truth-conditions of quantification over properties.

And once we consider this formulation of internalism we see that the above argument provides no problem for it. If we grant, as is presupposed in the above argument, that real numbers are objects in the domain of first-order quantification then it will be true according to moderate internalism that

(41) For every real number there is a property that is the property of being larger than that real number.

According to internalism the truth-conditions of this sentence can be spelled out as (in semi-formal notation):

(42) $\forall r \exists \vec{v} \bigvee_P ([_{nom}P(v_i)] = $ being larger than $r)$

And (42) is true, as can be seen as follows. Fix an arbitrary number r. One of the disjuncts in the disjunction will be

(43) (being larger than $v_i = $ being larger than r)

with a variable v_i bound from the outside by an (infinitary) existential quantifier. Since this variable ranges over real numbers, in particular

---

[14] See the end of s. 3.2 for the distinction between extreme and moderate internalism.

number r, there is a value to the variable that makes this disjunct true, namely r. So, (42) is true.

Real numbers, as objects of the domain of first-order quantification, can be the values of the variables that occur in the infinitary disjunctions, which are bound from the outside by the (infinitary) existential quantifiers. So, the more objects there are in the domain of first-order quantification, the more properties are loosely expressible, and the stronger is quantification over properties. The arguments from objects thus rely on a version of internalism that is based on using eternal predicates as the basis of expressibility. They do not affect the present version of internalism.

4.2.2. Arguments from "Closure Principles"

A second argument against internalism about properties is based on considerations that properties are closed under certain principles. In the simplest form these are principles of the kind that for any two properties there is a property that is the conjunction of the two. So, if being a dog is a property, and being a cat is a property, then being a dog and a cat is also a property. This is, of course, a very innocent form of a closure principle, but others are not so innocent. To argue against internalism using closure principles one will have to find a closure principle C such that

(i) we have good reason to believe that properties are closed under principle C, and
(ii) properties being closed under C is incompatible with internalism about properties.

We will in this section look at whether or not there are any good arguments of this kind.

A principle that seems to meet condition (ii) is:

(P1) For every set S of properties there is a property of having all the properties in S.

(P1) seems to be incompatible with internalism because of the argument:

Let's agree that how many properties are expressible depends on what objects there are in the domain of first-order quantification. So, if there are κ many objects in this domain, and if the base language is countable then there will be κ many properties that can be loosely speaker expressed.[15] However, there are more than κ many properties. Since what properties there are is closed under principle (P1) and since there are 2^κ many sets of loosely speaker expressible properties there are at least 2^κ many properties. For every set of loosely speaker expressible properties there is a property of having all these properties, and for every such set this resulting property is different. Thus there are at least 2^κ many properties.

This objection has several problems. First, but not most importantly, the argument begs the question against the strict internalist, who thinks that properties are not objects or entities, and are thus not available to be collected into sets. Sets of properties can only be built if properties exist as entities. But according to strict internalism, properties are not entities.[16] Thus to talk about sets of properties is to assume that properties are entities, which is one of the issues at stake here. Secondly, and more importantly, if we allow sets of properties, and if we accept sets in general, then these sets will be in the domain of the first-order quantifiers. In particular, the assumption in the above argument that there are only κ many objects in the domain of first-order quantification is false if there are also 2^κ many sets of properties, or sets of any kind. Thus the above argument really is a version of an argument from objects, with the difference that it uses sets, rather than real numbers. Such arguments, we have seen, should not bother the moderate internalist. Cardinality arguments using sets of properties are thus no threat to moderate internalism.

One might attempt, though, to give a related argument that does not rely on using sets. An opponent of internalism might argue that there are certain principles we should accept that tell us that properties are closed under certain operations, without ever taking recourse to sets of properties. A simple example of this would be the claim that properties are closed under conjunction. This can be formulated quite innocently as

(44) If P is a property and if Q is a property then P and Q is a property.

Some principles like this, it seems, will have to be accepted by anyone, and their acceptance does not beg any question against internalism or

---

[15] κ is an infinite cardinal number. If there are only finitely many objects then there will be countably many expressible properties.

[16] According to the other kind, loose internalism, properties are language-dependent entities.

externalism.[17] Such principles take the form of a schema that claims that if there are certain properties then there are also other properties. Can we specify a schema of this kind that would refute internalism?

No. Every such schema that we can specify is compatible with internalism. In fact, it is implied by internalism.[18] Expressible properties are closed under expressible closure conditions. Whatever the right-hand side of a closure condition would say, it would give us a predicate for expressing the relevant property. If the schematic letters stand for expressible properties then we will have predicates that express them, and the expressible closure condition will give us a recipe to construct a new predicate that expressed the new property which the condition claims there is. Thus any example of a schema that expresses a closure condition is compatible with internalism.

I conclude that cardinality considerations do not refute internalism, even though they seem on the face of it to be a serious problem for internalism. Cardinality considerations would work against a simple form of internalism, where only eternal predicates are allowed to express properties, or where expressibility is understood as language expressibility. Moderate internalism is not threatened by these problems.

4.3. Paradoxes

One quite different argument against internalism doesn't claim that internalism does not accommodate all the properties, but rather claims that internalism allows for too many properties. This might be especially striking because of what we have seen in the above section. Are properties really closed under all these expressible closure conditions? There is, of course, *property elitism*, the metaphysical view that there are only few and only very special properties, which disagrees with this.[19] According to one version of property elitism, for example, properties are not closed under disjunctions, and in fact there are no disjunctive properties at all. Such views, however, rely on heavy duty and

---

[17] Some such principles might beg the question against some forms of property elitism to be discussed below.
[18] Properly formulated, of course. In our case it would be the universal closure of
  (62) If $[_{nom}P]$ is a property and if $[_{nom}Q]$ is a property then $[\,[_{nom}P]$ and $[_{nom}Q]\,]$ is a property.
[19] The classic example is Armstrong in e.g. (1978, 1989), and others.

186 | *Thomas Hofweber*

controversial metaphysics. Simply because internalism isn't compatible with property elitism isn't an argument against it. Internalism, as a view about the metaphysics of properties, is naturally incompatible with several other competing views about the metaphysics of properties. There are, however, other arguments against internalism that argue that internalism admits too many properties. These arguments are not based on metaphysical considerations, but rather on the paradoxes. What these arguments try to establish is that not every predicate expresses a property. A simple argument of this kind is:

> Even though we can't give an example of a property that isn't expressed by any predicate (in our language), we can give an example of a predicate that doesn't express a property. It is the predicate:
>
> (AP) does not apply to itself
>
> If this predicate would express a property, P, then we can ask whether or not P applies to itself, i.e. whether or not $P(P)$ holds. And we can see that P does apply to itself iff it does not apply to itself. Contradiction. Thus there can be no property that is expressed by this predicate.

It is a not an uncommon reaction to conclude that this paradox shows that there is no property that is expressed by (AP). In particular, there are predicates that express no property, contrary to internalism. However, this reaction is premature.

The above argument relies on the fact that the lesson to draw from this paradox is that there is no property expressed by this predicate. This is problematic for several reasons. For one, it seems true to say that there is a property that seems to lead to paradox, or that puzzled logicians for decades, namely the property of not applying to oneself. But more importantly, this account of denying that there is such a property doesn't really solve the paradox. The paradox can be formulated in such a way that it doesn't even take recourse to properties. Thus trying to solve the paradoxes by adopting a certain view in ontology, that certain properties do not exist, does not get at the heart of the problem, and provides only an ad hoc way to block a certain formulation of the paradox, but not a solution to the paradox. We can also formulate the above paradox using only predicates, and not properties. Here is the modified version:

> Predicates are satisfied by objects. So, "is a dog" is satisfied by Fido. Predicates can also be satisfied by predicates. For example, "is short"

is satisfied by "is short". Now, call a predicate "heterological" if it does not satisfy itself. So, "is short" does not satisfy "heterological". Does "heterological" satisfy "heterological"? By the usual reasoning: it does iff it doesn't. Paradox.[20]

The above version of the paradox can't be resolved by claiming that certain properties don't exist, or that certain predicates don't express properties, since we never took recourse to properties. In particular, no one would conclude from this paradox that there is no such predicate as "heterological". So, if denying that there is such a property as not applying to oneself doesn't solve the paradox, but only blocks the particular formulation of the paradox, then this doesn't give us a reason to believe that there is no such property. Denying that "doesn't apply to itself" expresses a property doesn't solve the paradox. It can at most require us to give the paradox a slightly different formulation.

We have seen that these paradoxes don't require an internalist to claim that some predicates don't express a property. But an internalist does not have to take this route. An internalist will have to spell out anyway what will count as a predicate in making more precise what the infinite disjunctions and conjunctions will look like. It is an option for an internalist to spell this out in such a way that "does not apply to itself" is not a predicate. I don't want to pursue this here, however.

How the paradoxes can be solved, if at all, is of course a completely different story. We only need to note here that internalism and externalism don't seem to be importantly different in that respect. In particular, paradoxes are no more in conflict with internalism than they are in conflict with anything else.

4.4. Diagonalization

One further more or less technical argument has to be dealt with. It uses the technique of diagonalization, and aims to show that no language can express all properties, since by diagonalization we can construct a property that wasn't expressible in that given language.[21] This argument tries to show that the properties expressible in a given language are a proper subset of all the properties, but it doesn't try to do this

---

[20] This is, of course, Grelling's paradox.
[21] These arguments are called diagonal argument since they use the "diagonal" $R(x, x)$ of a binary relation $R(x, y)$.

188 | *Thomas Hofweber*

using a cardinality consideration. There are many ways in which this argument can be formulated more precisely. The details of the formulation aren't important for our present discussion, as we will see. I'll give an example of an argument using diagonalization that aims to show that internalism has to be false. Here is one:

> In every language there will be some property not expressible in that language. Suppose you have some language L, and let's assume that L can talk about its own syntax, say via some coding. We'll see that there is a property not expressible in L. Consider a language L^* which extends L in the following way. L^* has a two-place predicate SAT_L such that $SAT_L(x, y)$ holds just in case y is a code for the formula Φ of L and Φ holds of x. Now, take the property expressed by $\neg SAT_L(x, x)$, call it D. D is not expressible in L. Suppose it is. Then there is some predicate of L that expresses it, say Ψ. It will have some code, say z. Then $\Psi(z)$ holds iff $\neg SAT_L(z, z)$ holds. But the latter holds just in case $\Psi(z)$ doesn't hold. Contradiction. So, $\neg SAT_L(x, x)$ is not expressible in L.

The above argument doesn't show what one might think it shows for our discussion here. The language L indeed can't express the property D *unless it gives rise to semantic paradoxes*. If L already contains its own satisfaction predicate then the extension to L^* would lead to nothing new. But then, of course, we could formulate a semantic paradox in L, using exactly the argument that was given above. So, the argument only shows that there is a property that L doesn't express under the assumption that L does not contain its own satisfaction predicate. Now, the natural language English does contain its own satisfaction predicate. It can be expressed with the words "(the English expression) y truly applies to x" or "(the English expression) y is satisfied by x". So, if the above language L is supposed to be English then the extension to L^* is not a proper extension. L^* is just English again. The argument given is then simply a version of the paradox we discussed in the previous section. The diagonal predicate $\neg SAT_{English}(x, x)$ is nothing but a formal version of the predicate "does not apply to itself".

The argument thus does not show that there are properties inexpressible in English. It only shows that if a language does not contain its own satisfaction predicate then it doesn't express all properties, and if it does contain its own satisfaction predicate then it gives rise to paradoxes. One can make the same point more easily by considering truth instead of satisfaction. If a language does not contain its own truth predicate then it does not express all properties (namely the property of being a true sentence of that language), and if it does contain its own truth predicate then it gives rise to paradoxes. For the natural language English the latter of these options applies in both cases. In particular one should thus not conclude from the above argument that there are limits to what can be expressed in our own language.

How the paradoxes are to be dealt with is, again, another story, one that the internalists and the externalists alike will have to deal with. Diagonal arguments of the above kind point to the paradoxes, not to limits in what is expressible.[22]

4.5. Modal Arguments

Somewhat different arguments against internalism uses modal claims of some kind or other. Such arguments claim that internalism gets the truth value of certain modal claims wrong. In this section I will look at several examples of this and argue that they provide no problem for internalism rightly understood. Here it will be important to distinguish claims that we have good reason to believe to be true no matter what philosophical theory about modality or the nature of properties we adopt, and claims that themselves express a substantial metaphysical view about modality or properties. The latter, of course, can't always be accommodated. Internalism is itself one of the possible views about talk about properties, and it can't accommodate claims that characterize opposing views. However, there are no modal claims I know of that seem to be clearly correct and that are incompatible with internalism.

Let's look at some examples. A common strategy to argue against internalism is to claim that internalism gets wrong the truth value of utterances in counterfactual situations in which there are no language users. The idea is that since internalism uses conjunctions and disjunctions over classes of predicates (or sentences) that in such circumstances the disjuncts would be empty. But this is, of course, mistaken. A sentence such as

(45) If there had not been any languages then Fido would nonetheless have a property,

comes out as

---

[22] I'm indebted to Rich Thomason for pushing the issues in this section.

(46) If there had not been any languages then nonetheless V_P (Fido is P),

which is equivalent to

(47) If there had not been any languages then nonetheless either Fido is a cat, or Fido is a dog, or Fido is...

which, of course, is true. The underlying mistake here is to think that internalists equate quantification over properties with quantification over predicates. They don't. They merely make the claim that quantified statements over properties are equivalent to infinite disjunctions and conjunctions, all of which can be formulated in one's language and are sufficiently similar.

Another example apparently in conflict with internalism is

(48) There might have been different fundamental physical properties.

This is ambiguous between:

(49) Different properties might have been the fundamental physical properties.
(50) There might have been different properties than there are, and some of them might have been fundamental physical properties.

The first is no problem for internalism, since internalism can easily grant that even though being an electron is not a fundamental physical property, it might have been. So, this reading of (48) just says that different properties than the ones that are actually the fundamental ones might have been the fundamental ones. Accepting this as well as rejecting it is compatible with internalism.

The second reading of (48) requires that there might have been different properties than there are, and some of them might have been fundamental. This consists of two conjuncts. The second one poses the same problem as the first reading of (48) and thus is no problem. We will have to look at the first conjunct:

(51) There might have been different properties than there are.

Acceptance of this is closely tied to acceptance of

(52) There might have been different objects than there are.

In fact, there are some plausible considerations that (52) implies (51). Here is a common argument for this. I'll formulate it as it is usually given first, in an externalist framework. After that we will see how it carries over to an internalist framework.

Suppose you think that there might have been some objects that in fact there aren't. Let Joe be one of them. Then being Joe's brother is an object-dependent property. Object-dependent properties, just like object-dependent, or singular, propositions, exist only if the objects on which they depend exist. So, the property of being Joe's brother exists only if Joe exists. And if Joe might have existed, but doesn't, then there might have been a property which in fact there isn't, namely being Joe's brother. Or so the externalist's reasoning.[23]

Now, according to internalism a quite analogous situation obtains. What properties there are is affected by what objects there are. This comes from the interaction of the infinite disjunctions with the first-order variables that are bound from the outside. In our case, we have

(53) It is possible that there is a property P such that there actually is no property Q such that $P = Q$.

According to internalism this is equivalent to

(54) $\Diamond(\exists \vec{v} \vee_P [_{nom}P]$ is a property & $@\neg\exists \vec{w} \vee_Q [_{nom}Q]$ is a property & $[_{nom}P] = [_{nom}Q])$

And this is true if there might have been different objects than there are. If that is so then the variables $\vec{v}$ and $\vec{w}$ can range over different domains and thus there can be instances of P and Q that will be different. Just take *being identical to a* and *being identical to b*, for a an object which there might have been, but in fact there isn't, and b any object which in fact exists.[24]

Internalism does not have absurd consequences about the truth values of modal claims. This is not to say that internalism will be able to accommodate everyone's intuitions about modal claims. Some modal claims will be incompatible with internalism. But such claims will themselves express substantial metaphysical views. Internalism is one

---

[23] Not everyone accepts object-dependent properties, of course. This example is merely used to show how it is often argued that what properties there are depends on what objects there are, and how internalism mirrors this reasoning.

[24] To be precise, the above argument uses the principle that what objects are not named in our language can differ from one world to another.

contender among such views and thus shouldn't be rejected because it doesn't agree with its competitors.

5. CONSEQUENCES AND APPLICATIONS

5.1. Summary about Properties

We have started out by looking at two general views about talk about properties. One view, externalism, takes such talk to be about some mind-and language-independent domain of entities. The other view, internalism, takes quantification over properties to be merely a logical device to increase expressive power in a language-internal way. It claims that such quantified statements are truth-conditionally equivalent to infinite disjunctions and conjunctions over the instances that can be formulated in that language. Internalism seems to have a serious problem with inexpressible properties that quite directly seems to refute it. We have seen in the above sections that this is false. Internalism, understood not as extreme internalism but as moderate internalism, resists attempts to refute by such arguments. Moderate internalism can accommodate the fact that there is a sense in which different languages express different properties. Moderate internalism is compatible with the inductive argument, and with several more technical arguments that attempt to refute internalism with inexpressible properties. We have seen no reason to reject moderate internalism from considerations about inexpressible properties.

If what I have said so far is correct then internalism is a serious contender in the debate about properties. Of course, we have seen no reason so far why one might think that internalism is true. This is a substantial and further question. To decide whether or not internalism or externalism is true we will have to look at different issues. Among them are

1. What is the function of our talk about properties? Why do we talk about them in the first place?
2. What is the semantic function of property nominalizations, such as "being a dog"? What is the correct understanding of quantifier-free talk about properties, such as 'Being a philosopher is fun,' or 'Redness is a sign of ripeness'?

3. What is the correct understanding of ordinary uses of quantifiers over properties?

These are the important and hard questions. Strict internalists, loose internalists, and externalists will differ in the answers they will give to these questions. And who is right in the end depends on who has the better answers to these, and other, questions. A direct refutation of internalism with expressibility considerations is not going to work. Once that is clear we can focus on the important questions. In a series of other papers I have given more positive reasons to accept a version of strict internalism. This internalist view is based on a view about quantification in natural language, the relation between quantifiers and ontology, a defense of an internal–external distinction about ontological questions, the semantic function of that-clauses and property nominalizations, and other issues.[25]

There are, however, some important questions about expressibility that are closely related to the debate we have been engaged in so far. These are about how different languages do in fact differ in what can be expressed in them. But before we can look at this, let's see how what has been said so far applies to talk about propositions, and why this debate is important more generally.

5.2. Inexpressible Propositions

So far we have focused on properties. The same considerations and arguments, however, carry over to propositions. We will not go through the same issues again in the case of propositions. This would not only be tedious, but is also unnecessary, since one can argue directly that there are inexpressible properties if and only if there are inexpressible propositions. If ϕ is an inexpressible property then

(55) that Joe is ϕ

is an inexpressible proposition. And if that p is an inexpressible proposition then

---

[25] For the main idea of this view and some issues that motivate it, see Hofweber (2005, and forthcoming a) with an emphasis on noun phrases, or (2000) with an emphasis on quantifiers. For more on noun phrases from a more general point of view, see Hofweber and Pelletier (forthcoming). For a discussion about quantification and ontology, and the internal–external distinction, see (Hofweber, forthcoming b or 2005).

(56) believing that p

or

(57) being hungry even though p

is an inexpressible property. But besides that, it seems clear that whatever reason one might have to believe in inexpressible propositions will give rise to reasons to believe in inexpressible properties and vice versa. These issues run in parallel, and so do the arguments to the conclusion that they provide no problem for internalism. The moderate internalist's proposal about the modeling of the truth-conditions of quantification over properties carries over directly to a model for the truth-conditions of quantification over propositions. The only difference is that properties are shadows of predicates, whereas propositions are shadows of sentences. According to internalism, quantification over propositions is equivalent to infinite disjunctions and conjunctions, but now the instances of the disjunctions and conjunctions involve sentences, not predicates. And just as in the case of properties, the relevant disjunctions and conjunctions will involve extra free variables that are bound from the outside by infinitary quantifiers.

5.3. An Application: Minimalist Truth

The claim that there are inexpressible properties and propositions plays an important role in the endgame of several philosophical debates. One obvious case is the debate about the metaphysics of properties and propositions itself. But this is not the only case. I would like to point to one example here where internalism has a quite direct impact and would substantially help a certain position in an important debate, the debate about minimalist theories of truth. I will restrict the applications of internalism to other debates to this example, and I will try to be brief.

The assumption that there are inexpressible propositions gives rise to a powerful argument against minimalist (or deflationary) theories of truth. Such theories claim that truth is really a metaphysically thin notion whose function is mainly to give us increased expressive power of certain sorts. In particular, minimalists about truth stress the importance of the Tarski biconditionals

(TB) It's true that p iff p.

(or an appropriate generalization thereof) for an account of the function of talk about truth. They closely tie the function of talk about truth to the increased expressive power it gives rise to, and they claim that truth is a metaphysically thin notion. Minimalism about truth is thus motivated by considerations congenial to the ones that motivate internalism.

One of the standard objections against minimalist theories of truth, the *incompleteness objection* (see Schmitt 1995: 141), relies on there being inexpressible propositions. The objection goes thus:

> Since there are propositions inexpressible in present English the concept of truth isn't captured by all the instances of (TB). The predicate 'true' applies even to propositions that can't be expressed in our language, as in
>
> > (58) What the best philosopher in the year 3000 will write will be true.
>
> What this philosopher will write might not be English, and might not be translatable into English. But our concept of truth nonetheless applies. So, the concept of truth goes further than minimalists would have it, we need a substantial notion of truth that applies more widely and more generally.

To accommodate ascriptions of truth to inexpressible propositions, or sentences, or utterances, in foreign languages that can't be translated into English, minimalists have taken quite radical measures, and they have thereby made their views quite implausible. Paul Horwich (1990), for example, thinks that the axioms of the theory of our truth predicate consist in all the propositions of the same form as the ones expressed by the instances of (TB). Many of them will not be expressible in English but nonetheless they are axioms of the theory of our concept of truth. Hartry Field (1994), bases his form of minimalism not on ascription of truth to propositions, but on ascription of truth to utterances. He also accepts that there are utterances that express propositions that are not expressible in our present languages, and bites the bullet by accepting that our concept of truth can meaningfully be applied only to utterances that one can understand. Truth of other utterances makes sense only via some translation to ones that one can understand, and doesn't make sense to ones that can't be translated.

The viability of internalism is obviously most central to this debate, and in particular to what formulation a minimalist theory of truth should take. Neither Horwich nor Field give any arguments for there being inexpressible propositions. That there are is a shared assumption in the debate. Moderate internalism can help a minimalist theory of truth in dealing with this objection.

At the beginning of this chapter we discussed the sentence (1) involving a truth predicate where it gives rise to increased expressive power. Sentence (1) involves quantification over propositions:

(59) For all p if Jones said that p in the trial then it's true that p.

If internalism is correct about quantification over propositions then truth is attributed only to expressible propositions (ones that are loosely speaker expressible). Thus the incompleteness objection vanishes. The same holds for (58):

(60) For all p if the best philosopher in the year 3000 writes that p then it's true that p.

That minimalists could deny that there are inexpressible propositions is a well-known option, but this option is always portrayed as a last and desperate move. For example, Schmitt (1995: 142) writes that "This way of replying must surely be a last, heroic resort," and later calls it "in the realm of the preposterous" (ibid.). But with the distinction between extreme and moderate internalism, and with keeping different notions of expressibility apart, we have seen that this is not at all so.[26]

5.4. Isn't There More to the World Than What We Can Say about It?

Even if there are no direct arguments against internalism using expressibility considerations, one might feel a bit of unease with the internalist view about expressibility. According to an internalist there is an important sense in which the world can be fully described, and all objects can be completely characterized, *by us*. But we might ask for an explanation how that could possibly be so. Wouldn't it be a complete miracle if we could say everything there is to say about the world we live in? And even if we can say everything there is to say, why is this so?

---

[26] In what sense different languages differ in expressive strength will be discussed shortly.

Inexpressible Properties, Propositions | 197

There is one clear way in which this can be made sense of, but this is hardly a way that an internalist would want to be committed to. It would be no wonder that we can express all properties that objects have if a form of idealism is true. If the world and the objects in it are a product or construction of our mind then it might be no wonder that our expressive resources completely capture the world. An idealist could claim that the world as we experience and describe it is a product or construction of our minds, and that our concepts play a central role in this construction. Without going into the details, it might seem possible that an idealist of this kind could claim that all aspects of the world can be captured in our language since after all the world is our product, and it should be no surprise that our products can be fully captured by us.

The internalist's explanation of why we can say everything there is to say is different. It is not because the objects we describe somehow depend on our descriptive abilities. Rather it is based on a view about what it is that we ask when we ask about expressing everything. The internalist's explanation for why we can express everything is based on a view about how general talk about properties and propositions, talk that involves quantification over them, relates to particular talk about properties and propositions, one that doesn't involve quantifiers over them, or that is not about properties and propositions at all. According to the internalist quantification over properties and propositions is merely a generalization over the instances, rightly understood, in one's own language. Thus when we ask whether or not we can say everything there is to say we quantify over propositions. And if internalism is right then this quantifier will be a generalization over the instances in our own language. Thus no wonder the answer is that we can say everything there is to say.

The argument that an explanation for the alleged fact that we can fully describe the world requires a form of idealism or pure luck is based on an externalist thinking about properties. True enough, for an externalist complete expressibility would be a surprise and would require a substantial explanation. If properties and propositions are out there independently of us, it would indeed be a surprise if we can express them all.

An internalist can and should claim that the world and its objects exist independently of us and that objects have the properties they have independently of us.[27] Objects have properties independently of us in

---

[27] Except, of course, response-dependent properties and the like.

198 | Thomas Hofweber

the sense discussed above, namely that Fido would still have the property of being a dog even if there were no humans, which comes down to that Fido would still be a dog even if there were no humans. This is the beauty of internalism: the world and the objects in it exist independently of us, objects have the properties they have independently of us, but still, properties are mere shadows of predicates, our predicates.

So far we have mainly focused on arguments that attempt to refute internalism using considerations about expressibility. It is now time to look at a more positive proposal about expressibility.

6. THE EXPRESSIBILITY HYPOTHESIS

6.1. The Hypothesis

Everyone agrees that in *some* sense different languages differ in their expressive strength. What properties and propositions speakers of these languages are able to express differs in some sense. The tricky part is to say more precisely in what sense they differ and why and how this difference comes about. And, of course, there is the additional tricky question whether or not there is a sense in which they do not differ. In the above we have seen two important ways in which different languages differ with respect to expressive strength. First, there can be a difference between what can be expressed using eternal sentences or predicates in different languages. Secondly, there is a difference between what contexts are in fact available to speakers of a certain language. These two differences in expressibility are clearly present, and it is not too hard to see why they are there (we will talk more about this below). But are there any substantially different ways in which different languages differ in expressive strength? And are there limits to what languages in general can express? What we have seen so far suggests a hypothesis about expressibility that says 'no' to these questions. It gives rise to a picture about expressibility that is congenial to internalism and to a picture about how and why languages differ in what can be said with them:

(EH) *The Expressibility Hypothesis.* Different languages can differ in what can be expressed in them with context-insensitive expressions, and what speakers of these languages can in fact express in them.

However, all languages agree on what speakers can express with them in arbitrary contexts.[28]

Of course, not every system of symbols deserves to be called a 'language'. The expressibility hypothesis is clearly false if we allow traffic signs, or C++, or the dance of a bee to be a language. These should clearly not count as a language for our purposes, and all first human languages should clearly count as languages. How to mark the differences more precisely is a substantial and interesting question that we won't be able to address properly here. The expressibility hypothesis is interesting and controversial enough even when restricted only to human languages. But as a first approximation, for a system of symbols to be a language it has to satisfy at least some minimal conditions: it has to allow for the expression of basic logical concepts, as well as certain other basic concepts. These basic concepts will be discussed further below. The expressibility hypothesis can be empirically refuted, and empirically confirmed, by considering how different languages in fact differ from each other in expressive strength. This is a substantial task, and the considerations given below in support of the expressibility hypothesis can only be considered to be a sketch of an outline of issues that deserve a more thorough investigation. Nonetheless we shall have a closer look at the expressibility hypothesis and how it relates to internalism in this chapter.

6.2. *Internalism and the Expressibility Hypothesis*

The expressibility hypothesis and internalism about talk about properties and propositions are congenial, but independent. Internalism does not imply the expressibility hypothesis. Internalism and expressive chauvinism[29] are consistent. Internalism might be true, and it might

---

[28] This hypothesis has to be distinguished from one that has been endorsed by Searle (1969). Searle's hypothesis is that

(H1) For every proposition p, if you can think that p then you can say that p.

i.e. the content of any thought can be articulated in language. The present expressibility hypothesis is different. It states that

(H2) For every proposition p, if someone can say that p in some context then everyone can say that p in the right context.

i.e. everyone can express any proposition that anyone can express, in the right context.
[29] See s. 3.1, where this notion was introduced.

be true that our language expresses everything there is to express, even though other languages don't. Not that we should believe this. These two positions are, however, consistent with each other.[30] But the expressibility hypothesis implies that expressive chauvinism is false. If it is true then all languages will be equal when it comes to what speakers can express with them in arbitrary contexts, which is what the crucial clause of the expressibility hypothesis says:

(61) For every proposition p, if a speaker of some language L_1 can express p in some context then for every language L_2 there is some context C and some sentence Φ of L_2 such that an utterance of Φ in C by a speaker of L_2 expresses p.

So, internalism about talk about properties and propositions can be true and at the same time the expressibility hypothesis can be false. So, the former does not imply the latter.

And the expressibility hypothesis does not imply internalism. It is consistent with the expressibility hypothesis that propositions are language-independent entities, and that there are propositions that are not expressible in any language, in any context. Let's call a proposition that is not loosely speaker expressible in any language a *completely alien proposition*. That there are completely alien propositions is consistent with the expressibility hypothesis, but not with internalism. Sentence (61) says only that what is loosely speaker expressible in one language is loosely speaker expressible in any other. This is consistent with the claim that some propositions are not loosely speaker expressible in any language. Internalism requires, however, that all propositions are loosely speaker expressible in our own language. Thus the expressibility hypothesis does not imply internalism.

But internalism and the expressibility hypothesis go together. To accept the expressibility hypothesis and deny internalism would be to accept that even though any proposition expressible in a language at all is expressible in every other language, there nonetheless are completely alien propositions, propositions not expressible in any language whatsoever. It is hard to see what reason one might have for this view. And to accept internalism but deny the expressibility hypothesis would require

---

[30] It might even be that internalism is true for every language, but still our language expresses more than every other one. If internalism is true for some language L then quantification over propositions in that language will be equivalent to infinite disjunctions and conjunctions formulated in that language. It might nonetheless be so that one language can express strictly more than another.

one to accept a form of expressive chauvinism. Again, it isn't easy to see how this could be justified.

6.3. Expressive Change

To see that the expressibility hypothesis is a reasonable proposal, let's look a little bit more closely at how languages differ in expressive strength, and why they differ in it in this way. It is particularly instructive to look at how the expressive power of a language differs over time. One very important aspect of this is the process of *de-contextualization*. In this process a language is modified in such a way that speakers of it are able to express a certain proposition without them having to be in a certain context. A good example of this is the introduction of a name into the language.[31] Suppose I like to talk about a certain object o. I can always do that if o is around, and I can refer to o using a demonstrative. But when o is not around and isn't in the right spatial or temporal relation to me then talk about o becomes impossible or at least tedious. To get around the requirement of having to be in a special spatial or temporal relationship with o I can introduce a name for o. The expanded language I now speak relieves me of the requirement of being related to o in a certain way to be able to talk about o. But what I can say now (in any context) and what I could have said before (in special contexts) is the same. The only thing that has changed is that the expansion of the language has made what I can say more independent of what contexts I have to be in to say it. In this chapter we have focused mainly on reference to an object in a context. Other ways in which the context of a speaker might have an impact on what can be said can be understood analogously.

A second, somewhat more general, way in which languages evolve over time is *lexical addition*. In this process the language gets expanded with a new word that expresses what was before only expressible in a complicated way. A good example of this is to introduce a new, simple predicate for a complex phrase that for some reason or other has acquired greater importance over time, and been used more and more often. This would be analogous to an explicit definition, in the simplest case. But this way can be and often will be mixed with the first way in which languages differ. A new word will be introduced that allows

---

[31] Not via a description. The case of introducing a name via a description is discussed below.

speakers of the expanded language to communicate in a simple way independently of being required to be in a certain context that before could only be said in a complicated way while being in a certain context. A mixed case is introducing a name via a description. Not only does it allow one to continue talking about an object even if it changes its properties, it also allows one to talk about it in a simpler way than by having to pick it out via a possibly quite complicated description. In addition, such a description might contain context-sensitive elements, and introducing a name rids the speaker of having to be in a particular context to describe the object successfully.

What de-contextualization and lexical addition will occur in a language over time will heavily depend on what the interests and needs of the speakers in the language community are. Objects that are important will get named, complex phrases that are or become important will be the basis for lexical addition. In addition, what objects and contexts are in fact available to speakers of that language will have a great impact, too, for how the language will evolve.

So, we see that there are several completely unproblematic ways in which what can be said in a language, and how it can be said in different languages, can differ:

- different languages differ in what can be said by speakers of them independently of the requirement of being in a certain context;
- different languages differ in how easy it is to say something, i.e. how many words are needed to say it;
- speakers of different languages will in fact have different contexts available to them to make utterances in.

These ways in which languages differ are unproblematic and together sufficiently strong to give rise to the impression that what can be expressed with a language is something quite independent of and external to the language. These considerations account for many externalist intuitions, and why the expressibility hypothesis seems radical. But moderate internalism accommodates all of them. Is there any reason to believe that there is a difference in what can be said in different languages that goes beyond these, or analogous, considerations? How might it come about that different languages indeed do express propositions that can't be expressed in the other language, even in arbitrary contexts?

6.4. Holism and the Expressibility Hypothesis

One way in which I can see this to be the case is holism. If holism is right then, leaving subtleties aside, there aren't two sufficiently different languages that can express the same proposition. Holism is a real alternative to the expressibility hypothesis, but I won't argue with it here. I personally find little reason to believe holism to be true, but if you do then the expressibility hypothesis is not for you. Holism and the expressibility hypothesis describe the two extreme ends of the spectrum about how languages differ in what can be expressed in them. Holism says, again leaving subtleties aside, that nothing that can be said in one language can be said in another one. The expressibility hypothesis says, also leaving subtleties aside, that everything that can be said in one language can be said in every other one. If you are like me and you find no reason to accept holism then the expressibility hypothesis should be a serious candidate for you. It makes sense of how languages differ in expressive strength and lexical set-up. It makes sense of why we think that what can be said in one language isn't all that can be said (by taking recourse to the different notions of expressibility). And it gives us an account of how and why different languages differ in what can be said with them without collapsing into a position that doesn't allow for the same thing to be expressible in different languages, even radically different languages spoken by speakers in different locations and at different times.

We who reject holism should take the expressibility hypothesis as a working hypothesis about what is expressible and how different languages differ in what can be expressed in them. The expressibility hypothesis might be too naive, and might ultimately have to be rejected. But if it fails we should see why precisely it isn't enough, and what gives rise to different expressive strength that isn't already captured by the cases discussed above. There might be some reason to reject the expressibility hypothesis as stated, but this reason is only a modification of one of the themes we have already discussed. But maybe there is a reason to reject the expressibility hypothesis altogether which is not based on a particular wording of the hypothesis. If we could see such a reason we would have learned something very substantial and important about our languages or our minds.

One tempting line of reasoning to refute the expressibility hypothesis is based on the observation that what is expressible in a language according to the expressibility hypothesis depends on the basic concepts

204 | Thomas Hofweber

that are articulated in the language. Not everything expressible in a language can come from de-contextualization and lexical addition, or related processes. Some expressive resources have to be basic. Now, suppose it is true that if two languages articulate the same basic concepts then what is loosely speaker expressible by predicates and sentences in them is identical. Might there not be different languages that express different basic concepts? And if so, wouldn't what is loosely speaker expressible in these languages be different? Isn't that reason to give up the expressibility hypothesis?

It is certainly conceivable that other creatures speak a language that contains different concepts as the basic concepts. This is compatible with the expressibility hypothesis. One such case would be that even though for us negation and disjunction are the basic truth functional operators, for them it's negation and conjunction. Still, though, for both of us all truth functions are expressible. What is required for this kind of argument to refute the expressibility hypothesis is that there are creatures whose basic concepts are not even expressible by us. And this is, of course, much more controversial, and in fact repeats one of the controversies we had above. Can we really make sense of the idea that other people or other creatures have some basic concepts that we can't express at all? If you like holism you might find this plausible, and if you tap your externalist intuitions you might have little problem with it. But independently of that I see little reason to accept it, and to give such considerations an important status in our deliberations about what large-scale view about expressibility and talk about properties and propositions we should accept. The expressibility hypothesis makes sense of why and how languages differ in their expressive power. Unless we find plausible reasons to reject it I think we should work with it. It's our best bet.

7. CONCLUSION

The main aim of this chapter was to show that internalism is not refuted by considerations about expressibility. Internalism seems to be committed to expressive chauvinism, and this is a very implausible view. However, once we distinguish extreme from moderate internalism, and once we distinguish several notions of expressibility, it becomes clear that issues about expressibility and how they relate to internalism are not as simple as they might at first seem. As we have seen in this chapter, moderate internalism can accommodate claims to the effect that for every real number there is a property of being larger than that number, that there might have been different properties than there are, and that not every property is expressible in every language ("expressible" rightly understood). In addition, internalism is congenial to a view about expressibility, captured in the expressibility hypothesis, which is a plausible hypothesis about expressive change, at least for those among us who don't believe in holism. Internalism is not implied by this view about expressibility, since this view does not rule out that there are completely alien propositions. But should we believe that there are propositions inexpressible by any speaker in any language in any context? The answer to this question will partly depend on the answer to the question of what we do when we talk about propositions in the first place. In this debate we try to understand our own talk about properties and propositions. What function this talk has will be central to determining whether or not internalism or externalism is true. What we do when we talk about and quantify over propositions will be part of the story about whether or not the statement "there are completely alien propositions" is true. If externalism about talk about propositions is right then it might be true, if there indeed is a completely alien proposition out there. But if quantification over propositions has a function more congenial to the internalist then it will be false, whatever is out there in the world. Part of what is at issue in answering this question is understanding our own language, in particular what we do when we talk about properties and propositions.

To decide how this talk should be understood will involve a number of further and substantial issues, ones that do not directly relate to considerations about expressibility. These will be issues partly in the philosophy of language, and partly in metaphysics. They will include issues about the function of property nominalizations and quantifier-free talk about properties, whether or not that-clauses are referring expressions, issues about the role of properties in accounts of laws of nature and causation, and many more. These are the issues where the debate between externalism and internalism, and ultimately between minimalist and substantial approaches to the metaphysics of properties and propositions, will be settled. How this will go is, of course, a completely different story. The goal of the present chapter is merely to make sure that internalism and minimalism are not ruled out because of considerations about expressibility.

University of North Carolina at Chapel Hill

REFERENCES

Armstrong, D. (1978). *A Theory of Universals*. (Cambridge: Cambridge University Press).
—— (1989). *Universals: An Opinionated Introduction*. (Boulder, Colo.: Westview).
Bach, K. (1997). "Do Belief Reports Report Beliefs?", *Pacific Philosophical Quarterly*, 78: 215–41.
Barwise, J. (1975). *Admissible Sets and Structures* (Berlin: Springer Verlag).
Carnap, R. (1956). "Empiricism, Semantics, and Ontology", in *Meaning and Necessity* (Chicago: University of Chicago Press), 2nd edn.
Field, H. (1994). "Deflationary Views of Meaning and Content", *Mind* 103: 249–85.
Hofweber, T. (2000). "Quantification and Non-existent Objects", in A. Everett and T. Hofweber (eds.), *Empty Names, Fiction, and the Puzzles of Non-Existence* (Stanford, Calif.: CSLI).
—— (2005). "A Puzzle about Ontology", *Noûs*, 39: 256–83.
—— (forthcoming *a*). "Innocent Statements and their Metaphysically Loaded Counterparts".
—— (forthcoming *b*). "Neo-Carnapian Approaches to Ontology".
—— and Pelletier, J. (forthcoming), "Encuneral Noun Phrases".
Horwich, P. (1990). *Truth* (Oxford: Blackwell).
Keisler, H. J. (1971). *Model Theory for Infinitary Logic* (New York: North-Holland).
King, J. (2002). "Designating Propositions", *Philosophical Review* 111/3.
Quine, W. V. O. (1980). "On What There Is", in *From a Logical Point of View* (Cambridge, Mass.: Harvard University Press).
Schiffer, S. (1987). *Remnants of Meaning* (Cambridge, Mass.: MIT).
—— (1994). "A Paradox of Meaning", *Noûs*, 28: 279–324.
—— (1996). "Language Created, Language Independent Entities", *Philosophical Topics* 24: 149–67.
Schmitt, F. F. (1995). *Truth: A Primer* (Bouldes, Colo.: Westview).
Searle, J. R. (1969). *Speech Acts* (Cambridge: Cambridge University Press).
Yablo, S. (2000). "A Paradox of Existence", in A. Everett and T. Hofweber, (eds.), *Empty Names, Fiction and the Puzzles of Non-Existence* (Stanford, Calif.: CSLI).

8. Aristotle's Constituent Ontology

Michael Loux

I

In both Aristotle and Nicholas Wolterstorff we meet with a distinction between two styles of metaphysical explanation. They use different language in setting out the distinction. Wolterstorff speaks of relational and constituent ontologies;[1] whereas Aristotle tells us that we can make the substance of sensible particulars either something that exists "apart from the sensible objects" or something that is "immanent in them" (994^{a}15–16); but the contrast they want to mark is, I believe, the same contrast. The context for the distinction is a certain philosophical project, the project Aristotle calls identifying the substance of familiar sensible particulars. Put in general terms, this project is that of explaining why familiar particulars have the character they do, why, that is, they fall under the kinds and exhibit the properties we, in our prephilosophical thinking, associate with them.[2] The underlying idea is that familiar particulars exhibit whatever character they have derivatively or

---

[1] Wolterstorff (1970: 111 ff.) and (1991: 540–1, 547–8).

[2] All references to Aristotle's work are from Barnes (1984). Aristotle explains the locution "the substance of x" at 1017^{b}15–17. For a discussion of this text, see Loux (1991: 148 ff.). Although Aristotle restricts talk about the substance of a thing to talk about the principle in virtue of which the thing belongs to its proper substance kind, I am assuming an extension of the notion to cover not just the case of genuine Aristotelian substances but also the case of what Aristotle calls coincidentals (73^{b}9). Just as being for a familiar particular that is a substance is being a geranium, being a dog, or being a human, so being for a familiar particular that is a coincidental is being a musical man, being a white horse, or being an overweight rhinoceros; and I am assuming that in the latter cases no less than the former, we can engage in the project of identifying the cause of the being or the substance of the thing. The expressions 'separate' and 'immanent'/'in' can be used to mark a variety of contrasts; but at 996^{a}15–16, the operative contrast is that between an account that makes the substance of a thing something that is "in" it in the sense that it is a proper constituent, component, or metaphysical part of the thing and an account that makes the substance of a thing something that exists apart from the thing. Clearly, the force of 'separate' here is parasitic on its opposition to 'immanent'/'in'. See 998^{a}21–3 for the same use of 'immanent' and 1080^{a}37–1080^{b}2 for an explicit formulation of the contrast at work in 996^{a}15–16. I give a detailed argument for this reading of the relevant texts in Loux (2004).

dependently. As Aristotle puts it, they have their character in virtue of another (*kat' allou*). But the items from which familiar objects derive their character have their own distinctive character non-derivatively or, to use again Aristotle's language, in their own right (*kath hauto*).[3] Where the two approaches differ is in their accounts of character derivation. Those who endorse what Wolterstorff calls the constituent approach tell us that the items from which familiar particulars derive their character are constituents or components of sensible things; they are something like ingredients or parts of those things. On what Wolterstorff calls the relational approach, by contrast, the items from which familiar sensibles derive their character are not 'immanent in' those sensibles. As Aristotle's characterization has it, they exist "apart from the sensibles," and it is in virtue of standing in some non-mereological relation to those items that familiar particulars have the character they do. Different proponents of the relational strategy give different names to the relation at work here. They speak of participation, exemplification, instantiation; nor are their accounts of the precise nature of the relation always the same. Indeed, some refuse to speak of a relation here at all. As they see it, no account of character derivation that invokes the concept of a relation can fail to be viciously regressive. They speak instead of non-relational ties or nexus;[4] but they agree that it is in virtue of standing in their favored tie or nexus to the non-derivative possessors of character that familiar particulars have whatever character they do.

Proponents of the two strategies differ, then, in their metaphysical characterizations of familiar particulars. Proponents of the constituent strategy take familiar particulars to have a mereological structure other than that we prephilosophically associate with them. As these ontologists see it, ordinary objects are composites, complexes, or wholes made up of or constituted by metaphysically prior items, things that have an essential identity independent of the wholes into which they enter. The items in question are to be contrasted with the common-sense parts of a familiar particular. Indeed, the constituents of a sensible particular are responsible for its common-sense mereological structure no less than any other aspect of its character. Relational ontologists, on the other hand, will deny that familiar particulars have any but a common-sense

[3] For this use of the *kat' allou/kath hauto* contrast, see 1031^{b}13.
[4] See e.g. Strawson (1959: ch. 5) and Bergmann (1967: 24 ff.).

mereological structure. The only parts sensible particulars have are their common-sense parts, whether they be functional parts such as hands, legs, hearts, and lungs or strictly material parts such as the stuffs or particles out of which they are made. Indeed, relationists will typically accuse constituent ontologists of something like a category mistake.[5] They will say that the items responsible for a familiar particular's character are abstract entities, and they will deny that abstract entities can coherently be construed as constituents, components, or ingredients of concrete particulars. Familiar particulars can, nevertheless, stand in metaphysically significant non-mereological relations with, or be tied to, those abstract entities; and in virtue of doing so, they have whatever character we prephilosophically attribute to them.

Examples of the two strategies are easy to come by. Certainly the Russell of *The Problems of Philosophy* is endorsing the relational style when, having denied that what he calls ideas "exist in the world of sense", he goes on to tell us that "Whatever we may attempt to say about things in the world of sense, we can only succeed in saying that they participate in such and such ideas which, therefore, constitute all their character."[6] Russell credits Plato with the introduction of this style of metaphysical explanation; and it is members of the Platonic Academy who provide Aristotle with his stock examples of metaphysicians who "separate" the substance of familiar sensibles. Plato's own theory is, of course, the paradigm here; but Aristotle seems to have taken Speusippus' claim that numbers are the principles of familiar sensibles to be another account that "separates" substance.[7] Wolterstorff does not feel the need to give specific examples of the relational strategy. He takes it to be the standard pattern at work in recent ontology and so assumes that there is no need for particular examples, but it is clear that the sort of account he takes to be paradigmatic here is one like that found in Alvin Plantinga's work, where familiar particulars get their character by entering into a

---

[5] In Loux (2002: 124–5), I have what I call an Aristotelian raise this objection against bundle and substratum theorists. The Aristotelian is one who endorses the sort of account of substance we meet in the *Categories*, where there is no hint of a constituent approach, rather than the self-consciously constituent account presented in the *Physics* and developed, especially, in *Metaphysics* Z and H. There are important and much debated questions about just how we should understand the ontology of the *Categories* and its relationship to the later constituent ontology of the middle books of the *Metaphysics*. For opposing views, see Loux (1991) and Wedin (2000).

[6] Russell (1912: 92).

[7] I take 1080^b 15–16 to be a reference to Speusippus.

variety of exemplification relations with properties, relations such as essential exemplification and contingent exemplification.[8]

Aristotle's examples of those who make the substance of sensibles something "immanent in them" include his materialist predecessors, both those who made the substance of things some sort of stuff (what we call gunk) and those who took individual particles (our physical simples) to be the ultimate carriers of character, as well as the Pythagoreans who, as Aristotle sees it, made numbers the "elements" of sensible particulars.[9] In giving examples of constituent ontologists, Wolterstorff points both to the work of medieval philosophical theologians who construed the essences or natures of particulars as something like ingredients in them[10] and to the writings of Gustav Bergmann, where virtually every metaphysical claim gets couched in the language of constituents and wholes.[11] And we could add to the roster of constituent ontologists. Certainly, those empiricist critics of substance who insisted that familiar particulars are nothing but bundles of empirically manifest qualities were endorsing a version of the constituent strategy; and more recently David Armstrong has recommended the constituent approach when he suggests that we construe familiar particulars as nothing more than very complex states of affairs whose ultimate components are universals and what he calls "thin particulars".[12]

Three caveats regarding the distinction between the constituent and relational styles are in order. First, the contrast initially appears to be one between two theories of universals; but as our examples indicate, it is broader than that. Certainly contemporary relational ontologists construe universals as the non-derivative bearers of character; but as we have noted, Aristotle's Speusippus did not. He made numbers rather than properties or attributes the substance of sensible particulars; and although Aristotle often reads Plato as making universals responsible for the character of sensible particulars, he sometimes interprets the Forms not as universals at all, but as something akin to eternal paradigmatic particulars (997^a34–998^b13). Aristotle's favorite examples of immanentists made material stuffs or particles the substance of the

---

[8] See Plantinga (1974), where the relational approach expresses itself in virtually every chapter.
[9] See *Metaphysics* A. 3–4 for Aristotle's discussion of these views.
[10] Wolterstorff (1991: 540–1).
[11] Wolterstorff (1970: 111) and (1991: 547).
[12] Armstrong (1989: 94–5 and (1997: 183–90).

particulars made out of them. Now, one might suppose that these materialists were confused; one might suppose, that is, that what they should have said is that it is the defining properties of their chosen material elements that are the ultimate carriers of character. It is, however, not implausible to think that they took the material elements to be the sources of and, hence, prior to the properties associated with them. In any case, we do not have to look to esoteric examples from pre-Socratic philosophy to find constituent ontologists who make something other than universals the ultimate sources of character. Trope theorists make particular or individual properties the constituents of ordinary objects that are responsible for the character those objects have;[13] and, of course, even those constituent ontologists such as Bergmann and Armstrong who make universals constituents of ordinary objects want to deny that universals exhaust their constituents. Both think that universals constitute an ordinary object only in conjunction with a further constituent. Bergmann calls it a bare particular[14] and Armstrong, as we have noted, a thin particular.

Second, the classification of ontological theories into the relational and constituent might seem to be both mutually exclusive and collectively exhaustive; but it is neither. For one thing, there can be ontological theories that invoke both strategies. Consider a two-step theory that makes tropes constituents of familiar particulars and holds that while tropes confer on familiar particulars any character they might have, those tropes are instantiations of universals (we might call them trope-types) that are not constituents of any objects at all. For another, there are ontologies that endorse neither strategy. Consider the extreme nominalist who insists that we take the facts expressed by our non-philosophical character ascriptions to be irreducibly basic and so in no need of explanation.[15] Nominalists of this persuasion are, of course,

---

[13] See e.g. Williams (1953).
[14] See Bergmann (1967: 24–5). See also Allaire (1963).
[15] See e.g. Quine (1954: 10 ff.). Another possible example here is the framework we find in Aristotle's own *Categories*. Clearly, there are no "separate" explanatory principles in that work, but neither is there any talk of constituents or components. One might argue that the *Categories* is not a genuinely metaphysical treatise, at least not in the sense that it seeks to identify the substance of familiar particulars (what it calls primary substances). If this is right, then the central question is why we do not find the metaphysical project in that early treatise. Is it because, not having developed the hylomorphic theory, Aristotle does not yet see himself as a proponent of a constituent ontology? Or is it because he is doing proto-ontology rather than ontology in the *Categories*; that is, is he identifying the

rejecting the metaphysical project underlying our distinction. For philosophers who embrace that project, on the other hand, the relational and constituent ontologies seem to be the obvious theoretical options; and while a two-step ontology of the hybrid sort just delineated is possible, a theory invoking both patterns of explanation strikes us as redundant. For the philosopher who feels the need to provide an account of the character familiar objects display, the natural choice is that between the two options Aristotle and Wolterstorff lay out for us.

Finally, one might think that there are decisive reasons for favoring one of the two approaches over the other. Certainly, proponents of the two views try to convince us that this is so. It is in this spirit that relational ontologists accuse those constituent ontologists who make abstract entities constituents of concrete particulars of a category mistake. In the same spirit, constituent ontologists deny that it is possible for spatiotemporal particulars to stand in the required dependency relations to items completely outside space and time or for beings like us to acquire knowledge of such items. The charges on both sides are familiar, so familiar that they are likely to strike us as pieces of worn-out rhetoric rather than serious philosophy. In any case, it is difficult to believe that any of these charges can settle things one way or the other. If there is a moral here, perhaps it is the one Wolterstorff draws: the need for tolerance in ontology.[16] We should encourage proponents of both styles to lay out fully articulated versions of their respective approaches. Rather than raising a priori objections, we should attempt to understand how the styles work themselves out and to evaluate them in terms of their fruitfulness in illuminating metaphysically significant relations and in solving metaphysical problems on a variety of fronts.

II

When Aristotle first presents us with the contrast between theories that "separate" substance and those that make it "immanent in" sensible substances, he can seem to be an impartial commentator on a debate to which he is not a party. But, of course, he is anything but neutral here.

---

data for the project of ontological explanation rather than carrying out that project? These questions are just a few of those that this early text raises.

[16] Wolterstorff (1991: 535, 541).

Although some scholars have denied this, Aristotle's own account of character derivation falls squarely into the constituent camp.[17] He holds that a substance such as a human being or a horse falls under the natural kind it does because it is a composite whose constituents are the appropriate form and a parcel of the appropriate sort of matter; and he thinks that what he calls coincidentals—things such as a musical man or a white horse—have the character they do in virtue of being composites of a substance of the right kind and the appropriate item from one of the accidental categories.[18] We have, then, a multilayered structure of constituents and wholes. Coincidentals are composites of a substance and an accident; and a substance, in turn, is a composite of matter and form; and the mereological structure can run deeper; for the matter for a substantial particular can itself be a composite involving a lower level matter and form; and that same type of structure can be repeated at still lower levels.

But while it may be clear that the immanentist or constituent strategy is operative here, little attention has been paid to the role that strategy plays in shaping Aristotle's account of familiar particulars. Especially in discussion of matter and form, we meet with talk of components and constituents; but there is little serious reflection on the philosophical commitments implied by this sort of talk. There is, of course, a more general difficulty here. It is not that we have a thoroughly articulated conception of the constituent strategy that commentators have failed to apply in their discussions of Aristotle's metaphysics. The constituent strategy itself stands in need of clarification. Little has been done to identify its overall structure or its theoretical implications. To be sure, proponents of the strategy have had things to say here, but their comments have had an internalist cast: they seem to be addressed to philosophers already at home in the constituent strategy; and they have

---

[17] I argue in detail for this claim in Loux (2005). One might find it puzzling that I should think it necessary to argue this point at all and even more puzzling that I would spend more than fifty pages arguing it. Aristotle's theory, one might have thought, is the paradigm of an immanentist or constituent theory. I agree. Unfortunately many (perhaps, most) recent commentators do not. It has become almost routine to deny that the hylomorphic theory is to be understood in constituent terms; hence, the need for an extended argument.

[18] See 73^b 6–9, 179^a1–2, 1029^a20–3, 1038^b4–6, 1041^b5–7, 1043^a7–11, and 1049^a34–6. For a detailed discussion of these texts and the overall theory they express, see, once again, Loux (1991) and Loux (2005). See also F. Lewis (1982, 1991: chs. 3–6).

been sketchy: nothing like general principles for understanding talk about constituents and wholes emerges from these comments. Accordingly, if we are to understand Aristotle's account of character derivation as an instance of the constituent approach to ontological issues, we need to get clearer on just what that approach entails.

The core idea is that each familiar object is a complex or coarse-grained entity made up or composed of a plurality of simpler, more fine-grained entities. We have followed Wolterstorff in labelling ontologies that reject immanent sources of character in favor of those that are "separated" relational, but we cannot overlook the fact that relations play a crucial role in the constituent strategy as well. The fine-grained entities of that strategy enter into relations with each other and in virtue of doing so make up or compose the coarse-grained entity that is a familiar particular. But the relation into which the fine-grained items enter is unique or distinctive; it is not to be identified with or assimilated to other more familiar relations responsible for composition. Properties can be conjoined to make up a single conjunctive property, but property conjunction is not the relation at work in constituent ontologies. If relevant at all to the constituent strategy, property conjunction would not serve the purposes of any but bundle theoretic versions of the strategy; but even there its relevance is dubious since familiar particulars are not themselves properties. Objects of categorially the same or different types can be related as members of a single set; but set-theoretical composition is not the relation tying constituents into wholes. Sets are abstract entities, but what the constituents of those ontologies are supposed to make up or compose are concrete particulars. We have spoken of mereological structure, but we have been speaking loosely. There is a narrower, technical use of the term 'mereology' where it refers to the logic of parts and wholes, and that logic identifies a relation between objects that gives rise to something that is a whole made out or composed of those objects. However, the relation tying the fine-grained entities of a constituent ontology is more demanding than that tying the parts of the sums or fusions of formal mereology. Whereas the constituents of a physical composite are spatiotemporally compresent throughout the time they compose the composite, the items making up a mereological sum or fusion can be as spatially disparate as you please; and even if we impose the appropriate spatiotemporal restrictions, we are not likely to capture the relation at work in constituent ontologies. It is difficult to see how the restricted relation will fail to apply to the case of a familiar object's common-sense parts, and there is a further difficulty constituent ontologists often have with the attempt to reduce the relation of constitution to mereological composition. They tell us that whether restricted or not, mereological composition is such that if a plurality of objects compose a thing, they compose just one thing; but these constituent ontologists want to claim that one and the same plurality of objects can simultaneously constitute numerically distinct composites.[19]

But there is a further, more general difficulty with the attempt to assimilate the relation between the constituents making up an ordinary particular to any of the relations underlying these more familiar forms of composition. Those relations tend to be such that if it is possible for a plurality of objects to enter into any one of them, then the entities in question do enter into that relation. But constituent ontologists invariably tell us that it is possible for the items constituting a familiar particular to exist without constituting it. Familiar particulars are contingent entities; their non-existence is possible. Accordingly, constituent ontologists say that where certain objects go together to constitute a familiar particular, they do so only contingently.

So constituent ontologists agree that there is a *sui generis* relation that contingently binds a plurality of metaphysically simpler items into a composite whole. But they do not all agree about the identity of that relation. Bundle theorists restrict the constituents of familiar particulars to first-order properties, and they tell us that the first-order properties constitutive of a familiar particular bear to each other a relation that gets variably labeled as compresence, collocation, consubstantiation, or combination.[20] It is a relation the relevant properties only contingently bear to each other; and the labels suggest that it is merely spatiotemporal coincidence. But while bundle theorists will agree that it may be by way of their occupying a single region of space at a given time that we recognize the compresence or collocation of the properties constituting a physical or material particular, they refuse to identify the relation with spatiotemporal coincidence. For one thing, they typically want to be relationists about space and time and to hold that the frameworks of space and time presuppose the framework of fully articulated physical

---

[19] See e.g. Armstrong (1997: 178–83). The difficulty with this claim is that not all those interested in formal mereology endorse the idea that if certain objects have a sum, they have just one sum. See e.g. Simons (1987: 1–3).

[20] See e.g. Williams (1953), Ayer (1954), and Castañeda (1974).

or material particulars. Accordingly, they will insist that facts of property compresence are prior to spatial and temporal facts. For another, many bundle theorists want to follow Hume in endorsing a bundle theoretic treatment of minds as well as material objects; and they will hold that where we have minds, compresence gets expressed not by spatiotemporal coincidence, but by some sort of psychological relation between properties.

Like bundle theorists, substratum theorists recognize the need for a relation that only contingently binds the constituents of a familiar particular. They tell us that the items constitutive of a familiar object are tied together by the relation/nexus of exemplification: one item—a substratum, bare particular, or thin particular—exemplifies the properties that together with it constitute a familiar object;[21] and they insist that a crucial difference between their concept of exemplification and other notions that go by that name (whether the notion at work in relational ontologies or that operative in our everyday prephilosophical thought and talk about familiar objects and the properties we say they have or possess) is that their notion of exemplification is not one that gets divided into the essential/necessary and the contingent/accidental: since it is the tie/relation binding the constituents of merely contingent composites, it is a categorial or structural fact about this relation that it binds objects only contingently. What it binds are objects from different metaphysical categories; and the product of the relation is something with a distinctive ontological structure. What results is not a mere "togetherness" of constituents, but rather the fact that one constituent exemplifies the other. So the product of the relation is an item belonging to a third metaphysical category—a fact or a state of affairs; and according to substratum theorists, familiar particulars are to be identified with such facts or complexes of such facts.[22]

Aristotle's account of the constitution of familiar particulars is structurally of a piece with that of the contemporary substratum theorist. As we have noted, there are two cases here. The first involves the matter and form that go together to constitute an individual substance falling under a natural kind—something like a geranium, a horse, or a human being; the second involves the substance and accident that together

---

[21] See e.g. Bergmann (1967: 24 ff., Armstrong (1989: 88 ff.), and Allaire (1963).

[22] The idea that ordinary objects are to be understood as facts/states of affairs or complex structures of such is prominent in both Bergmann (see 1967: 24 ff.) and Armstrong (see 1989: 88 ff.).

constitute a coincidental—a musical man or an overweight rhinoceros. In both cases, Aristotle tells us, the relation whose obtaining gives us the composite is predication, where predication is a metaphysical relation between non-linguistic objects (1029^{a}21–4). So the form is predicated of the matter to yield an Aristotelian substance, and the accident is predicated of the substance to deliver a coincidental, and Aristotle is explicit in holding that in both cases the relation is merely contingent. Indeed, although Aristotle is credited with being the father of essentialism, the only forms of basic or primitive predication he recognizes are both cases of contingent or accidental predication. As he sees it, it is only if we make the tie connecting the constituents of familiar particulars one that obtains merely contingently that we can explain the fact that those particulars are one and all both generable and corruptible. What he claims is that the coming to be of an ordinary object is simply a matter of its constituents coming to be related in the appropriate way, and its passing away is their ceasing to be related in that way; and predication is the way the constituents are related.[23]

How, then, does essential predication enter the picture? Where the subject of the predication is a familiar particular, the answer is clear: essential predication is a derived form of predication; its obtaining is simply a matter of the obtaining of one of the two basic or constitutive cases of predication.[24] For Aristotle, an essential predication is *de re* necessary; but what is central to the notion of essential predication is that it is what-predication: the predicated universal marks out its subject as *what* it is. Thus, a biological species is essentially predicated of its

[23] See, in this connection, *Physics* A. 7–9, where the subject/thing predicated distinction gets introduced to explain how coming to be and passing away are possible. Aristotle is explicit in maintaining that this account holds both for the case that is the focus of his account, the case of a coincidental such as his musical man, and for the case of a genuine substantial individual—the case of a biological organism (190^{a}33–190^{b}4). The idea that the coming to be and passing away of a familiar concrete particular is a matter of the "coming together" or "coming apart" of its constituents also dominates *Metaphysics* Z. 7–9.

[24] See Loux (1991 chs. 4, 5) for a detailed discussion of this idea. There remains a question about the ontological status of substance species. One might find it tempting to construe Aristotle as an eliminativist about these universals; but as I argue in Loux (1991), that reading does not square with his repeated claim that the individuals falling under substance species are fully real, fully substantial. Likewise, one might want to read Aristotle's doctrine of form predication as embodying a reductionism about substance species; but as I argue in section VI, that reading of Aristotle is also misguided. The moral, I take it, is that the claim that a given universal is analyzable in terms of metaphysically prior items entails neither eliminativism nor reductivism about that universal.

members. The species *horse* is essentially predicated of Funny Cide: what Funny Cide is is a horse. That predication's obtaining, however, consists in the fact that the substantial form associated with the species is contingently predicated of the appropriate matter—the matter that composes Funny Cide; and presumably a parallel story holds where some hybrid universal such as *musical man* is predicated of the appropriate coincidental. What the coincidental is is a musical man, but that essential predication's obtaining involves nothing more than the appropriate accident's (here, *musical's*) being contingently predicated of the appropriate substance (here, the relevant human being).

Initially, however, this may seem puzzling. The musical man is essentially a musical man. The man, on the other hand, is a substance and not a coincidental, so it is difficult to see how, on Aristotle's theory at least, he could qualify as a musical man. But even if Aristotle were to allow that the expression 'musical man' can be truly applied to the man, the fact remains that he takes the man to be only contingently musical. Accordingly, Aristotle must deny that the man is essentially a musical man. So Aristotle is committed to the claim that the musical man is, but the man is not essentially a musical man. But there is only one thing here—the man who happens to be musical. After all, we do not give two votes—one to the man and another to the musical man. But if there is just one thing here, then it looks as though Aristotle is committed to the claim that it both has and lacks the property of being essentially a musical man, and that seems to represent a violation of the Indiscernibility of Identicals.

But do we really have a violation of the principle here? Aristotle, at least, would deny that we do. The Indiscernibility of Identicals tells us that, necessarily, if a thing, x, and a thing, y, are identical, every property of x is a property of y and vice versa.[25] But, then, we have a violation of the Indiscernibility of Identicals only if the man and the musical man are numerically identical; and Aristotle denies this. It is not too difficult to see why. On Aristotle's constituent ontology, the musical man is a composite and the man is a proper constituent of that composite; and surely a thing and each of its proper constituents are non-identical.

But did we not say that the man and the musical man are one thing? We did, but to get an untoward result, we need the additional premise

---

[25] For Aristotle's commitment to the Indiscernibility of Identicals, see 202^{b}15–16.

that numerical identity and numerical unity are one and the same thing, and Aristotle rejects that premise. He distinguishes between two types of unity/sameness—accidental unity/sameness and unity/sameness in being; and only the latter corresponds to our notion of numerical identity.[26] Now, Aristotle thinks that a composite is one with each of its proper constituents. Thus, the musical man and the man occupy precisely the same region of space; to point to one is to point to the other; and whatever we do to the one we do to the other. But these facts obtain merely contingently. If the man were not musical, there would be no such thing as the musical man and none of the adduced facts would obtain. It is, however, only contingently that the man is musical; and the contingency displays itself in the fact that the man and the musical man have different life histories. They come to be at different times; and if the man should somehow lose his musical skills before he dies, they would likewise pass away at different times. So while one, the man and the musical man are only accidentally one; and since Aristotle denies that accidental unity is numerical identity, he can consistently deny that the fact that the musical man is essentially musical, but the man only contingently musical, represents a violation of the Indiscernibility of Identicals.

But if Aristotle thinks that the man and the musical man are non-identical, is he not committed to what we nowadays call collocated objects? Well, he explicitly denies that it is possible for numerically distinct material objects to have the same proper place or, as we would put it, to occupy precisely the same region of space (209^a5–7);[27] and he means that it is impossible for this to happen at a single time. Notice, however, that the man and the musical man do not provide a counter-example to this principle since while non-identical, they are accidentally one and so their spatial coincidence is not a case of numerically *two* collocated material objects. But quite apart from the distinction between unity and identity, there is nothing really puzzling about the fact that the man and the musical man have the same proper place; for while we can certainly say that the coincidental we call the musical man occupies that region of space, its doing so is not a self-standing state of affairs. The musical man's being in that place is a kind of logical product of two

---

[26] See e.g. *Topics* A. 7 for Aristotle's account of the distinction. For detailed discussions of the distinction, see F. Lewis (1982, 1991: ch. 3).
[27] See also 998^a13–19, where we get two applications of this principle.

more basic facts: first, that a certain man occupies that place and, second, that the man is musical. And, of course, the man in question is a proper constituent of the composite that is the musical man. So it is only because a proper constituent of the musical man is in a place that we can say that the composite is.

Indeed, while it is not false to say that the musical man is in the relevant place (call it P), the state of affairs consisting in its being in P should not be understood to involve an accident's being predicated of the coincidental. There is an accident here, namely, being in P, and it is predicated of a subject, but its subject is not the coincidental, but something that is a proper constituent of the coincidental—the man. It is a central feature of Aristotle's doctrine of coincidentals that where predication is restricted to the primitive composite-forming relation, accidents can be predicated of substances and nothing else. Indeed, he explicitly denies that, in the relevant sense, accidents can be predicated of coincidentals ($1007^{b}2$ ff.). Accordingly, in the strict sense, there is no such thing as a white musical man, a six-foot musical man, or a 165-pound musical man. That is, there are no genuine composites answering to such expressions as 'the white musical man' or 'the six-foot musical man'. The operation that generates composites is predication, and accidents can only be predicated of substances. But it does not follow that it is false to say that the musical man is white, is six feet tall, weighs 165 pounds, and occupies P. These claims are all true, but the states of affairs that constitute their truth-conditions are not the sorts of ontological configurations that underlie what appear to do very similar claims—the claim that the man is white, the claim that the man is six feet tall, the claim that the man weighs 165 pounds, and the claim that the man occupies P. The latter claims all express genuine metaphysical predications: each expresses the fact that a particular accident is metaphysically predicated of a substance. The corresponding claims about the coincidental are true, but they do not express cases of predication ($83^{a}15$–19). What

(1) The musical man is white

expresses is a fact of coincidental unity or sameness. It expresses the fact that a certain coincidental is accidentally one with/the same as something of which the accident *white* is metaphysically predicated. So there is a predication on the horizon, but the coincidental is not the subject of that predication; the substance that is one of its proper constituents is.

III

But while it is a merely contingent fact that the items comprising a familiar particular go together to constitute that particular, the particular has its constituents necessarily. Call this latter claim Constituent Essentialism. For the constituent ontologist, intuitive support for Constituent Essentialism is strong. According to constituent ontologists, a familiar particular is nothing more than a composite of ontologically prior items: what it is for a familiar object to exist is for there to be certain metaphysically more basic items standing in a particular contingent relation or tie. But, then, it is difficult to see how any constituent ontologist could deny that its constituents are essential to an ordinary concrete object. The claim seems to be something like a principle in the good old Aristotelian sense of being a starting point for a certain philosophical project—here, the project of constituent ontology; and I know of no constituent ontologist who does not endorse the claim.[28]

Evidence that Constituent Essentialism is something like a framework constraint on any ontology that instantiates the constituent strategy is to be found in the fact that constituent ontologists endorse it despite what initially looks like a deeply counterintuitive consequence of the claim. If we follow most constituent ontologists, then we will construe the properties we prephilosophically associate with a familiar particular as its constituents; but, then, if we are constituent ontologists, we seem forced to deny that a familiar particular can remain numerically identical through changes in its properties, and that denial strikes us as strongly counter-intuitive. Nevertheless, constituent ontologists routinely accept the counter-intuitive consequence.[29] Both substratum and bundle theorists regularly deny that ordinary objects can remain literally identical through changes in their properties. And they seldom

---

[28] It might be thought that Russell and (following Russell) Albert Casullo are constituent ontologists who reject Constituent Essentialism, but this is not clear. Both deny that the characteristic claim of the bundle theory should be understood as a necessary truth; but denying that every possible world, W, is such that all the concrete particulars of W are nothing but complexes of compresent properties is compatible with holding that each actually existent concrete particular has its constituents necessarily. One need merely deny that any actually existing concrete particulars exist in any of the worlds where the bundle theory is false and concreta have constituents other than their properties. For Russell's statement of the view that the bundle theory is only contingently true, see, for example, Russell (1948: 295). See Casullo (1985) for the elaboration of this view.

[29] See, once again, Bergmann (1967: 34), Armstrong (1997: 148–59), and Casullo (1985).

express any hesitation about rejecting the prephilosophically compelling idea of identity through change. We do not find substratum or bundle theorists in a state of philosophical anxiety over the costs of Constituent Essentialism. That suggests that they do not see themselves as faced with a philosophical trade-off here, and that can only be because they take Constituent Essentialism to be a framework constraint on the very project of ontology as they practice it, that is, on ontology in the constituent mode. The inevitable results are either some sort of error theory about our prephilosophical beliefs about change or what can strike us as a revisionist account of persistence through change in the form of some version of the temporal parts or perdurantist theory.

I believe that Aristotle agrees with other constituent ontologists in endorsing Constituent Essentialism. Nonetheless, his own account of the structure of familiar particulars allows him to endorse as well the prephilosophical datum of literal identity through change. What I am suggesting here can seem problematic on a number of fronts. Let me take the problems in order. First, the claim that Aristotle is a Constituent Essentalist can seem problematic even apart from questions about identity through change in properties. The difficulties here do not include Aristotle's silence on the issue of Constituent Essentialism. Perhaps we never find Aristotle explicitly endorsing the thesis;[30] but we seldom find any constituent ontologist formulating and explicitly endorsing Constituent Essentialism, and the reason is obvious. It is found in the intuitive status of the thesis as a framework constraint on constituent ontology. The commitment constituent ontologists have to the principle is taken to be too obvious to require any formal pronouncements on their part, and we can assume that this holds no less for Aristotle than for more recent practitioners of constituent ontology.

Nor is the difficulty that Aristotle regularly allows familiar objects— his substances—to remain identical through changes in their parts. Certainly, he allows this. The paradigms of his substances are living beings—plants, animals, and human beings, and he takes it to be obvious that they can lose and gain parts. This happens in the normal course of their biological careers. Animals molt: they lose their skins, shells, or feathers; and they grow new ones. Plants defoliate and later sprout new leaves; and human beings lose hair, teeth, and nails and replace them with new ones. Furthermore, there are the catastrophic

---

[30] But see 317^{a}23–6, which is very close to a statement of the thesis.

changes that can befall organisms, where they lose parts such as fingers, claws, branches, and the like. But the fact that Aristotle countenances identity through changes of both these kinds does not, by itself anyway, entail that he rejects Constituent Essentialism. What follows is merely that he rejects what has been called Mereological Essentialism, the view that the common-sense parts of a thing are essential to it. The common-sense parts of a thing are not, however, what we have been calling its constituents; and provided it is possible to lose or gain a common-sense part without losing or gaining a metaphysical "part" or constituent, one can endorse Constituent Essentialism while rejecting Mereological Essentialism. And whether or not the former thesis is counter-intuitive, the idea that it is impossible for a living being to remain identical through a change in its common-sense parts does run counter to our prephilosophical intuitions.

But can one reject Mereological Essentialism while continuing to endorse Constituent Essentialism? It might seem that Aristotle at least cannot. The changes we have mentioned may not themselves represent changes in the items Aristotle counts as a thing's constituents, but it is difficult to see how any of those changes could occur without the departure or accession of matter. And in addition to the changes we have mentioned, there are the progressive patterns of change that mark the biological careers of all plants, animals, and human beings: they grow or increase in bulk and they decline, diminishing in bulk; and those changes cannot occur without a change in the organism's matter. So the matter of a living being is constantly changing: at each stage in the career of one of Aristotle's substances, we have a different matter. Its matter, however, is a constituent of a substance: a substance's matter and form together constitute the substance. But, then, it looks as though changes in a thing's common-sense parts do ultimately involve changes in the thing's constituents; and if they do, then one cannot reject Mereological Essentialism without rejecting Constituent Essentialism.

Now, most constituent ontologists would readily accept this conclusion, for not only do they deny the possibility of identity through change in properties, they deny as well that change in parts is possible. Nor is this surprising, for the latter kind of change can be understood to be an instance of the former. For each item that counts as a common-sense part of a thing, there is a property, namely, the property an object has just in case that item is one of its parts. Aristotle, however, would find it disconcerting if it were to turn out that the denial of Mereological

Essentialism entails the denial of Constituent Essentialism. He takes the claim that things can remain identical through changes in their parts to be the expression of a prephilosophical truism, but he is also a constituent ontologist and would not, I think, quarrel with the claim that Constituent Essentialism is a framework principle of the constituent approach to ontological questions about character.

The fact is that Aristotle would deny that any of the changes we have been discussing eventuates in a matter non-identical with that present before the change. Aristotle explicitly tells us that in cases where a substance undergoes growth or decline (that is, cases where the substance increases or decreases in bulk), the substance's matter remains numerically identical (321^a22–5);[31] and it is fairly clear that he would say the same thing about the related cases where a substance loses or gains a part. In such cases, he concedes, there is a change in the matter: it becomes greater or less. Along with the substance it constitutes, it increases or decreases in bulk. But that sort of change, he insists, is merely an accidental change, the sort of change that is compatible with the persistence of the changing thing as one numerically identical object. The matter retains its substantial identity and changes merely in its quantitative determinations. The product of the change is not a new and different thing. What we have after the change is identical with what we had before; it is just larger or smaller than it was before. But, then, while the phenomena in question—change in common-sense parts, growth, decline—are incompatible with Mereological Essentialism, they are not incompatible with Constituent Essentialism. One can endorse the latter while rejecting the former, and Aristotle can preserve the prephilosophical intuitions he is anxious to defend without rejecting a framework principle of his chosen style of ontology.

But, of course, the argument for this claim presupposes that it is possible for the matter constitutive of a substance to retain its identity through changes in its properties—its quantitative properties; and the idea that a thing can retain its identity through a change in any of its properties is one we have found constituent ontologists regularly rejecting. Their reasons for rejecting the idea would seem to bear on what Aristotle calls the matter for a substance no less than on the substance itself. As Aristotle sees it, the matter for a familiar living being is itself a

---

[31] See also 317^a32 ff. and 319^a11 ff., both of which show that Aristotle construes quantitative changes in the matter as accidental changes rather than substantial changes or cases of unqualified coming to be or passing away.

composite object, a hylomorphic structure with its own lower-level proper constituents; and the argument against identity through change in properties is just that since any such change would result in a thing with new and different constituents, identity through such a change would be incompatible with a lynchpin of constituent ontology, the thesis of Constituent Essentialism. So we are back to our central question: can a constituent ontologist consistently endorse identity through change in properties?

The answer, I take it, is that constituent essentialists can consistently endorse identity through change in properties provided they distinguish between the properties constitutive of an object and the properties with respect to which the object changes. Traditional substratum and bundle theorists make no such distinction.[32] They hold that all the properties we prephilosophically associate with an object and speak of the object as having or possessing are its constituents. But, then, the doctrine of Constituent Essentialism compels them to deny that there is literal identity through change in properties and to endorse instead either an error theory with regard to our prephilosophical beliefs about identity through change or some substitute for those beliefs. Aristotle, by contrast, denies that the various universals we think of a substance as instantiating count as its constituents. On his hylomorphic account, the only entities constitutive of a substance are its matter and form and while the form is a universal, it is not a universal predicable of the substance itself. It is predicated of the matter constitutive of the substance.[33] To be sure, its predication of the matter entails that certain other universals are predicated of the composite substance whose form it is. As we have seen, in virtue of the fact that the substantial form is predicated of its proper matter, the substance species correlated with the form is essentially predicated of the constituted composite substance; and, of course, other essential predications involving the composite are entailed by the species predication. But the form is predicated exclusively of the matter; and while the species predication and any essential predications it entails are all derived predications, the form's predication of the matter is a case of primitive or basic predication. As we have seen, it is not the only such case. Form predications result in composite substances falling under substance-kinds; and those composite substances are

---

[32] See e.g. Bergmann (1967: 6).
[33] See, again, 1029^a20–3, 1038^b4–6, and 1049^a34–6 and my discussion of this claim in Loux (1991: chs. 4, 5).

subjects for the other case of primitive or basic predication—the case where what is predicated is an item from one of the dependent categories. Like form predications, predications of this second sort hold only accidentally. The subject of any such predication has an essential identity that is independent of the thing predicated. The universal that gets predicated is not a constituent of the thing that is its subject. The subject is always something like a horse, a geranium, or a human and the constituents of things like these are the appropriate matter and the appropriate substantial form.

So we have cases of predication where the subject is a familiar particular—an Aristotelian substance—but the predicated universal is not a constituent of the thing of which it is predicated. Accordingly, the predication holds or fails to hold without jeopardy to the identity of its subject, so that with regard to these universals, we can have what we have been calling change in property without any violation of Constituent Essentialism. Like form predications, the predications in question do result in composites, the sort of composites we have been calling coincidentals. Given the predication consisting in the man's being musical, we have the existence of the musical man. Its constituents are the relevant man and the accident predicated of him. Although coincidentally one with/the same as the man, the musical man is not numerically identical with the man. The substance that is the man is a proper constituent of the composite that is the musical man; and although the accident is predicated of the man, it is not in the basic or core sense predicated of the coincidental of which the man is a proper constituent. Just as its substantial form is not predicated of the composite substance, so *musical* is not predicated of the musical man, at least not in the primitive or basic sense. Indeed, no accidents are predicated of the musical man (1007^b2 ff.). We can, of course, say that the musical man is musical, pale, courageous, or six feet tall; but, as we have noted, none of these claims express predications whose subject is the musical man. If true, what they express are cases of coincidental sameness or unity. If true, what the sentence

(2) The musical man is pale

expresses is the fact that the musical man is coincidentally one with something of which pale is predicated, namely, the man. Such sentences can, of course, vary in their truth value over time. When the relevant man comes to be well tanned, (2) becomes false. The coincidental that is the musical man, however, does not itself undergo a change; one of its constituents does; and when that constituent changes so that he is no longer musical, the coincidental that is the musical man ceases to exist. Unlike the man, the musical man cannot survive that change; and Constituent Essentialism tells us why. According to that doctrine, the items constitutive of an object are essential or necessary to it. For it to be true that the musical man exists, there must be a composite whose constituents are the man and *musical*; and no such composite exists when the man ceases to be musical.

So Aristotle's coincidentals are like the composites of a substratum or bundle theory: the only non-Cambridge changes they can undergo are generation or corruption: changes in which they come to be or pass away. But because Aristotle distinguishes between the universal constitutive of a substance and those predicated of a substance, he can consistently endorse a constituent analysis of substances while accommodating the prephilosophical intuition that substances can remain numerically identical through change.

IV

For constituent ontologists, then, a familiar concrete particular is a composite, a thing made out of metaphysically more basic constituents. Now, some constituent ontologists think that we can give the complete recipe for an object simply by identifying its constituents. Others, however, insist on the need to identify the order in which those constituents are put together.[34] The latter want to include relations among the constituents of familiar objects, and they point out that where we have non-asymetrical relations, precisely the same objects can constitute numerically different complexes; thus, aRb and bRa. We can capture both views if we say that for constituent ontologists, the existence of a concrete particular consists in the fact that its constituents are put together in some determinate order. Suppose an object, x, has constituents $a_1, \ldots a_n$ put together in a particular order. As we have seen, while constituent ontologists will take the fact that $a_1 \ldots a_n$ are put together in that order to be contingent, they will insist that the resulting

[34] Aristotle, I take it, endorses the former view and David Armstrong, the latter. See, again, Armstrong (1997: 178 ff.).

composite, x, has essentially or necessarily the property of being constituted by $a_1 \ldots a_n$ in the relevant order. And they will add that x has this property uniquely. Indeed, virtually every constituent ontologist will take it to be a necessary truth that no two objects have precisely the same constituents arranged in precisely the same way;[35] and this claim is, once again, something like a framework principle of constituent ontology. On that view, an object is nothing more than its constituents as put together in a certain way; but, then, necessarily if a thing, x, and a thing, y, have exactly the same constituents put together in the same order, x is numerically identical with y.

We can call this claim the Principle of Constituent Identity. I have said that it is something like a framework constraint on constituent ontology. It is no surprise, then, that it has played a central role in debates between constituent ontologists; in particular, in debates between bundle theorists and substratum theorists. The dialectic here is familiar. Without sounding all the bells and whistles in the dialectic, we can say that bundle theorists restrict the constituents of familiar objects to the properties we associate with them, and they tell us that for a particular concrete object to exist is for its properties to be compresent; and they view compresence as symmetrical. Typically, however, they construe properties as universals, so they hold that where distinct objects have, as we say, the same property, there is a single item that enters into the constitution of each; but, then, they are committed to the claim (known as the Identity of Indiscernibles) that it is impossible for numerically distinct concrete particulars to have exactly the same properties.[36] There seem, however, to be obvious counterexamples to the Identity of Indiscernibles,[37] and substratum theorists argue that to account for the possibility of these counterexamples, we must concede that each familiar particular incorporates a constituent over and above its properties—the differentiating constituent called a bare particular.[38] Pretty clearly, the Principle of Constituent Identity is what structures

---

[35] One might take Herbert Hochberg to be an exception. In Hochberg (1960), he rejects what I have call the Principle of Constituent Identity. Interestingly, in conversation, Hochberg has agreed that his account of familiar particulars is not, strictly speaking, a version of what we have been calling constituent ontology.

[36] One finds this reasoning set out in Ayer (1954). For a discussion of the dialectic in question, see Loux (2002: ch. 3).

[37] See Black (1952) for a much discussed counterexample.

[38] See Allaire (1963) for a clear formulation of this line of argument.

this whole interchange. It is only because they endorse the principle that bundle theorists find themselves committed to the Identity of Indiscernibles, and it is only by appeal to the principle that substratum theorists are able to use counterexamples to the Identity of Indiscernibles to show the need for diversifying or differentiating constituents.

If, as I have claimed, the Principle of Constituent Identity formulates a framework constraint on the enterprise of constituent ontology, then we can expect to find the principle in Aristotle. The fact is that we do. Although Aristotle does not explicitly formulate the principle, it is clear from a famous text at the end of *Metaphysics* Z.8 that he endorses it. Aristotle says: "But when we have the whole, such and such a form in these flesh and bones, then we have Callias and Socrates. And they are different because of their matter (for that is different); but they are the same in their form; for the form is indivisible" (1034^a5–8).[39] The problematic Aristotle is addressing here is precisely the problematic we have been discussing. The question is: how do things whose constitutive universals are exactly the same manage to be numerically different? On Aristotle's own version of a constituent ontology, of course, each composite has just a single constituting universal, and where the composite is a substance rather than a coincidental, that universal is a substantial form. Now, since Callias and Socrates belong to the same lowest-level substance kind, they have precisely the same constituting universal—the substantial form associated with their common proper kind, and it is a monadic universal. So Callias and Socrates overlap; they share a constituent. How, then, is it that they are numerically different? The assumption is that since they are numerically different, they must differ in a constituent; and Aristotle tells us that they do; they have numerically diverse parcels of matter as constituents.

Pretty clearly, the Principle of Constituent Identity underlies the reasoning behind this passage. Indeed, the implied pattern of argument is precisely that of the substratum theorist who uses the possibility of numerically diverse, yet qualitatively indiscernible concrete objects to show that each concrete particular has a constituent over and above its constituting property—a diversifying or differentiating constituent. What Aristotle is claiming is that since Socrates and Callias are indiscernible with respect to their constituting universal, each must have an

---

[39] Other texts where we meet with the idea that matter is the principle of numerical diversity include 277^b26–279^b4, 1018^a6–7, and 1058^b5–10.

additional constituent numerically different from any constituent found in the other; and Aristotle argues that on his hylomorphic version of a constituent ontology that is precisely how things work out: there are numerically different parcels of matter; the single shared form is predicated of each to give us the numerically diverse composites that are Callias and Socrates.

This, however, cannot be the end of the story. Since Socrates and Callias are members of a single lowest-level kind, their respective parcels of matter are indiscernible as to kind: both are parcels of flesh and bones. Aristotle, however, wants to construe flesh and bones as hylomorphic composites in their own right. Accordingly, it appears that the problematic that confronted us in the case of Socrates and Callias arises for their matter as well. We have two parcels of matter indiscernible as to form. More precisely, in each individual, we have both flesh and bones, with a single form in the flesh in each and a single form in the bones in each. But, then, what is it that makes the parcels of flesh and bones numerically different in the two cases? They must be numerically different if they are to account for the numerical diversity of our original substances, Socrates and Callias. Since the parcels of matter are indiscernible as to form, it looks as though the only account we can provide for the numerical diversity is the sort of account we gave in the case of Socrates and Callias: each of the parcels of matter has a constituent over and above its constitutive universal—some lower-level matter. But, presumably, we will be confronted once again with parcels of matter that are the same in kind, and so our original problem will confront us once again.

Aristotle, of course, refuses to countenance the possibility of an infinite regress in material causation (994^a1–4). At some point, he insists, we will arrive at an original matter—a matter that has nothing else for its matter. Initially, at least, it would seem plausible to think that we should look to that matter to find a final resolution of our difficulty. But here we face a vexed problem of interpretation. Commentators tell different stories about the matter Aristotle is supposed to take as original.[40] Some hold that, for Aristotle, there is no matter more basic than the four elements—fire, earth, air, and water; whereas others take him to hold that there is a matter common to the four elements, a

---

[40] For a discussion of this controversy, see Loux (1991: chs. 2, 7).

matter which combines with the appropriate pair from the contraries hot/cold and wet/dry to give us fire, earth, air, or water.[41]

What the Principle of Constituent Identity requires is that at some level in the ontological analysis of any composite substance we meet a constituent that is found in no other composite substance and incorporates no constituent found in any other composite. So we need many such diversifying constituents, as many as there are individual hylomorphic composites. Unfortunately, if there is a matter common to the four elements, if, that is, the traditional doctrine of prime matter is true, it will not, by itself, give us the required diversifying constituents. The texts that seem to support a doctrine of prime matter tell us that it is something that "in its own right is neither a particular thing, nor of a particular quantity, nor otherwise positively characterized" (1039^a24–5). It is difficult to see how anything meeting this austere characterization could be the sort of thing that in its own right could be parceled out, cut up, divided, or partitioned to give us numerically different constituents. And the fact is that it needs to be parceled out, cut up, divided, or partitioned in some way. Unlike the bare particulars of the substratum theory, prime matter is not a preindividuated bearer of numerical diversity. What it composes is itself just an undifferentiated or homogeneous mass of stuff—fire, earth, air, or water; and if we are able to make sense of the idea of numerically different portions, bundles, or parcels of prime matter, it is only because we are able to make sense of the numerically different portions, bundles, or parcels of the elementary stuffs it composes. If we take prime matter to enter into Aristotle's metaphysical thinking, we have to suppose that its division or diversification is parasitic on the division or diversification of the stuffs whose matter it is.[42]

So even if the original matter (the matter that has no matter) is prime matter as traditionally conceived, we are not going to meet the required diversification of material constituents at a level prior to that at which we have the four elements of fire, earth, air, and water. Taken by itself, each is, as we have noted, an undifferentiated or homogeneous mass of stuff. Accordingly, we will have a resolution of our difficulty at the level of the elements only if these undifferentiated stuffs are partitioned or

---

[41] A crucial text in this debate is 329^a25–32, where Aristotle seems to be arguing from the phenomenon of elemental transformation to the existence of a matter common to the four elements.

[42] See Code (1995: esp. 410) for confirmation of this idea.

parceled out to yield discrete and separate bundles or portions. What is it that might do the partitioning or parceling? The intuitive answer would seem to be space and time: spatiotemporal location does the dividing. Now, Aristotle has no theory of space. He speaks instead of the places (both common and proper) that things occupy. Furthermore, he seems to want to endorse some version of what we call presentism and to deny that time is a dimension in which things are spread out. So his way of expressing the intuition about what we call spatiotemporal location would be to say that what gives us a diversity of parcels of any of the elements at a time is the fact that the parcels have numerically distinct proper places at that time.

Initially, this might seem problematic. Although Aristotle will concede that the individual places familiar objects occupy have an existence that is independent of the particular concrete individuals that happen to occupy them at a given time, he will insist that the whole framework of places is parasitic or dependent on the whole framework of material substance.[43] But what we are trying to get here is the framework of individual material substances, so it might appear problematic to appeal to a diversity of places in our account of the numerical diversity of material substances. It may, however, be that appearances are deceiving us here. Aristotle never tells a complete and satisfying story of just how the ontological dependence of places is supposed to work itself out; but there is a certain picture of this dependence that it is plausible to think he rejects. This is a picture in which we have an ontological "moment" where there are masses of stuff (fire, earth, air, and water) in search, so to speak, of places to occupy. Aristotle seems to have thought instead that given the totality of stuff that is the four elements, we are thereby given a rudimentary framework of places: each of the four elements, recall, has its own natural place. That rudimentary framework may be sufficient to give us the partitioning or dividing that Aristotle's theory demands. Of course, Aristotle never explicitly endorses the claim that it is places that diversify material constituents. What we have is merely the Z.8 claim about the material diversity of Socrates and Callias. But since he refuses to countenance the preindividuated bearers of numerical diversity we meet in the substratum theory, the claim about Socrates and Callias and its theoretical underpinning in the

---

[43] See *Physics* IV. 1–5 for Aristotle's discussion of place. The dependence here is supposed to be a special case of the dependence of accidents on substances.

Principle of Constituent Identity leave us little option but to attribute to Aristotle this sort of account of the numerical diversity of material constituents.

V

Not all those who count as constituent ontologists number universals among the items constitutive of familiar concrete particulars, but many do. For those who do, various questions about the instantiation of constituting universals arise. Central here are questions about what is called the Principle of Instantiation or the Principle of Exemplification.[44] The principle is often formulated as the claim that there are no uninstantiated or unexemplified universals, and it might be thought that this principle is something like a framework constraint not on constituent ontology in general, but on any version of constituent ontology that makes universals constituents of familiar particulars. To evaluate this claim, we need to become clearer on the principle.

First, our initial formulation of the principle does not make explicit its modal status. Is the principle supposed to hold only contingently, so that while in our world every universal is instantiated, there are possible worlds where universals exist uninstantiated? One would think not. One would think that what is at issue here is the possibility of uninstantiated universals. Accordingly, I will assume that the principle tells us that it is impossible that there be uninstantiated universals.

Second, our understanding of this stronger, modal claim will depend on our views about the nature of time. If we are eternalists and take time to be a fourth dimension in which things are spread out, then we will understand existence as existence at some time or other; and if we disapprove of uninstantiated universals, we are likely to express our disapproval by saying that, necessarily, every universal is such that at some time or other it is instantiated.[45] On the other hand, if we are presentists, then we will think of existence as existence now or existence at the present time; but, then, if we have problems with the concept of

---

[44] In Bergmann (1967: 43, 88), we meet what Bergmann calls the Principle of Exempification. It has two parts: (1) that there are no unexemplified universals and (2) that every particular exemplifies at least one universal. What I am here calling the Principle of Instantiation is the idea at work in (1) taken by itself.

[45] As Armstrong does. See (1989: 75–82).

uninstantiated universals, we are likely to express our concern with a much stronger version of the Principle of Instantiation, one telling us that necessarily every universal is now or currently exemplified.

As I have suggested, there is good reason to think that Aristotle endorses some variant of what I have been calling a presentist account of time and even better reason to suppose that he endorses the Principle of Instantiation;[46] but, then, he would seem to be committed to this more demanding formulation of the principle. That formulation can, however, strike us as problematic. It conjures up the picture of a world whose pool of existing universals is unstable, with universals coming into and going out of existence willy nilly as the vagaries of contingent fact shift. But, perhaps, no such unruly ontology is entailed by a presentist reading of the principle. Anyone who endorses the principle in any of its formulations will want to distinguish between our thought and talk about what count as basic or fundamental universals and our discourse about other less fundamental ways of being. The claim will be that while the metaphysician needs to tell a convincing story about our thought and talk about contents like *being a pink unicorn* and *being a left-handed hoplite*, that story does not require the postulation of a ground-level universal corresponding to every such content; and the defender of the Principle of Instantiation, whether eternalist or presentist, will want to restrict the principle to the case of fundamental or basic universals.[47]

But even with this restriction, the presentist version of the principle we have attributed to Aristotle would seem to result in an ontology with some residual instability. For Aristotle at least, the basic universals include those that ground an individual organism's membership in its proper biological species; but, then, will not facts about evolution play havoc with the pool of universals? And there is a related problem here, a more general problem that would seem to confront the eternalist defender of the Principle of Instantiation no less than the Aristotelian presentist. Whether we are eternalists or presentists, it would seem, we must concede that the roster of uninstantiated universals varies across possible worlds. Accordingly, while denying that there are any possible

[46] The evidence for a presentist account is largely indirect. See 5ª26–7, 218ª2–3, 5–6. For evidence that Aristotle endorses the Principle of Instantiation, see 14ª7–14.

[47] The underlying idea here is one that is expressed nicely in David Lewis's suggestion that what we are calling constituent ontologists should endorse a "sparse" theory of universals. See D. Lewis (1986).

worlds that number among their inhabitants unexemplified universals, we must hold that basic universals that are instantiated in our world go uninstantiated in other possible worlds. But, then, whether eternalist or presentist, the defender of the Principle of Instantiation appears committed to the view that universals—basic or fundamental universals—can turn out to be merely contingent beings.

Now, some defenders of the Principle of Instantiation will cheerfully accept the idea that it is a metaphysically contingent fact just which universals there are, a contingent fact, they say, it is the business of our best empirical sciences to establish for us.[48] There is, unfortunately, a cost to this idea. It seems to force us to deny that singular propositions about universals are necessary truths. If we are realists about universals, we will hold that sentences such as

(3) Red is a color,
(4) Courage is a virtue,

and

(5) Triangularity is a shape,

express propositions that are genuinely about universals; and the propositions in question appear to be necessary truths. But if the universals in question are merely contingent beings, it is difficult to see how these propositions could be necessarily true. And it will not do to respond by denying that colors, moral virtues, and geometrical shapes are basic universals; for whatever universals we take to be fundamental, provided we concede that each of them is such that in some possible world it goes uninstantiated, we will find that the problems associated with (3), (4), and (5) arise in their case.[49]

---

[48] See Armstrong (1989: 87–8, 1997: 36–7).

[49] Michael Rea has suggested that the defender of the Principle of Instantiation might reply by telling us that while each of (3)–(5) is a contingent truth, there are necessary truths in the environment that explain our inclination to construe (3)–(5) as necessary truths. For (3), there is the proposition (call it (3')) that if red exists, then red is a color. But as Rea nicely points out, this strategy faces a serious problem. To account for the necessity of (3'), the defender of the Principle of Instantiation will need to endorse either some sort of counterpart theory for properties or a theory of haecceities for such things as red. But Rea makes the point that counterpart theory for properties is highly implausible, and the appeal to haecceities here will work only if we construe them as necessarily existing entities; but, then, why not say the same for red? Here, as elsewhere, I am indebted to Rea for a careful reading of an early draft of this chapter.

Aristotle himself endorses the general line of argument at work here and concludes that basic universals are necessary beings (1039^b20–1040^a7). Given his adherence to a presentist reading of the Principle of Instantiation, he is committed to a doctrine of the eternality (or better: necessary eternality) of the biological species. He is committed, that is, to denying that it is so much as possible that there be a time at which one of the universals underlying the biological species goes unexemplified. That seems to imply that Aristotle is committed to rejecting current biological theory; and there is independent evidence that he would reject it. In *Physics* II. 8, we find Aristotle giving specifically biological reasons for rejecting a protoevolutionary theory we find in Empedocles, and it is difficult to understand his arguments in that chapter without reading into them a general indictment of any evolutionary theory in biology.[50] All of this points to a problem we cannot hope to resolve here—just how a contemporary presentist who agrees with Aristotle in endorsing both the Principle of Instantiation and the idea that the universals underlying the biological species are necessary beings is to accommodate the evolutionary theory at work in contemporary biology.

Setting this thorny issue aside, let us return to our central issue and ask whether it is true that the Principle of Instantiation is entailed by acceptance of the constituent strategy. Although we seldom meet with explicit pronouncement of this claim, the general consensus, I think, is that it is. There is an assumption that when we restrict ourselves to philosophers who endorse the existence of universals, what divides what we have been calling relational from constituent ontologists just is their opposing verdicts on the Principle of Instantiation.[51] The idea is that in each case we have a single package of views, all of which come to pretty much the same thing. Among philosophers who think that universals provide us with the source of any character familiar particulars display, we have our Platonists and our Aristotelians. Platonists reject the Principle of Instantiation and hold that there are (or, at least, could be) uninstantiated universals. Obviously the existence of those universals cannot involve their being immanent in spatiotemporal particulars; and equally obviously all universals have the same ontological status, the

---

[50] See, especially, the argument presented at 198^b17–199^a8.

[51] Surely, this is the picture at work in Armstrong (1989: 75–82) and Loux (2002: 47–50). A similar picture is at work in Fine (1993). See e.g. p. 60.

same style of existence. But, then, universals exist "apart" from familiar particulars; they exist outside space and time; and concrete particulars derive their character by standing in some non-mereological relation to these separately existing universals. Aristotelians, by contrast, reject the idea of separately existing universals. The universals responsible for the character of spatiotemporal particulars are immanent in those particulars; they confer character on them by being their constituents. But, then, for these constitutive universals at least, the Principle of Instantiation would seem to be inevitable. If the basic or ground-level universals are things that are immanent in or constitutive of familiar particulars, then the idea that a basic or fundamental universal could go uninstantiated would seem to be incoherent.

Now, all this makes for a familiar picture; but it is not difficult to find problems in the picture. If we focus merely on the case of constituent ontology, it is not clear why it should be mandatory for proponents of that strategy to endorse the Principle of Instantiation in their account of the universals constitutive of familiar concrete particulars, what we might call basic first-order universals. To suppose otherwise is to suppose that the constituent ontologist is committed to identifying the existence and the instantiation of a basic first-order universal; but the constituent ontologist is no more committed to that identification than the relational ontologist. If it is instantiated, a basic first-order universal will be immanent in at least one spatiotemporal particular; it will be a constituent in that spatiotemporal particular. But while conceding that each basic first-order universal can be a constituent in some concrete particular, constituent ontologists can deny that it must be; and they can deny that this involves endorsing a Platonic theory of separated universals. They can point out that while the Platonist thinks it a category mistake to suppose that a universal is immanent in a spatiotemporal particular, they think this is possible; and they can argue that the standard picture at work in Platonic theories—that of a world of separated universals—typically rests on a mistake, the mistake of supposing that if universals are not to be found in space and time, then they must exist, so to speak, somewhere else—in some realm outside space and time. Constituent ontologists can deny that uninstantiated universals need to be "located" anywhere at all. Likewise, they can deny that allowing uninstantiated universals makes one a relational metaphysician. While denying that it is a necessary truth that each basic first-order universal confers character, constituent ontologists can hold that where one does, it does so by being a constituent of some contingently existing concrete particular.[52]

The fact is that we occasionally find constituent ontologists who appreciate these points and reject the Principle of Instantiation. I am thinking of those bundle theorists who construe the properties constitutive of familiar objects as necessary beings that are only contingently exemplified.[53] But among constituent ontologists, these bundle theorists are clearly in the minority; and that explains, I think, why they get overlooked when we construct the pictures I have been discussing. What we typically find is that those constituent ontologists who make universals constituents of objects endorse the Principle of Instantiation for those universals; and there can be no denying that there is something attractive, if not compulsory, in the coupling of these two ideas. If you think of basic first-order universals as things that confer character by being literal constituents in things, it is not unnatural to take the next step and write that constitutive role into the essence of those universals.

And where we find this move being made is in the work of those constituent ontologists who insist that we distinguish between the universals constitutive of an object and some further constituent that is supposed to be the literal exemplifier, instantiator, bearer, or subject of the constituting universals. A substratum theorist such as Armstrong is one example, and obviously Aristotle himself is another. Armstrong has his thin particular instantiating the universals which together with it constitute the relevant "thick particular"; and Aristotle has the universals constitutive of individual substances—substantial forms—predicated of the appropriate parcels of matter and the universals constitutive of coincidentals—accidents—predicated of the appropriate individual substances. And in both thinkers, the idea of universals as things that are instantiated by or predicated of something else gets written into the very essence or nature of constituting universals.

---

[52] In the same way, it seems possible for a relational ontologist to endorse the Principle of Instantiation. Relational ontologists who make universals the non-derivative bearers of character are committed to denying that the exemplification of a universal, U, by an object, x, consists in U's being immanent in or a constituent of x; they are committed to holding that exemplification is a *sui generis* relation/tie of a non-mereological sort. It is certainly consistent with these claims, however, to hold that necessarily every universal is exemplified. It may, of course, not be immediately obvious why anyone would want, in this way, to couple the relational strategy with the Principle of Instantiation, but there is nothing incoherent in doing so.

[53] This sort of view can, I think, be found in Castañeda (1974).

Armstrong rejects the bundle theorist's conception of universals as self-standing quasi-substances in favor of the idea of universals as "ways things are";[54] and Aristotle tells us that his constituting universals—both substantial forms and accidents—are "suches" rather than "thises" (1033^b20–5). He denies that they are "definite objects" of the sort we meet in Platonic Forms: each is instead "how" its subject is. So in both thinkers, we have the idea that there are certain basic, ground-level universals and that they get instantiated by being immanent in or constitutive of familiar concrete objects; and in both thinkers, the constitutive role of these universals gets expressed in the claim that each such universal is how some other constituent in a concrete object is or in the claim that each is a *way* some other constituent is. But this claim is not taken to express a merely contingent fact about the relevant universals. On the contrary, it is supposed to express a structural fact about the categorial form of these fundamental, ground-level universals. What those universals are is just ways other things are or how other things are. But the effect of understanding these universals in these terms is to make the Principle of Instantiation necessarily true for their case. The idea that a thing that is nothing more than a way something is or how something is could exist without anything to be that way or 'that how' is well-nigh incomprehensible.

VI

So Aristotle's account of concrete particulars features themes central to the constituent approach to questions about character derivation. Like other constituent ontologists, he takes familiar particulars to be items with something like a mereological structure: they are composites or complexes made up of ontologically more basic entities. He thinks that the entities constitutive of familiar objects confer on the complexes into which they enter whatever character we associate with those complexes, and he holds that among the constituents of familiar objects at least some have their own distinctive character non-derivatively. Furthermore, he agrees with other proponents of the constituent strategy in holding that where certain objects, $a \ldots n$, go together to comprise or constitute a given particular, it is a contingent fact that they do so; and

---

[54] Armstrong (1989: 96–8).

he joins other constituent ontologists in thinking that a composite particular has its constituents necessarily: while no mereological essentialist, he is what I have called a constituent essentialist. And, like other constituent ontologists, he endorses what I have called the Principle of Constituent Identity. He thinks, that is, that it is metaphysically impossible for numerically distinct objects to have exactly the same constituents arranged, configured, or structured in precisely the same way. Finally, he agrees with the majority of those constituent ontologists who number universals among the constituents of familiar objects in claiming that some version of the Principle of Instantiation holds for the basic or fundamental universals constitutive of familiar concreta. He takes it that what it is for such a universal to exist is for it to be instantiated by being immanent in or constitutive of one or more concrete particulars and, accordingly, he denies that it is possible for any of what I have called basic first-order universals to go uninstantiated.

But while Aristotle's account of familiar particulars conforms to the overall pattern of a constituent ontology in all these respects, there is one important way in which it differs from other instances of that ontological strategy. I touched on this difference very briefly and indirectly in the previous section when I mentioned that Aristotle takes the universals underlying the various biological universals to be basic or fundamental universals, but I made no effort to indicate the significance of Aristotle's treatment of the relevant universals or to show how that treatment makes his account unique among those exhibiting the constituent strategy. Here, I want to bring out these points in detail. A good starting point is to note that constituent ontologists typically share a certain outlook about familiar concrete particulars. It is difficult to characterize this outlook without resorting to vague and unhelpful generalities. What one wants to say here is that constituent analyses are typically reductive. The difficulty with invoking the contrast between reductive and non-reductive accounts in this context is that there is no fixed parameter for applying the contrast. In an obvious way, any account telling us that items of a certain kind, K, are composites or things having proper constituents can be described as reductive—reductive, at least, as compared with an account that characterizes the Ks as unanalyzable simples. If this is the sort of contrast we have in mind, then the suggestion that a constituent ontology might be anything but reductive must strike us as something of an oxymoron.

There is, however, a more demanding sense in which a constituent account of the members of a kind, K, might be reductive: the account might provide a constituent-whole analysis of the Ks that has the result that the form of being displayed by the Ks turns out to be a construction out of lower-level forms of being, that is, forms of being that can be found outside the context of the Ks in structurally and functionally more elementary objects. The fact is that constituent accounts of familiar concreta typically are reductive in this more demanding sense.[55] Many of the classic examples of bundle-theoretic accounts of familiar objects take purely phenomenal properties—colors, sounds, shapes, and the like—to exhaust the ultimate constituents of familiar concrete particulars; and classic defenders of bare particulars typically follow their lead in making elementary phenomenal features constituents of ordinary objects; nor is this surprising since defenders of bare particulars typically present their own account of the structure of familiar particulars as one that grows out of the bundle theorist's account. We are supposed to get the bare particular theorist's recipe for familiar particulars by taking the bundle theorist's recipe and supplementing it with the bare differentiating or diversifying constituents required to account for the possibility of numerically different, yet qualitatively indiscernible particulars. More recent defenders of the constituent strategy would reject the extreme empiricism underlying these classic versions of the strategy. Nonetheless, their accounts share the reductive outlook of their constituent predecessors. Thus, we meet with the claim that the sort of properties that should lie at the core of our account of the structure of familiar objects are those that play a non-eliminable role in our best scientific theory and we find constituent ontologists making the fundamental properties of theoretical physics the sorts of items ultimately responsible for whatever character ordinary physical objects have.[56]

And it is not difficult to see why the constituent strategy should so regularly be coupled with a reductive analysis of familiar concreta. On the one hand, the constituent approach can seem an especially attractive vehicle for the expression of antecedently held reductive beliefs. On the

---

[55] One exception may be found in a pre-Aristotelian constituent ontologist—Anaxagoras, who, by Aristotle's telling, defended a radical form of antireductionism that posited an irreducibly basic kind of constituent for every sort of character displayed by familiar particulars.

[56] Certainly this is the thrust of the account defended in Armstrong (1989 and 1997).

other, it can seem that to construe familiar concrete objects as complexes or composites of ontologically more fundamental items is *eo ipso* to endorse an account that analyzes whatever forms of being those concrete objects display in terms of lower-level forms of being, the forms of being exhibited by their ontologically more fundamental constituents. But however natural the connection between the constituent and reductive strategies may seem, it is not inevitable.[57] Not every version of a constituent ontology has to be reductive in the sense that it construes the forms of being associated with all familiar concrete objects as mere constructions out of lower-level forms of being. To see this, consider an account that tells us that the familiar concrete objects falling under a kind, K, are complexes or composites, but insists that among the proper constituents of the Ks, there is one that is necessarily such that, first, it is found in all and only the Ks and, second, it has no proper constituents of its own. So the account is positing a constituent that is necessarily idiosyncratic to the Ks and that is not itself subject to any kind of ontological analysis. The idea is that the constituent in question has a distinctive character of its own, that it has that character non-derivatively, and that the character is necessarily such that any complex into which the bearer of that character enters is marked out as a member of the kind K. So while the account concedes that being a K involves a plurality of proper constituents, it insists that one of those proper constituents has a character that is *sui generis* or unique to the Ks. Accordingly, the account concedes that there may be more to being a K than incorporating this idiosyncratic constituent, and it concedes that to identify the extra feature or features, one may need to make reference to what can be called lower-level principles—proper constituents of the Ks that can be found outside the context of the Ks in lower-grade structures. Nonetheless, the account is telling us that a thing's being a K presupposes its having as a proper constituent an unanalyzably basic principle whose own character insures that any complex into which the principle enters is a K. What the account is telling us is that there is a principle that is, as we might put it, equideterminate with the kind K; that is, it is necessarily such that it is instantiated always and only in things that instantiate the kind K and the account is identifying that principle as what Aristotle calls the primary substance of the Ks:

---

[57] A few sentences from the next three paragraphs were taken from Loux (2005).

according to the proposed account, the principle non-redundantly induces or delivers precisely the form of being all and only the *K*s display. An account of this sort is denying the possibility of wholly and completely analyzing the being of the *K*s in terms of lower-level forms of being, so while a form of constituent ontology, it is not a case of a reductive analysis.

But if no account that instantiates the proposed pattern is a case of reductive metaphysics, then we have found a crucial respect in which Aristotle's own version of the constituent approach differs from other more typical versions of that approach; for Aristotle's account of one sort of composite—the sort that is a biological organism (a plant, an animal, or a human being)—is an instance of precisely that pattern. As I suggested in the previous section, what Aristotle tells us is that, for every species, *S*, of living being, there is a primitive or unanalyzably basic universal that is necessarily such that it is a proper constituent in all and only the members of *S* and that it is the primary substance of each of the complexes whose proper constituent it is.[58] It is, of course, the substantial forms associated with the various biological species that are constituents of this sort. Substantial forms are predicable items. Their incorporation in a complex presupposes a subject of which they can be predicated, and that subject is provided by some parcel of the sort of stuff that counts as matter for the species in question. So while equideterminate with the species, the form is not coextensive with the species. Although instantiated always and only *in* things instantiating the species, it is not instantiated *by* any of those things. It is predicated of the matter, whereas the species is predicated of the complex composed

---

[58] This is not, I think, a controversial claim on my part. The idea that the substance of the *K*s must be equideterminate with *K* is certainly implicit in 1017^b15–16 and 1038^a25–30. It is at work again in 1043^a3–11 as well as 1041^b25–31 and 1043^b22–33, both of which assume the account developed in *Physics* B. 1, where the equideterminacy thesis is also operative. I would argue that the thesis is also at work in Z. 13's initial argument (1038^b7–14), where, I would claim, Aristotle is arguing that, if *K* is a substance universal, it is impossible for a universal more general than *K* to be the substance of the *K*s; and I find it plausible to see the equideterminacy thesis as implicit in the argument of 1038^b30–4 as well. There, I would claim, Aristotle is attacking the idea that the substance of the *K*s can be some sort of construction out of universals more general than *K*. The same theme is at work, I think, at 1038^b30–4. Where *S* is the substance of the *K*s, then, no universals generic with respect to *S* are among the constituents of the *K*s. Indeed, such universals are not fundamental or basic universals at all: they are something like abstractions from fully determinate universals; only the latter are basic or fundamental. See 1038^a6–7, 1040^b21–5, and 1058^a3–4.

of the matter and the form; and while the form is the primary substance of the members of the species, its own proper character does not exhaust the character or kind of being associated with the species. But it is what *first* or *originally* delivers or induces that form of being. Any instance of the kind of matter that is its subject can exist outside the context where we have a member of the relevant species. What gives us the existence of an individual member of the species is the predication of the form. So while its character does not exhaust the form of being it underwrites, it is what is initially responsible for that form of being; and, of course, so long as it is there as a proper constituent, we have a thing with that form of being. And whereas the matter that is its subject is what Aristotle calls a *kat' allou* being, a composite whose own peculiar character derives from metaphysically prior constituents, the form is not subject to any type of ontological analysis. Whatever character or kind of being the form displays, it displays *kath hauto*, or in its own right. So the form has its own proper character non-derivatively, and that character is necessarily such that all and only the complexes into which it enters exhibit the kind of being associated with the species.

These themes all bear on the abstract, structural properties of form. They belong to what, in two different senses, we can call formal ontology, and they get presented and elaborated in the very difficult central books of the *Metaphysics*. In Book II of the *Physics* and in some of the biological treatises, Aristotle approaches these topics in more substantive terms by focusing on the causal and explanatory role of form.[59] Central in these contexts is the idea that the being characteristic of a biological kind gets expressed in a behavioral pattern peculiar to its members, and the claim is that the relevant pattern derives from some irreducibly basic principle internal to the members of the kind—what Aristotle calls the nature of the kind. So we have once again a repudiation of reductive accounts of biological kinds, but here what gets repudiated is the more particular idea that the behavioral repertoire unique to a kind can be explained in terms of causal principles that apply outside the kind in the explanation of lower-grade phenomena. The claim, on the contrary, is that we can explain the pattern of behavior definitive of a biological kind only by reference to a principle equidetermiate with

---

[59] See, especially, *Physics* B. 1, 8–9 as well as *De Partibus Animalium* I. 1. The line of argument I spell out here is primarily from *Physics* B. 1. It is interesting to note how Aristotle supplements the account of *Metaphysics* Z and H with an appeal to these themes. See 1041^b30 and 1043^b22–3.

the kind. We must posit, for each natural kind, a primitive or irreducibly basic causal principle; and at this point in the argument Aristotle appeals to his own constituent theory as the proper ontological framework for the expression of these causal claims.[60] The proposal is, first, that we construe the sort of causal explanation required here as a special case of the general form of explanation at work in our account of character derivation and, second, that we invoke Aristotle's own version of the constituent approach in our explanation of character derivation. The proposal enables us to interpret the internality of a nature in terms of the notion of a proper constituent in a composite, and we can understand the causation of the nature as a case of a proper constituent's determining the character of the composite into which it enters. Here, the constituent marks out its containing composite as a member of its proper substance kind by endowing it with the behavioral repertoire definitive of the kind. And, of course, within the ontological framework of Aristotle's own constituent theory, the demand that the nature be an irreducibly basic or primitive causal principle can be accommodated. The substantial form of a living being is a proper constituent that is equideterminate with the kind it supports, and it is a constituent that nonderivatively or primitively has the sort of character that fits it out to play its proper role in marking out the living being as a member of the kind. But, then, the substantial form is precisely the sort of thing required to play the causal role of a nature.

In these same contexts, Aristotle fleshes out these claims about the causal role of substantial form by arguing that natures function telelologically, that the causation at work here is an instance of final causation.[61] One component in this claim bears on the process of biological development that takes us from the embryo to the mature flourishing member of the kind. That process is the backbone of the behavioral pattern characteristic of the kind, and Aristotle argues that the formal nature is the final cause of the process.[62] The argument centers on the claim, first, that the process owes its identity to the state in which it culminates and, second, that the state is one where we have the mature member of the species displaying the nature in its

---

[60] In *Physics* B. 1, the relevant appeal comes at 193^b32 ff. In *Physics* B. 8, a similar appeal is made at 199^a30-3.

[61] The *locus classicus* for this argument is *Physics* B. 8, but *De Partibus Animalium* I. 1 and *De Anima* II. 1 are also important texts here.

[62] See 193^b7–18, 198^a25–7, and 1032^a18–25.

full-blown form. But there is a further component to the claim that biological natures function teleologically. Aristotle argues that natures impose a top-down organization on the members of the relevant kind in the sense that the nature dictates a specific pattern of functional organization in which the various organic parts of a living being get their identity from the role they play in the overall functional economy imposed by the nature. What we have, then, is a single, unified form of being or life that spreads itself over the parts and subordinates them to the whole, with the result that no satisfactory account of the relevant form of being or life can be anything but holistic.[63]

The idea that there is this sort of pattern of functional organization associated with a substantial form might tempt some to characterize forms as what are nowadays called structural universals.[64] This characterization is, in a number of ways, misleading; nonetheless, the characterization incorporates an important insight about substantial form and the sort of overall organization displayed by anything that has a substantial form. It turns out, however, that there is a certain irony in the fact that talk of structural universals is an appropriate vehicle for capturing the insight.

What exactly is a structural universal? Unfortunately, it is difficult to find anything like a rigorous definition of the notion in the literature. The notion is typically introduced informally as the idea of a universal that is exhibited by a mereologically complex object whose various parts instantiate certain other universals according to a specified configuration or pattern.[65] Where U is a structural universal instantiated by a mereologically complex object, x, there are other universals, $U_1, \ldots U_n$, such that each of the parts, $a_1 \ldots a_n$, of x instantiates an appropriate universal from $U_1 \ldots U_n$. The example we regularly meet in the literature is the universal *being a methane molecule*. That universal is a structural universal because there are certain other universals, $U_1 \ldots U_n$, such that a molecule instantiates *being a methane molecule* just in case each of the different atoms making up the molecule exhibits an appropriate universal from $U_1 \ldots U_n$.

Notice that in explaining what a structural universal is, I have used the expression 'mereologically complex object'. The aim is to make

---

[63] This idea gets formulated repeatedly. One especially clear and explicit formulation is found at 415^b15–21; another, at 641^a18–20.
[64] As it has Dory Scaltsas. See Scaltsas (1994: 110).
[65] For discussion of this concept, see e.g. D. Lewis (1986) and Armstrong (1997: 47–55).

explicit that the concepts of part and composite/whole at work in discussions of structural universals are not the concepts of constituent and composite/whole at work in immanentist or constituent ontologies. To be sure, some objects (Aristotle's individual substances, for example) count as composites in both uses of the term 'composite'; but the concept I have marked by the term 'mereologically complex object' is the idea of the fusion or sum of what I have been calling the common-sense parts of a thing.

Now, it is easy enough to see how talk of structural universals might be thought to capture the idea that the substantial form of an organism is its nature and involves a determinate pattern of structural and functional organization. Nonetheless, the claim that substantial forms are structural universals is not an altogether appropriate vehicle for the expression of this idea. A structural universal is one instantiated by something that is a mereologically composite object. Where we have a substantial form, the relevant mereologically complex object is the individual living thing—the individual plant, animal, or human being. Unfortunately, in Aristotle's theory, the substantial form is not instantiated by or predicated of the individual living being whose form it is. On the contrary, the substantial form is predicated of something that, like it, is a proper constituent of the individual biological organism—its proximate matter.

But while the substantial form cannot be a structural universal, its predication of the matter does induce the predication of a universal that satisfies our rough characterization of a structural universal. In virtue of the form's being predicated of the matter, the species associated with that form is predicated of the individual organism. So the species is predicated of or is instantiated by something that is, in the requisite way, mereologically complex; and that predication holds just in case the common-sense or spatially determined parts making up the mereologically complex object exhibit the sort of structural and functional organization associated with the nature or form. So even if the substantial form is not itself a structural universal, its predication entails the predication of a universal that is, by our rough account, structural; and the claim that this universal is structural highlights an important set of facts about the functional organization of a typically Aristotelian substance.

There is, however, a certain irony in all this. Current discussions of structural universals invariably focus on the question of whether there are any such universals. The question is whether, having postulated the various individual universals instantiated by the various parts of a mereological composite, we need to posit a further universal instantiated by the whole. The worry is that such a universal would be redundant; its instantiation would involve no new facts over and above those involved in the instantiation of the individual universals by the parts of the mereological composite.[66] There is, however, an assumption at work in this dialectic. The assumption is that where we have a structural universal (or, at least, a candidate for status as such), the determination of facts is always from the bottom up. The assumption is that the instantiation of a structural universal by a mereological composite must rest on or be determined by the instantiation of universals by the parts of that composite. The idea is that facts about wholes must supervene somehow on facts about parts.

It is important, however, to notice that the rough characterization of structural universals at work in the dialectic is, in fact, one that is neutral with respect to direction of determination. It applies not merely in the case where a universal's instantiation by a mereological composite is determined by facts about the composite's parts, but also in the case where the relevant facts about parts are determined by the whole's instantiation of the structural universal. What is remarkable is that participants in the debate over structural universals have failed to recognize this fact; they have failed to see that, as they characterize it, the notion of a structural universal applies within the context of a holistic theory such as Aristotle's where we have determination from the top down no less than within the context of a thoroughgoing reductionism where the determination is from the bottom up. Evidently reductive prejudices are so deeply ingrained that the neutrality of the concept just gets overlooked.

The irony, then, is that a notion tailored to play a central role in a dialectic whose controlling assumptions are so thoroughly reductionist should apply within the context of an antireductive theory such as Aristotle's. In that theory, it is a necessary truth that each genuine substance is the sort or kind of thing it is if and only if each of its common-sense parts has the appropriate character. But the direction of determination here is from the top down. It is because the composite living being is a member of its proper biological kind that its parts have

---

[66] See D. Lewis (1986).

the properties they do. They have the character they do in virtue of being integrated components in the single overarching functional economy that is the ongoing life of, say, a geranium, a dog, or a human being; and we misunderstand the determination at work here if we take it to involve antecedently existing entities that come to have new properties in virtue of standing in new relations to other antecedently existing things. The parts of a living being are things that get defined functionally: the roles they play in the overall vital economy are built into their essences, so that, as we put it earlier, they get their identity from their integration in the whole.

As we have seen, what strictly speaking counts as a structural universal is the biological species; but it is not the universal whose instantiation is ultimately responsible for the special top-down organization in which the parts of a biological organism get their identity from the role they play in the overall functional economy that is the relevant kind of life. The substantial form is that universal; it is a primitive causal principle; and it is what makes Aristotle's ontology unique among those that implement the constituent strategy. His ontology includes composite beings which, nonetheless, exhibit an irreducibly unique or autonomous form of being. That form of being just is the form of life that expresses itself in the functional organization and behavioral repertoire definitive of a biological kind; and what insures the autonomy of that form of being is the fact that anything that enjoys it does so in virtue of having as a proper constituent an irreducibly basic causal principle the substantial form—that is equideterminate with that form of being.

University of Notre Dame

REFERENCES

Allaire, E. (1963) "Bare Particulars", *Philosophical Studies* 14: 1–8.
Armstrong, D. (1989) *Universals* (Boulder, Colo.: Westview).
—— (1997) *A World of States of Affairs* (Cambridge: Cambridge University Press).
Ayer, A. J. (1954) "The Identity of Indiscernibles", in id., *Philosophical Essays* (London: St Martin's Press).
Barnes, J. (1984) *The Complete Works of Aristotle*, 2 vols. (Princeton, NJ: Princeton University Press).

Bergmann, G. (1967) *Realism* (Madison, Wis.: University of Wisconsin Press).
Black, M. (1952) "The Identity of Indiscernibles", *Mind* 61: 153–64.
Castañeda, H. N. (1974) "Thinking and the Structure of the World", *Philosophia* 4: 3–40.
Casullo, A. (1985) "A Fourth Version of the Bundle Theory", *Philosophical Studies* 47: 95–107.
Code, A. (1995) "Potentiality in Aristotle's Science and Metaphysics", *Pacific Philosophical Quarterly* 76: 405–18.
Fine, G. (1993) *On Ideas* (Oxford: Oxford University Press).
Hochberg, H. (1960) "Universals, Particulars, and Predication", *Review of Metaphysics* 14: 87–102.
Lewis, D. (1986) "Against Structural Universals", *Australasian Journal of Philosophy* 61: 343–77.
Lewis, F. (1982) "Accidental Sameness in Aristotle", *Philosophical Studies* 42: 1–36.
—— (1991) *Substance and Predication in Aristotle* (Cambridge: Cambridge University Press).
Loux, M. (1991) *Primary Ousia* (Ithaca, NY: Cornell University Press).
—— (2002) *Metaphysics*, 2nd edn. (London: Routledge).
—— (2005) "Aristotle on Matter, Form, and Ontological Strategy", *Ancient Philosophy* 25: 81–123.
Plantinga, A. (1974) *The Nature of Necessity* (Oxford: Oxford University Press).
Quine, W. (1954) *From a Logical Point of View* (Cambridge, Mass.: Harvard University Press).
Russell, B. (1912) *Problems of Philosophy* (Oxford: Oxford University Press).
—— (1948) *Human Knowledge: Its Scope and Limits* (London: George Allen & Unwin).
Scaltsas, T. (1994) *Substances and Universals in Aristotle's Metaphysics* (Ithaca, NY: Cornell University Press).
Strawson, P. F. (1959) *Individuals* (London: Methuen).
Wedin, M. (2000) *Aristotle's Theory of Substance* (Oxford: Oxford University Press).
Williams, D. C. (1953) "The Elements of Being", *Review of Metaphysics* 7: 3–18.
Wolterstorff, N. (1970) "Bergmann's Constituent Ontology", *Noûs* 4: 109–34.
—— (1991) "Divine Simplicity", *Philosophical Perspectives* 5: 531–52.

9. The Relation between General and Particular: Entailment vs. Supervenience

Phillip Bricker

I. INTRODUCTION

I say (with many others): the world is a *thing*, the *biggest* thing, the *mereological sum* (or *aggregate*) of all things. Truth is determined by the distribution of fundamental, or perfectly natural, properties and relations over the parts of this biggest thing. For want of a better name, call this the *thing theory*.[1] Some say instead: the world is a *fact*, the *most inclusive* fact, the *conjunction* (also mereological sum) of all the facts. Truth is determined by (some sort of) correspondence to the facts. Call this, following Armstrong, *factualism*.[2] The dispute between the thing theory and factualism can be traced, of course, to the opening lines of Wittgenstein's *Tractatus*, where it received second billing:

1   The world is all that is the case.
1.1   The world is the totality of facts, not of things.[3]

Could there be a starker division between fundamental ontological theories of the world?

The paper that became this chapter was part of Metaphysical Mayhem VII at Syracuse University in August 2002 and was presented to the Philosophy Department at Arizona State University in February 2003. It expands on material presented to the Philosophy Department at New York University in February 1999. Thanks especially to Daniel Nolan, Laurie Paul, and Ted Sider for their comments.

[1] David Lewis is a prominent thing theorist. See the opening paragraph of *On the Plurality of Worlds* (1986).

[2] Armstrong's version of factualism is presented in *A World of States of Affairs* (1997). Armstrong prefers 'state of affairs' to 'fact'. Although I will stick with the shorter term 'fact', be warned that 'fact' herein is a philosophical term of art, ontologically loaded unlike its natural language homonym. Facts are immanent: part of the furniture of the world.

[3] Ludwig Wittgenstein, *Tractatus Logico-Philosophicus* (1921).

On closer inspection, however, the division appears less stark. A factualist need not reject things; nor need a thing theorist reject (all) facts. For each thing accepted by the thing theorist, there is an associated fact accepted by the factualist saying that the thing has the nature that it does. A factualist can identify things with their associated facts at no ontological cost: (some) facts are also things.[4] In the other direction, a thing theorist can identify the fact associated with a thing with the thing itself: things are also facts. Some metaphysicians may protest: the thing and its associated fact differ in their modal existence conditions, and so cannot be identified; a red ball, for example, can exist without being red, whereas whenever the associated fact exists, the ball exists and is red. But an enlightened factualist or thing theorist, one who appreciates the inconstancy of *de re* modality, need no more reject the identity of things with facts on this basis than, say, the identity of statues with hunks of clay; in both cases, *counterpart relations* may be multiplied, not entities within the world.[5]

The factualist, however, is not yet satisfied: even if things are facts, they cannot be *all* of the facts. For there is a distinct fact for each (sparse) property had by a thing, the fact that the thing has that property; there is a multiplicity of facts for each thing. And, the factualist may continue, this is an *immanent* multiplicity, lest the world be impoverished in causes and effects.[6] But whether a thing ontology is too coarse, say, to capture the causal structure of the world belongs to the traditional dispute over the reality and nature of properties; it is not what divides factualists from thing theorists. A trope theory, for example, can provide for an immanent multiplicity of causes and effects without positing anything but things and the tropes that are their parts; an enlightened trope theorist can then identify facts with tropes, and sums of tropes.[7]

As long as one considers only the case for (positive) *particular* facts, it seems, the dispute between factualists and thing theorists is either subsumed under a more general dispute over *de re* modality, or is

---

[4] Armstrong holds that things—what he calls "thick particulars"—are facts, in both cases taking intrinsic nature to be essential. See (1997: 125–6).

[5] See Lewis (1986: 248–63) for the general case. For an application of counterpart theory to the case at hand, see Lewis (2003).

[6] See, e.g. Armstrong (1989b: 28–9). Lewis (2003) provides a non-immanent multiplicity.

[7] In his (1989b: 113–27), Armstrong acknowledges that tropes can do much of what he requires of states of affairs. I do not agree, however, that tropes must be "non-transferable".

transformed into a dispute over realism about properties. But when one considers instead the case for *general* facts, one comes up against a genuine disagreement. If a factualist can successfully argue that general facts exist as something "over and above" particular facts and particular things, then the thing theorist is in trouble.

In this chapter, I focus on two contrasting arguments: Russell's well-known argument, endorsed and bolstered by Armstrong, that general facts are needed in addition to particular facts because general truths are not *entailed* by particular truths; and an argument, endorsed by Lewis among others, that general facts are not needed in addition to particular facts because general truths (globally) *supervene* on particular truths.[8] Needless to say, as a thing theorist, I reject the former argument and accept the latter. My goal, however—difficult to attain in matters of fundamental ontology—is to present my main arguments from a neutral perspective, so that they will have force even from within the factualist framework: a factualist, no less than a thing theorist, should dispense with general facts.[9]

In what follows I tacitly restrict attention to *first-order* particular facts and their *first-order* generalizations. Some factualists hold that *second-order* facts involving relations between universals are needed to ground the distinction between laws and accidental regularities. Their arguments, however, threaten only nominalist versions of thing theory, not thing theory generally. In any case, the issues raised by the problem of laws cut across the issues raised by the problem of generality; in this chapter, I set the former aside.

I begin with some clarifications, and some basic assumptions. As a thing theorist, I may well be asked: what is a thing? Don't expect a definition, however. Things are basic for the thing theory. I can give examples: people and puddles and protons are things. But I can't say much of anything as to what makes people and puddles and protons things without taking sides on metaphysical disputes—three-dimensionalism vs. four-dimensionalism, absolutism vs. relationism about space and time, realism vs. non-realism about properties (universals or tropes)—with

---

[8] See David Lewis's (1992: 201–7) discussion of the supervenience of truth on being. Brian Skyrms is a factualist who rejects general facts because they supervene on (first-order) particular facts; see his (1981: 199–206).

[9] The arguments for and against general facts apply, with some changes, to the case of negative particular facts. In this chapter, however, for reasons of space, I omit explicit discussion of negative particular facts.

respect to which I intend the thing theory to be neutral. I will assume, however, that aggregates of things are things, and that spatiotemporal parts of things are things. But non-spatiotemporal parts of things (if any—for example, universals or tropes) are not things. Finally, I believe that any respectable thing theorist will follow Hume in denying necessary connections between (mereologically) distinct things; but since the Humean thesis is disputed, I will be careful to flag those arguments that depend on it.

What, according to the factualist, are facts? The best way, I think, to get a handle on facts is by way of their relation to *propositions*. Propositions, I will suppose, are necessarily existing, non-linguistic entities.[10] Truth-conditions for propositions are classical: for any proposition and any possible world, the proposition is (definitely) true at the world, or its denial is (definitely) true, but not both. Propositions represent the way the world is from "without"; they do not belong to the basic inventory of the world, all of whose members contingently exist. Facts, on the other hand, are immanent; they are part of the world; they ground the truth and falsity of (contingent) propositions. To each fact there corresponds a unique (up to necessary equivalence) true proposition (*truth*, for short): necessarily, the fact exists if and only if the corresponding proposition is true. But, whereas the propositions are *abundant*, so that every sentence (with definite, classical truth-conditions) expresses some proposition, the facts are *sparse*. Only a select minority of the truths correspond one–one with the facts.

Which truths so correspond? Start with the (first-order) *atomic propositions*: all propositions that predicate a fundamental property of a basic particular, or a fundamental n-ary relation of an n-tuple of basic particulars.[11] All factualists hold that, for each true atomic proposition,

---

[10] Since in this chapter I am concerned only with contingent truth, propositions may be taken to be classes of possible worlds. But it wouldn't matter for what follows if instead propositions were taken to be sentences (better: equivalence classes of necessarily equivalent sentences) of some sufficiently idealized language, say, with predicates for fundamental properties and relations, and names for basic particulars. And it wouldn't matter for most of what follows if some propositions were taken to exist contingently, existing only when the entities they are about exist.

[11] I assume that for our world, or any world, both the factualist and the thing theorist can speak of the *particulars* that exist at the world, and the *fundamental* (or *perfectly natural*) properties and relations instantiated by particulars at the world. I call a particular *basic* just in case it instantiates some fundamental property or relation; thus I do not suppose that basic particulars must be mereologically simple. Note that, for the factualist, facts are not constructed from particulars, properties, and relations. Rather, facts are basic,

there is a unique *atomic fact*; and that the atomic facts are *ontologically basic*, part of any complete inventory of what there is. But are these atomic facts *all* the (first-order) facts? Define a (first-order) *general proposition* to be the result of applying a universal quantifier to a qualitative property; the general proposition is true (true at a world *w*) just in case every particular (every particular existing at *w*) instantiates the property.[12] A property is *qualitative*, roughly, if it can be defined using Boolean operators and first-order quantifiers from the fundamental properties and relations (including the part–whole relation).[13] For example, if F and G are fundamental properties and R is a fundamental relation, then *being G if F*, *bearing R to something*, and *having a part that is F and bears R to a part that is G* are all qualitative properties; and their generalizations, *all Fs are Gs*, *everything bears R to something*, and *everything has a part that is F and that bears R to a part that is G* are all general propositions. Now, the question to be addressed is this: must the factualist posit general facts in addition to the atomic facts to serve as ontological ground for true general propositions? Or are the general truths *determined* by the atomic truths?

Clearly, the issue will turn on what is meant by "determined". Perhaps it helps somewhat to note that the determination relation in question is non-causal, and holds of necessity. But more must be said: a mere logical or functional determination is not to the point unless it carries with it ontological force. Thus, if the atomic truths *determine* the general truths, in the relevant sense, then the general propositions hold or fail to hold *in virtue of*, or *because of*, the holding or failing to hold of the atomic propositions. In this case (I argue below) general facts needn't be added to the inventory; the atomic facts suffice. On the other hand, if the atomic truths *fail* to determine the general truths,

and particulars, properties, and relations are somehow abstracted from facts. Cf. e.g. Armstrong (1989a: 43).

[12] The restriction to qualitative properties is a convenient stipulation: it allows me to ignore questions of *de re* modality when considering truth-conditions for the general propositions; but it doesn't unduly limit the scope of my arguments, since the case for general facts applies with equal force to the qualitative and the non-qualitative propositions.

[13] A more formal treatment would take place within a framework of algebraic logic: the qualitative properties (and relations) are defined recursively by the application of Boolean, quantificational, and combinatorial operators to the fundamental properties and relations. For an illustration of one such framework, see Quine (1960). (But the framework would need to be generalized to take advantage of the resources of infinitary logic, including infinite Boolean operators and, perhaps, infinite strings of quantifiers.)

in the relevant sense, then the atomic facts do not suffice; additional entities will need to be added to serve as ontological ground for the general truths—presumably, for the factualist, general facts. Call the relevant determination relation between propositions *ontological determination*.

What has given the debate over general facts its longevity, I believe, is that there are two relations between propositions—entailment and supervenience—either of which, at first glance, might plausibly be taken to be necessary for ontological determination. Often it makes no difference which is taken to be necessary because entailment and supervenience coincide. But for the case at hand, one must choose: taking entailment to be necessary and taking supervenience to be necessary lead to opposite results. In what follows, I will argue that when entailment and supervenience diverge, it is only supervenience that is necessary for ontological determination; failure of entailment carries no ontological force.

II. THE NON-ENTAILMENT OF GENERAL TRUTHS BY PARTICULAR TRUTHS

Russell famously argued, during his logical atomist stage, for the existence of general facts. In *The Philosophy of Logical Atomism* (1918) Russell writes: "you cannot ever arrive at a general fact by inference from particular facts, however numerous" (p. 235). He later concludes from this: "you must admit general facts as distinct from and over and above particular facts" (p. 236). In short, Russell argues: the atomic truths do not *entail* the general truths; therefore, general facts are needed in addition to atomic facts.[14] Call this the *Non-Entailment Argument*. The argument tacitly supposes that entailment, of some sort, is a necessary component of ontological determination. What is entailment? Although I suppose that Russell had in mind some notion of *formal* entailment (within an ideal language), I suggest instead that we take the relevant entailment relation to be *strict implication* defined

---

[14] Armstrong endorses Russell's argument, and gives it a truthmaker twist. I discuss Armstrong's variation in section VI. Frank Ramsey (1927) objected to Russell's argument for general facts along different lines. But Ramsey's objection rests on a modal fallacy. For a diagnosis, see Hazen (1986).

in terms of possible worlds.[15] Let A and B be classes of propositions.[16] B *entails* A iff every world at which every member of B is true is a world at which every member of A is true. (B entails a single proposition Z iff B entails $\{Z\}$.) Note that, on this interpretation of 'entails', necessary general truths are trivially entailed by the atomic truths, and so should be excluded from the scope of the argument. The main premise of the Non-Entailment Argument, then, is:

> *Non-Entailment Thesis*: Some contingent general truth is not entailed by the class of atomic truths (if there are any contingent general truths).

As stated, the Non-Entailment Thesis is a claim about truths at the actual world: a *local* thesis. A stronger, *global* thesis, generalizing over all worlds, is:

> *Global Non-Entailment Thesis*: At any world (at which there are contingent general truths), some contingent general truth is not entailed by the class of atomic truths.

In this section, I will examine arguments for versions of the Non-Entailment Thesis, ultimately defending a version even stronger than Global Non-Entailment. In the final section, I reject the Non-Entailment Argument. I claim that the Non-Entailment Thesis does not give reason, even from within the factualist framework, for positing general facts as anything "over and above" the atomic facts.

Arguments for all versions of the Non-Entailment Thesis start from a *base* world, perhaps the actual world, and then move to an *expanded* world at which the atomic truths at the base world still hold, but some general truth at the base world fails to hold. (I say a world w is an *expansion* of a world w' just in case the atomic truths at w include all the atomic truths at w', and at least one more.) There is more than one way, however, to choose an expanded world, and the choice may matter.

---

[15] Interpreting entailment as strict implication does not prejudice the case. If entailment is strict implication, it is more difficult to show that general truths are not entailed, but (presumably) easier to show that non-entailment has ontological import; and I will be challenging only the latter.

[16] I adopt the following convenient policy. Formal definitions and proofs are given within a framework of classes allowing, if need be, for proper classes (e.g. "the class B entails the class A"); informal discussion is carried out within a framework of plurals (e.g. "the Bs entail the As"). This is a distinction of style, not substance. All such occurrences should be interpreted the same way; for purposes of this chapter, it won't matter which.

Let me illustrate with respect to a simple world, schematically described. Suppose that at the base world there are just four atomic truths: Fa, Ga, Hb, and Rab.[17] Thus the world contains two basic particulars, three fundamental properties, and one fundamental relation. The general proposition, *all Fs are Gs*, is true at this world. Is it entailed by the atomic truths? No. *First Method of Argument.* Expand the base world *vertically* by adding a property to an already existing particular: in this case, add F to b so that Fb but not Gb is true at the expanded world. Then, the atomic propositions true at the base world are still true at the expanded world, but the general proposition, *all Fs are Gs*, is false. *Second Method of Argument.* Expand the base world *horizontally* by adding a new basic particular: in this case, add a new particular c standing in relation R to a and to b, and having just one fundamental property F, so that Fc but not Gc is true at the expanded world. Then, again, the atomic propositions true at the base world are still true at the expanded world, but the general proposition, *all Fs are Gs*, is false. Thus, on either method of expansion, it is shown that the atomic truths do not entail the (contingent) general truths.

But this is much too quick. There are positions in the metaphysics of modality on which one or both of these methods of arguing may be blocked. I will briefly outline the difficulties faced by these methods. Then, I will show how, given the metaphysical assumptions that I accept, the argument for the Non-Entailment Thesis can be improved.

The first method of argument might seem preferable to the second—expanding the base world vertically rather than horizontally—because it makes no assumptions about the possibility of alien (basic) particulars (or alien fundamental properties and relations).[18] But the first method's scope is limited, in two ways. First, the method works for some general truths, but not for others. Whether it works depends, for one thing, on the logical features of the property being generalized. Thus, if the property has the feature, *is preserved under vertical expansion*—whatever has the property continues to have it in any vertically expanded world—then the first method is blocked. For example, the proposition, *everything is F*, for a fundamental property F, cannot be falsified by a

---

[17] If particulars can exist without instantiating any fundamental properties, then Hb can be omitted. If particulars can coexist unconnected by fundamental relations, then Rab can be omitted as well.

[18] Alien properties and individuals—and their cost—are discussed by Lewis (1986: 91–2, 158–65).

vertical expansion. For another thing, whether the first method works depends on contingent features of the base world. For example, suppose we add to the simple world considered above a fifth atomic truth, Gb. Then, *all Fs are Gs* is again true, but cannot be falsified by a vertical expansion: something which is G *if* F cannot be made to be *not* G and F by adding properties, because everything at the base world is G.

The first method's scope is limited in a second way. Thus far, I have spoken uncritically of atomic propositions, as if all theorists would agree as to what proposition Fa expresses when a basic particular a instantiates a fundamental property F. But, of course, different ways of "identifying" particulars across worlds, different accounts of individual essence, result in different propositions being labeled "the atomic propositions".[19] Now, if individual essences can *exclude* fundamental properties, if particulars can necessarily *fail* to have a fundamental property, then there is no guarantee that in vertically expanding the base world, some atomic truth at the base world won't be falsified. For example, with respect to the simple world considered above, if b's individual essence excludes F, there will be no expanded world at which Fb is true, and so the argument is blocked.

More generally: say that a basic particular a at world w has a *vertically exclusive* essence iff in some vertical expansion of w, a does not exist. The first method of argument for the Non-Entailment Thesis cannot be counted on if vertically exclusive essences are allowed. But vertically exclusive essences would seem to be unexceptionable: an electron essentially has the fundamental properties it has—say, a particular mass property, charge property, and so on—and essentially has *no more*.

The second method of arguing—expanding the base world horizontally—can be applied much more generally. It can be applied to any contingent general truth, irrespective of the property generalized or the contingent features of the base world. And the restriction on essences is much less severe. Say that a basic particular a at world w has a *horizontally exclusive* essence iff in some horizontal expansion of w, a

---

[19] I remain neutral throughout this chapter on issues of "transworld identification" except when considering my own modal view, in which case my counterpart theoretic bias comes to the fore. Note that a counterpart theorist should distinguish between atomic *predications*, which have truth values only at a single world, the world that includes the particular in question, and atomic *propositions*, which have truth values at every world, truth values that depend on the choice of a counterpart relation. The atomic predications are metaphysically basic for a counterpart theorist, not the atomic propositions.

does not exist. The second method cannot be counted on if horizontally exclusive essences, such as *being the only F*, are allowed. But I know of no modal theorists who identify atomic propositions by way of essences of this sort. The second method, then, appears far superior to the first as a way of supporting the Non-Entailment Thesis.

But the second method isn't for everyone because of its reliance on aliens, on there being basic particulars at the expanded world that do not exist at the base world. Of course, when the base world is a simple world, such as considered above, this is not a problem; plenty of actual particulars are alien to the simple world. But when the base world is the actual world, as it must be to argue for the Non-Entailment Thesis, there may be a problem for certain strict actualists: those who hold that any basic particular that exists in any non-actual possible world also exists in the actual world. (Actualists who are anti-haecceitists face no problem, however, since for them horizontal expansions can add new, qualitatively different basic particulars without adding alien properties, and thus without violating actualist scruples.)

The second method, however, has a serious limitation for anyone, actualist or not, who holds that some worlds are "maximal" and cannot be horizontally expanded. For, in that case, it is a contingent matter whether the actual world can be horizontally expanded as the argument requires, and the argument for the Non-Entailment Thesis, and thus for general facts, will depend on a contingent premise. That's no way to argue for fundamental ontology. Certainly it would be better to establish the Non-Entailment Thesis entirely from premises that are necessary and a priori.

But enough meddling in other philosophers' modal affairs. Since my strategy is to give the factualist the Non-Entailment Thesis, and reject the Non-Entailment Argument, it is enough if I explain why, on the modal metaphysics I accept, the Non-Entailment Thesis holds. A revision of the second method will allow me to do this without relying on premises that are contingent.

First, I allow as a genuine metaphysical possibility what might be called *universal actualization*.[20] The best way to illustrate the possibility I have in mind is from a realist perspective; ersatzists and fictionalists

[20] The view set forth in this and the next paragraph is defended at length in my "Island Universes and the Analysis of Modality" (2001). (The version on my web site—<www.umass.edu/philosophy/faculty/bricker.htm>, accessed 9 July 2005—includes the section numbers that were inexplicably omitted from the published version.)

can translate into their framework in familiar ways. Thus, consider Leibniz's God surveying the realm of possible worlds prior to actualization. I suppose that within each world the parts are all interconnected (by spatiotemporal relations, or other external relations), but that the parts of distinct worlds are wholly disconnected from one another.[21] On the standard assumption, Leibniz's God must actualize exactly one world: necessarily, one and only one world is actual. But what prohibits Leibniz's God from actualizing two (or more) worlds? Or, dropping Leibniz's God from the picture: why exclude the possibility that two or more worlds together are actual? No good reason, I fear; only custom. If two (or more) worlds are actual, then actuality includes two disconnected parts: island universes. If *all* worlds are actual, then actuality includes every possibility: every possible individual is actual.

If we allow the possibility that two (or more) worlds are actual, then there are more possibilities (for the whole of actuality) than there are worlds: every world is a possibility, but so is every plurality of worlds. Propositions, then, will have to be assigned truth values relative not just to single worlds, but to pluralities of worlds.[22] For example, the proposition, *island universes exist*, is false at any single world, but true at any plurality of worlds. (Truth at a plurality of worlds is not, of course, to be identified with truth at each world in the plurality; rather, one is to suppose actuality is the aggregate of the worlds in the plurality, and then to ask what is true of that aggregate.) Then, the standard analyses of possibility and necessity must be adjusted to accommodate the change in truth-conditions for propositions: a proposition is *possible* iff it is true at some world, or at some plurality of worlds; a proposition is *necessary* iff it is true at all worlds, and at all pluralities of worlds.[23]

I also need a modest assumption about essences: necessarily, any particular that exists would still have existed, and would have had the same fundamental properties and stood in the same fundamental relations to other particulars, had the world been (qualitatively) exactly the same

---

[21] For defense, see my (1996).

[22] What is a "plurality"? I use 'plurality' as a way of staying neutral between three ways of presenting the view: classes, aggregates, or a framework of plurals. I prefer the latter, but the differences won't much matter for present purposes.

[23] This raises a terminological problem. Usually when I write 'world' in this chapter, what I really mean is 'world, or plurality of worlds'. But since my own view rears its head only in this section, and in one paragraph of the final section, it does little harm that I speak with the vulgar.

except for the addition of island universes.[24] It follows that, if a world or plurality of worlds is included in a larger plurality of worlds, then the atomic propositions true at the former are still true at the latter; atomic truths are not falsified by the addition of island universes. More generally, when a particular instantiates a qualitative property at a world or plurality of worlds, it does so also at any larger plurality of worlds.

It is now a simple matter to establish the Non-Entailment Thesis without relying on a contingent premise by establishing the Global Non-Entailment Thesis. Indeed, I will establish an even stronger thesis, claiming that, necessarily, *no* contingent general truth is entailed by the atomic truths, with necessity understood as quantification over worlds, and pluralities of worlds. This will be seen to follow from the fact that, at the plurality of all worlds, all general truths—equivalently, all negative existential truths—are necessary truths; for example, if there aren't any unicorns in the plurality of all worlds, then, necessarily, there aren't any unicorns.

> *Strong Global Non-Entailment Thesis*: For any world or plurality of worlds W, any contingent general proposition true at W is not entailed by the class of atomic propositions true at W.[25]
>
> *Proof*: Consider any world or plurality of worlds W. Let P be any contingent general truth at W. (If there are none, then the non-entailment claim holds vacuously.) Let U be the plurality of all worlds. Given our assumption about essences, the atomic propositions true at W are all true at U since W is included in U. But P is false at U. For, being contingent, P is false at some V included in U, and, making use of our assumption once again, any counterexample to P in V is also a counterexample to P in U.[26]

---

[24] The assumption for relations requires that island universes be *absolutely isolated*: no part of one stands in any fundamental (external) relation to any part of another. Note also that, in interpreting modality *de re* on this view, counterpart relations must be taken to be relative to worlds and to pluralities of worlds (because pluralities of worlds overlap). In particular, where W and V are distinct worlds or pluralities of worlds, a is a particular existing at W, and b is a particular existing at V: b may be a counterpart of a at V, even though b, presumably, is not a counterpart of a at the plurality of worlds that includes V and W: a is its own counterpart at any plurality of worlds that includes W.

[25] Of course, the definition of entailment now reads: a class of propositions A entails proposition Z iff at every world *or plurality of worlds* at which all the members of A are true, Z is true.

[26] It might appear that the proposition, *everything coexists with some F* (where F is any contingently instantiated fundamental property), is a counterexample to Strong Global

III. THE SUPERVENIENCE OF GENERAL TRUTHS ON PARTICULAR TRUTHS

Standing in opposition to the Non-Entailment Argument is the *Supervenience Argument*: general truths supervene on atomic truths; therefore, general facts are not needed in addition to atomic facts. (A stronger version, to be discussed below, concludes: therefore, there are no general facts.) The argument tacitly supposes that supervenience, not entailment, has ontological import. I will defend that assumption in due course. First, I consider the supervenience claim. As with the Non-Entailment Thesis, it comes in both a local and a global version:

Supervenience Thesis: If a world agrees with the actual world on all atomic truths, then it agrees also on all general truths.

Global Supervenience Thesis: If any two worlds agree on all their atomic truths, then they agree also on all their general truths.[27]

Since it is unlikely that anyone would accept the local version while rejecting the global version, I will focus entirely on the latter in what follows, what I call the *Supervenience of the General on the Particular*.

For the thing theorist, the Supervenience of the General on the Particular is almost automatic. The actual world is a thing. Other worlds, then, are things as well (for the realist about worlds; but it will do no harm to speak from a realist perspective because ersatzist or fictionalist thing theorists will *represent* other worlds as things, and the realist arguments will carry over). The intrinsic qualitative nature of a thing, including a world, is determined by the distribution of fundamental properties and relations over its parts. The qualitative nature of a

---

Non-Entailment; for this proposition is entailed by any atomic truth of the form *a is F*. But *everything coexists with some F* is not a general proposition as herein defined because the property, *coexisting with some F*, is not a qualitative property. It depends on the distinction between the actual and the merely possible, and, if island universes are possible, that distinction cannot be defined in qualitative terms. *Being spatiotemporally related to some F* is a qualitative property; *coexisting with some F* is not. (This is the only argument in the chapter for which the restriction of general propositions to qualitative propositions plays an essential role.)

[27] Two asides. First, it is more common nowadays to define global supervenience as a relation between classes of properties, rather than classes of propositions. Couching the discussion in terms of properties is obviously inconvenient for the case at hand, though it could be done by turning propositions into properties of worlds. Second, the distinction I draw between global and local theses—applying to all worlds, or just to the actual world—is not the distinction that originally gave Global Supervenience its name.

world, then, is determined by its atomic truths, and worlds that agree on atomic truths agree in their intrinsic qualitative nature: they are *qualitative duplicates*. Moreover, since worlds are biggest (interconnected) things—parts of distinct worlds stand in no fundamental relations to one another—worlds that agree on atomic truths are *qualitatively indiscernible*, agreeing in both their intrinsic and extrinsic qualitative nature.[28] Now, for the thing theorist, propositions are properties of worlds. In particular, a general proposition, *everything is Q*, is the property, *having every part be Q*. But *having every part be Q* is a qualitative property given that Q is qualitative. Therefore, worlds that agree on atomic truths, being qualitatively indiscernible, agree on any general truth, *everything is Q*.[29]

The factualist will not be impressed by this argument. But I think the factualist has good reason, from within her own framework, to accept the Supervenience of the General on the Particular. To see why, ask what sort of world would have to exist in order for such supervenience to fail. Thus, suppose worlds w and w' agree on atomic truths. Then they agree on all matters of particular fact: for any particular, basic or not, and any qualitative property, the particular instantiates the property at both worlds, or at neither.[30] Now suppose some general proposition, *everything is Q*, holds at w but not at w'. Then, the existential proposition, *something is not Q*, holds at w'. But there is no particular a at w' such that a is not Q; for if there were, *a is not Q* would be true at w as well, which contradicts everything being Q at w. So, at w', a true existential proposition is *unwitnessed* by any particular. Rejecting the Supervenience of the General on the Particular requires embracing worlds at which existential truths lack witnesses. But what is objectionable about that?

It is customary and proper, for thing theorist and factualist alike, to place the following two demands on a theory of possible worlds: worlds must be *possible*, in a broad metaphysical or logical sense; and worlds must be *determinate*, leaving nothing unsettled. These demands constrain

---

[28] See Lewis (1986: 62-3), on the distinction between duplicates and indiscernibles.

[29] For the thing theorist, Supervenience of the General on the Particular is an instance of what Lewis has dubbed (following Bigelow) the *Supervenience of Truth on Being*: "truth is supervenient on what things there are and which perfectly natural properties and relations they instantiate" (Lewis 1992: 207). A stronger version of Supervenience of Truth on Being holds that truth supervenes on what things there are (full stop). That corresponds to the Subject Matter Principle to be introduced below. (To avoid confusion, the weaker version might better be called the *Supervenience of Truth on Particular Truth*.)

[30] Again, any proof of this must await a rigorous account of the qualitative properties.

which classes of propositions can be the class of truths at some world. Thus, according to the first demand, truth—that is, the class of true propositions—is *consistent* at any world (where consistency is a modal notion, perhaps primitive, perhaps reduced to *possibilia*). The second demand is sometimes expressed by saying that truth, in addition to being consistent, is *maximally* consistent at any world: no proposition could be added to the truths without falling into contradiction. Truth is maximally consistent just in case it is consistent and *complete*: for any proposition, either that proposition or its denial is true. But requiring only that truth be maximally consistent, or consistent and complete, at every world falls short of capturing the idea that worlds are determinate. Truth must be *witnessed* as well: every existential truth must be witnessed by some particular; that is, if an existential proposition is true at a world, the property being existentially generalized holds of some particular existing at the world. Let *Completeness* be the thesis that truth at any world is complete; *Witnessing* the thesis that truth at any world is witnessed.

To clarify the relation between Completeness and Witnessing, it is useful to consider a "world" that everyone agrees is not in general determinate: the "world" of a work of fiction. Suppose, for example, there is a story, "Who Killed Peter Rabbit?", that has only four characters (among sundry objects): Flopsy, Mopsy, Cottontail, and Peter. Suppose it is true in the story that someone kills Peter, but it is never revealed who did it. (For the sake of the illustration, pretend that *killing* is a fundamental relation.) Then truth in the story violates Witnessing, because there is no character (or object) in the story that witnesses the existential proposition in question. Now consider two versions of the story. On one version, it is revealed that either Flopsy, Mopsy, or Cottontail is the killer, but not who. In this case, Completeness is violated as well as Witnessing: for example, neither the proposition that Flopsy killed Peter, nor its denial, is true in the story. This is one way for the story to fail to be determinate. On the second version, it is revealed that neither Flopsy, Mopsy, nor Cottontail (nor Peter himself) is the killer. In this case, there need be no violation of Completeness: the story could be filled out so that, for every proposition, either it or its denial is true in the story. But, Witnessing is still violated: for any character in the story—indeed, any actual or possible individual—it is not true that he or she (or it) is the killer. Clearly, the "world" of the story fails to be determinate no less in the second version than in the first: someone killed Peter, but who the killer is remains undetermined.

Once it is appreciated that Completeness and Witnessing are two independent demands on truth and that both are needed to capture the idea that worlds are determinate, it is hard to justify holding on to the former while rejecting the latter. If the factualist concedes, as most factualists will, that truth at any world is maximally consistent, and thus complete, it would be arbitrary to then deny that truth need be witnessed as well.

But might a factualist choose to give up *both* Completeness and Witnessing? Could the idea that worlds are determinate be just a stale piece of thing propaganda? Perhaps the following argument for Completeness and Witnessing will carry some weight. I suppose that the factualist works within a framework of classical logic, and that the meaning of the Boolean operators and the quantifiers is given by the standard Tarskian truth-conditions. But meaning has modal force: the Boolean operators and the quantifiers must have these truth-conditions, not just at the actual world, but at all possible worlds. Now suppose we were to allow a world at which truth is not complete: some proposition p is such that neither it nor its denial, *not p*, is true at the world. But, presumably, the proposition, *p or not p*, is true at the world, since tautologies are necessary truths. And that violates the standard Tarskian truth-conditions for disjunction: a disjunction is true iff at least one of its disjuncts is true. To reject Completeness, then, is to suppose that there is a world at which disjunctions do not have their standard truth-conditions. That, I claim, is incoherent, and thus worlds at which truth is not complete should be rejected.

The argument applies, *mutatis mutandis*, to Witnessing. For suppose we were to allow a world at which truth is not witnessed: there is a true existential proposition, *something is Q*, even though for every particular a existing at the world, it is not true that a is Q. That violates the standard Tarskian truth-conditions for existential propositions. To hold that existential propositions behave in this way, I claim, is incoherent. Worlds at which truth is not witnessed, no less than worlds at which truth is not complete, should be rejected.

IV. SUPERVENIENCE AND ENTAILMENT COMPARED

General truths, I have argued, supervene on, but are not entailed by, atomic truths. Thus supervenience and entailment do not always

Entailment vs. Supervenience | 267

coincide. In this section, I consider just how these notions relate to one another. Before going any further, however, it would be wise to head off a potential terminological confusion. Armstrong, as already mentioned, is a staunch defender of the Non-Entailment Argument. But this might seem to conflict with his espousal of what he calls "the doctrine of the ontological free lunch" applied to supervenience: "what supervenes is no addition of being"; "the supervenient is ontologically nothing more than its base".[31] Thus Armstrong apparently accepts the premise of the Supervenience Argument that supervenience has ontological import. But wait: Armstrong also appears to accept the other premise of the Supervenience Argument, the Supervenience of the General on the Particular.[32] How, then, can he avoid the conclusion of the Supervenience Argument? Why aren't general facts free for the eating?

The mystery is solved as soon as one realizes that Armstrong has a non-standard notion of supervenience, at least as applied to propositions. He defines supervenience in terms of possible worlds as follows: "*Q* supervenes on *P* if and only if there are *P*-worlds and all *P*-worlds are *Q*-worlds."[33] In this definition, '*Q*' and '*P*' may range over any manner of entity. But when applied to (contingent) propositions, the definition amounts to equating 'supervenience' with 'entailment' (between single propositions), rather than what is standardly called 'supervenience'—namely, global supervenience.[34] Thus—returning now and henceforth to standard usage—Armstrong applies the doctrine of the ontological free lunch only to entailment, not to (global) supervenience; he would not use the doctrine to support the Supervenience Argument. On the contrary, according to Armstrong, because the General is not

---

[31] Armstrong (1997: 12–13).

[32] Armstrong (1989a: 94). Specifically, Armstrong concedes that two worlds could not "be exactly alike in all lower-order states of affairs" and yet differ in their "totality states of affairs". For Armstrong's account of totality states of affairs—his version of general facts—see his (1997: ch. 13).

[33] Armstrong (1997: 11) seems to be aware that his use of supervenience is, in some way, non-standard. He writes: "supervenience *in my sense* [my emphasis] amounts to entity *P entailing* [his emphasis] the entity *Q*, but with the entailment restricted to the cases where *P* is possible".

[34] Given the proliferation of supervenience notions, it is with some reluctance that I label any "non-standard". But the classic formulations of supervenience are *discernibility* theses—there can be no difference of one sort without a difference of some other sort—not *entailment* theses. (Two *loci classici* are Hare (1952: 145) and Davidson (1970: 88).) Even Kim, who promulgated entailment formulations for "strong" and "weak" supervenience, called the discernibility formulations "canonical" (1987: 80). See also the following footnote.

entailed by the Particular, one must pay with an ontology of general facts.

I return now to the question: how exactly are supervenience and entailment related to one another? Are there conditions, say, on the base propositions—conditions not satisfied in the present case—under which these notions do coincide? In comparing supervenience and entailment it is important to compare like with like: local with local, global with global. For maximum generality, I will compare global with global. The definitions, for arbitrary classes of propositions A and B, are as follows. (Recall, the A-truths (B-truths) at a world are all and only those propositions in A (B) that are true at the world.)

> A *globally supervenes* on B iff for any worlds w and w', if the B-truths at w coincide with the B-truths at w', then the A-truths at w coincide with the A-truths at w'.
>
> A is *globally entailed by* B iff for any world w, the B-truths at w entail the A-truths at w.

Or, equivalently, unpacking for easy comparison:

> A is *globally entailed by* B iff for any worlds w and w', if every B-truth at w is a B-truth at w', then every A-truth at w is an A-truth at w'.

Clearly, entailment is a stronger notion than supervenience:

> *Claim*: Whenever A is globally entailed by B, A globally supervenes on B as well.
>
> *Proof*: Suppose A is globally entailed by B. Consider any two worlds, w and w', whose B-truths coincide. Then, every B-truth at w is a B-truth at w', and every B-truth at w' is a B-truth at w. Since A is globally entailed by B, this gives: every A-truth at w is an A-truth at w', and every A-truth at w' is an A-truth at w. In other words, the A-truths at w and at w' coincide, as was to be shown.

For an example where both global entailment and global supervenience hold, let B be the class of atomic propositions, and A the closure of B under (finite or infinite) conjunction. (That is, A is the smallest class that contains B, and contains all conjunctions of whatever it contains.)

We already have before us one example—the atomic propositions and the general propositions—where supervenience holds and entailment fails. For a second, more revealing, example, let B again be the class of atomic propositions, and let A be the class of all denials of atomic propositions. Supervenience holds because whenever worlds assign the same truth value to propositions, they assign the same truth value to their denials. But entailment fails to hold: any two worlds, one of which is a (vertical or horizontal) expansion of the other, provide a counterexample. Consideration of this example suggests a simple condition under which supervenience and entailment coincide:

Claim: Suppose that B is closed under denial: the denial of any proposition in B is in B. Then: if A globally supervenes on B, A is globally entailed by B.

Proof: Suppose B is closed under denial, and that A globally supervenes on B. Let w and w' be such that every B-truth at w is a B-truth at w'. Then, also, every B-falsehood at w is a B-falsehood at w'. For let Z be any B-falsehood at w. Not Z is a B-truth at w (because B is closed under denial), and so *not* Z is a B-truth at w', making Z a B-falsehood at w'. Thus, the B-truths at w and w' coincide. Since A globally supervenes on B, the A-truths at w and at w' coincide as well, from which it follows that every A-truth at w is an A-truth at w', as was to be shown.

We are now in a position to see why supervenience and entailment often can be, and are, substituted for one another without ontological consequence. The majority of global supervenience theses on the market involve base propositions that are closed under denial; so, for ontological purposes, it wouldn't matter if the corresponding global entailment thesis were considered instead.[35] Thus, one often takes the qualitative propositions as the base and asks whether the laws of nature, or

---

[35] In Kim's seminal work on formulations of supervenience, the base properties and supervenient properties were assumed to be closed under Boolean operations. That allowed Kim to prove the equivalence of the discernibility and entailment formulations for "strong" and "weak" supervenience (1984: 64; 1987: 81–2.) (What I have called "global entailment", of course, is the entailment formulation that corresponds to global supervenience.) Others, however, have sometimes been less careful in their discussions of supervenience. For example, Chalmers (1996: ch. 2), in an influential discussion, introduces supervenience (applied to properties) as a discernibility thesis (p. 33), but then claims that "in general, when B-properties supervene logically on A-properties, we can say that the A-facts *entail* the B-facts" (p. 36, his emphasis). Moreover, he explicitly does not take the A-properties and B-properties to be closed under denial: "supervenience theses [for capturing materialism] should apply only to *positive* facts and properties" (p. 40, his emphasis). Later, supervenience is *redefined*, in effect, as a (local) entailment thesis because the original discernibility thesis is deemed inadequate to capture the ontological thesis of

counterfactuals, or propositions about causation, or about chance, globally supervene. Since the qualitative propositions are closed under denial, they supervene just in case they are entailed. Similarly, supervenience of the mental on the physical, or the evaluative on the descriptive, could just as well be presented in terms of entailment. But when the base propositions are the atomic propositions, as in the case at hand, supervenience and entailment come apart. Now it matters whether it is supervenience, or only entailment, that entitles one to an ontological free lunch.

V. THE SUPERVENIENCE CRITERION DEFENDED: THE SUBJECT MATTER PRINCIPLE

In this section, I defend the Supervenience Argument: general truths supervene on atomic truths; therefore, general facts need not, and should not, be added to the fundamental inventory of what there is. There are two familiar obstacles to arguments of this sort: one having to do with the relation between supervenience and determination (or dependence), the other having to do with the relation between supervenience and reduction. I will take them in turn.

Ontological determination, I said earlier, supports such locutions as "in virtue of": the determined propositions hold or fail to hold *in virtue of* the holding or failing to hold of the determining propositions. It has often, and rightly, been pointed out that supervenience cannot by itself be taken to be such a relation of ontological determination.[36] Supervenience is *necessary covariation*: if the truth values of the supervenient propositions vary between two worlds, then the truth values of the base propositions must vary between them as well. Necessary covariation, however, is not asymmetric. There are classes of propositions such that each necessarily covaries with the other. But, certainly, we would not want to say that each ontologically determines the other. For example,

materialism. I suspect a typical reader will not be aware that the original discernibility notion of supervenience has been replaced by a non-equivalent entailment notion (also called "supervenience"). Another example: Horgan (1993: 566–7) uses the discernibility and entailment formulations interchangeably without (explicitly) making any closure assumption that would justify such usage. For further discussion of how the discernibility and entailment notions differ, and why they should be kept apart, see McLaughlin (1995: 24–30).

[36] See especially Kim (1990: 142–9).

the denials of atomic propositions supervene on the atomic propositions; but also *vice versa*. Yet, surely, it is the atomic propositions that are ontologically basic, not their denials. Thus, supervenience, characterized as necessary covariation, falls short of ontological determination.

So far, so good. But here approaches to the problem diverge. The approach I favor asks: what must be added to supervenience to get ontological determination? How is ontological determination to be *analyzed* in terms of supervenience? The other approach rejects attempts at analysis. Supervenience, it is claimed, is a superficial relation that must be *explained* by some deeper, metaphysical relation of ontological determination. On this approach, to try to analyze ontological determination in terms of supervenience would be to put things wrong way around.[37]

I reject the second approach. Primitive ontological determination is dark and mysterious, and primitive modality, to boot. Why buy into the framework of possible worlds if not to rid the world of such creatures of darkness? Otherwise, one buys the dog and does the barking oneself.

How, then, might ontological determination be analyzed? Although I have no detailed analysis to offer, I think the ingredients of a correct analysis are clear enough. We need here, as in so many other analytic endeavors, the notion of a fundamental, or perfectly natural, property or relation. But since we are concerned with supervenience of *propositions*, rather than properties and relations, we will need a derived notion of fundamental that applies to classes of propositions. Then, a plausible sufficient condition on ontological determination can be formulated: A is ontologically determined by B if B is fundamental, and A supervenes on B. This condition, of course, is quite limited in application; but it will be enough for moving on with.

First, let us see how this partial analysis applies to our example with symmetric supervenience. We say: the denials of atomic propositions hold or fail to hold *in virtue of* the holding or failing to hold of the atomic propositions, not the reverse. Why? Surely, the class of atomic propositions is a fundamental class; it consists entirely of predications of fundamental properties and relations. Although supervenience goes in both directions—either class of propositions is logically definable in terms of the other using Boolean negation—only one direction corresponds with the true order of analysis. Fundamentalness of the base propositions supplies the direction, and turns supervenience into

---

[37] This is more or less the view Kim (1993: 165–9) takes.

ontological determination. Nothing more is needed to justify use of the "in virtue of" locution.

The partial analysis applies to the case of general propositions in exactly the same way: the general propositions are ontologically determined by the atomic propositions because the atomic propositions are fundamental, and whatever supervenes on what is fundamental is ontologically determined by it. Note that the argument does not require a *premise* that the general propositions are *not* fundamental. Perhaps we start out unsure whether (some of) the general propositions are fundamental. After the supervenience thesis is established we *conclude* that they are not. For, a constraint on any correct analysis of 'fundamental' applied to classes of propositions is: if two (non-overlapping) classes of propositions are fundamental, neither supervenes on the other.

Some philosophers claim to find the distinction between properties and relations that are fundamental, and those that are not, mysterious, whether couched within a realist theory of universals or tropes, or a nominalist theory of natural properties and relations, or objective resemblance. An analysis of ontological determination in terms of fundamental properties and relations would leave them still in the dark. But, even to these philosophers I can say: better one mystery than two, and there is no hope of running an analysis in the other direction. Moreover, although these philosophers may endorse some primitive modal notions, and make use of them in constructing a framework of possible worlds, once that framework is available they will presumably want to hold the line and analyze further modal notions, such as ontological determination, in terms of possible worlds and non-modal notions. The notion of fundamentality, being non-modal, meets that standard.

The second familiar problem involves the relation between supervenience and reduction. I have claimed that, under the right conditions, supervenience goes hand in hand with ontological determination. But ontological determination, as characterized, is a relation of conceptual or analytic priority; I have done nothing to justify my use of the adjective 'ontological'. Let it be granted that the general propositions hold or fail to hold in virtue of the atomic propositions holding or failing to hold. Why should this have any ontological consequence as to the existence of general facts?

Philosophers who make use of notions of supervenience in their theories and analyses appear to be divided by this issue into two camps: roughly half take supervenience to be a reductive relation (at least when it is assumed the base propositions are fundamental), roughly half take it to be non-reductive.[38] Indeed, for the former being reductive is essential to supervenience (when the base propositions are fundamental), for the latter being compatible with non-reduction is essential. Strange goings on! Sometimes, no doubt, the disagreement is superficial: different notions of reduction are being invoked, or restricted supervenience theses are at stake. Here, of course, only ontological reduction and unrestricted supervenience theses (quantifying over all worlds) are at issue. But even when the discussion is narrowed in this way, a fundamental disagreement sometimes remains. What might it be?

What provides the link between supervenience and ontological reduction, I think, is (a version of) the Humean denial of necessary connections between distinct existents. Disagreement on the Humean principle, then, is a likely source of disagreement on the relation between supervenience and reduction. (It is no accident that the modern champion of the Humean denial, David Lewis, is also a chief proponent of the reductionist camp!) Whenever one class of propositions supervenes on another, there are necessary connections between the subject matters of the two classes. The only way to avoid such necessary connections is to maintain that the subject matter of the two classes is not distinct.

Here is a way of making these ideas more precise. I will need the notion of a subject matter of a class of propositions: all the entities that the propositions are about, in one sense of 'about'. Say that a (non-empty) class of actual or possible entities E is a *subject matter* for a (non-empty) class of propositions A iff the existing or failing to exist of members of E entails the truth or falsity of members of A. More exactly, where X is any (contingent) proposition saying for each member of E whether or not that member exists, and Z is any proposition in A: E is a *subject matter* for A iff either X entails Z or X entails *not* Z.[39] (E is

---

[38] Lewis and Armstrong are chief proponents of the reductionist view. Lewis's most complete statement is in "Reduction of Mind" (1994: 412–15); Armstrong states his view in (1989a: 103–5) and (1997: 12–13). As we have seen, however, Armstrong applies his "doctrine of the ontological free lunch" to entailment, not to (what I have been calling) supervenience when it differs from entailment. The widespread view that supervenience is compatible with non-reduction was promoted, in large part, by Davidson (1970).

[39] My use of "subject matter" here, as the class of entities the propositions are about, should not be confused with David Lewis's related but ontologically non-committal use of "subject matter" according to which subject matters are partitions of logical space,

a *subject matter* for a single proposition P iff E is a subject matter for $\{P\}$.) Note that this is an *intensional* notion of subject matter. In one sense of 'about', if asked what the proposition, *there are no unicorns*, is about, I correctly answer (as a thing theorist): "nothing" (assuming there are no actual unicorns). In another sense, I should answer: "all actual and possible unicorns". It is the latter sense that I have in mind. Note also that subject matters are not required to be minimal, much less unique.[40] Indeed, when E is a subject matter for A, every class that includes E is also a subject matter for A; the class of all actual and possible entities is a subject matter for any class of propositions (assuming it has a subject matter at all).

It might be useful to present some elementary facts about subject matters that follow immediately from the definition. First, any subject matter for a proposition P is also a subject matter for its denial, *not P*, and vice versa. Second, if D is a subject matter for a proposition P and E is a subject matter for a proposition Q, then the union of D and E is a subject matter both for the conjunction, *P and Q*, and for the disjunction, *P or Q*. Third, any (non-empty) class is a subject matter for a necessary or an impossible proposition. Finally, if D is a subject matter for a class of propositions A, and E is a subject matter for a class of propositions B, then the union of D and E is a subject matter for the union of A and B.

Now, I would like to put forward for consideration, by thing theorists and factualists alike, the following fundamental principle of ontology:

Subject Matter Principle. Every (non-empty) class of propositions has a subject matter.[41]

This principle expresses in a direct way the (strong) Supervenience of Truth on Being.[42] Factualists should find this principle agreeable; if

---

roughly, all the ways a world could be with respect to the subject matter. See his "Relevant Implication" (1988).

[40] In special cases, a proposition will not have a minimal subject matter. Consider, for example, *there exist infinitely many things*. Any "co-finite" class of *possibilia* is a subject matter for this proposition, that is, any class consisting of the entire universe of *possibilia* with finitely many entities removed. (The parallel observation that this proposition lacks a minimal class of truthmakers is due, I believe, to Greg Restall.)

[41] If the identity of indiscernible worlds is rejected—as it is by me in my (2001)—then the Subject Matter Principle must be restricted to propositions that never differ in truth value between indiscernible worlds. (Qualitative propositions, for an anti-Haecceitist.)

[42] Not to be confused with the weaker version of the Supervenience of Truth on Being considered earlier which asserts only that Truth supervenes on Particular Truth. See n. 29.

anything it is too weak—weaker, for example, than the Truthmaker Principle accepted by many factualists (see section VI). Thing theorists, however, will find the principle plausible only if they are willing to deviate from ordinary ascriptions of essential properties: when determining which things make up the subject matter for a class of propositions, intrinsic nature must be taken to be essential; a counterpart of a thing is always a duplicate of the thing. Otherwise, the thing theorist will be hard-pressed to find a subject matter for predications of properties ordinarily not taken to be essential, such as color or shape applied to macroscopic objects: the existence of some particular red ball will not entail that the ball is red. This is a substantial commitment, but one that I happily accept. I thus endorse the Subject Matter Principle.

How does the notion of subject matter apply to atomic and general propositions? Consider an atomic proposition, a *is* F. For a thing theorist, a itself provides a subject matter for a *is* F (assuming a is essentially F). For a factualist, a subject matter is provided by the atomic fact, a's being F. (If the proposition a *is* F is false, then a's being F is a merely possible fact.) Now consider a general proposition, *everything is* F, for a fundamental property F. For a thing theorist, its subject matter is the class of all actual and possible *non-Fs* (assuming that a *non-F* is essentially a *non-F*). What is its subject matter for a factualist? It follows immediately from the definitions that if A supervenes on B, and E is a subject matter for B, then E is a subject matter for A. Applying this to the case at hand: The general propositions supervene on the atomic propositions. The atomic facts, according to the factualist, are a subject matter for the atomic propositions. Therefore, according to the factualist, the atomic facts are a subject matter for the general propositions. If we take the Subject Matter Principle to be our guide in the ontological enterprise—as I think we should—we arrive already at the weak conclusion of the Supervenience Argument, that general facts are not *needed* in addition to atomic facts. For, the notion of a subject matter provides a clear sense in which the atomic facts are an *ontological*

The Subject Matter Principle is roughly equivalent to Bigelow's (1988: 133) weakened Truthmaker Axiom: "If something is true, then it would not be possible for it to be false unless either certain things were to exist which don't, or else certain things had not existed which do." It also turns out to be equivalent to a simple (one-way) difference-making principle: for any two (discernible) worlds w and w', either something exists at w but not at w', or something exists at w' but not at w. For an illuminating discussion of the relation between various truthmaking and difference-making principles, see Lewis (2001).

ground for the general propositions: the truth or falsity of any general proposition is fixed by the existing or failing to exist of the atomic facts. That nothing more should be required of an ontological ground will be further argued in section VI.

What of the strong conclusion of the Supervenience Argument, that general facts do not exist? The Subject Matter Principle, by itself, is compatible with there being a realm of general facts alongside the atomic facts—a second, separate subject matter for the general propositions. If ontological determination is to make the reduction of that which supervenes not merely permissible, but obligatory, we will need to invoke, in addition to the Subject Matter Principle, some version of the Humean denial of necessary connections.

Say that two subject matters are *distinct* just in case no member of one is identical with, or overlaps, any member of the other. I propose calling on the Humean denial in the following convenient form:

Non-Distinctness of Subject Matters. No contingent proposition has two distinct subject matters.

The Non-Distinctness of Subject Matters follows from the Humean denial. For suppose some contingent proposition P has two distinct subject matters, D and E. Then, whether the entities in D exist or fail to exist is not independent of whether the entities in E exist or fail to exist.[43] That is to say, there are necessary connections between distinct existents.

How does Non-Distinctness of Subject Matters apply to the Supervenience of the General on the Particular? As already noted, for the factualist, the atomic facts (actual and possible) are a subject matter for the general propositions. Now suppose there existed a general fact distinct from the atomic facts. Since, necessarily, a fact exists if and only if its corresponding proposition is true, it follows that this general fact would all by itself be a subject matter for the general proposition to which it corresponds. But then this general proposition would have two distinct subject matters—the general fact and the atomic facts—violating the Non-Distinctness of Subject Matters. It follows—at least for the factualist with strong Humean scruples—that there are no general facts.

---

[43] Why? Let X be a proposition entailing P that says, for each entity in D, whether it exists or fails to exist; such a proposition exists because P is contingent and D is a subject matter for P. Let Y be a proposition entailing *not P* that says, for each entity in E, whether it exists or fails to exist; such a proposition exists because *not P* is contingent and E is a subject matter for P. X and Y are incompatible.

The factualist may well balk at this last step in the Supervenience Argument. Humean scruples come more easily to a thing theorist than a factualist. For one thing, there is the perennial problem of determinates and determinables. More relevant to the present case, there is the problem that general facts, were they to exist, would by their very nature stand in necessary connections with particular facts. So any argument against general facts that invokes the Humean denial can fairly be accused of begging the question. I would be content, however, in conversation with such a factualist, to retreat from the claim that general facts do not exist to the claim that general facts are not needed in addition to atomic facts. Atomic facts are subject matter enough for the general propositions.[44]

VI. THE NON-ENTAILMENT CRITERION REJECTED: THE TRUTHMAKER PRINCIPLE

In the previous section, I argued that even a factualist has reason to accept (at least the weak conclusion of) the Supervenience Argument and deny the need for general facts. In this section, I examine the Non-Entailment Argument, and try to pinpoint where it goes wrong. The Non-Entailment Argument, recall, is: the general truths are not entailed by the atomic truths; therefore, general facts are needed in addition to atomic facts. A natural way to try to bridge the gap between failure of entailment and the need for general facts is to invoke a truthmaker principle—every truth has a truthmaker—and argue that general facts (or, at any rate, non-atomic facts) are needed to serve as truthmakers for general truths. The Non-Entailment Argument then becomes a species of the Truthmaker Argument frequently employed by Armstrong to support the existence of facts ("states of affairs").[45]

To begin, we need a precise formulation of the Truthmaker Principle. I will begin with a "local" version that applies only to the actual world: *actual* truths have *actually existing* truthmakers. And I will consider the weaker, plural version which demands, not that there be a single entity

---

[44] Perhaps the factualist will be swayed instead by Ockham's razor to abandon general facts. But I, for one, do not think Ockham's razor has any force in metaphysics.

[45] See especially (1997: 13–14, 113–19, 196–201). Armstrong's rendition of the Non-Entailment Argument is extremely brief, though it is clear that the Truthmaker Principle plays a crucial supporting role.

that serves as a truthmaker, but only that there be some plurality of entities that serve jointly as truthmakers.[46] A plurality of entities *makes true* a proposition when their joint existence entails the proposition. Restating in terms of worlds and classes gives: a (non-empty) class of actual entities E provides *truthmakers* for a (non-empty) class of truths A iff every world at which every member of E exists is a world at which every member of A is true. (E provides *truthmakers* for a single truth Z iff E provides *truthmakers* for $\{Z\}$.) Then,

Truthmaker Principle. Every (non-empty) class of truths has truthmakers.[47]

For the factualist, the atomic facts are truthmakers for the atomic truths. In this case, the correspondence between truthmakers and truths is one–one. In general, however, the correspondence is one–many and many–one. For example: a truthmaker for a truth is also a truthmaker for the many disjunctions with that truth as one of its disjuncts (one–many); but also an existential truth, *something is F*, for fundamental F, has as truthmaker the many atomic facts Fa, Fb, and so on (many–one). The Truthmaker Principle thus supports a "correspondence theory of truth" according to which a proposition is true just in case there exists some fact (or facts) that bears the truthmaker relation to the proposition; but it is a stripped-down correspondence theory, because the facts are sparse, and the correspondence provided by the truthmaker relation is many–many, and not one–one.

The Truthmaker Principle, if sound, can bridge the gap in the Non-Entailment Argument. For suppose, for *reductio*, that the atomic facts were all the facts. By the Truthmaker Principle, the general truths must have truthmakers. So, the atomic facts would be truthmakers for the general truths; that is, the existence of the atomic facts would entail the general truths. But, necessarily, an atomic fact exists just in case the corresponding atomic proposition is true. So, the atomic truths would entail the general truths, contradicting the Non-Entailment Thesis (assuming there are contingent general truths). Therefore, the

---

[46] Whether or not this is equivalent to requiring a single truthmaker for every truth depends on one's views on unrestricted mereological composition, and mereological essentialism.

[47] Note that the truthmaking relation here defined is uninteresting for necessary truths: any (non-empty) class of entities is a truthmaker for a necessary proposition. But it does no harm to include this case. For discussion, see Restall (1996).

atomic facts cannot be all the facts: the general truths must have truthmakers beyond the atomic facts—presumably, for the factualist, general facts. With the Non-Entailment Argument thus expanded, it is clear that the Truthmaker Principle goes hand in hand with the view that failure of entailment is what matters for ontology, not the holding of supervenience.

At this point, one might expect that a proponent of the Supervenience Argument would simply reject the Truthmaker Principle. But it is not that simple. An enlightened thing theorist can, and should, accept the Truthmaker Principle, properly interpreted. Ironically, it is only the factualist, I shall argue, who should reject the demand for truthmakers.

I begin by considering the Truthmaker Principle from the thing theorist's perspective, asking: what *thing* (or *things*) could make a general truth true? Take, for example, the general proposition that all planets are less than 10^{30}kg in mass. Suppose for the sake of argument that this proposition is true. The planets, whether taken singly or jointly, seem deficient as truthmaker: all the planets might exist just as they are and yet an extra jumbo planet greater than 10^{30}kg exist as well. A truthmaker for this proposition must somehow include, not only the planets, but the spaces between the planets. But such a truthmaker is not far to seek. Although no proper part of the world will do as truthmaker for this or any other (contingent) general truth, the world as a whole does the job just fine, where the world is understood to be the biggest thing. The world as a whole makes it true that there are no planets greater than 10^{30}kg simply by having no such planets among its parts.

Armstrong would disagree: no thing could be a truthmaker for a (contingent) general truth; since the world is indeed a truthmaker for all truths, the world is not a thing. Why couldn't a thing be truthmaker for a general truth, according to Armstrong? Because any thing might have been a proper part of some bigger thing. If the world is a thing, then we will have to say that the world might have been a proper part of a bigger world. (Consider, for example, a possible world containing a series of cosmic oscillations—big bang, big crunch, big bang, and so on—and suppose one of the cycles is a duplicate of our world.) If our world might have been a proper part of a bigger world, then it might have existed in its entirety while there also existed outside its bounds a planet greater than 10^{30}kg in mass. So, the existence of the world does not entail that no such planet exists. To ensure truthmakers for general propositions,

Armstrong is driven to introduce "totality facts", higher-order facts that exist in addition to the atomic facts that constitute things.

But the thing theorist who accepts the inconstancy of *de re* modality has a ready response. Though we say that the world might have been part of a bigger world, we also say, with no less propriety, that the world might have been bigger than it is. (For example, the world might have contained a series of cosmic oscillations.) Both of these claims are naturally and straightforwardly interpreted as modality *de re*; moreover, the very same possible world (say, with cosmic oscillations) can serve to establish both claims. To establish the first claim, we identify the world by intrinsic character alone, so that counterparts of the world must be duplicates of the world. To establish the second claim, we identify in part by extrinsic character, taking it to be essential to a world that it be a world, that is, the biggest thing there is; on this way of identifying, counterparts of worlds must be worlds. Don't ask: which is the *right* way of identifying, the way that captures the *real* essence of the world? Rather, follow the lead of ordinary discourse and let attributions of essence vary with context. It is ordinary indeed, and unobjectionable, to say that general truths are made true by the world as a whole, all the while understanding by 'world' the aggregate of all things. In this "truthmaking" context, both intrinsic and extrinsic aspects of the world are taken to be essential: only duplicates of our world that are themselves worlds are counterparts of our world.[48]

If we interpret the Truthmaker Principle in a way that allows the extrinsic character of the truthmaker to be relevant, then the truthmaker relation is not an internal relation: it does not supervene on the intrinsic character of its *relata*. Armstrong objects that the truthmaker relation must be internal. Why? I can discern two arguments in his writing. In one, he suggests that if the truthmaker relation is not internal, then we will have to allow, a priori, that "anything may be truthmaker for any truth".[49] But here Armstrong seems to have conflated "not internal" with "*purely* external". A *purely* external

---

[48] Again—as with the Subject Matter Principle—if the identity of indiscernible worlds is rejected, then the Truthmaker Principle should be restricted to propositions that are true at all worlds indiscernible from the actual world. (Of course, stipulating that identity is essential to worlds, that a world has only itself as counterpart, would trivialize the Truthmaker Principle.) For an extended discussion of the essential properties of worlds, but one from a rigid essentialist perspective, see Bigelow (1990).

[49] Armstrong (1997: 198).

relation, indeed, is not in any way constrained by the intrinsic character of its *relata* (taken separately). For example, if distance relations are purely external, then any two distinct things can stand in any distance relation to one another. But one can deny that a relation is internal without denying that it is constrained by the intrinsic character of its *relata*. From the fact that intrinsic character isn't *all* that matters, one cannot conclude that intrinsic character doesn't matter at all. When I say that the world, *qua* world, has as part of its essence the extrinsic property of being the biggest thing, that is compatible with saying that some or all of its intrinsic nature is also essential. Thus, one can deny that the truthmaker relation is internal without holding that "anything may be truthmaker for any truth".

A second argument that the truthmaker relation must be internal is hinted at in a number of places.[50] Suppose, the argument goes, that an entity may be a truthmaker for a proposition in virtue of its *extrinsic* character. Then the entity is not by itself sufficient as truthmaker, it is only sufficient in conjunction with something else; that something else must also be brought into the truthmaker. But here I suspect a conflation between "extrinsic" and "relational".[51] Relational properties are always extrinsic; but extrinsic properties need not be relational. The property, being the biggest thing, is extrinsic (i.e. not intrinsic) because it can differ between duplicates. But it is not relational: an entity need not stand in any (external) relation to something else in order to have it. One cannot conclude from the fact that truthmaking depends on an extrinsic property of a thing—for example, the property of being the biggest thing—that there exists some entity distinct from the thing that must be "brought into the truthmaker".

I conclude that, so far as general truths are concerned, a thing theorist is free to accept the Truthmaker Principle by holding, at least in truthmaking contexts, that the world is essentially a world. Does this do anything to advance the conclusion of the Non-Entailment Argument, as recently expanded? Even if we suppose that the thing theorist accepts atomic facts, say, by identifying them with the tropes that things are composed of, one only gets so far as the conclusion that some truthmaker is needed in addition to the atomic facts. For the thing theorist, that

---

[50] e.g. ibid. 115–16.
[51] Armstrong uses "intrinsic" and "non-relational" interchangeably throughout his work. See e.g. ibid. 91–2.

extra truthmaker is just the world, the biggest thing. Note that the world may be an *extra* truthmaker even if it is identified with the aggregate of the atomic facts: the world *qua* aggregate can be allotted different truthmaking capabilities than the atomic facts taken plurally (or, equivalently, than the class of atomic facts).[52]

Although I accept the Truthmaker Principle, I accord it no fundamental ontological importance. I say this not because taking the world to be truthmaker for every (contingent) truth, as I do, trivializes the principle. It does not. (For example, if someone insisted, *per impossibile*, that there were brute counterfactual or dispositional truths, I would not allow that the world made them true; for, on my view, the fundamental properties and relations that hold among parts of the world are all categorical, not modal.) The Truthmaker Principle lacks ontological importance because, although it is true, and even known a priori to be true, it is not *necessarily* true, whereas all fundamental ontological principles hold necessarily. And because it is not necessarily true, the connection it makes between failure of entailment and the existence of extra truthmakers is not necessary either.

How can the Truthmaker Principle fail to be necessary? Here I need to return briefly to my view, introduced above, that not all possibilities for actuality are possible worlds. Consider again Leibniz's God surveying the realm of possible worlds. I said that an industrious God might have actualized more than one world, even all the worlds. I say no less that a lazy God might have actualized no world at all, in which case nothing contingent would have existed: no world, and no truthmakers for the contingent truth, *nothing exists*. There is thus a possibility (though not a possible *world*) at which the Truthmaker Principle is false: the possibility of nothing.[53] However, because the possibility of

---

[52] I suppose a thing theorist could introduce a limited multiplicity of truthmakers for general truths by taking the aggregate of all the Fs to be a truthmaker for the general truth, all Fs are Gs (for any G). This could be done by saying that, in truthmaking contexts, the extrinsic property, including all the Fs, is an essential property of the aggregate of all the Fs. Again, these extra truthmakers would be no addition to the thing theorist's ontology. But here, I fear, the thing theorist can no longer claim any support from ordinary discourse. And an awkward problem arises in case all Fs are Gs and there is only one F.

[53] For some defense of this view, see my (2001: esp. 47–9). To accommodate the possibility of nothing, the analysis of possibility must be further expanded to read: a proposition is *possible* iff it is true at some world, or some plurality of worlds, or at nothing, where a proposition *is true at nothing* (intuitively) iff it would have been true had no world been actualized. All (contingent) existential propositions are false at nothing; all universal propositions are vacuously true.

nothing is controversial—and, in particular, rejected by Armstrong[54]—I will not suppose it in discussing the factualist view.

I turn now to consider the Truthmaker Principle—and the Non-Entailment Argument—from the factualist perspective. The strategy of holding on to the Truthmaker Principle by allowing the world to be composed entirely of atomic facts while taking the world nonetheless to be a truthmaker for general truths is not available to the factualist. For, as noted in the introduction, for any fact, necessarily, the fact exists if and only if its corresponding proposition is true. I take this to be constitutive of what facts are *vis-à-vis* their role as truthmakers. But now suppose that the world is merely the aggregate—i.e. the conjunction—of all the atomic facts. Then, necessarily, if all the atomic facts exist, then the proposition that is the conjunction of all the atomic truths is true, and so the world exists as well—even if additional atomic facts exist. The world could not have any (horizontally or vertically) exclusive essential properties, such as the property: being the *totality* of atomic facts. And so the world could not be the "extra truthmaker" required by the Non-Entailment Argument. The factualist, then, must choose: accept the Truthmaker Principle and posit general facts, or reject the Truthmaker Principle.

I have already argued, in effect, that a factualist with a Humean bent should reject the Truthmaker Principle. In the previous section, I invoked the Humean denial of necessary connections to defend the Supervenience Argument. If the Supervenience Argument is sound, the Non-Entailment Argument is not, and, for the factualist, the culprit must be the Truthmaker Principle. But the Non-Entailment Argument can be attacked directly without relying on Humean principles. According to the Non-Entailment Argument, general facts are needed because the general truths are not entailed by the atomic truths. But when we look more closely at *why* such entailment fails—when we look to a *proof* of the Non-Entailment Thesis—we find nothing to support the need for general facts. Entailment fails because there are two worlds, w and w', such that all the atomic truths at w are true at w', but some general truth at w is false at w'. What grounds this difference in general truths between w and w'? There are atomic propositions true at w' that are not true at w. Thus, for the factualist, there are entities that exist at

---

[54] See his (1989a: 24–5).

w'—atomic facts—that do not exist at w. This difference in the existence of atomic facts is all that the proof needs to ground the difference in general truths, and establish the failure of entailment. No mention of general facts here: nothing beyond atomic facts need be posited to exist either at w or at w'.

The argument generalizes. Consider any case in which a class of propositions A supervenes on, but is not (globally) entailed by, a class of propositions B. Then, by failure of (global) entailment, there are worlds w and w' such that every B-truth at w is a B-truth at w', but some A-truth at w is not an A-truth at w'. What grounds the difference in A-truth at w and w'? Supervenience ensures that the difference can be grounded entirely in the subject matter for B. For, by supervenience, since w and w' differ with respect to A-truth, they must differ with respect to B-truth. Whatever entities, then, ground the difference in B-truth also ground the difference in A-truth: no special subject matter for A is required. Thus, whenever (global) entailment fails and supervenience holds, there is a full and adequate explanation for the failure of entailment in terms of the difference in B-truth, and the subject matter of B.

If the factualist rejects the Non-Entailment Argument, as I have argued she should, the Truthmaker Principle goes with it. I recommend that the factualist accept in its place the Subject Matter Principle of the previous section. To compare these two principles properly we need to consider the "global" version of the Truthmaker Principle that applies, not just to the actual world, but to all possible worlds:[55]

> *Global Truthmaker Principle.* For every (non-empty) class of propositions A and every world w, the A-truths at w have truthmakers at w.

(The truthmaking relation is now relativized to worlds: a (non-empty) class of (actual or possible) entities E provides *truthmakers* at w for a (non-empty) class of propositions A iff every member of E exists at w and, for any world v, if every member of E exists at v, then every member of A is true at v.)

> *Claim.* The Global Truthmaker Principle implies the Subject Matter Principle.

---

[55] On my view, it would be further generalized to apply to all possibilities for actuality.

Proof. Let A be any non-empty class of propositions, and Z any member of A. Let w be any world. By Global Truthmaker (and excluded middle), either Z has truthmakers at w or *not Z* has truthmakers at w. Let E_w^Z be any class that provides truthmakers for Z at w or that provides truthmakers for *not Z* at w. Let E^Z be $\cup_w E_w^Z$. We need to show that E^Z is a subject matter for Z. Consider any proposition X saying for each member of E^Z whether or not that member exists. If X is impossible, then it trivially entails Z (as well as *not Z*); so suppose that X is possible. X is compatible either with Z or with *not Z*. Suppose first that X is compatible with Z, and let v be a world at which both X and Z are true. Consider E_v^Z. X entails that each member of E_v^Z exists (since X is true at v, each member of E_v^Z exists at v, and E_v^Z is included in E^Z), which in turn entails Z (because E_v^Z provides truthmakers for Z). So, X entails Z. By a similar argument, if X is compatible with *not Z*, then X entails *not Z*. It follows that E^Z is a subject matter for Z. Finally, let E be $\cup_{Z\ in A} E^Z$. E is a subject matter for A, as was to be shown.

We have the following proportional analogy: the Subject Matter Principle is to supervenience as the (Global) Truthmaker Principle is to (global) entailment. If the factualist concedes that only failure of supervenience, not failure of (global) entailment, has ontological import, then she should accept only the Subject Matter Principle.

In the opening paragraph of this chapter I said—being intentionally vague—that, for the factualist, truth is determined by (some sort of) correspondence to the facts. If the factualist trades in the Truthmaker Principle for the Subject Matter Principle and allows that the atomic facts are all the (first-order) facts, what remains of correspondence? Even less, certainly, than the stripped-down correspondence supported by the Truthmaker Principle. Correspondence becomes more holistic: it can no longer be said, except in special cases, that an individual truth corresponds with anything less than all the facts. But it can still be said that truth in its entirety corresponds with the facts in their entirety: for any world, the (first-order) truths at that world are determined by the atomic facts that exist at the world. Moreover, this plural correspondence between truths and facts is one–one: worlds that differ with respect to (first-order) truth differ with respect to the existence of atomic facts as well. The correspondence relation is now, of course, a relation of supervenience, not entailment. Whether such plural correspondence is enough, terminologically speaking, to count as a "correspondence theory of truth", or a "factualist theory", is an empirical matter of usage. Metaphysically speaking, it is correspondence enough.[56]

University of Massachusetts Amherst

REFERENCES

Armstrong, D. M. (1989a) *A Combinatorial Theory of Possibility* (Cambridge: Cambridge University Press).
—— (1989b) *Universals: An Opinionated Introduction* (Bouldes, Colo.: Westview).
—— (1997) *A World of States of Affairs* (Cambridge: Cambridge University Press).
Bigelow, John (1988) *The Reality of Numbers* (Oxford: Oxford University Press).
—— (1990) "The World Essence", *Dialogue* 29: 205–17.
Bricker, Phillip (1996) "Isolation and Unification: The Realist Analysis of Possible Worlds", *Philosophical Studies* 84: 225–38.
—— (2001) "Island Universes and the Analysis of Modality", in G. Preyer and F. Siebelt (eds.), *Reality and Humean Supervenience: Essays on the Philosophy of David Lewis* (Lorham, Md.: Rowman & Littlefield), 27–55.
Chalmers, David J. (1996) *The Conscious Mind: In Search of a Fundamental Theory* (Oxford: Oxford University Press).
Davidson, Donald (1970) "Mental Events", in L. Foster and J. W. Swanson (eds.), *Experience and Theory*, (Amherst: University of Massachusetts Press); repr. in id., *Essays on Actions and Events* (Oxford: Oxford University Press, 1980), 207–25.
Hare, R. M. (1952) *The Language of Morals* (Oxford: Clarendon).
Hazen, Alan (1986) "A Fallacy in Ramsey", *Mind* 95: 496–8.
Horgan, Terence (1993) "From Supervenience to Superdupervenience: Meeting the Demands of a Material World", *Mind* 102: 555–86.
Kim, Jaegwon (1984) "Concepts of Supervenience", *Philosophy and Phenomenological Research* 45: 153–76; repr. in *Supervenience and Mind* (Cambridge: Cambridge University Press, 1993), 53–78.

---

[56] This paper was part of Metaphysical Mayhem VII at Syracuse University in August 2002 and was presented to the Philosophy Department at Arizona State University in February 2003. It expands on material presented to the Philosophy Department at New York University in February 1999. Thanks especially to Daniel Nolan, Laurie Paul, and Ted Sider for their comments.

—— (1987) " 'Strong' and 'Global' Supervenience Revisited", *Philosophy and Phenomenological Research* 48: 315–26; repr. in *Supervenience and Mind* (Cambridge: Cambridge University Press, 1993), 79–91.

—— (1990) "Supervenience as a Philosophical Concept", *Metaphilosophy* 21: 1–27; repr. in *Supervenience and Mind* (Cambridge: Cambridge University Press, 1993), 131–60.

—— (1993) "Postscripts on Supervenience", in *Supervenience and Mind* (Cambridge: Cambridge University Press), 161–71.

Lewis, David (1986) *On the Plurality of Worlds* (Oxford: Blackwell).

—— (1988) "Relevant Implication" *Theoria* 64: 161–74; repr. in *Papers in Philosophical Logic* (Cambridge: Cambridge University Press, 1998).

—— (1992) "Armstrong on Combinatorial Possibility", *The Australasian Journal of Philosophy* 70: 211–24; repr. in *Papers in Metaphysics and Epistemology* (Cambridge: Cambridge University Press, 1999).

—— (1994) "Reduction of Mind", in Samuel Guttenplan (ed.), *A Companion to the Philosophy of Mind* (Oxford: Blackwell), 412–31; repr. in *Papers in Metaphysics and Epistemology* (Cambridge: Cambridge University Press, 1999).

—— (2001) "Truthmaking and Difference-Making", *Noûs* 35: 602–15.

—— (2003) "Things *Qua* Truthmakers", in Hallvard Lillehammer and Gonzalo Rodriguez-Pereyra (eds.), *Real Metaphysics* (London: Routledge), 25–38.

McLaughlin, Brian P. (1995) "Varieties of Supervenience", in Elias Savellos and Umit Yalcin (eds.), *Supervenience: New Essays* (Cambridge: Cambridge University Press), 16–60.

Quine, W. V. O. (1960) "Variables Explained Away", repr. in *Selected Logic Papers* (Cambridge, Mass.: Harvard University Press, 1995).

Ramsey, F. P. (1927) "Facts and Propositions", repr. in *Foundations: Essays in Philosophy, Logic, Mathematics and Economics* (New York: Humanities Press, 1978), 40–57.

Restall, Greg (1996) "Truthmakers, Entailment and Necessity", *Australasian Journal of Philosophy* 74: 331–40.

Russell, Bertrand (1918) *The Philosophy of Logical Atomism*, repr. in Robert Charles Marsh (ed.) *Logic and Knowledge* (London: Routledge, 1992), 177–281.

Skyrms, Brian (1981) "Tractarian Nominalism", *Philosophical Studies* 40: 199–206.

Wittgenstein, Ludwig (1921) *Tractatus Logico-Philosophicus* trans. D. F. Pears and B. F. McGuinness (London: Routledge & Kegan Paul).

10. Epistemicism and Semantic Plasticity
John Hawthorne

Introduction

I shall endeavor in this essay to make vivid a kind of puzzle that arises when Timothy Williamson's epistemicist machinery[1] is applied to borderline cases of (a) personhood and (b) semantic properties. My aim will be to raise some concerns about his development of the epistemicist view, and then to explore an alternative way of thinking about epistemicism. What follows is very much a progress report on unfinished business, but I hope there is enough progress to warrant the report.

§1

Consider a sorites series in which a subject S has his hair removed, one hair at a time, beginning with a full head of hair, ending with no hair at all. At the beginning, S is clearly not bald. At the end, S is clearly bald. However, there will be occasions where S is neither clearly bald, nor clearly not bald: at those times, S is a borderline case of baldness. Williamson's epistemicism combines the following theses about borderline cases of baldness:

(1) The relevant instances of excluded middle hold. Supposing that our subject is now a borderline case of baldness, it is nevertheless true that

   S is bald or ~S is bald.

I am grateful for conversations with and comments from Cian Dorr, Hartry Field, Kit Fine, Hud Hudson, David Manley, Stephen Schiffer, Ted Sider, Ryan Wasserman, Peter van Inwagen, Dean Zimmerman, audiences at Oxford, MIT, NYU, and Syracuse, and especially Timothy Williamson.

[1] See his *Vagueness* (London: Routledge, 1994).

(2) Bivalence holds for any baldness ascription to S. Thus, whether or not S is now a borderline case of baldness
'S is bald' is true or 'S is bald' is false.

(3) If S is a borderline case of baldness, then we are unable to know whether or not S is bald.

(4) Not all ignorance is due to vagueness. In borderline cases, vagueness has a distinctive source, namely: if we had used the word 'bald' ever so slightly differently, we would have picked out a different property by 'bald'. We are insensitive to the ways that slight differences in usage make a difference to the semantic value of our terms. When ignorance is due to that kind of insensitivity, we suffer ignorance that is due to vagueness.

How does the kind of insensitivity in (4) make for ignorance? Well suppose 'bald' is true of S, but it is also true that if we had used the term 'bald' ever so slightly differently, 'bald' would have been false of S. If we are insensitive to the ways that slight differences in usage makes for a difference in semantic value, then insofar as we actually believe S is bald, there will be close worlds in which we make a mistake in a relevantly similar situation. Thus even if we believe that S is bald and get it right, we do not *know* that S is bald.

In a borderline case of baldness, (*a*) there are a plurality of candidate semantic values, where a semantic value is a candidate for 'bald' insofar as, for all we are able to know, it is the actual semantic value of the term 'bald', (*b*) one of the candidates is the actual semantic value, which in turn determines the actual truth value of the relevant baldness ascription, and (*c*) some of the candidates hold of the case at hand, and others do not. Here is a bit of terminology: let us say that a term is "semantically plastic" when (*a*) slight differences in usage make for differences in semantic value and (*b*) we are insensitive to the ways in which difference in usage makes for a difference in semantic value.

§2

Assuming that persons are material beings, it is natural to think that the predicate 'is a person' is vague. Here are four relevant considerations:

1. To begin: there is vagueness about when a person comes into existence. Even if, for example, one is convinced that a person

begins with conception, there will be vagueness at the beginnings of personhood owing to vagueness as to when conception actually takes place. (Think of the trajectory of sperm, slowly approaching and entering the egg. It is clearly a vague matter when conception occurs.) In general, all views about the beginnings of personhood use vague predicates in the favored criterion. Thus, even granting any given one of those views, vagueness along the temporal dimension will not disappear.
2. And unless one believes that persons enjoy life (or at least existence) everlasting, there will be vagueness as to when a person's existence comes to an end. Once one remembers that such predicates as 'dies' and 'is braindead' and so on are vague, the relevant thesis about persons should be obvious enough.
3. Further, there is vagueness as to where the spatial boundaries of a person lie. There are, for example, certain atoms in the vicinity of my surface such that it is a vague matter whether or not they are parts of me.
4. There is vagueness as to whether various less sophisticated beings count as people.

§3

Suppose that there is a speck of dirt—call it Tony—such that it is a vague matter whether or not the sentence 'The person sitting down has Tony as a part' (hereafter S1) is true. Let us try to describe the vagueness of this case using epistemicist machinery. What we should say, it seems, is that there are a multitude of candidate semantic values for the term 'person' such that the truth value of S1 differs according to which of those candidates is adopted as the interpretation of 'person'. The point presumably extends to personal pronouns. It will thus presumably also be a vague matter whether or not the sentence 'He has Tony as a part' (pointing at the person in the chair) is true (hereafter S2). And this will be because there is a range of candidate semantic values for 'he' such that the sentence differs in truth value according to which semantic value in the range is adopted. Suppose S2 is true. There will be a meaning that could very easily have been given to 'he' such that S2 is false.

This semantic picture invites us to posit a plentitude of overlapping objects in the vicinity of the chair. Only one of them falls within the extension of 'person'. Only one of them is the referent of the personal pronoun 'he'. Insofar as the object in question has Tony as a part, then S1 and S2 are true. But owing to semantic plasticity, there are a variety of candidate semantic values of 'person', each of which associates some object or other with the definite description 'The person in the chair'. While some of the candidate semantic values associate an object containing Tony as a part with the definite description 'The person in the chair', others will not.

Let us focus on two of the candidates, one containing Tony as a part, the other not. Call them Grubby and Clean. Suppose Grubby and not Clean falls within the actual extension of the term 'person' in English (though of course we would be unable to know this). Then S1 and S2 are both true. But there is a possible tribe that uses the word 'person' ever so slightly differently, so that Clean and not Grubby falls within the extension of the term 'person' in their mouths and S1 and S2 in their mouths are false. Such a tribe might even be actual. Pretend that there exists a tribe of Twinglish speakers that uses 'person' in such a way that 'person' is true of Clean and not Grubby. Then when a Twinglander says 'The person sitting in the chair has Tony as a part' he will express a false proposition even though we say something true.

There are a variety of overlapping objects on the chair. Only one of them is a person. That is, only one of them falls under the extension of the actual semantic value of 'person'. The same holds, presumably, for such predicates as 'thinks', 'talks', and so on. Only one of the objects thinks. Only one of them talks. The one that is the person is also the one that thinks and talks. Others of the overlapping objects fall within the extension of candidate semantic values for 'thinks', 'talks', and 'is a person' (in the sense of candidacy explained). Suppose Grubby thinks and talks. If our use of 'think' and 'talk' had been ever so slightly different in certain ways then 'think' and 'talk' would have applied to Clean. Let us say that an object thinks* iff it falls within the extension of one of the candidate semantic values for 'thinks'. We could similarly introduce the predicates 'person*' and 'talks*'. There are many objects on the chair that are persons*, which think*, and which talk*. But only one of them thinks, talks, and is a person.

Why do I insist that only one of the objects is a person? Well, I take it that as a feature of our usage we do not allow that many objects at a time are people when those objects mereologically overlap almost entirely. If semantic values are going to respect that aspect of usage then each candidate semantic value for 'person' will allow only one of the objects on the chair to fall within its extension.[2]

What makes, say, Grubby and not Clean the thinker? If we could know the answer to that question then (says the epistemicist) it would not be a vague matter whether Tony is part of the person. We cannot know what it is about our use of 'thinks' that determines one of the candidate semantic values to be the actual one. Our knowledge of semantic relations is incapable of extending that far. And that is precisely why ignorance arises in the case at hand.

Call the approach just sketched the 'Simple Epistemicist Treatment of Persons'.

§4

There is a problem for the simple epistemicist treatment. Let me illustrate it by an example. Suppose a Twinglander is sitting in a chair. Suppose that the Twinglander uses 'thinks' and 'person' ever so slightly differently (and is otherwise very much like an ordinary English speaker), so that the semantic value for 'thinks' and 'person', as used by the Twinglander, is different from ours. In particular, let us suppose that Grubby and Clean are both in the chair, our use of 'person' is such that it is true of Grubby and not Clean, and the Twinglander's use of 'person' is such that it is true of Clean and not Grubby.

Here are some very obvious truths:

(1) The Twinglander is the person sitting on the chair.
(2) The person sitting on the chair is the only thing on the chair that is able to talk and think.
(3) When the person sitting on the chair says 'I' the person is referring to himself.
(4) If the person sitting on the chair says something of the form 'a is F' then that claim is true iff the predicate 'F' in the mouth of that person is true of the thing referred to by 'a'.

---

[2] Even if one goes against that aspect of usage and counts many of the objects sitting on the chair each as a person, some of the issues that follow will arise. For even if there are many persons on the chair, there will presumably be certain objects for which it is vague whether or not those objects are persons at all.

Let us add to these obvious truths the added facts provided by our epistemicist-driven description of the scenario:

(5) Grubby is the person sitting on the chair (and Clean is not);
(6) 'is a person' in the mouth of the Twinglander is true of Clean and not Grubby.

Suppose the Twinglander says 'I am a person'. We can deduce: (*a*) Grubby says 'I am a person', (*b*) Nothing else on the chair says 'I am a person', (*c*) Grubby is referring to himself, (*d*) 'I am a person' as uttered by Grubby is true iff 'is a person' in the mouth of Grubby is true of Grubby, and (*e*) 'is a person' in the mouth of Grubby is not true of Grubby. All of this leads us to conclude that when the Twinglander says 'I am a person', the Twinglander expresses a false proposition and that nothing in the vicinity says something true. The same argument could have been run, *mutatis mutandis*, for 'I think' and 'I talk'. We should now conclude further that if our use of 'person' and 'think' had been ever so slightly different, then the sentences 'I think' and 'I talk', in our mouths, would have been false. This casts a skeptical shadow over the actual world: on a safety-driven conception of knowledge, the presence of mistakes at close worlds undermines knowledge at the actual world. Clearly, something has gone terribly wrong.

Let us get a bit clearer about the source of the problem. As things have been set up, it is *our* standards for 'person', 'thinks', 'talks', and so on that determine which of the candidate objects is an object that is self-referring, but it is an object's own, potentially different, standards that determine the extension of 'is a person', 'thinks', 'talks', and so on in its own mouth. It is our own standards that determine which objects are objects that are capable of engaging in the activity of drawing boundaries. In short, our standards determine which objects are boundary drawers. But it is the potentially different standards of the boundary drawer that determine where the extension of 'thinks' and 'person' in its mouth are to fall. Suppose the set of boundaries corresponding to 'person' that are drawn by a boundary drawer do not include its own boundary. Then were that boundary drawer ever to self-ascribe that predicate it would make a mistake.

Let us say that a person uses a close variant of 'person' iff the semantic value of 'person' in the mouth of that person is a candidate semantic value for 'person' in English. Assuming that 'person' is semantically plastic, it seems very easy for a variant of 'person' in the mouth of a boundary drawer to be false of the boundary drawer. That is just to say that it is easy for a person to be such that she uses a close variant of 'person' in a way that is false of that person. The same holds for 'thinks'. The trouble is that we do not want to say that there are close variants of 'thinks' and 'person' such that those predicates are falsely self-ascribed. For it is all too easy to self-ascribe those predicates—'I' thoughts will do the trick.

The simple epistemicist model needs supplementation or revision. I shall explore three approaches.

§5

Strategy A: One response is to deny that self-ascription is easy for close variants of English. One might insist that when the Twinglander says 'I think', the Twinglander is not referring to himself by 'I' but is referring to, say, Clean. On this model 'I think' in the mouth of the Twinglander is much more like 'he thinks' than it may first appear. In brief: whenever a person uses a close variant of 'thinks' in such a way that the person does not fall within the extension of that predicate, then the person will have no readily available device for self-reference and in particular will not self-refer when that person uses what would naturally be taken as a cognate of 'I'.

This view may not be as bad as it first appears. In particular, it is worth bearing in mind a certain potential symmetry between me and the Twinglander. For on this view the Twinglander may point in my direction and say 'He cannot refer to himself', where 'he' in the Twinglander's mouth refers to something that mereologically overlaps me, but which is not identical to me, and that satisfies 'person', 'talker', 'thinker', and so on in *his* mouth. So the proponent of this view can do something to deflate the suggestion that we are really special by being able to self-refer.

We should also bear in mind that, almost inevitably, the epistemicist is going to have to learn to live with a mass of strange counterfactuals. Suppose I want not to be bald. It seems at first blush to be true that if I had gone to the pub last night, I would still have wanted not to be bald. But suppose that if I had gone to the pub, the evening's conversation would have induced slight differences in use that shifted the meaning of 'bald' ever so slightly. Then it would seem that, strictly speaking, the counterfactual is false, since at the closest world where I go to the pub

I do not stand in the desired relation to the proposition actually expressed by 'I am not bald'.

All that said, I remain unimpressed by the view that self-reference fails in close variants of English. There is something exceedingly strange about a view according to which, at close worlds, many people (perhaps most people) do not have linguistic devices of self-reference. Relatedly, it is extremely natural to think that if a pronominal device has the conceptual role of the first-person pronoun in a person's cognitive life, then that pronoun will be a device of self-reference. The thought is a little rough-and-ready, owing to the rough-and-ready nature of the concept of "conceptual role", but has some force nevertheless. 'I' thoughts in the Twinglanders belief-box will have stereotypical roles in practical reason and so on that make it utterly natural to suppose that they are devices of self-reference. While the meaning of 'bald' may be fragile, 'I' does not seem to be so easily purged of the character that Kaplan described for it.[3]

§6

Strategy B: Return to the case of the Twinglander. Suppose that by the standards of the Twinglander, 'person' is true of Clean. In short, Clean is the object that counts as the utterer of 'I'-talk by the standards of the Twinglander. Perhaps the concept of a person is distinctive in that it defers to the self-conception of people: an object can only count as a boundary drawer insofar as its draws its own boundaries *at* its own boundaries.[4] On the hypothesis that Grubby is a person, Grubby counts Clean but not Grubby as the referent of 'I'. That counts as a *reductio* of the idea that Grubby is a person at all.

Example: Suppose there is an Englander and a Twinglander each in a chair. The intrinsic environment is pretty much the same for each. There are, inter alia, two objects, $Grubby_E$ and $Clean_E$, in the Englander's chair

---

[3] See 'Demonstratives,' in J. Almog et al. (eds.), *Themes from Kaplan* (Oxford: Oxford University Press, 1989).

[4] This is not to say, of course, that a person cannot radically misdescribe himself. He may think himself an immaterial being when in fact he is material. And so on. The point is that we must allow questions of who the person is to march in step with questions about what is picked out by "I" in the person's mouth. Thus once we concede that, overall, the pattern of usage in the person's mouth privileges x over y as the referent of 'I', it is no longer an option to nevertheless reckon y as the person/thinker/utterer.

and two objects, Grubby$_T$ and Clean$_T$, in the Twinglander's chair. Suppose the Englander's self-descriptions (without him knowing it) privilege Grubby$_E$ and the Twinglander's self-descriptions (without him knowing it) privilege Clean$_T$. Then 'person' in the Twinglander's mouth is true of Grubby$_E$ and Clean$_T$. Something analogous holds for the Englander. Each defers to the other's self-description as the prime semantic determinant of which object is the referent of 'I' thoughts and, in turn, of which object falls within the extension of 'person'. (I am here abstracting away from the question as to what it takes to be a person beyond being a thinker that can self-refer.)

Our simple epistemicist position claimed, in effect, that people could very easily have used the term 'person' in slightly different ways such that they did not fall under the extension of 'person' in their mouths. Our revised position denies this.

§7

Let us turn to the diachronic case. Suppose I begin life with the self-conception of a Twinglander and towards the end of my life move towards the self-conception of an Englander. (Of course, the shift might not be epistemically obvious to me: in fact if the shift is around borderline cases, it will not be.) Suppose my earlier self is sitting in a chair and my earlier self's usage privileges Grubby (where now let Grubby be an object that always has Tony as a part)[5] and not Clean (which never has Tony as a part) as the referent of 'I' thoughts. My later self, however, privileges Clean but not Grubby as the referent of 'I' thoughts. The natural way to apply the deferential conception is thus: my earlier self refers to Grubby with his 'I' thoughts and my later self refers to Clean with his 'I' thoughts. But this can't be right. My earlier self *is* my later self! But Grubby is not identical to Clean. When I look back on my earlier self, I want to say "I was referring to myself when I said 'I am hungry' ". If I am Clean then it cannot be that my earlier self refers to Grubby by 'I'. The problem is analogous to the earlier one. The ascribee's usage puts semantic pressure to count one thing as the referent of its 'I' thoughts, whereas the ascriber's standards on who is to count as a

---

[5] Let us assume that Tony remains within the close vicinity of the surface throughout the life of the individual.

thinker in the first place puts semantic pressure towards a different thing to count as the referent of 'I' thoughts. Where the target and the ascriber take themselves to be one and the same person, the 'to each his own' deferential strategy cannot be made to work.

At this point the epistemicist can appeal to externalist themes. Return to the case of 'bald'. It is wrong to think that the extension of 'bald' in my mouth is simply a matter of how *I* use 'bald'. My own use creates various semantic pressures, but I am a member of a linguistic community. The usage of others also contributes to the extension of the term in my mouth. Indeed, one reason—though not the only one—why I cannot know which value is the semantic value of 'bald' in my mouth is the fact that I am not privy to all the details of others' usage. Now what goes for my semantic relationship to others in the linguistic community may go for my later or earlier self. The extension of 'person' in my mouth—and relatedly, the referent of 'I'—may be constitutively determined by the usage of my later or earlier self. Suppose, to simplify, a community consisted of two individuals, A and B. A's usage of 'bald' may favor a cut-off at seventeen hairs. Roughly speaking: if A was the only member of the community, then the extension of 'bald' in his mouth would include all and only people with seventeen hairs or less. Suppose, meanwhile, B's usage favors a cut-off at fifteen hairs. This does not mean that B and A have different semantic values for 'bald'. The fact that they translate each other homophonically and use their own word to report the other's mental states creates semantic pressure against such a resolution. If God were to interpret them he would likely say that their terms have the same semantic value, adopting some appropriate weighting of the various semantic pressures at play.[6] We cannot know how the weighting would proceed, of course—our lack of knowledge of the details of the relevant laws of semantics is what gives rise to the

---

[6] We cannot say that God would respond that way in every such case. If we imagine a community that gradually shifts over time from being disposed to favor a cut-off that is at fifteen hairs to favoring a cut-off that is at 1,015 hairs, we will not tolerate the conclusion that the first means the same as the last, despite the fact that, from one time to the next, the shift in use is small and the homophonic pressures towards semantic uniformity great (we can imagine each without hesitation translates the utterances of recent community members in a homophonic way). We are faced here with a familiar situation: a relation R1 that might initially be thought to be sufficient for a relation R2 cannot be quite treated that way owing to the fact that the former is intransitive and the latter transitive. Intriguing versions of the same problem seem to arise for long-lived persons with evolving self-conceptions, though I shall not attempt to delve into the matter here.

phenomenon of vagueness (says the epistemicist). Similar remarks apply, *mutatis mutandis*, to the case at hand. If the earlier usage favors Grubby, the later Clean, but there is considerable semantic pressure for uniformity of semantic value across uses, then the matter is resolved by some (we know not what) weighting of semantic pressures to yield uniform semantic value. Perhaps the usage that favors Grubby loses out to the usage that favors Clean. In that case, both the early and later self use 'person' in such a way that the extension of 'person' includes Clean and not Grubby. In that case no utterance of 'I am a person' gets to be false: on both occasions, it is Clean that makes the utterance. Grubby is not a person at any time. Both utterances come out true since Clean is always, Grubby never, included in the extension of 'person'.[7]

§8

I have sketched a picture. Does it fit with the bare bones of epistemicism I began with? It is of course perfectly consistent with excluded middle, with bivalence, and with the thesis that borderline cases are beset by ignorance. What is less clear on this picture is that there is semantic plasticity in borderline cases. More specifically, it is not clear that the intension associated with 'person' could easily have been different. To make this vivid, consider a world W containing nothing but a Twinglander sitting in a chair. If 'person' is deferential in the way described and the Twinglander's usage favors Grubby, then I should say that Grubby is the person in that world. Could the intension of 'person' have easily been such that it did *not* deliver Grubby as the extension taking W as its argument? (I am operating here with a standard conception of intensions as functions from worlds to extensions.) It would seem that a word that was not deferential in the way described would not be a close variant of 'person'. But that inclines me to think that there is no close variant of 'person' that does not deliver the set containing Grubby as its value, taking W as argument. We want to say that it is a vague matter whether the person in W has Tony as a part. But it is not at all clear that the ignorance can be explained as a matter of semantic plasticity.

---

[7] And perhaps the use favors a third object that has Tony as a part early on but has Tony slightly beyond its mereological boundaries later on. If the pattern of use described can induce that kind of extension then the relevant changes in use would have the effect of making the person shrink. It would be odd were diets of this kind possible.

§9

(An aside: suppose one adopts the epistemicist picture sketched thus far. Given the plenitudinous ontology in the background and the willingness to defer to self-conceptions as the determinants of boundaries, it is at least natural to extend the picture to allow that some people have wildly different boundaries simply on account of wildly different self-conceptions. To make this vivid, consider a community of Eggers. An Egger believes that he or she came into existence as a human Egg. An Egger will say that fertilization made him or her gendered (and in general a lot more interesting). But on an Egger's self-conception, his or her existence began with an egg. Embrace the plenitudinous ontology suggested by epistemicism and it is very natural to suppose that there is at least an object—don't ask yet whether it is a person—that comes into existence at the time that the egg does, endures for seventy or eighty years, and has all the intrinsic requirements for thought later in life. Assume the deferential perspective and, it becomes very natural to say that these are the objects that the Eggers refer to by means of their 'I' thoughts. Some people, then, come into existence prior to fertilization. Not us, perhaps.[8] But the Eggers do. Is this a *reductio* of the deferential conception of persons? I shall not try to settle this matter here.[9])

§10

Strategy C:[10] One might say in these cases that vagueness in spatiotemporal boundaries does not, despite first appearances, have its source in any vagueness associated with the term 'person' (and in the associated personal pronouns), but rather in vagueness associated with other pieces of vocabulary. Suppose it is a vague matter when I came into existence. It might be claimed that there is some particular object o, such that it is definite that 'person' is true of o, and definite that 'I' in my mouth refers to o, but that the location of o is indefinite owing to

---

[8] I shall not investigate the delicate issues of transworld identity here.

[9] A few people have raised the following puzzle: What of someone whose usage favored the cosmos as the preferred boundary (and who thus thought of himself rather on the model of a many-headed hydra)? While we might defer to the Egger, we will not be so ready to defer to the Cosmos. I leave the issue as a puzzle for the deferentialist.

[10] Thanks to Mark Johnston, Ted Sider, and Timothy Williamson for urging me to consider this strategy.

vagueness associated with the term 'occupies'. Now in the case of mereologically complex objects such as myself (assuming the falsity of Cartesianism), it seems clear that the location of the whole is derivative upon the location of the small parts. It would thus be strange to suppose it is a sharp matter as to whether any given atom is or is not part of a mereologically complex thing at each time but that the location of the thing is vague, unless there is vagueness in the location of particular atoms. But the latter is *not* plausibly the source of indeterminacy in my boundaries. So as far as I can tell, then, the most promising development of the current strategy will require positing vagueness in the concept of parthood: it is vague for various pairs x, y, that, at some given time, x is a part of y. Assuming semantic plasticity, this will require that we posit a variety of candidate semantic values for 'is a part of', ones that differ intensionally.

Some will consider this an extremely radical tack, almost as radical as the idea that 'exists' is vague. I think this reaction can likely be traced to a tendency to think of mereology as part of logic, and thus a tendency to think that 'part of' enjoys purity of the kind possessed by existence and identity. This will be reinforced insofar as one adopts an extensionalist mereology according to which x is identical to y iff x is part of y and y is part of x.[11] For then it will be particularly difficult to maintain vagueness for 'part of' in combination with precision for 'is identical to'.

I do not find such abstract logical considerations very pressing myself: I am not particularly drawn to extensionalism, nor to a logicist thesis about mereology. There is a more local problem, however. For consider a case in which it is vague whether or not a person comes into existence at all (imagine the room blowing up just as the sperm is entering the egg). In that case it seems extremely difficult to explain the vagueness of the case in terms of vagueness in 'part of', since here it is vague whether 'person' is true of anything at all. Similarly, consider a world where there is an explosion that renders it vague whether I come into existence. (Imagine the world is just like the actual world up to the freak explosion.) If it can be vague whether I exist at that world then there had better be something that exists there that is a candidate semantic value for 'I'.[12] Let us use 'Johnny' as a precise name for that object. It now

---

[11] And allayed insofar as one thinks that it is the time-indexed 'is part of at t' and not the time-less 'part of' that is fundamental.

[12] I assume, reasonably enough, that the unrestricted existential quantifier cannot itself be vague.

appears that 'I am Johnny' is indefinite. But it is hard to see in this case how the vagueness can be blamed on 'part of'.

I can think of only one promising escape. In other works, Timothy Williamson has defended a necessitarianism about objects according to which any object exists eternally and necessarily.[13] If one adopts that view, it is no longer coherent to suppose that there is a world where it is vague whether I exist at all. It is of course coherent to suppose that there is a world where, at some time, it is vague whether I am concrete. Further, it is coherent to suppose that there is a world where it is vague whether I am ever concrete. But this kind of vagueness *can*, perhaps, be blamed on 'part of'. Suppose that, for one of the candidates for 'part of', there is a world w where I never have atoms as parts, but that on another precisification of 'part of', I do have atomic parts at w. On this conception, there are worlds where, while I definitely exist, it is vague whether or not I ever, so to speak, descend into the atom-filled void. Acknowledging a restricted use of 'exists' to mean 'concretely exists', there is a sense in which it is vague whether I exist at that world, though the vagueness can be placed squarely on the shoulders of 'part of'.

I recommend strategy B to non-necessitarian epistemicists. However, strategy C may very well turn out to be preferable if we assume a necessitarian setting. Strategy B makes trouble for the semantic plasticity component of Williamson's view. Strategy C does not. Considerations of personal identity thus appear to forge an interesting bridge from his version of epistemicism to necessitarianism. (Not that one needs to rely on such a bridge in order to motivate necessitarianism.)

§11

The issues I have raised are far from unique to epistemicism. Consider the main competing theory of vagueness,[14] supervaluationism. The supervaluationist uses supertruth and superfalsity as her primary concepts of semantic evaluation. A sentence is supertrue iff it is true on all precisifications and superfalse iff it is false on all precisifcations. A borderline case is one where the relevant sentence is true on some precisifications, false on others. Suppose 'He has Tony as a part' is a

---

[13] See e.g. 'Existence and Contingency', *Aristotelian Society*, sup. vol. 73, 1999 pp. 181–203.

[14] See Kit Fine, 'Vagueness, Truth and Logic,' *Synthese* 30, 1975.

borderline case (where 'Tony' is precise). That will be because there are various precisifcations of 'he', some of which contain Tony as a part, others not. Here too we have a plenitude of objects required by the semantics. Suppose further that we embrace the analog of semantic plasticity: small shifts in use generate small shifts in the range of acceptable precisifications of a term. Suppose now a Twinglander has a slightly different set of acceptable precisifications for 'person' than I do. Now the competing pressures described above will arise. On the one hand, I want to say that the Twinglander self-refers by 'I'. This encourages me to treat all and only the acceptable precisifications of 'The Twinglander' in my mouth as acceptable precisifications of 'I' in the Twinglander's mouth. But suppose some of the acceptable precisifications of 'The Twinglander' in my mouth are not acceptable precisifications of 'person' in the Twinglander's mouth. Then there is a threat that 'I am a person', in the mouth of the Twinglander, will not come out supertrue (similarly for 'I think'). Such a sentence will have to be reckoned borderline. This result is intuitively unacceptable. The same theme is in play. We have competing pressures on the reference of 'I', generated on the one hand by my conception of a person and on the other hand by the self-conception of another. It is thus relatively straightforward to recast the issues just discussed within the alternative semantic framework of supervaluationism. A shift from epistemicism to supervaluationism will thus not make the problems go away, so long as semantic plasticity is maintained.

§12

I now turn to the case of semantic predicates. Timothy Williamson is happy to suppose that his picture extends to such predicates as 'refers' and 'is true'. Thus, in a reply to a commentary by Stephen Schiffer, he writes:

semantic ascent preserves vagueness. For example, since it is clear that something is bald if and only if it is in the extension of 'bald', 'bald' has the same borderline cases as 'in the extension of "bald" '.

My general explanation of the ignorance that constitutes vagueness extends to semantic terms. Although someone may judge truly 'Baldness is the property of having fewer than 3,832 hairs on one's scalp', the judgement does not express knowledge, for whatever produced a judgement in those words could very easily have done so even if the overall use of 'bald' had been very slightly shifted (as it could very easily have been) in such a way that it referred to the property of having fewer than 3,831 hairs on one's scalp, in which case the judgement then made in those words would have been false. What produces the judgement does not produce true judgements reliably enough to produce knowledge.... To extend this explanation of our non-semantic ignorance to an explanation of our semantic ignorance, note that in the envisaged counterfactual circumstances the sentence ' "Bald" refers to baldness' naturally still commands assent (clearly, 'bald' refers to baldness). In those circumstances, the false judgement in the words 'Baldness is the property of having fewer than 3,832 hairs on one's scalp' goes with a false judgement in the words " 'Baldness' refers to the property of having fewer than 3,832 hairs on one's scalp". Although someone may use the latter words to make a true judgement in the actual circumstances, the judgement does not express knowledge, for what produces it does not produce true judgements reliably enough to produce knowledge. Thus the account explains equally why we are not in a position to know that 'baldness' refers to the property of having fewer than 3,832 hairs on one's scalp.[15]

I think that this passage obscures an important distinction. Let us distinguish semantic plasticity—the phenomenon whereby the intension associated with a term could easily have been different—from extensional plasticity—the phenomenon whereby the extension of a term could easily have been different. Suppose I am moody. I fall under the extension of 'happy at noon, 15 April 2004'. Being moody, I could very easily have failed to fall under the extension of that predicate. Thus, there are close worlds where the extension of that predicate is different to what it actually is. But *that* phenomenon obviously does not by itself indicate that 'happy' is semantically plastic. Now if 'bald' is semantically plastic in the way that Williamson envisages, that certainly means that, say, 'expresses' (conceived of as a relation between a noise token and a property) is extensionally plastic. A noise token may in this world express a property P, baldness, and yet at a close world that noise token not express that property. (Similarly, if we allow 'c means p by noise type n' to express a three-place relation between a phonetic or graphemic type, a community, and a property, then the semantic plasticity of 'bald' will make for extensional plasticity with regard to that ternary predicate.) Moreover, it is plausible enough

---

[15] 'Reply to Commentators', *Philosophy and Phenomenological Research*, 57/4 (December 1997), 947–8.

to think that such extensional plasticity, coupled with our insensitivity to the ways that slight shifts in use make for differences in semantic value, will undermine the possibility of knowledge of the propositions expressed by the relevant metalinguistic claims in borderline cases. The words " 'Baldness' refers to the property of having fewer than 3,832 hairs on one's scalp" could easily have expressed a falsehood. And given our insensitivity to the shifts in semantic value, one who accepted that sentence would not plausibly express knowledge thereby. But none of this shows that semantic terms are themselves semantically plastic. And thus none of this shows that ignorance in the metalinguistic claims can be traced to the semantic plasticity of one or more terms that are used in them. If we assume with Williamson that vagueness requires semantic plasticity, then while we may grant that semantic ascent preserves ignorance, we are still owed a justification of the passage's opening claim that semantic ascent preserves vagueness.

§13

We have seen that the considerations adduced by Williamson in the quoted paragraph do not demonstrate that semantic terms are semantically plastic. But is there any positive reason to think that they are not? Interestingly, the puzzle adduced earlier can be reproduced here. We generated havoc earlier by allowing our standards for what counts as a person to draw boundaries in different places to cognate terms (terms used at close worlds with almost indistinguishable conceptual roles) used by various counterfactual people themselves. What happens if we allow, say, the predicate 'true' to draw boundaries in a way that fails to match the boundaries drawn by people at close worlds who use a term with a conceptual role that bears the hallmark of our use of 'true'? Havoc similarly results.

Let us suppose that 'true' is semantically plastic, so that its intension at close worlds differs from its actual intension. Here, I am thinking of 'true' as a predicate of utterance tokens, so that its semantic value will be a function from worlds to sets of utterance tokens.[16] Suppose, then, that

---

[16] The ontology of words is obviously a tricky business. The points that I am making can, however, be recast in terms of other different semantical frameworks, including, for example, one that takes 'true' as a predicate of utterance types—where an utterance type is

at a nearby world W the semantic value of 'true' was slightly different, so that each utterance of a particular sentence S by a particular community C fell under the extension of the semantic value expressed by our term 'true' (given W as argument), but did not fall under the extension of the semantic value of 'true' as used at W. Let us assume, as required by the Williamson picture, that at that world the use of 'true' is only ever so slightly different, so that the fundamental features of its conceptual role at our world—in particular the behavior gestured at by the "T-schema"—are intact.

Consider now an utterance of

'S' is true iff S

made by an inhabitant of W. By hypothesis the right-hand side of the biconditional is true. How about the left-hand side? By hypothesis, 'S' does not fall within the extension of 'true' as used by the community at that world. Thus, the community would be saying something false by the left-hand side. Thus, if the community were to utter the relevant biconditional, the left-hand side would be false, the right-hand side true. The biconditional would be false. Assuming semantic plasticity, we have been led to conclude that at close worlds, certain counterparts of the T-schema are false! This seems just as bad as conceding that at close worlds people do not self-refer by 'I'. Note that in both cases we supposed that a certain conceptual role is accompanied by a certain semantic achievement: a pronoun with the conceptual role of 'I' has self-reference, a predicate with the conceptual role of 'true' will yield true instances of the associated T-schema. In both cases, semantic plasticity induces a detachment between the relevant conceptual role and the associated semantic achievement.[17]

As in the case of 'I', one might try to soften the blow. "After all," it may be said, "while counterparts of the T-schema are false at close worlds, they are true*, where the property of being true* is the property expressed by 'true' at close worlds." But I take it that this is not

individuated by a combination of phonemic/phonetic considerations and a specified community of users.

[17] Some people have suggested to me a salvage that goes by way of reinterpreting 'iff' at close worlds. It does not seem plausible that logical operators are semantically plastic in the relevant respect. Moreover one can redo the puzzle so that instead of considering a statement ' 'S' is true iff S', we consider an *inference* from ' 'S' is true' to 'S' (where the paradoxical result is that at close worlds the inference is invalid).

satisfactory. Truth is the norm by which we evaluate both our actual and counterfactual selves. The response requires us to think that at nearby worlds truth doesn't really matter. As such, it is not acceptable. (Consider an analogous conversation in ethics, where one tries to let one's counterpart off the hook by combining a concession that he is cruel with the observation that he is not cruel*, where cruel* is what he means by 'cruel'.)

Untoward results can also be reproduced for 'refers', 'expresses', 'designates', and so on. Suppose, say, that 'refers' is semantically plastic, so that while tokens of some counterfactual name n refer to x, the pair $<n,x>$ does not fall under the extension of 'refers' as used at that (nearby) world. Consider now the claim

'n' refers to n

as used at that counterfactual world. That claim is true just in case the pair picked out by the flanking singular terms falls under the extension of the binary predicate. The referent of " 'n' " is the name itself. By hypothesis the referent of 'n' is x. By hypothesis the pair $<n, x>$ does not fall under the extension of 'refers', as used by members of the counterfactual community under consideration. Thus certain instances of the "disquotational schema for reference" come out false at nearby counterfactual worlds. Once again, an intolerable result.

The lesson, I take it, is that we should be very cautious about positing semantic plasticity for semantic vocabulary. Not only does the quoted passage from Williamson fail to provide any reason for embracing it; there are powerful reasons for rejecting it.

§14

Insofar as we are sympathetic to epistemicism, we are left with a residual problem. What exactly is distinctive of the ignorance due to vagueness? I have argued that it is implausible that our ignorance concerning the boundaries of personhood can be traced to semantic plasticity. But this does not seem to be a good reason for denying that in some very reasonable sense, 'person' is vague. We should similarly allow that in some very reasonable sense, certain claims of the form

'bald' is true of people with less than N hairs

are borderline, even though the vagueness of such claims cannot be traced to the fact that certain terms occurring in them are semantically plastic. (Even if 'bald' is semantically plastic, that does not mean that " 'bald' " is.) Now we have noted that semantic terms may well be beset by extensional plasticity in borderline cases. But we cannot say that, in general, ignorance due to extensional plasticity makes for the kind of ignorance associated with borderline cases. Suppose a particle moves rapidly between point A and B—so rapidly that we cannot in principle discern whether, at a given time, the particle is at location A or B. Consider the claim 'The particle is at A at noon.' There is extensional plasticity, sure enough. Suppose 'is at A at noon' is true of the particle. That predicate could easily have been false of the particle. But this case does not in any way have the feel of a case in which there is ignorance due to vagueness.

So let us reexamine the question as to what the epistemicist should say about the ignorance that is distinctive of borderline cases. Let us begin with an epistemicist picture of the metaphysics of semantics. It would be very strange indeed to deny that semantical facts (and propositional attitude facts) supervene on a ground floor comprised of a certain distribution of fundamental properties across space-time (which will be microphysical, assuming that some broad naturalistic picture is correct). The epistemicist is thus happy to believe that there is some sort of function from fundamental distributions to semantical facts. Call that function 'F'. Meanwhile, semantical ignorance about a certain noise type may have at least two different sources. On the one hand, we may be ignorant of various facts about the ground floor which serve as input to F. Such facts will, let us suppose (or pretend[18]), straightforwardly encode this or that fact about how the noise type is used by some member of the community, by fellow members of the community, the causal relations of that noise type to this or that feature of the world, and so on. Let us call this source of ignorance about semantic facts *ground-floor ignorance*. On the other hand, we may have a rather incomplete grasp of F itself, so that even if one were (idealizing now) to have a full grip on the array of fundamental facts, one would still not be in a position to discern the semantical facts on the grounds that one's grasp of how the latter depends on the former is radically incomplete. Let us imagine that the

---

[18] This involves a bit of oversimplification, since facts about macro-organisms, words, and causal relationships to other macro-objects will not themselves really be fundamental.

nature of F could be captured by a set of semantical laws that describe how semantical facts depend on the ground floor. Insofar as we didn't know what the semantical laws were, we would have ignorance not traceable to ground-floor ignorance. Let us call the second kind of ignorance *semantico-nomic ignorance*.[19]

Now it is quite clear that in a borderline case, Williamson supposes the ignorance not merely to be rooted in ground-floor ignorance: even if one knew all of the relevant ground-floor facts, one would not be able to make the ignorance go away. Suppose that the ground-floor facts are captured by P, and that Q includes the relevant semantic facts about the extension of some predicate. The problem is not merely that we do not know that P. It is that we are in no position to know that P ⊃ Q, even though that material conditional is presumably a necessary truth. Ground-floor omniscience would not remove our insensitivity to the true semantic mechanisms.

Notice now that this picture provides a plausible epistemicist account of ignorance due to vagueness that does not proceed by way of semantic plasticity: in cases which we call "ignorance due to vagueness", we have a sentence that expresses a proposition P such that our principled inability to know whether P is rooted in semantico-nomic ignorance. Even if, say, some claims of the form

(1) Tokens of 'big number' as used by community C are true of any number greater than 154

are not semantically plastic, we may have a principled ignorance of their truth values that is rooted in semantico-nomic ignorance. Hence our ignorance of (1) will count as "ignorance due to vagueness".

One might worry that the picture just sketched disrupts a safety-based conception of knowledge according to which belief is knowledge just in case there is no danger of error—that is, no error at "close worlds".[20] Suppose someone dogmatically believed some claim S of the form (1) above. Clearly such a person would not know that S even

---

[19] There may be other kinds of ignorance that do not fall into the two categories I have just described. Suppose that there are higher-order natural kinds and fundamental but inscrutable principles about how they depend on the ground floor. (Suppose, for example, that phenomenal properties are like that.) Our ignorance about whether bats have a certain quale might not then depend either on ground-floor ignorance or ignorance about how semantical laws work. It would then depend on ignorance of some principles of psychophysics that hold of necessity. (Thanks to Hartry Field here.)

[20] I am grateful for conversations with Williamson here.

if it were necessarily true. Williamson provides us with a vision of how semantic plasticity explains ignorance in borderline cases: Suppose someone were to accept dogmatically a borderline claim S. Even if S is true, then, owing to semantic plasticity, S would express a falsehood at "close worlds". Thus, at close worlds, the dogmatist could make a mistake. His actual belief thus turns out not to be safe and so the dogmatist does not know S. Eschew plasticity for S and no similar explanation is available. Someone who dogmatically accepted S would, it seems, express a truth at close worlds and so, by a "safety"-theoretic test, count as knowing that S is true.

Is this a real problem for the current brand of epistemicism? I don't think so. To use the preceeding line of thought against that account is to presuppose an all-too-crude safety-theoretic account of knowledge (one that advocates of safety-based accounts—including Williamson—will be at pains to distance themselves from). We all know that if someone dogmatically cleaves to Goldbach's conjecture, that will not in itself secure knowledge. But, given that there seems to be no semantic plasticity in the relevant mathematical language, such a dogmatist would not be in error at close worlds. In that case, we are hardly inclined to use a crude safety-based account as grounds for admitting that the dogmatist knows Goldbach's conjecture after all (assuming that it is true). We instead refine our conception of what knowledge comes to. Similar remarks apply to semantico-nomic ignorance, *mutatis mutandis*.

§15

It is not clear that the semantic plasticity gloss on ignorance due to vagueness has to be jettisoned altogether. Return to (1), namely:

(1) Tokens of 'big number' as used by community C are true of any number greater than 154.

Consider an instance of (1), S, that is not semantically plastic. S is plausibly *about* a term that is semantically plastic. When it comes to evaluating sentences in our own language, semantical claims like S, made about ourselves, will be evaluated by way of sentences that do not contain semantical vocabulary. Thus,

(2) Utterances of '154 is a big number' in my community are true

in my language, will be evaluated by me (on the simplifing assumption that there is no context dependence) by way of

(3) 154 is a big number.

Suppose, as I have been suggesting, (3) is semantically plastic but (2) isn't (or, at any rate, it isn't once 'my community is made precise'). If (3) is vague, then so is (2) on the grounds that indefiniteness transmits across known equivalences.[21] We cannot, then, quite say that indefinite sentences are semantically plastic. But there is a thesis that is still arguably defensible—call it the Modified Plasticity Thesis—according to which, when a sentence in our own language is vague, the canonical means for evaluating it will be via a plastic sentence.

Note, though, that if we adopt strategy B above for handling personal identity issues, then it is not clear that even the Modified Plasticity Thesis is correct. And that is because, on that view, 'person' is vague without being semantically plastic. On that view, then, sentences such as 'Some person has Clean as a part' are not semantically plastic.[22] Someone who adopted that strategy can endorse the view that vagueness turns on semantico-nomic ignorance, but cannot endorse even the Modified Plasticity Thesis. (The thesis fares even worse when we face up to the proliferation context-dependence in our language).

§16

Suppose I introduce a predicate 'is a dommal' by a pair of stipulations: Let 'is a dommal' be true of dogs and false of non-animals.[23] My stipulations do not settle whether

---

[21] Assuming that Definiteness satisfies the distribution principle of normal modal logic and that knowing P implies definitely P, then it just won't do to say (2) is definite but (3) is indefinite. For it is known by me that (2) implies (3). So it is definite that (2) implies (3). By distribution, definitely (2) implies definitely (3). By contraposition, indefinitely (3) implies indefinitely (2).

[22] Thanks to Nicolas Silins here.

[23] The dommal example figures in both *Identity and Discrimination* (Oxford: Oxford University Press, 1990), 107, and *Vagueness*, p. 213, though Williamson's take on the example changed between books.

Another interesting kind of case to consider is where symmetric constraints are at work. Suppose I stipulate that Fs are dommals and Gs are gommals, that everything is to be either a dommal or a gommal, and that nothing is to be both a dommal and a gommal. It is dangerous to say that in such cases the terms have no semantic value, since similar phenomena may be prevalent in subtler form in natural language. In the pure case, I would suppose that the epistemicist should say that one of the stipulations fails to hold (it being unknowable which). I shall not pursue the matter here.

(4) Cats are dommals.

Williamson accepts bivalence here. On his preferred picture, the truth value is determined by a default principle, the two candidates being, roughly,

P1: A sentence is false unless one has done enough to secure its truth,

and

P2: A sentence is true unless one has done enough to secure its falsehood.

Williamson seems to think that he knows which default principle is the true one, but such an epistemic stance does not seem very plausible to me. Do we really have access, a priori or otherwise, to the relative merits of P1 and P2? I reckon it better to combine bivalence with an admission of principled ignorance: we do not know (4) owing to semantico-nomic ignorance.

Imagine a sorites sequence of cases in which, at one end,[24] a community is very firmly in favor of P1, and thus finds 'Cats are dommals', as introduced by a member of their community, obviously false; and at the other end, a community that is very firmly in favor of P2, and thus finds 'Cats are dommals', as introduced by a member of that community, very obviously true. Imagine that we are somewhere in the middle, accounting for the borderline status of 'Cats are dommals' in our mouths.

Do we at last have a case where it is plausible to think that the meaning of 'true' is intensionally shifty? Should we say that the community at one end means one thing by 'true' (governed by P1) and that the community at the other end means another thing by 'true' (governed by P2)? Such a reaction would conflate intensional with extensional considerations. After all, it is reasonable here to think that each community ought to be deferential to the other. Suppose I am in a community that favors P1. Suppose I look at a community that is heavily in favor of P2. Should I, using 'false' in my mouth, say that 'Cats are dommals' is false, even as uttered by the community of P2 followers? This seems like the wrong reaction. It seems much more natural to suppose that when I say 'Cats are dommals', that is false, and

---

[24] Thanks to Timothy Williamson and a member of an Oxford audience for bringing sorites series of this sort to my attention.

expresses one proposition, but when the community of P2 lovers says 'Cats are dommals', they express a quite different proposition. And that is because the practices of my community determine 'dommal' in my mouth to have the same intension as 'dog', but the practices of that community determine 'dommal' in their mouths to have the same intension as 'animal'. Thus the P1 lovers should only endorse a principle such as P1 when it is suitably restricted to their linguistic locale. No one in the sorites sequence should think that P1, unrestricted, might be a necessary truth. On this conception, which I take to be the most plausible way of thinking about the case, the intension of 'true' is invariant along the sorites sequence. (It is interesting to notice the structural affinities between this case and the discussion of deference above.)

§17

Let us turn to the phenomenon of semantico-nomic ignorance itself. The picture is one according to which semantic mechanisms transcend our grasp of them in a deep and principled way. Some will find this deeply intolerable. It is interesting, here, to note a contrast between our attitudes towards mathematics and semantics. In the realm of mathematics, the view that there are evidence-transcendent features of this or that mathematical structure, while hotly debated, is not regarded as extreme or bizarre. Yet analogous views about semantics are apt to strike readers as somewhat outrageous. This reaction is at least in part rooted in a reluctance to recognize semantical properties as natural kinds, joints in nature with distinctive real essences. This "hyperinflationary" conception of semantical properties would not, of course, suffice to establish the current brand of epistemicism. But it would render the idea of semantico-nomic ignorance rather more palatable and thus help to make my favored version of epistemicism a going concern.

Let me thus offer a few preliminary motivating remarks in support of hyperinflationism. Consider first the following frequently voiced concern about epistemicism: For any predicate, there are ever so many functions from use to extension that "fit" the use of that predicate. What on earth could it be that makes one of those functions special in such a way that 'true of' should be specially associated with it? Shouldn't we instead make every attempt to do justice to the thought that each of the functions provides an equally good candidate extension?[25]

The concern needs refinement. Recalling Kripkenstein,[26] none of us (or hardly any of us) think that quus is an equally good candidate semantic value for 'plus' in the mouths of our earlier selves as plus (where plus and quus are functions that differ only with regard to pairs of natural numbers whose sum we are unable to entertain due to our finitude). But both candidates "fit" use in some fairly obvious sense, since each interpretation is equally charitable with regard to our actual and counterfactual use of 'plus' (so long as suitable compensating adjustments are made in the interpretation of other pieces of arithmetical vocabulary in which generations about addition are stated). The lesson generalizes to non-arithmetical vocabulary. Bizarre interpretations can be concocted to "fit" use which none of us are very inclined to think are acceptable interpretations.

In response to all this, some will go the way of Kripkenstein's skeptical solution,[27] combining a suitably disquotationalist story about our truth predicate with a recognition that there are no deep objective constraints on the acceptability of a translation. The Quine-Field[28] development of this view would have us believe that an ascription of truth to some utterance made by my earlier self (or some interlocutor) has to be relativized to a translation scheme. Semantico-nomic ignorance will have no place in that framework. Indeed, the chasm between such theorists and the current brand of epistemicism is far too vast for me to hold out much hope of closing it here. (For many of us, it is cost enough for that view that it relinquishes all hope of salvaging straightforward truth for claims made by our earlier selves and our fellows.)

Of more interest to me here is the Lewisian reaction to Kripkenstein,[29] one which allows the distinction between natural and gerrymandered properties to do work in the foundations of semantics. Roughly speaking,

---

[25] The relevant notion of "fit" deployed in such arguments is typically left unexplained, but I take it that talk of an interpretation "fitting" use of some term is tantamount to a claim that some interpretation provides some reasonably charitable interpretation of our settled dispositions to use a term.

[26] Saul Kripke, *Wittgenstein on Rules and Private Language* (Oxford: Blackwell, 1982).

[27] See *Wittgenstein on Rules and Private Language*, ch. 3.

[28] See W. V. O. Quine, *Word and Object* (Cambridge, Mass.: MIT Press, 1960) and Hartry Field, *Truth and the Absence of Fact* (Oxford: Oxford University Press, 2001).

[29] See David Lewis, 'New Work for a Theory of Universals', and 'Putnam's Paradox', in *Papers in Metaphysics and Epistemology* (Cambridge: Cambridge University Press, 1999).

the picture maintains that there are two desiderata on interpretation, namely: (*a*) The Requirement of Charity: *ceteris paribus*, interpret us so that our claims come out true so interpreted; and (*b*) The Requirement of Eligibility: *ceteris paribus*, interpret us so that our predicates get assigned more rather than less natural properties as their semantic values.

On Lewis's picture, naturalness of reference is what explains there being a fact of the matter as to what something refers to: more specifically it is the comparative naturalness of one candidate over others that explains why a term determinately refers to that candidate. What makes a plus interpretation more acceptable than a quus interpretation? Well, while both interpretations may do equally well on the score of charity, one interpretation scores far higher with regard to eligibility. Thus the quus-interpretation can be discounted. Consider by contrast the case of 'bald'. Each "candidate" semantic value is, intuitively, equally natural. So neither charity nor eligibility can break the tie.

There is a second role that naturalness plays in the Lewisian account, namely, naturalness begets semantic stability. If we refer to a highly natural property by some term t, which is more natural than properties in the vicinity, then the semantic value of t often remains stable despite quite significant shifts in use.

It seems as if the epistemicist has little to gain from a Lewisian distinction between natural and non-natural properties.[30] Such reaction would be far too hasty, I think. Let me explore a few themes in that connection, making vivid those ways in which a Lewisian distinction between natural and non-natural properties can serve as a springboard for hyperinflationism.

1. Suppose one were to embrace the Requirement of Eligibility, along with an objective distinction between natural and unnatural properties. This is already to recognize the existence of deep principles about semantics that transcend the ken of ordinary folk. Perhaps one might think that we semantic theorists can appreciate the plausibility of such a requirement and even know that it is probably true. But it would be outrageous to suggest that ordinary linguistic competence brings with it

---

[30] As noted, it does not, prima facie, help with predicates such as 'bald'. Moreover, Lewis would certainly have thought that there is no uniquely best way to weight charity versus eligibility when it comes to assigning semantic value. If one interpretation scores slightly better on charity, another slightly better on eligibility, then both will likely stand as acceptable interpretations that can be supervaluated over.

knowledge of any such principle. To claim that such a principle is known "implicitly" by ordinary folk is to court further confusion: to claim that those principles that describe how terms refer are automatically known implicitly by people simply on account of their ability to refer is, in truth, no more plausible than the claim that those principles that describe how we maintain our balance are automatically known implicitly by people simply on account of their ability to avoid falling over. The eligibility requirement does not govern the semantics of ordinary folk by being known implicitly by them. Rather, it governs the semantics of ordinary folk (if it does so at all) by virtue of being a correct (if partial) account of the nature of semantical relations. Accepting the eligibility requirement is, obviously, not yet to accede to epistemicism. But to accept it is to embrace the existence of fundamental semantic mechanisms that are beyond the ken of ordinary folk, a move that should provide real encouragement indeed to the epistemicist.

2. The version of epistemicism I am interested in is best served by a metaphysic according to which semantic properties—reference, truth, and so on—are themselves natural kinds, joints in nature. Where a property marks a natural kind, we are open to the thought that it has a "real essence" that transcends our ordinary understanding of it, even one that in some respects transcends our cognitive capacities. The fundamental metaphysical task of my epistemicist, then, is to render plausible the picture of semantic properties as joints in nature. Does the Lewisian metaphysics help or hinder in this way?

First, some preliminaries. Lewis embraces a plentitude of properties, some of which are metaphysically "haloed"—that is, natural. More precisely, there is a continuum from more to less natural properties, with perfectly natural properties at one end, and increasing "gruesomeness" as one moves along the continuum. Which *are* the natural properties? Even supposing that we think that everything supervenes on physics, the issue is not settled. For if we accept a natural property framework, we must choose between an austere physicalism on the one hand and what might be called an "emergentist" framework on the other. According to the austere physicalist, the perfectly natural properties will only be found at the microphysical ground floor, relative naturalness being a matter of definitional distance from the perfectly natural properties: to calibrate the naturalness of a property, see how complicated the definition of that property would be in a "canonical" language in which each predicate corresponded to a perfectly natural property.[31] From such a perspective, the property of, say, being a chair will likely turn out hopelessly unnatural, far less natural than, say, the disjunctive property of being either a hydrogen atom or being fifteen feet from a quark. (Indeed, it wouldn't be surprising if the canonical definition of a chair was infinitary.) The "emergentist" by contrast, believes that naturalness is not a matter of mere definitional distance from the microphysical ground floor. (This kind of emergentist can of course allow that everything supervenes on the microphysical.) Perhaps being a cat is far more natural than certain properties far more easily definable in Lewis's canonical language. On the emergentist conception of things, there is no algorithm available for calibrating naturalness in terms of a perfect microphysical language.

Now Lewis's own development of the eligibility view certainly provides a hindrance to the picture of semantical joints—joints delineated by semantic predicates themselves—since his physicalism is an austere one. Though lacking the space to develop the point here, I suspect that we find hereabouts a fundamental tension in his world-view. On the one hand he wishes the eligibility requirement to dispel the specter of rampant indeterminacy presented by Kripkenstein and Quine. Yet on the other hand, he offers us an austere physicalist account of what eligibility comes to. It does not seem that the two perspectives can be reconciled. How can the eligibility requirement provide some reasonable measure of determinacy for 'gavagai' if the property of being a rabbit turns out to be hopelessly gruesome? Far better, it seems to me, to opt for an emergentist physicalism, in which semantical joints remain a live option.

We can go further. As we have noted, the eligibility framework offers a useful perspective on the presence and absence of semantic plasticity. Suppose there is a highly natural property that distinguishes itself among the properties that "fit" the use of a predicate reasonably well. The other "candidates" are far less natural and so the highly natural property easily wins the semantic competition. Even if the use of the term had been slightly different, the highly natural property would win the competition, since even a slightly lower score *vis-à-vis* a gruesome property on the score of charity would be trumped by a far higher score

---

[31] See Lewis, 'Putnam's Paradox', 66.

in naturalness. Using language that has recently become popular: the highly natural property serves as a reference magnet. But we have seen above that semantical predicates are not semantically plastic. The reasonable conclusion seems to be that semantical properties are reference magnets and therefore highly natural themselves. Epistemicism is not yet forced upon us, but a suitable metaphysical underpinning for such a view—one replete with semantic magnets—is now in place.

In conclusion: I identified two themes in Lewis's own use of natural properties in semantic theory. First, we encountered the idea that a fact of the matter about reference typically requires there being a highly eligible referent. The epistemicist metaphysic I am envisaging denies this. There is a fact of the matter concerning the reference of 'bald', but it is not explained by the naturalness of the referent of 'bald'. There is, of course, a way in which one might still be able to pay lip-service to the idea that reference to a particular property is begotten by naturalness. For there being a fact of the matter as to what 'bald' refers to is, on this picture, explained by the eminent naturalness of the reference relation itself.

Second, we found the idea that eligibility begets semantic stability. This idea can be taken on board, pretty much as it stands, by the current brand of epistemicism. 'Bald' is plastic, on account of the non-eligibility of its referent. 'Refers' is stable, on account of the high eligibility of its referent.[32]

§18

Do I suppose myself to have offered absolutely decisive arguments for the 'magnet' version of epistemicism over Williamson's? I do not.

---

[32] Suppose one says that 'true', as a predicate of utterances, is semantically stable. Here is a possible problem. I write down a string of marks. There is a question of the boundaries of the utterance. Suppose some bit of ink, call it Ink, is such that it is borderline whether or not it is part of the utterance. It seems that it may be that while 'true' in my mouth expresses a property that applies to a thing with Ink, a nearby community may go a different way. The problem is not obviously solved by shifting to a picture according to which the fundamental semantical relations concern mental representations, since their boundaries can be vague as well. The concern is not decisive. The earlier discussion is not irrelevant. For example, think back to strategy C above. That can be replayed here. Perhaps the vagueness in this case turns on the vagueness of 'part of'. In that case, there may be no vagueness concerning which object 'true' applies to, only vagueness concerning which are the parts of that object. I am grateful for discussions with Cian Dorr here.

Let me end by sketching what I think is the best strategy to pursue for one who repudiates semantic magnets and wishes to stick closely to Williamson's original vision. I will make a number of simplifying assumptions. Let us imagine that there is one community to a world, that sentences are worldbound, that each community speaks a language that is not context-dependent, and that languages contain their own truth predicate.[33]

Let us distinguish domestic ascriptions of a close variant of 'true', which are ascriptions of the predicate to sentences *in the language of that predicate*; from foreign ascriptions, which are ascriptions to sentences in a language that isn't the language of that predicate. Suppose communities C1 in Alpha and C2 in Beta are close variants of each other. Let the *home extension* of a variant of the truth predicate be defined thus:

> *Home extension*: A sentence S is part of the home extension of a close variant v of the truth predicate iff S is in the language that v belongs to and v is true of S.

We can now state a thesis of *domestic stability* for 'True'.

> 'True' (as we use it) is domestically stable just in case a sentence is part of the home extension of a close variant of 'true' iff 'true' is true of it.

Suppose, now that 'true' is domestically stable. At some close variant community C, if our predicate 'true' is true of a sentence S in the language of C, then the variant of 'true' in C will be true of S as well. But this is not yet semantic stability. For it is quite compatible with domestic plasticity that the variant of 'true' that is in C is false of some sentence of *our* language that 'true' is true of. Consider, for example, this scenario: there is a sentence of our language S1, and a sentence of their language S2, such that: (i) The intension of our term 'true' includes both S1 and S2, but the intension of their variant of 'true' includes S2 but not S1 (and indeed, the intension of their variant of 'false', while not including S2, does include S1). This scenario is quite compatible with domestic stability but not with semantic stability. Now, crucially, domestic stability is enough to ensure that close variants of

---

[33] If these assumptions are relaxed, the relevant points can still be made, but are a little harder to both state and see.

instances of the T-schema are true. So it turns out that one can save the original Williamson approach from the argument given earlier by combining domestic stability with semantic plasticity.

Let 'true*' be the close variant of 'true', and assume the scenario just described. It is false that, for any variant of 'true*' something is part of the home extension of that variant iff 'true*' is true of it. After all 'true' is a close variant of 'true*' and while S1 is part of the home extension of 'true', 'true*' is not true of it.

Does this mean that while we would be quite correct in uttering the thesis of domestic stability, the nearby community would be making a mistake when uttering the counterpart of that thesis? And wouldn't that make us incredibly lucky? To think so is to miss out on the fact that 'true of' may not be semantically stable.

Let 'true' and 'true of' name our expressions, and 'true*' and 'true of*' be a pair of close variants. Let *being true of** be the relation that is meant by 'true of*'. In the scenario described, 'true' is true of S1 and S2, 'true*' true of S2 but not S1. Supposing for simplicity that these are all the pertinent facts, we can say that 'true' is domestically stable but that a domestic stability thesis for 'true*' isn't true.

Suppose, however that 'true' is true of* S1 but not S2, and that 'true*' is true of* S1 and S2. Let some sentence S be part of the home extension* of a variant of 'true*' iff S is in the language of the variant and the variant is true* of it. Suppose the community of 'true*' users utters the sentence that we use to express domestic plasticity. We can allow that they would be saying something true (and not merely true*), since they would be saying that if something is a close variant of 'true*', then a sentence is part of the home extension* of that variant iff 'true*' is true* of it.[34] Each community gets to speak the truth by the variants of the domestic plasticity thesis owing to the fact that shifts in 'true' are accompanied by compensating shifts in 'true of'.

Similar considerations can be raised for a community with 'true' and 'says that' as their basic ideology. We certainly want close variants of the schema:

if 's' says that S then 's' is true iff S

---

[34] In the toy scenario described, something is a close variant of 'true*' iff it is a close variant of 'true'. In other cases, extra complications will arise via the fact that the close variant relation is not transitive.

to have only true instances. If we now allow that 'true' is not domestically stable, then we are in trouble. For we certainly want disquotational instances of " 'S' says that 'S' " to be true at close variant communities. Suppose, then, that S2 is true but that " 'S2' is true*" is false, and that S2 belongs to the language of 'true*'. Then

If 'S2' says that S2 then ('S2' is true* iff S2)

will have a true antecedent and false consequent. Assuming, then, that we want disquotational instances of " 'S' says that S" to come out true at close variant communities, we must think of 'true' as domestically stable.

But we do not have to think of 'true' as semantically stable. Let 'Talking donkeys are impossible' and 'Talking donkeys are impossible*' be S1 and S2 respectively. Suppose further:

'Talking donkeys are impossible*' says that talking donkeys are impossible.

Suppose 'Talking donkeys are impossible' and 'Talking donkeys are impossible*' are both true. Compatibly with all this I can allow that the variant community speaks the truth in saying:

'Talking donkeys are impossible' is false*

and

'Talking donkeys are impossible*' is true*.

Suppose this was true:

'Talking donkeys are impossible' says that* talking donkeys are impossible*.

Then there will be a false instance of the schema:

If a sentence S says that* P then S is true* iff P.

For, given that 'Talking donkeys is impossible*' is true, and " 'Talking donkeys is impossible' is true*" is false, then

If 'Talking donkeys are impossible' says that* talking donkeysare impossible*, then ('Talking donkeys are impossible' is true* iff talking donkeys are impossible)

would contain a true antecedent and a false consequent. But we can allow the schema in question to have all and only true instances by allowing for compensating adjustments in the meaning of 'says that'. In particular, we can allow that

" 'Talking donkeys are impossible' says that* talking donkeys are impossible*"

a sentence in the variant language, is false. Once again, we can perfectly well combine domestic stability with semantic plasticity.

§19

I have, in effect, tried to develop two competing versions of epistemicism. It should be clear that I have a mild preference for the metaphysically inflationary version. But my main aim has been to map out the conceptual terrain, rather than to advance a view with any confidence.[35] At the very least, I hope that this discussion will serve as a useful springboard for future treatments of semantic plasticity and epistemicism.

Rutgers University

---

[35] After all, the discussion will seem inevitably simple-minded once one takes stock of the literature on semantic paradox. It may turn out to be obligatory in that setting to complicate the picture of a few simple semantic magnets, especially if one wishes for a treatment that is compatible with a commitment (for any given truth-predicate) to bivalence. Note, though, that this falls short of allowing some variant of a truth-predicate to be false of a sentence that the truth-predicate is true of. One might thus complicate the picture by (at a first pass) allowing for a range of 'truth' magnets of increasingly wider intensions, but none with competing intensions (in the sense that the intension of some variant of 'true' never includes a possible sentence that is also delivered by the intension of some variant of 'false').

Part IV

METAPHYSICS AND THEISM

11. God and the Problem of Universals

Brian Leftow

We sort things into classes we find natural: we call some animals cats, some dogs, etc. In so doing we attribute being cats, dogs, etc. to them. Theories of attributes are answers to the question, "what exactly makes it correct to attribute to something (say) being a cat?" Some philosophers, realists, think that what makes it correct is that this animal has a real constituent, cathood, in common with all other cats: there is a single entity, a universal, cathood, in which (so to speak) all cats overlap. Other philosophers, nominalists, deny that there is such a thing as cathood. Recent theories of attributes typically do not assume that God exists. There are at least two reasons for this: most philosophers do not think it likely that God exists, and even more do not see how the existence of God could ever bear on the theory of attributes. It was not always thus. In the debate's medieval heyday, the players were all theists. Many saw God's existence as intensely relevant to this issue. Aquinas, for instance, rejects Platonist theories of universals because "it seems contrary to the faith to hold, as the Platonists did, that the Forms of things exist in themselves".[1] Ockham wielded against Scotus principles based finally on his understanding of God's omnipotence.[2] I'd like to show that the medievals were at least partly correct: if there were a God, this would have dramatic implications for the problem of universals. In particular, it would (I believe) blunt the force of all standard arguments for realism. When I've argued this, I consider what sort of nominalism theists ought to adopt about attributes only creatures have and take up objections to the sort I suggest. I then turn to attributes creatures share with God. These turn out to require a different (but still nominalist) treatment. The sorts of nominalism I suggest provide a novel form of argument for God's existence.

---

[1] Aquinas, *ST* Ia q. 84 a. 5.
[2] As the anonymous author of the *Tractatus de Principiis Theologiae* makes plain.

Suppose, then, that there is a God, a necessarily existent being necessarily omniscient, omnipotent, eternal, and Creator of all concrete things other than He. I now suggest that this should remove all intuitive pressure toward Platonist versions of realism. Once I've argued this, I suggest that it should also remove all intuitive pressure toward non-Platonist realism.

GOD AND PLATONISM

Platonist theories of attributes hold that universals can and do exist unexemplified: that whether or not there ever were cats, there would be a universal, cathood. One motive for attribute-Platonism is modal. Platonists want uninstanced universals to provide truthmakers for necessary truths–uninstanced necessarily existing cathood to make it true before cats exist that were anything a cat it would be a mammal.[3] But God can do this work. An omniscient God has all possible concepts. If God is necessarily existent and omniscient, then in all possible worlds, God has His actual concept *cat*.[4] It is simple parsimony to let divine concepts do as much work as they can once they're in one's metaphysic. So if we start with God on the scene, we ought to make use of His concepts. The contents of God's actual cat-concept can make it true in all possible worlds that if anything is a cat as actually conceived (@-cat), it is a mammal. It's crucial here that we do not assume Platonism—but of course we should not in this context, since we are considering arguments *for* Platonism, and whether they work if there is a God. Suppose then that God stipulates that cats shall be mammals, forming His cat-concept so that this is part of it. There is nothing Platonic to say Him nay. And the rest of reality is bound by His stipulation. As necessarily God is Creator, necessarily any concrete thing other than He instances

---

[3] So e.g. Michael Loux, *Substance and Attribute* (Dordrecht: D. Reidel, 1978), 95; Roderick Chisholm, *On Metaphysics* (Minneapolis: University of Minnesota Press, 1989), 141–2.

[4] This claim does not assume that cats as actually conceived necessarily are possible. But if there is a possible or possibly possible or etc. world in which there are cats as actually conceived, then in any other world, such cats are at least an *im*possible sort of entity, on a par (though perhaps only contingently so) with the round square. So given that cats in fact exist, in any other world, God has the concept of a cat as at least an impossible sort of entity. Of course, cats and round squares aren't in all respects on a par, even in worlds in which cats are impossible.

one of His concepts and exists because He has created it so. So necessarily, before cats ever exist, God has His actual cat-concept, and its contents plus God's position as Creator guarantee that were there @-cats, they would be mammals. If God necessarily has this concept, then this truth necessarily is provided for. We can also get this result without assuming that God necessarily has His actual cat-concept. If God actually conceives only mammal cats, then in every possible world in which there are @-cats, they are mammals, and the ultimate root of this fact is that God's concept @-*cat* stipulates this. Suppose this so and now consider worlds in which there are no @-cats. In these worlds, the closest @-cat worlds will all be mammal cat worlds. The reason for this will ultimately be the contents of God's concept @-*cat* in worlds in which He has this concept.

Chisholm argues Platonism thus: "Consider the...statement...' there are shapes that are not exemplified'... Such statements... cannot be paraphrased into statements referring only to individuals. This... constitutes at least a *prima facie* justification for accepting (that) there *are* properties, some... exemplified and some... not."[5] So too, virtue is its own reward even if no one is virtuous. Now Chisholm's point may be at root modal. We do think there is such a thing as the shape of a Euclidean triangle, even if there are no such triangles. But our reasons to think this may boil down to its being possible that something have that shape: "there *is* an unexemplified shape" may assert no more than that something can have that shape. This possibility can rest on God's possessing the relevant concept. If there is a non-modal point here, divine concepts can do what needs doing. For an unexemplified shape to exist presumably amounts to there being something x not located in space-time such that things come to have a particular shape just in case they come into a suitable relation with x. Fine: why can't a divine concept be a value of x?

Tooley shows compelling advantages in an account of natural laws as relations among universals.[6] Tooley argues a Platonist account of these universals thus: the universe could so vary that life never evolved

---

[5] Chisholm, *On Metaphysics*, 141–2. Presumably Chisholm has only actual individuals in view—admit merely possible (i.e. non-existent) individuals, and such paraphrases as "some possible individual has a shape no actual individual has" heave into view. But (say I) there *are* only actual individuals, so that's fine.

[6] Michael Tooley, *Causation* (New York: Oxford University Press, 1987), *passim* but esp. 137–42. See also Evan Fales, *Causation and Universals* (New York: Routledge, 1990).

without varying in basic natural laws. For instance, the earth's having had a different orbit would not have entailed a difference in natural law. So if

life never evolve[d] because the earth is too close to the sun, it [could] still be a basic psychophysical law that whenever organisms are in a certain complex brain state, they have experiences with a certain specific quality of redness, even though... [there are], by hypothesis, no sentient organisms, and *a fortiori* no experiences of the red variety. But if laws are relations among universals, then [this] cannot be a basic law... unless the relevant universals exist.[7]

So the universal *phenomenal redness* must exist even if no experiences of red ever do. But God could provide for such laws. Natural necessities could rest entirely on God's concepts and volitions.[8] Perhaps the reason these brain states must give rise to those experiences, even if there are no brains, is that God would allow no other result.

I've claimed that an appeal to God's mind can undercut motivations to Platonize attributes. But Platonists can try to turn the tables on me. Attribute-Platonists can appeal to God's mental content. If we need Platonist attributes to make sense of this, then in the end, appeal to God's mind leaves us as much reason to Platonize as we had originally. There are at least four tacks a Platonist can take here.

Attributes and Content

Before Creation, one divine mental state was God's knowing that

1. were there any cats, they would be mammals, not
2. were there any cats, they would be vegetables.

Why was its content (1), not (2)? Surely (we think) something must account for its having had one content, not the other. When we think a state has a content, it's natural to think that something is the content it has, that having a content is having a relation to some sort of object. It seems natural to say that the state was or was a consequence of God's grasping the nature of cats, what it is to be a cat, the attribute *being a cat*. So it also seems natural to say that there was a divine mental state

---

[7] Tooley, *Causation*, 114.
[8] See e.g. Del Ratzsch, "Nomo(theo)logical Necessity", in Michael Beaty, (ed.), *Christian Theism and the Problems of Philosophy* (Notre Dame, Ind.: University of Notre Dame Press, 1990), 184–207.

whose content included the attribute. If so, the attribute existed and was an unexemplified (Platonist) universal, unless mental states can have non-existent intentional objects. Further, it existed *really* rather than "merely intentionally" if there are no multiple modes of being, and instead things either simply exist or simply do not. Perhaps God's mental activity produced this attribute. Perhaps it merely grasped something that was there anyway. Either way, the attribute existed and was not exemplified.

But we needn't think this way, even if we grant the large ontological assumptions this argument makes. We could treat being contentful, and contentful one way rather than another, as a primitive fact about mental states or events. If we bring the attribute into the story of God's mental content, the story goes this way: a particular state includes the attribute *being a cat* and so is or leads to God's knowing (1). Why does it include the attribute? It just does.[9] That's just the state's nature, as a brute fact; that's where explanation stops. Without the attribute, the story goes: the state is or leads to God's knowing (1). Why? It just is (or does). That's its nature, as a brute fact; that's where explanation stops. Either way, explanation stops at a brute fact about the nature of a mental state. Why, really, is the one resting-point any better than the other? In fact, the two resting-points might be the same. For each may really come down to saying that God knows what He does because He thinks a certain way. God thinks a certain way, such that His thought grasps or includes an attribute and so He knows (1), or God simply thinks a certain way, such that He knows (1). If we rest finally in a brute fact about God's thinking either way, why prefer the more baroque story to one with cleaner, attribute-free lines?

The Platonist might regroup here. "You speak of the nature of a mental state. Natures are attributes, and natures of mental states needn't be instanced: God in a world without Adam has no mental state instancing the nature *knowing that Adam exists*. Or if you don't want to treat states as subjects of attributes, you can rephrase this: there is an attribute of knowing that Adam exists. In a world without Adam, this attribute exists but is not instanced." One reply is that "the nature of x" can be ontologically innocent. Rather than invoking a distinct entity, it can be just a way to say "x insofar as it makes it true that P", for some

---

[9] Later I introduce the notion of a state's "targeting" an attribute. Bringing this in wouldn't alter the argument in any important way, so I ignore it here.

P necessarily true of x. In any event, why exactly are we supposed to think that if Adam does not exist, there is such an attribute as knowing that he exists? The only reason I can see is that it is possible to know that Adam exists. And we can deal with this by a simple wrinkle on an argument above: God's concepts can provide for this possibility. On the other hand, if God necessarily knows that (1), the property of having content (1) (or of knowing that (1)), is necessarily exemplified; it cannot exist uninstanced. It's at best an Aristotelian universal.[10] Of course, if I say no more than this, then while I block Platonism, I leave an issue Aristotelians can exploit. I take this up in my discussion of Aristotelian universals. A Platonist might regroup here yet again, and suggest a non-modal account of what makes attributes Platonist: not that they *can* exist unexemplified, but that they are, say, intrinsically indifferent to exemplification. We could cash this out as follows: even if they are necessarily exemplified, if they *weren't* exemplified, they would still exist—and this counterpossible's truth is overdetermined, by the semantics that renders all counterpossibles trivially true and the nature of the attribute. But what argument could the Platonist offer for this claim?

Attributes and Causal Powers

A second appeal to divine mental content runs this way. The (1)-vs.-(2) difference has causal consequences. Because God's state has content (1), not (2), when God made cats, they came out mammals, not vegetables. Some real thing must account for any difference in causal role, and so for the state's giving God the power to produce mammal but not vegetable cats (or perhaps just being that power, or being a power that gives God that power among others). Surely the natural candidate here is a real attribute, *being a cat*, which helps give the state its content. But if it is necessary that (1), in a world without cats, God would still know that (1). So we should be Platonists about attributes: God grasps them whether or not they are exemplified.

I am skeptical of this proposed explanation. What does the attribute really contribute to it? Without the attribute, we can say: here's a

---

[10] If God does not necessarily know (1), He still necessarily knows things involving (1): again, cats are necessarily at least an impossible sort of entity, given that they actually exist. There necessarily *is* such a thing as being a cat, whether or not it is possibly exemplified in every possible world.

mental state with certain roles in God's thinking and willing, such that when that state guides God's action, He produces mammal cats. Why does it have these roles? It just is that way: it just does. Perhaps its having them *is* its having a particular mental content, one purely narrow, not involving the existence of anything that might also exist beyond God's "head". The real thing that accounts for the difference in causal role is not some constituent of the state but simply the state itself, which is a (1)-rather than (2)-state. With the attribute, we can say why the (1)-state has its roles: some divine state (perhaps the (1)-state itself) grasps this attribute, and this helps give God's (1)-state its causal roles. *But why did the state grasp this attribute, not another?* No answer: it just did. It just does have the causal role of grasping one attribute, not another, and because it does so, it guides God's action to mammalian cats. Here the attribute seems an idle wheel. Either way, some divine mental state has an ultimate brute causal role. Why not just say directly that the (1)-state is such that God will if He acts on it make mammal cats? On pain of infinite regress, there have to be differences in causal role that aren't further accounted for. What's the advantage to seeing the ultimate brute power involved as one to grasp an attribute rather than one to guide action a certain way? Nor does talk of aptitude to guide action bring Platonist attributes into the picture. A Platonist attribute can exist unexemplified. If God is necessarily omniscient, He necessarily has any concept He can have, and so any such aptitude is necessarily exemplified.[11]

Broad Content

Another Platonist attempt might focus on the relation between the content of God's concepts and items outside God's mind. There are two notions of what it is for a mental state's content to be narrow. On one, a mental state has narrow content just if it does not involve items outside the mind: it does not have such items as constituents, nor does

---

[11] There are complications here about singular concepts: some argue that God can have a singular concept of a particular creature only if that creature actually exists. (So e.g. Christopher Menzel, "Temporal Actualism and Singular Foreknowledge", in James Tomberlin (ed.), *Philosophical Perspectives V* (Atascadero, Calif.: Ridgeview Press, 1991), 475–508. If that's true, then if some creatures exist contingently, there are (singular) concepts God has only contingently. I hold that God has singular concepts of possible creatures whether or not they exist, but I can't discuss the matter here.

its identity depend on any such items, nor therefore does its existence entail the existence of external items. On another, a mental state has narrow content just if it is insulated from differences in the external world: that is, just if there are not external circumstances such that were they different, the state's content would *ipso facto* be different, even if what was in the thinker's "head" were in all intrinsic respects identical. A mental state's content is broad just if it is not narrow.

Now in the second sense, a divine mental state grasping a Platonist attribute can't thereby have broad content. Platonist attributes don't differ intrinsically from world to world. So it's not the case that the content of a divine mental state grasping one could have been different due to an intrinsic difference in the attribute without there having been any difference in God's internal state, for the content of the divine state could not have been different due to an intrinsic difference in the attribute. If a divine mental state *produces* a Platonist attribute as its content, it's hard to know what to say about narrowness in the first sense: is the attribute "in" or "outside" God's mind? But if a divine mental state grasps an attribute that was there externally independent of any divine mental activity, making it that state's content, that state's content is broad in the first sense. A Platonist can allege that benefits would flow from calling God's mental content broad in this sense. For by calling the content of this divine state broad, we could ascribe to God knowledge of external attributes with all the epistemic advantages of our knowledge of our own mental states' narrow contents. If the content of God's mental states is broad, He knows items in the world by knowing the contents of His own mind: by grasping the nature of cats in His mind, He grasps with introspective security and transparency the very entity which exists extra-mentally.[12] So (a Platonist might contend) we ought to see God's mental states as grasping Platonist attributes to secure these advantages.

But this wouldn't commend Platonism over Aristotelianism—since God could equally have broad-content mental states involving natures that exist only if exemplified. For that matter, it doesn't commend Platonism over nominalism, since God could also have broad-content states involving particulars (why not?), and on some sorts of nominalism,

---

[12] This argument glosses over a large debate: *is* it possible for states with broad content to afford the epistemic benefits theories of narrow content traditionally allowed to introspectively founded belief? For discussion, see Peter Ludlow and Norah Martin (eds.), *Externalism and Self-Knowledge* (Stanford, Calif.: CSLI, 1998).

that's all that would be needed to have broad-content states involving those particulars' natures. Moreover, we can have the advantages for free. The mere fact that an attribute in the external world can only be as God thinks and wills it to be is enough to guarantee God's knowledge of it is every bit as complete and secure as He could have by introspection, whatever the status of His mental content. There is nothing particularly worthwhile about *getting* knowledge introspectively. What matters is that the world be as transparent to God as our (narrow) introspective contents are to us, and that He knows it as securely as we know narrow contents by pure introspection. These claims are true whatever we say about His mental content.

Pre-Creative Intentionality

There is another way thoughts about God's mental content might move one toward attribute-Platonism, which was actually involved in the Platonist's first attempt. Some find it puzzling that God, or anyone, can have thoughts genuinely *about* items that in no way exist. For if possibilism is false, as all the right-thinking believe, what does not exist has no properties. But then in particular what does not exist has no converse intentional attributes, like being referred to or being the subject of a thought. So if God has a concept *of* an attribute, it seems to follow that the attribute exists. Since (surely?) not all attributes of which God has concepts have instances, there are then attributes that exist uninstanced.

This line of thought broaches deep issues I cannot discuss here. But I will make a suggestion. If there are unexemplified attributes, the divine conceivings whose contents they are either do or do not produce them. If a conceiving brings one to be, presumably something about it, logically before the attribute exists, determines that the conceiving will bring *that* attribute to be—directs it to produce *that* attribute, not another. Whatever that is, why can't such a targeting, on its own, without producing an attribute, make the conceiving state one directed toward one attribute, not another? In fact, this targeting surely *does* direct the state toward that attribute—that's why, on this view, it does produce that attribute. But then we can just suggest that the state's "aboutness" consists in this targeting, deleting all reference to the targeting *producing* an attribute, and hold that due to this targeting, if God in the right way acts on what He in this state conceives, He'll produce a particular extra-mental attribute, perhaps by producing an instance of it. Such a state would grasp (target) what the attribute would be like if God did produce it. And note that if I have a mental state that grasps just what an attribute would be like but not the attribute itself, and am fully cognizant of what that state will produce if appropriately called-on, I have a wholly adequate conception of the attribute, yet the attribute does not acquire so much as a converse-intentional attribute.[13]

Suppose now that a divine conceiving grasps an unexemplified attribute that exists independent of it, outside God's mind. We have very little idea how this would work. And as I see it we can't here follow our usual procedure in thinking about God's mind and to some extent model it on our own case. For I do not believe that there *are* unexemplified attributes, nor then that we ever do grasp any such things (whatever "grasping" is). But if there were unexemplified attributes, our "grasping" of them could not be perceptual. All perception is founded on causal relations to the things perceived, and abstract, uninstanced attributes could not cause us to perceive them. So we could not acquire concepts of them directly, by relations involving the attributes themselves. We would form our concepts of them by working with materials acquired elsewhere. The most reasonable view would surely be that we "grasp" them simply by imagining things that have them, or imagining what it would be to have them—in mathematical cases, perhaps led by mathematical-inductive reasoning. Then what would make it the case that we grasp an unexemplified attribute, if ever we did so, is simply that we get right what does in fact exist. But if this is the best story, then it would be the case that something about the act of (say) imagining, logically before it produced the content perceiving which constitutes grasping an attribute, makes that act "target" one imaginative content, and so one attribute, rather than another. And given this much, the reasoning proceeds as before: the "aboutness" of God's relevantly similar state would consist in the same sort of targeting, etc.

Thus (I submit) there is no case for attribute-Platonism in God's mental content. And so (I submit) if there is a God, there is no argument for attribute-Platonism, and a good argument against it from parsimony: if the arguments for Platonism represent appeals to all the

---

[13] Here again, of course, the Platonist might ask about what sort of property of the state this "targeting" would be—how I'm to account for it. And here again the answer is that whatever this is, it is at most an Aristotelian universal. It is exemplified in every possible world, if God is necessarily omniscient.

intuitions Platonists can marshal, then God can soak up all Platonist intuitions with no added ontological bloat. If we start from God, then, we should conclude that Platonism is false.

ARISTOTELIAN REALISM

Aristotelians hold that while universals do not exist unexemplified, they exist in their instances: the property of being a cat, again, in all cats. There are five main arguments for this view. There is also an Aristotelian appeal to properties of God's mental content to consider.

One Aristotelian argument runs roughly this way: things appear to share properties. Different tokens appear to be of the same type. This apparent fact can't be explained away. So there must be some philosophical account of it. Only realism will do: either no form of nominalism gives an adequate account of this, or some forms of nominalism do, but on balance a realist account still comes out best.[14] One main factor determining which theory comes out best here is economy: if a nominalist account can give as robust and explanatory an account of this as a realist theory, the nominalist theory automatically wins. If appeal to God's concepts counts as a form of nominalism—of which more anon—this argument is undercut. Appeal to God is more economical, and we see shortly that it does in fact provide an explanation of apparent sameness of type.

Cats form a real kind or natural class. Cats and sneezes do not. One argument for Aristotelian universals comes from the need for something to account for the unity of natural classes, and so to distinguish them from non-natural classes: universals present in all and only the members of natural classes would do this, and (Aristotelians allege) either nothing else will, or nothing else will as well.[15] This is a worry about the objectivity and correctness of schemes of classification: if there aren't real universals, what makes only some classes natural? The short

---

[14] In, *Nominalism and Realism* (New York: Cambridge University Press, 1978). D. M. Armstrong took the tack that no form of nominalism works. In *Universals* (Boulder, Colo.: Westview, 1989), he went for the weaker claim that on balance, realism works best.

[15] Armstrong, *Universals*, 13–14. Obviously this argument recommends only theories of "sparse" universals, on which only natural properties are real universals, rather than theories on which there is a real universal for (nearly) every concept that can be formed, however outré.

answer here is that divine concepts can do the needed work. Suppose that God creates things in various kinds—that is, to instance various divine kind-concepts. Then those are the kinds to which things really belong: they have all and only the kind-traits God wills them to have. (Where else could a kind-nature come from, if God is on the scene?) Then a scheme of classification will be correct just if it divides things as do the divine general concepts that really sort things into different kinds, and objective if correct because these kind-divisions do not come from us. The natural classes are those that satisfy certain general divine concepts. This sort of appeal to God accepts the naturalness of classes (equivalently, real facts of sameness of type) rather than trying to explain them away. And it offers a genuine explanation of apparent sameness of type—even a causal explanation of it, which realism cannot as such give.[16]

Now given God's omniscience, a question arises here. God has both a concept all and only cats satisfy and a concept all and only cats and sneezes satisfy. We can wonder why just one of these determines a natural class. Isn't something like a real universal all cats share still needed here to make the natural/non-natural distinction? I think not. One option is to say that the natural classes are just those determined by the concepts to satisfy which God created. The rest, one can say, represent concepts by which God noticed what would be out there in the world He'd decided to make, but which He did not act in order to instance. Perhaps God acted in order to make cats and acted in order to make clouds, but merely noted and accepted that if He so acted, His concept of being a cat or a cloud would also apply. This is ultimately a distinction that involves causation. For concepts God acted to satisfy are among the causal conditions of His creative act. Concepts He did not act to satisfy are not. Distinctions between items causally involved in a particular result and items not so involved are as real and objective as any one can find. So this approach provides an objective basis to distinguish natural from non-natural classes.[17]

---

[16] To explain the "as such": realists can of course try to explain all cats' being of the same type in terms of descent from common ancestors. This is a causal explanation. But it is not a distinctively realist explanation. Nominalists could say the same.

[17] A question worth considering: does this imply that had God willed to create not cats but cats-or-sneezes, or cats-or-non-events, these would have been the natural properties—with the world looking exactly the same? That is, does this view force us to be skeptics about our judgments of naturalness? Nothing about the view that which properties are natural depends on how God made the world entails that He might have done otherwise in

Some have argued that we need universals to explain how distinct things can satisfy common predicates.[18] I do not regard this as a promising argument, but I'll note anyway that God can do the work here as well. Perhaps what makes it the case that "__ is a cat" applies to both Boots and Puff is that both causally depend in the right way on the same divine concept. You might object here that if you see a cat, you notice that it is a cat—you pick up perceptually on that in it which makes it correct to call it a cat. But you can't see a divine concept. If you can't see a divine concept, you can't see a relation to a divine concept. I reject a premise here. You can't see quarks, but you can see what it looks like to bear certain relations to a quark, for you can see what it looks like to be a cat, and whatever is a cat bears to a great many quarks such relations as __ *has as a part*__ . So too, perhaps what you see is what satisfying a divine concept looks like.

A fourth realist argument is that we need universals to explain, explicate, or ground resemblance: what makes two cats perfectly similar in species is that both are cats, and this, it's alleged, must be explained by their having cathood in common.[19] This is not *quite* the natural-class worry in another guise: classes may be natural without involving perfect similarity among their members, or even perfect similarity in a single respect. Again, this argument doesn't seem to me to have much hope of pushing one into realism. Two cats are alike because both are cats, but why think that both being cats has to be explained by a common constituent? If there is any work to do here, God can do it. What makes two cats perfectly similar in species—both cats—can be their depending causally on the same divine concept. At any moment at which both exist, God sustains both. He keeps them in being and intentionally keeps them cats.[20] So both are cats because of divine acts among whose causal conditions is the same general divine concept. And this (obviously) is a genuine *causal* explanation of their likeness.

---

these respects, or that if He had, the world would look the same to us. Perhaps God would guarantee that we perceived as natural whichever properties He'd made so. And perhaps God's concept *cat* just is the kind of concept He would no matter what make a natural kind: perhaps that's just how His mind works. If so, it isn't in fact possible that He make being-cat-or-sneeze a natural property.

[18] This line of thought of course goes back to Plato.
[19] For variations on this see Loux, *Substance and Attribute*, 44–53.
[20] "Aren't they essentially cats?" Well, we don't have to assume this. If they are, then keeping them cats is part and parcel of keeping them in existence. If they're not, then God keeps them cats though He has the option to make something else of them.

A last realist argument appeals to abstract reference.[21] It's claimed that there is no adequate nominalist paraphrase for such claims as that

orange is more like red than blue is.

This is true only if "orange" refers. So if there is nothing nominalistically acceptable for it to refer to, orange must refer to some single color, found in all orange things. Here again, God can ride to the rescue. Consider the paraphrase that depending on God's concept *orange* is more like depending on God's concept *yellow* than depending on God's concept *blue* is. This has to work. For what it really does is analyze the property-expressions in the original in terms of a theory, that to have a color is to depend on a divine color-concept. This theory is an isomorph of Plato's version of Platonism, that to have an attribute F (for appropriate F) is to depend on the Form of F, with God's concepts taking the place of Platonic Forms. So if Platonism would give an acceptable rendering of the original—as none deny—so does appeal to God's concepts. Of course, if God's concepts take the place of Platonic Forms, one wonders: is this just a version of Platonism itself? There will be more to say about this, but for the moment, note that Platonism as introduced above is belief in *universals* that exist uninstanced. Plato's Forms were not universals: they were not present *in* any of their instances. Plato was an odd sort of nominalist, if realism be understood as belief in immanent universals. So even if this *were* a form of Platonism, it would be nominalist on the account above. Of course, if God's concepts are so like Platonic Forms, the question arises whether they're any ontological improvement on the Forms: if appeal to God brings the Forms (in effect) with it, you may think, better to avoid God. I take this up below.

With God in one's ontology, there is reason to think that one should not believe in universals—unless such things as dependence on God's concept *orange* turn out to be universals. But there's no obvious reason they must.[22] Theists, then, should be nominalists.

---

[21] See Armstrong, *Nominalism and Realism*, 58–61, and Loux, *Substance and Attribute*, 54–88.

[22] I've suggested analyzing property-terms quite generally in terms of dependence on divine concepts. These could well be particular *cases* of dependence: tropes. Or for that matter, Boots's dependence on God's concept *cat* could be an ordered pair, <Boots, cat>. We needn't even commit to relation-tropes here; some sort of nominalism about relations might do.

THEIST CONCEPT-NOMINALISM

What sort of nominalism sits best with theism? Appeal to God is not a taxi one can step off when one likes. If a theist ought to do as much with God as he can before appealing to other entities, a theist ought to look for the least commissive version of nominalism, the one that brings in the least that is outside God. For attributes God and creatures do not share, one might first consider a theist version of concept-nominalism. Concept-nominalism is the view that for an appropriate range of Fs, to be an F is just to fall under "the" concept of an F. I'll consider some main objections to concept-nominalism and point out that a theist concept-nominalism escapes almost all of them. And it should not be surprising that it does, for theist concept-nominalism, again, is akin to Plato's version of Platonism, a theory which if nominalist is at least unusual for nominalism.

I begin with perhaps the most basic unease one might have with human concept-nominalism: can't we have the wrong scheme of classification? Concept-nominalism allows that individual humans can make mistakes. We do not all command perfectly the concept-schemes we learn. But if there is such a thing as "the" conceptual scheme of humanity as a whole, or of a given society, in (say) its ideal development as judged by its own strictly internal standards, couldn't that fail to match up with the real system of kinds there is? Not all share this worry—Putnam, for instance, would not. But for those who do, it's worth noting that God's conceptual scheme can't get it wrong, because things are what they are because God made them in accord with it.

D. M. Armstrong raises four sorts of problem for concept-nominalism generally.[23] One is that there are not enough actual human concepts to unify all actual natural classes. Thus human concept-nominalism hasn't enough raw material to carry through its program. A related point is that (apart from some obvious exceptions), it's possible for things to be F even if there is no human concept of F: in fact, this is actually so. If this is so, then of course as a general rule being F can't depend on the existence of the appropriate human concept. By contrast, God, as omniscient, has all possible concepts. So there is nothing a thing could be of which God would not have a concept. And His position as necessarily Creator would guarantee that there cannot be something that falls

---

[23] Armstrong, *Nominalism and Realism*, 27.

under no actual divine concept even if He somehow did not have all possible concepts.

Armstrong also raises a problem about causation. Their properties determine how and what things cause. So the causal order depends on the properties of things. It does not depend on the existence of human minds. But on human concept-nominalism, what properties things have depends on how they are related to minds. So on human concept-nominalism, the causal order does depend on the human mind. The theist rejoinder, of course, will be that while the causal order is independent of human minds, it is not independent of God's mind. So there is no dilemma here for theist concept-nominalism.

Armstrong also notes that if something is F, the human concept of F applies to it because it is F, not vice versa. But it just is not the case that God's concept of F applies because things are F. The vice versa holds here: Boots is a cat because God applies His concept *cat* to her, i.e. conceives and makes her to be a cat. You might think this claim confused. There are at least two ways a concept applies to things. A maker can apply a concept to a thing causally, molding it according to the concept. A concept applies to a thing descriptively just if its content is sufficiently close to describing it adequately. God's concept *cat*, you may think, does not apply to Boots in the descriptive sense till God's *causal* application of it has succeeded: first God makes Boots, then it is the case that His concept *cat* adequately describes Boots. But this, I think, gets the mechanics of creation *ex nihilo* wrong. As Creator, God simply stipulates: "I declare it true that Boots is a cat." As a result, Boots is a cat. It's because the concept applies descriptively—by divine fiat—that it applies causally, i.e. Boots comes to be a cat (also by divine fiat).

Being Intrinsic

One could also raise a worry about intrinsic properties: on human concept-nominalism it is not clear that any properties are really intrinsic, since on this view, with some obvious exceptions, for all F, whether something is F depends on its relations to something outside itself. But surely if we know anything at all about being intrinsic, such properties as being a dog are intrinsic. One can wonder, then, whether theist concept-nominalism also has a problem with the intrinsic. A response can begin by saying something about being intrinsic—first on a purely intuitive level, then in terms of developed accounts of being intrinsic.

God and the Problem of Universals | 341

Intuitively, a property F is intrinsic just if whether a thing is F is settled entirely within the thing's skin: roughly, just if being F is independent of whatever is or is not so outside the F-thing.[24] Let's ask what "outside" means in the case at hand. God is omnipresent. One can gloss this in terms of God's having a spatial location or in terms of His lacking all spatial location. If God has any location, He is everywhere, and so as truly within a dog as without. If He is in the dog, presumably His (narrow-content) concepts count as in the dog too: if my concepts are in my head and I am in the room, my concepts are in the room. If the universe ended at Fido's skin, God and His concepts would not exist outside Fido, but would just as truly exist within Fido: while God is not a part or property of Fido, God's presence within Fido counts as an intrinsic fact about Fido, it seems. This is not surprising. Relations to things within an item's skin count as intrinsic to the item. We ordinarily focus on parts and perhaps properties as intrinsic because we think of these as the only items that might ordinarily be within a thing's skin. If there is a God who is everywhere, though, these are not the only items.

If we do not say that God's concepts count as where God is, then since they aren't going to be anywhere else—God being omnipresent, there's nowhere else to be—we'll have to say that they're nowhere, and so have no spatial relations to anything. We must take up what to say if they do not regardless, for if God has *no* location, nor then do His concepts. So He and they are not outside anything—nor inside it. So if our intuitive characterization of the intrinsic is in terms of what's inside and outside a thing, we can't conclude at an intuitive level that relation to a divine concept is or that it is not intrinsic to Fido. And so on this account of omnipresence, at an intuitive level, the problem dissolves. For there is a problem only if being a dog is intrinsic and there is some reason to think that relation to a divine concept is not intrinsic to Fido.

The fact that we can't call relation to God intrinsic or non-intrinsic if He is non-spatial shows *inter alia* that the intuitive characterization won't do. A good account of the intrinsic ought to apply to any non-spatial

---

[24] There's an immediate problem with this intuitive formulation. Being a dog is intrinsic (I've said). But necessarily, if Fido is a dog, there either is or is not something else. If Fido is a dog and there is anything else, something is accompanied by a dog. If Fido is a dog and there is nothing else, there is nothing but a dog. So necessarily, if Fido is a dog, either something is accompanied by a dog or there is nothing but a dog: Fido's being a dog entails something about what's so outside Fido. Still, the claim in the text expresses the core intuition here. The problem merely shows that we have work to do to express the intuition properly.

things there might be—God, angels, souls, numbers. So let's consider developed accounts of the intrinsic. A property is intrinsic, intuitively, just if whether a thing has it is independent of what is or is not so outside it. If having the property is independent of what is so outside the property's subject, it is independent of whether the universe ends at its borders. There are various ways to explicate this thought in the literature. Lewis and Langton begin from a base account, that an attribute P is intrinsic just if both an accompanied and an unaccompanied object can both have and lack P, where an object is accompanied just if it coexists with a contingent thing distinct from itself.[25] The account becomes more complex to deal with difficulties involving disjunctive properties, but the complexities don't affect what I want to say, and so I'll ignore them. Doghood is intrinsic on the base account, regardless of whether God figures in its make-up. Lewis and Langton restrict accompaniment to contingent things because if there are necessary beings, it is not possible for anything not to coexist with them. Given this restriction, dependence on a necessarily existent God for an attribute doesn't affect whether the attribute is intrinsic: if God is also necessarily omniscient, He necessarily has the concept on which the attribute depends, for He could not fail to have any concept He possibly has, or possibly possibly has, etc. And there is something right about leaving God out of the picture. Our intuitions about which attributes are intrinsic just don't take God into account. If so, analyzing creaturely attributes as relations to God shouldn't count against their being intrinsic, if they count as intrinsic by ordinary intuitive criteria. That being a dog consists in a relation to a divine concept, and so nothing could be a dog without God, should leave it the case that as we *ordinarily* think of being intrinsic, Fido is intrinsically a dog. Yablo suggests an account based on refining a definition in part/whole terms, that F is intrinsic just if for all x that are parts of worlds W that are parts of worlds W^*, x has F in W just if x has F in W^*.[26] Clearly doghood is again intrinsic on this account, even if God figures in its make-up: necessary beings are parts of all worlds, and so relations to them and concepts they necessarily have are too. Now I'm not suggesting that Lewis/Langton or Yablo have had the last word

---

[25] Rae Langton and David Lewis, "Defining 'Intrinsic' ", *Philosophy and Phenomenological Research* 58 (1998), 333–45. See also Dean Zimmerman, "Immanent Causation", in James Tomberlin (ed.), *Philosophical Perspectives* 11 (Atascadero, Calif.: Ridgeview, 1997), 462–3.

[26] Stephen Yablo, "Intrinsicness", *Philosophical Topics* 26 (1998), 485.

on the intrinsic. But I think they start with an intuition that has to be at the core of the notion and suggest promising routes to developing it. If a theist concept-nominalist analysis of doghood keeps it intrinsic on their accounts, there is reason to think that doghood so analyzed may remain intrinsic on whatever account is the best explication of intrinsicality.

A Type Problem

The last of Armstrong's arguments I'll consider concern types: the concept of F that all Fs fall under, Armstrong asserts, is a type, not a token-concept. And falling-under is a type of relation. Now the first thought just seems a mistake. If I have a token dog-concept, every dog falls under it, whether or not I actually predicate it of any. So the concept-nominalist view can simply be that to be a dog is to fall under some token dog-concept. But still, there are problems in the vicinity. For Fido will fall under any such token. And this is because they all are tokens of a single type-concept—it is because of the type of concept a token dog-concept is. And so we face the question of how to analyze the fact that these tokens are of a single type. We can avoid this question only by not explaining why Fido falls under all token dog-concepts. But giving no account of this leaves a frustrating, unsatisfying theory: why just *these* tokens? And it also leaves the consequence that Fido's being a dog is massively overdetermined, since falling under any one token suffices for being a dog. This doesn't sound right. What makes Fido a dog is his having one property, being a dog. And surely falling under any single one of these concepts is enough to entail that Fido has this property. But why should this be so, if not because the concepts are all of a single type? Fido falls under a token concept because of the type to which the token belongs.

So Fido belongs to a type because he falls under a token concept because the token concept belongs to a type. Why then does the concept belong to a type? If we say that it is because *it* falls under a token concept because *that* concept belongs to a type—the concept-nominalist answer—we're off on an infinite regress. But it's unintuitive that an infinity of levels of concept figure in the explanation of as simple a fact as Fido's falling under a first-level species-concept. And the regress seems vicious. For we meet it in asking what it is for Fido to be of a type. The answer raises the question of what it is for a token dog-concept to be of a type. The answer we give if we're off on the regress is that it consists in the dog-concept's falling under a further concept because *that* concept is of a type. If our account of being of a type always invokes further cases of being of a type, we never get an explanation of what it is to be of a type. One could, I suppose, invoke type-theory of a different sort, and say that it is a mistake to seek an explanation of what it is to be of a type *simpliciter*. What one can have and should seek, the type-theorist can say, is just an explanation of what it is to be of a level-0 type, of a level-1 type, etc. On the type-theoretic move, what it is for Fido to be of a type at level 0 is for Fido to fall under a concept. That is a sufficient explanation of level-0 type-facts. There is nothing more to say. The concept invoked at level 0 is itself of a type, but this is being of a level-1 type, a matter irrelevant to the completeness and adequacy of our account of what it is to be of a level-0 type. But at least as a strategy in human conceptualism, this will run into a problem of too few concepts. We actually at this moment possess only a finite number of type-levels of concept. Suppose that we now have concepts up to level 27. Then there are not now any level-28 concepts. So it is not now the case that for a concept to be of a level-27 type is for it to fall under a concept at level 28. There are no such concepts. Since at any time we have constructed only a finite number of type-levels of concept, at any time, the type-theoretic move fails, for human conceptualism. Theists, of course, have infinite conceptual resources at their disposal. So if the type-theoretic move is acceptable in principle, theists could invoke it. But theists can give a simpler reply. For Fido to be a dog is for him to fall under a single *token* dog-concept, God's. So the regress never starts.

A Harder Type-Problem

Armstrong's second type-worry concerns the falling-under relation. Theist concept-nominalism has a problem here. On concept-nominalism, that Fido is a dog is really the fact that Fido falls under *dog*. That Fido falls under *dog* is really the fact that Fido and *dog* jointly fall under *falls under*. That Fido and *dog* jointly fall under *falls under* is really the fact that Fido, *dog,* and *falls under* jointly fall under *falls under*. Presumably this in turn amounts to the fact that Fido, *dog*, *falls under* and *falls under* jointly fall under *falls under*. But can the same concept fall under itself twice? Distinct tokens of the same type-concept can, if the concept is of (as it were) multiple adicity. But either theist concept-nominalism has but a single token-concept on hand, God's concept *falls under*, or theist concept-nominalism is forced to an infinity of divine token concepts of falling under, of ever-higher adicity. This is the theist concept-nominalist version of Plato's Third Man problem. And this regress seems vicious. We meet it in an effort to say what it is for Fido to fall under a concept. The answer now on offer is that this consists in some *other* set of items' doing so. If our account of falling under a concept always invokes further cases of falling under a concept, we never get an explanation of what it is for something to fall under a concept. Moreover, at each step in the regress, Fido's falling under a concept is analyzed as Fido falling under a concept along with some other items: the very thing we want explained appears in the purported explanation. This seems as clear a case of making no philosophical progress as one will ever meet.

Other theories of universals have their own worries here, of course. Concept nominalism's *falling under* is its substitute for the realist's exemplification. For Fido to be a dog, on any version of realism, is for him to exemplify doghood. This is so only if Fido and doghood jointly exemplify exemplification, and so on in exact parallel. On trope nominalism, for Fido to be a dog is for him to exemplify a trope of doghood, or perhaps for such a trope to be compresent with the rest of his tropes. But then a compresence-trope is compresent with the rest of Fido's tropes. If having every property or relation is a matter of a trope-bundle's containing an appropriate trope, this seems to require a further compresence to render compresence compresent with the rest. This brings Bradley's relation-regress to mind, but that hardly means that there's no problem here to deal with. On likeness nominalism, for Fido to be a dog is for him to be like a paradigm dog. This is so only if the relation between Fido and the dog is appropriately like paradigm likeness, and so on. On set-nominalism, for Fido to be a dog is for him to be a member of the set of dogs. This is so only if the relation between Fido and the set is a member of the set of membership relations, and so on. The last two generate regresses in which Fido does not reappear. Still, even without this feature, it's hard to see how we make philosophical progress here in any way we don't in the concept-nominalist case.

There is then a problem here that no extant theory of universals handles well. This does not entail that no extant theory of universals is true. And if all theories have the problem pretty well equally, it is not reason to reject any particular one of them. And so, in particular, it is not reason to reject theist concept-nominalism. It's also worth noting that the difficulty exists only for positions that insist on treating all attributes alike. But theories of attributes need not be one-size-fits-all. In the medieval context, for instance, Aquinas was a trope nominalist about lowest-level kinds and a different sort about higher-level kinds.[27] Realists can allege that the predicate "exemplifies" is like the predicate "is a barber who shaves all and only those who don't shave themselves": it doesn't express an attribute, something that might be exemplified, because it just can't. But this leaves them with no account of exemplification at all: they've ruled out an account in realist terms, and they can't accept a nominalist account, because that would court the question of why we should not just go nominalist in all cases. Trope theorists have a similar problem with exemplification or compresence: if we can do without a trope in this case, why not elsewhere? Here other sorts of nominalist seem to have an edge: as long as they do not lurch over into realism or tropism, they are free to mix and match different sorts of nominalist account. Theist concept-nominalists might want to consider a likeness-nominalist account of falling-under. Perhaps what it is for Fido to fall under God's concept *dog* is for the relation between Fido and *dog* (or whatever we parse talk of the relation into) to be like a paradigm case of falling-under rooted somewhere in God—say, God's falling under His concept *God*. This would not generate a difficulty about why we should not go likeness-nominalist throughout. In the case of attributes only creatures can have—the case for which I've recommended concept-nominalism—there is just nothing in God to resemble. There is no paradigm dog in God. There is only God's concept of a dog. And a concept does not resemble a dog *qua* dog.[28] And the suggestion that likeness to a created paradigm dog is what makes dogs dogs gets no traction if God is on the scene. If there is a God, Fido is a dog not because of what he resembles but because this is what God made him to be, in accord with His concept *dog*.[29] This is the deepest account of it.[30] The

---

[27] See my "Aquinas on Attributes", *Medieval Philosophy and Thedogy* 11/1 (spring 2003).

[28] Of course, any two things resemble each other in a host of ways: both Fido and God's concept of a dog are things of which God is aware, things of which God is aware He's aware, etc.

[29] Obviously his parents had something to do with it also. Just how created causes and God share responsibility for things' existence is too large a topic to broach here. But the whole point of the classical doctrine of divine conservation is to let theists say that God's responsibility for things' existence after Creation is underway is not essentially different from His responsibility for the existence of those things He brought to be at the first instant of Creation (assuming that there was one).

[30] That is, whatever Fido's parents' contributions, they are less fundamental than God's.

God and the Problem of Universals | 347

theist concept-nominalist theory of doghood just lets this deepest account do as a theory of attributes. Fido is related to God logically before he is related to anything else. For first (logically) he is created, and only then (logically) can he stand in any other relation. So if Fido's relation to God as Creator suffices to settle any particular fact about him, there is nothing left for anything else to settle. Fido's relation to God as Creator settles the fact that he is a dog. If so, there is nothing about his being a dog left for likeness to other dogs to settle.

IS IT JUST PLATONISM?

If one is a theist, one has God and His concepts on hand anyway. There is reason to think that these are all we need for an adequate theory of attributes only creatures can have. If this is correct, theists get their theory of these attributes—part of a full theory of universals—for free. Is it in fact the ontologically cheapest theory of universals? That depends on whether this is really Platonism coming in by the back door. There is a problem here, prima facie. If God is not in space and (as I hold) not in time, divine concepts are not either, and so qualify as abstract on one oft-met account of abstractness. If abstract entities occur in theist concept-nominalism's ontology, it is Platonist, in one sense of that term. It also threatens Platonism in another. For God has concepts that are not satisfied. These (one could argue) constitute attributes that are not exemplified. God has the concept *centaur*. So what it would take to be a centaur—namely, satisfying that concept—is determined. And what more is it for there to be an unexemplified attribute of centaurhood than for what it takes to be a centaur to be determinate, and set by an entity right relation to which would constitute being a centaur? I now argue in three ways that theist concept-nominalism is not Platonist in the first sense and provides an ontological "cost-savings" on standard Platonism. I then take up the second sense of Platonism.

To begin, divine concepts do not come out abstract on *all* ways to make the abstract/concrete distinction. A second criterion of abstractness many use is that abstracta cannot be causes or effects. If God does not simply have His concepts by nature, He causes Himself to have the concepts He has. For that matter, even if God has by nature the concepts He has, perhaps what His nature dictates is that He cause Himself to have these concepts. Further, divine concepts may have causal roles in God's mental economy. If divine concepts are not abstract (on at least some ways to make the abstract/concrete distinction) and take the place of attributes that are, theist concept-nominalism eliminates abstract ontology.

Another defense suggests an analogy. Human concept-nominalists claim to reduce our ontology by purging the extra-mental world of universals, saying that the ontology of predication involves in their place concepts and relations to them. Human-concept nominalists do not rest this claim on any particular account of concepts (save that they are mental particulars). Though certainly the concepts they appeal to exist in time, and in space also on some accounts of mind, nothing in nominalism requires that this be so. (Set nominalism is a form of nominalism about properties even if sets do not exist in space or time.[31]) Even if our concepts are not spatial—if, perhaps, we are all Platonic souls, or at any rate if mental particulars like concepts are not the sort of thing to have locations—nobody would claim that concept-nominalists merely shift our ontology elsewhere, or redefine it, rather than reduce it. For the concept-nominalist replaces universals with mental particulars that were in our ontology anyway. The theist who deals in divine concepts rather than Platonic abstract entities has as much right to the ontological-economy claim as the human concept-nominalist does. In fact, some theists hold that God is just a rather impressive Platonic soul, existing too in time but not space.[32] If this is right, theism that eliminates extra-mental entities in favor of divine concepts has as much right to an economy claim as concept-nominalist Platonic dualism. And of course whether one is a Platonic dualist does not affect whether concept-nominalism makes an economy: a commitment to materialism is no part of the concept-nominalist program. But it would be odd to say that theism is as economical as concept-nominalism if God is in time but not if He is not. Concept nominalism (if it works) takes universals off the books in favor of mental particulars—period. Concept-nominalism economizes on *kinds* of entity: there are concepts anyway, and so with universals dropped, there are fewer kinds of thing in heaven and earth than are dreamt of in Russell's philosophy. So too, if one is a theist, God and His concepts are there anyway, and so

---

[31] Some around Harvard have used "nominalism" to refer to a denial that sets exist. Obviously, I use the term differently.

[32] So in so many words Richard Swinburne, *The Christian God* (New York: Oxford University Press, 1994), 127.

every kind of entity one uses them to replace is one less kind of thing in one's ontology.

I add a third reply. When I say that God has concepts, my ontological commitment is not what it might seem. Having a concept makes us able *inter alia* to discriminate, recognize, have the sorts of experience associated with these, classify, use terms, and grasp, infer, affirm, and deny claims: broadly, to have a mental life of a certain sort. Having a concept is being in a mental state which is or gives us a set of powers; I recognize that you have the powers, infer that you are in the state, and express this by saying that you competently command the concept. In saying that God has concepts, the most I commit myself to is that there is in God whatever underlying reality makes it apt to speak of concept-possession. This reality may be just God's possession of certain powers. But it probably involves something more. In us, states that license talk of concept-possession are often dispositional: I have the concept of a kangaroo but rarely use it. Perfect-being considerations suggest that God is never unaware of anything He knows—that all His knowledge is occurrent, not dispositional. If this is so, every divine concept is always in use in some divine mental event. I suggest then that in the last analysis, the ontology of divine concepts is in terms of divine mental events and powers.[33] So my move is to replace an ontology of universals with one of divine powers and events involving God. There are powers and events anyway. So if I can make this move stick, I economize on kinds of entities.

But I am not yet out of the woods. On a popular view, an event is a particular having an attribute at a time, or something like a time.[34] On this view, talk of events does not free us from all abstract ontology: it leaves attributes in the picture. A concept-nominalist treatment of the attributes involved in the events to which one reduces God's having

---

[33] I hold that God is timeless. So this claim commits me to the existence of atemporal events. I defend these in "The Eternal Now", in Gregory Ganssle and David Woodruff (eds.), *God and Time* (New York: Oxford University Press, 2001). Another sort of indirect defense is in my *Time and Eternity* (Ithaca, NY: Cornell University Press, 1991), 290–7. For I there argue that an atemporal God can act. Actions are events. If you don't accept my arguments for atemporal events, restate the view above in terms of causally involved states: whether it is a state or an event, God knowing that cats are mammals has causes (in my view, His *making* the concept of a cat have the content it does) and effects (His making cats as He has). If you don't think a timeless God can be causally involved, you just don't think there can be a timeless God, since God is by nature an agent. As nothing in my argument here requires that God be timeless, we can differ over this another day.

[34] So Jaegwon Kim, "Events as Property-Exemplifications," in Jaegwon Kim, *Supervenience and Mind* (New York: Cambridge University Press, 1993), 33–52.

concepts would generate a vicious regress. So one needs here another account of events, but one a nominalist can love. Quine proposes that an event is simply "the content, however heterogenous, of some portion of spacetime".[35] As a theory of all events this has defects too numerous to mention. But I'll take from it the thought that it might be possible to treat at least some events simply as parts of some suitably chosen whole. Here's a thought, then: the divine life is the whole of what goes on for God. Things not in space and even not in time can have parts: algebra is part of mathematics. So perhaps we can say that a divine mental event is simply part of the divine life, part of what goes on for God. In one event this goes on, in another that. But "this" and "that" are just placeholders for descriptions of what goes on. They imply nothing about the inner constitution of those events. The events could well just be concrete particulars of which a nominalist can approve. Now divine mental events have content. So we must ask: what gives divine mental events content, if not appropriate involvement with some sort of abstract object? What makes an event God's employment of the concept *cat* if not some involvement with an abstract content of some sort? Events are causal relata. They have powers. If a rock's striking the window smashes it, it is able to; it is also able to have effects it did not actually have (it could have smashed a china vase next to the window, had one been there), and so has unused powers. Perhaps the ontology of God's mental content need invoke only divine powers and/or powers of and causings by certain events involving God. An event is an employment of *cat* because of its actual or possible relation to the production of cats, or of a divine conscious state appropriately characterized in terms of cats. The divine mental event that is God's thinking that P is simply that part of the divine life that has or would have effects suitable to having that content: God's thinking that Fido is a dog is that part of His life that would in conjunction with certain other divine mental events bring it about that Fido is a dog. It is the part of God's life that underlies a particular sort of divine power.

Talk of divine powers may seem only to shift the bump in the rug rather than flatten the rug out. For a power may be one to bring it about that P, for some P. So it might seem that talk of powers does not free us from propositions, states of affairs, and the like: Platonic entities. But that a power is one to bring it about that P does not entail that it involves an

---

[35] W. V. O. Quine, *Word and Object* (Cambridge, Mass.: MIT, 1960), 171.

entity, a proposition P, in its inner constitution. It may just be a brute fact about that power that this is what it does. For it to be correct to characterize the power this way, all that's required is that it be one that will bring it about that P, not that P somehow be part of its make-up. Mention of powers brings with it a further ontological question. Powers are properties of their possessors. So what sort of properties are these—tropes, perhaps? All divine powers are either powers God has by having His nature or powers of mental events or powers God has due to the mental events He undergoes. The first sort of power is uncontroversially part of the divine nature itself: having it is part of having deity.[36] So the problem of giving a theory of these powers is just part of the problem of giving a theory of the divine nature, deity, a matter to which I speak below. Many will find it plausible to parse the second sort into the third: I do so. A trope-free account of the third sort of power might run this way: for God to have the power to bring it about that P is for God to be such that possibly it happens that P as a result of God's activity. The only entity this truth-maker involves is God. It's up to fans of more commissive accounts of powers (trope or realist theories) to explain why this won't do.

Finally, what of unsatisfied divine concepts saddling us with Platonist attributes? As far as I can see, nothing forces us to concede this. A theist can consistently hold that for there to be an attribute of being a centaur, something must actually satisfy God's concept *centaur*. And the theist can then parse this attribute in nominalist terms.

ARISTOTELIAN UNIVERSALS AND DIVINE MENTAL CONTENT

We saw above that Platonists could at least try to appeal to God's mental content to reinstate Platonism about universals. I replied to Platonist

---

[36] Well, perhaps not *quite* uncontroversially. On a now-common account of natures, a thing's nature is just the conjunction of all the attributes it has necessarily. On this account, at least, there's no controversy. An older, Aristotelian tradition makes a distinction between a thing's nature and its proper accidents. Its nature is the core necessarily-had property that explains its having the rest of its necessarily-had properties. Its proper accidents are the rest that are so explained. This tradition might ask whether these powers are parts of the core attribute *deity* or instead among the proper accidents. God's having these, collectively, is His being omnipotent. So the real question on this account of natures is whether being omnipotent is part of having deity or instead something that supervenes on having deity. My money is on the "part" claim.

attempts that any properties God's conceivings etc. involve are at best Aristotelian universals. And so the Aristotelian, too, can try to turn the tables on me. "In place of an independent proposition (1), you've got a dependent property, within God, with the same content. But many divine mental activities involve (1): God knows that (1), is glad that (1), wants us to know that (1), etc. So the property of having this content is a universal—and for that matter, one we share in too. Again, you speak of divine conceivings as targeted. Being targeted is a property of conceivings. But many divine conceivings have targets. So these are universal properties—and again, our conceivings are also targeted." But all this does is point out that in the intuitive, pre-analytic sense, some things in God have properties in common with other things in God and with things in us. It is not an argument that we must explicate this commonality in terms of real universals. And appeal to divine concepts has blocked the arguments for universals. Now we can't appeal to divine concepts in the cases at hand. It's not being conceived as targeted that makes a conceiving targeted—on pain of infinite and probably vicious regress.[37] But we've shown by appeal to divine concepts that there are ways to undercut the realist appeal—that we needn't accede to it absent a showing that no nominalist alternative will do. The realist might reply, "well, for all you've shown, where appeal to divine concepts isn't available, realism wins". That supposes that where appeal to divine concepts doesn't provide a theist-nominalist alternative, nothing else does either. That remains to be seen.

Theist concept-nominalism won't do for attributes God Himself has, whether or not we share them. On a theist concept-nominalism, God would make Himself divine by thinking up a concept of deity He could fall under, make Himself conscious by thinking up a concept of conscious beings He could fall under, and make Himself a being who develops concepts by developing that concept and falling under it. All this gets things backwards. Because God first is a being who develops concepts, He develops that particular concept. Because God is first conscious, He can consciously employ concepts. Because He is first divine, He has the full powers deity imparts, which include the abilities to be conscious and to develop concepts. Some other theory of attributes will have to do in these cases. But this does not undo our argument so far.

[37] My thanks to Mike Bergmann here.

God and the Problem of Universals | 353

Platonism is a non-starter here. Its whole distinction from Aristotelian views is to allow for unexemplified attributes. If God has an attribute, it is not unexemplified. And if God does not, there is no bar to treating it in concept-nominalist terms. The arguments for Aristotelian realism get no traction in the case of the divine nature, deity. In its case there is no need to provide for the unity of natural classes, or explain the naturalness of some classes, or vindicate the objectivity and correctness of a classing, or explain why a predicate applies in common to distinct things, or explain how distinct things can be perfectly alike. There cannot be two things in the same possible world with deity (or so I'm prepared to argue). But God also has shared attributes. I think, though, that if we call on another divine attribute, we can deal with these.

God is powerful because He has deity. Other powerful things are powerful because they satisfy God's concept *powerful*. That the same divine concept applies to God and to something else doesn't entail that the concept applies to the two for the same *reason*. What unifies the natural class of non-divine powerful things is a causal-explanatory relation to God *via* a particular divine concept. What unifies the natural class of powerful things is an explanatory story involving deity and a divine concept. God is powerful because He has deity. Deity also gives Him the ability to form concepts, the disposition to omniscience that guarantees that He forms the concept *having power*, and the causal role in virtue of which everything else is powerful because it satisfies His concept of having power. So God is powerful because God has deity, and everything else is powerful ultimately because God has deity and wills to create powerful things. All the powerful things belong together in a single class because they have the right explanatory relations to the same single something—but it is not a universal property they share. Instead, deity is something analogous to a common causal contributor to all its members' belonging to that class. The same will apply for all other shared divine essential attributes: deity unifies all the relevant classes, and the classes are distinguished by the different divine volitions to which their non-divine members trace, and so more precisely by the concepts that provide the contents distinguishing these volitions from one another. This implies that if only God exists, the natural class of powerful things and the natural class of knowledgeable things are identical—but that is true. Now consider a shared divine contingent attribute, e.g. that of knowing that Leftow is male. God knows that Leftow is male because God has deity and God stipulates that Leftow is male. Anyone else knows that Leftow is male because God has deity and God stipulates that Leftow is male and God wills (either actively or merely permissively) that this individual know that Leftow is male. Here what unifies the class is a causal story involving deity and a particular divine mental content, taken as specifying a volition and the content of the knowledge in question. If this sort of thing works in the case of essential attributes, it works for non-essential ones as well.

If this is viable, then we needn't go realist for our account of divine attributes. But even if we avert the realist threat to theist concept-nominalism, there is still a nominalist threat. We can't appeal to theist concept-nominalism for the central case of *deity*. So it would seem that we need some other version of nominalism here. This raises a natural question as to why we should not use this version throughout. Why complicate matters? Further, God may have haecceities (attributes F such that necessarily, anyone in any possible world who is F is identical with anyone in any possible world who is F) or singularies (non-haecceities necessarily had by at most one item). Though haecceities and singularies are not universals, they are still a complication for theist concept-nominalists: they are attributes, and so any theory one invokes to deal with them will again raise the question of why we should not just use that theory throughout. Mention of this complication in God's case, of course, also forces us to consider haecceities and singularies of creatures. A theist concept-nominalist theory will do for them if one can vindicate the claim that God has genuinely singular concepts of creatures prior to creating any. I think one can indeed do so in the end, but this raises complications sufficient for a separate paper, and so I cannot tackle it here.

The problem of an adequate account of *deity* is broader than I can tackle here. I suspect that no theory of attributes is adequate to it, and that the proper conclusion to draw from this is that it is not an attribute at all. Whatever one makes of it, then, it will turn out to be something surprising. I suspect that divine haecceities are all in the end included in *deity*, and that singularies are a mixed lot, to be dealt with case-by-case. But the point to close on is this. There can't be two Gods. This just seems to be part of the concept of God. So whatever *deity* is, it isn't a universal. Neither is any haecceity or singulary. The claim that theism defeats realism appears to stand, at least so far.[38]

---

[38] My thanks to Dean Zimmerman and Michael Bergmann for comments.

A REALLY ONTOLOGICAL ARGUMENT

So I claim that there is genuine ontological economy to be had in a divine-concept theory of universals: it is not Platonism by the back door. Now Ockham bids us to posit nothing without need, but particularly nothing weird. Realisms deal in universals: lots of them, and objectionably strange. Ditto trope theories. Human concept-nominalism is manifestly inadequate. Human predicate-nominalism is just a linguistic transform of this. Set-nominalism is also an obvious failure, and brings the weirdness and ungainly profusion of sets with it. The best version of likeness-nominalism on offer solves its problems only by appeal to Lewis's modal realism.[39] This involves the existence in some space-time of every weird but possible thing conceivable—even deities. So a theory that gets along with just one space-time and one deity is both cheaper and less weird. Theism posits just one single unusual entity. It is a concrete thing, as against the abstracta of many other theories, and is recognizably like a person, and so perhaps less weird than many other entities. There's a case to be made, then, that Ockhamist considerations favor adopting theism as part of one's theory of universals.

Arguments in ontology for commitment to unusual entities come in several basic styles. Some seek to show that beliefs we hold entail that these exist: thus some have argued that a claim we believe, that there are perceptual illusions, entails that there are sense-data. Some seek to commit us to them by claiming that without them we have no adequate account of the truthmakers for truths we accept: thus Quine is driven to sets by his belief that mathematics needs them to come out true. Some try to show that the entities they defend provide good or best explanations for ranges of phenomena: one might also put the illusion argument for sense-data in this category. And some try to convince us that while our beliefs do not entail that the entities at issue exist, and perhaps we can have adequate accounts of truthmakers for truths of a certain sort without them, still the costs and benefits of admitting the odd entities suggest buying them. Thus Lewis argues the existence of his sort of possible worlds by showing that this posit, though not cheap ontologically, buys a host of analytical and theoretical benefits: given these, he suggests, it is on balance worth positing the worlds.

---

[39] Gonzalo Rodriguez-Pereyra, *Resemblance Nominalism* (New York: Oxford University Press, 2002).

Natural theology is the effort to add an unusual entity, God, to our ontology. The traditional arguments for God's existence are of either the entailment sort (ontological, cosmological) or the explanatory sort (design). What I've given here is really one part of a Lewis-style argument for God's existence, for one can show that just as theism gives one the cheapest and so best theory of universals, it buys most cheaply the best going ontologies of modality, mathematics, and morality. We might call this the *really* ontological argument, as it applies in God's case a style of argument genuinely used in ontology. The full argument, though, is a tale for another day.

12. A Theistic Argument against Platonism (and in Support of Truthmakers and Divine Simplicity)

Michael Bergmann and Jeffrey Brower

> Because it seems contrary to the faith to hold, as the Platonists did, that the Forms of things exist in themselves...Augustine substituted concepts of all creatures existing in the divine mind for the Ideas of things defended by Plato.
>
> —Thomas Aquinas, *Summa Theologiae* Ia q. 84 a. 5

Predication is an indisputable part of our linguistic behavior. By contrast, the metaphysics of predication has been a matter of dispute ever since antiquity. According to Plato—or at least *Platonism*, the view that goes by Plato's name in contemporary philosophy—the truths expressed by predications such as "Socrates is wise" are true because there is a subject of predication (e.g. Socrates), there is an abstract property or universal (e.g. wisdom), and the subject exemplifies the property.[1] This view is supposed to be general, applying to all predications, whether the subject of predication is a person, a planet, or a property.[2]

For comments on earlier drafts, we are grateful to Susan Brower-Toland, Jan Cover, Martin Curd, Brian Leftow, Trenton Merricks, Alvin Plantinga, Michael Rea, Michael Rota, William Rowe, Paul Studtmann, and Dean Zimmerman. Thanks are also due to the Purdue Research Foundation for a Summer Faculty Grant that supported work on this project.

[1] For convenience in what follows, we will often speak of "true predications" as shorthand for the more cumbersome (but also more accurate) phrase "the truths (or propositions) expressed by true predications". The latter, however, is what we always have in mind.

[2] Platonism thus involves what is often called an "abundant" (as opposed to a "sparse") theory of properties. Of course, philosophers since Russell have been aware that there is one sort of case to which this (or any other such unified) analysis of predication cannot be said to apply, namely, predications involving the predicate 'is non-self-exemplifiable'. As is well known, the assumption that there is a property corresponding to this predicate immediately leads to paradox (such a property must either exemplify itself or not, but in either case we get a contradiction). In what follows, we ignore this complication and

Despite the controversy surrounding the metaphysics of predication, many theistic philosophers—including the majority of contemporary analytic theists—regard Platonism as extremely attractive. At the same time, however, such philosophers are also commonly attracted to a form of traditional theism that has at its core the thesis that God is an absolutely independent being who exists entirely from himself (*a se*), whereas everything else is somehow dependent on him. This central thesis of traditional theism (which we'll call 'the aseity-dependence doctrine') led philosophers and theologians during the Middle Ages to endorse what is known as the doctrine of divine simplicity. According to this doctrine, God is an absolutely simple being, completely devoid of any metaphysical complexity whatsoever—where this implies not only that he lacks certain obvious forms of complexity, such as those associated with material or temporal composition, but also that he lacks even the minimal form of complexity associated with the exemplification of properties. The appeal of this doctrine is that it makes it completely clear that God does not depend on things in any way at all, not even in the way that wholes depend on their proper parts or that things depend on their properties (in order to exemplify them).

One of the main conclusions of this chapter will be that Platonism is inconsistent with the central thesis of traditional theism, namely, the aseity-dependence doctrine. The inconsistency is perhaps clearest in the case of Platonism and divine simplicity, which is the characteristic medieval expression of the aseity-dependence doctrine.[3] But our conclusion will be that Platonism is, in fact, inconsistent with the aseity-dependence doctrine itself (not merely its medieval expression), and, hence, that merely rejecting divine simplicity is insufficient to remove the contradiction.

---

continue to speak of Platonism, as well as any other theory of predication involving an abundant theory of properties, as a general or unified theory of predication, since it assumes that all predications *except those leading to Russell's paradox* can be explained in terms of properties or exemplifiables. For an example of a defense of Platonism that is considered by its author to be general and unified *in this sense*, see van Inwagen (2004).

[3] We can state the inconsistency as follows: Whereas Platonism requires all true predications to be explained in terms of properties, divine simplicity seems to require God to be identical with each of the things that can be predicated of him (more on this below). But then, if both are true, it follows that God is identical with each of his properties and hence is himself a property—which is absurd since, unlike properties, God is a person and persons can't be exemplified.

A Theistic Argument against Platonism | 359

In one sense, our conclusion should come as no surprise. There is a rich tradition of thinkers—from Augustine right down to the present—who have felt pressure from traditional theism to reject the existence of Platonic forms or properties.[4] Nonetheless, our argument stands out in important ways from other arguments in this tradition (though even if it didn't, it would still be worth pressing, if only because contemporary philosophers of religion seem to have lost sight of a significant tension that exists between traditional theism and Platonism, and hence continue to operate *as if* the two were perfectly compatible). Platonism, as we have characterized it, is a thesis involving two components: (1) the view that a unified account of predication can be provided in terms of properties or exemplifiables, and (2) the view that exemplifiables are best conceived of as abstract properties or universals. Most theistic arguments against Platonism have targeted only the second component. What distinguishes our argument is that it specifically targets the first. This difference is important, because it is often thought that the inconsistency of Platonism and traditional theism can be avoided merely by rejecting the Platonic view of properties in favor of another, such as the Augustinian view that properties are ideas in the mind of God.[5] Indeed, some contemporary Augustinians, most notably Thomas Morris and Christopher Menzel, have gone so far as to suggest that such a replacement will not only remove the original inconsistency, but also preserve the most attractive feature of Platonism from a contemporary point of view, namely, its conception of properties as necessary beings.

But if our argument is correct, the inconsistency between Platonism and traditional theism runs deeper than most theistic arguments suggest. Traditional theists who are Platonists, therefore, cannot avoid the inconsistency merely by dropping the Platonic conception of properties and replacing it with another—whether it be an Aristotelian conception (according to which there are no unexemplified universals), some form of immanent realism (according to which universals are concrete constituents of the things that exemplify them), a nominalistic theory of tropes (according to which properties are concrete individuals), or even the Augustinian account (according to which all exemplifiables are

---

[4] Aquinas alludes to this tradition in the *first* part of the epigraph that begins this chapter.
[5] Aquinas refers to this Augustinian view in the *second* part of the epigraph quoted at the beginning of this chapter.

divine concepts).⁶ In fact, as we shall be at pains to show, the inconsistency will remain so long as the traditional theist continues in *any* way to endorse the first of the two components of Platonism identified above—i.e. so long as she offers *any* unified account of predication in terms of exemplifiables, no matter how such entities are conceived.⁷

Assuming our argument is sound, the inconsistency can be resolved in only one of two ways: either by rejecting traditional theism (and hence becoming either a non-theist or a non-traditional theist) or by rejecting any unified account of predication in terms of exemplifiables (and hence adopting either a non-unified account of predication or a unified account that appeals to something other than exemplifiables). For those who want to hang on to their traditional theism, we shall argue that our argument naturally leads to a unified account of predication in terms of *truthmakers*. As will emerge, such an account of predication is precisely what is needed to defend the traditional doctrine of divine simplicity against the dominant objection it has faced in the last two decades. Thus, our argument for the claim that traditional theism is inconsistent with unified accounts of predication in terms of exemplifiables can be viewed as a theistic argument in support of both the truthmaker theory of predication and the traditional doctrine of divine simplicity.

Our discussion in the chapter proceeds as follows. In Section I, we consider some of the reasons that have been given for thinking that traditional theism is inconsistent with Platonism and then briefly examine the most important recent attempt to reconcile them by appealing to some form of Augustinianism. After these preliminaries, we lay out our argument for their inconsistency, focusing in particular on the inconsistency between the traditional theist's aseity-dependence doctrine and the Platonist thesis (also included in many non-Platonist accounts of predication) that a unified account of predication can be provided in terms of exemplifiables. In Section II, we explain how the conclusion of Section I naturally leads to a truthmaker theory of predication, which

---

⁶ Cf. Loux (1978, 1998) for Aristotelian realism; Armstrong (1978, 1989, 1997) for immanent realism; Campbell (1980, 1990) for trope theory; and Morris (1987) for the Augustinian view.

⁷ Hence, the argument will also work against those who understand predication in terms of property instances—that is, concrete individuals standing in a special relation (namely, instantiation) to the universals of which they are the instances—as well as against those who understand predication in terms of sets and conceive of sets as exemplifiables. For a property-instance conception of exemplifiables, cf. Mann (1982, 1983); for a set-theoretical conception of exemplifiables, cf. Oliver (1996: 21–5).

A Theistic Argument against Platonism | 361

in turn provides the materials needed to defend the traditional doctrine of divine simplicity against the dominant objection to it in the recent literature.[8]

I. AGAINST PLATONISM

Traditional (Western) theism has many ingredients, including among others that God is an omnipotent, omniscient, eternal, necessarily existing, perfectly good person. This list is not intended to be exhaustive (for our purposes it will be unnecessary to provide an exhaustive list). Rather it is intended to be representative of the sorts of things that traditional theists have said about God. In addition to the things just mentioned, there is a further component of traditional theism, one that will be especially important to our discussion in what follows, namely, the aseity-dependence doctrine discussed above. That doctrine, as we will be understanding it, may be stated as follows:

AD: (i) God does not depend on anything distinct from himself for his existing and (ii) everything distinct from God depends on God's creative activity for its existing.

Each of the components of AD follows straightforwardly from the traditional conception of God as an absolutely perfect or supreme being. Thus, (i) asserts that God *lacks* a certain type of imperfection (namely, dependency on another), whereas (ii) asserts that he *possesses* a certain type of perfection (namely, that associated with having creative power extending to *all* other existing things). Moreover, each of these components fits well not only with the traditional conception of deity, but also with certain authoritative statements within the tradition. Compare, for example, the first sentence of the Nicene Creed, which also seems to presuppose that God is the uncreated creator of all things:

---

[8] We should note up front that, in presenting this argument from *traditional* theism against Platonism and in defense of divine simplicity, we are not thereby committing ourselves to either the falsity of Platonism or the truth of divine simplicity, despite the fact that we are both theists. One can always avoid rejecting Platonism merely by availing oneself of a version of *non*-traditional theism, according to which things such as necessarily existing exemplifiables are *not* dependent on God. (See Wolterstorff 1970 for a defense of such a view.) Moreover, in the case of divine simplicity, one would have to do more than defend it against the dominant contemporary objection it faces (which is all we do here) to show that it is ultimately defensible.

"We believe in one God, the Father Almighty, Creator of heaven and earth, and of all things visible and invisible."[9]

Although we will be speaking in what follows of the dependence of creatures on God's creative activity, we do not mean to imply by this that created things have a beginning in time, nor even that they are contingent beings. As we understand it, the aseity-dependence doctrine is perfectly consistent with there being other necessary beings besides God, provided that they too depend on God as a created thing depends for its existing on its creator. With all this in mind, we can state the position on which we want to focus thus:

> T: Traditional theism (which includes AD) is true.

Our claim is that T is inconsistent with a group of theories concerning the metaphysical implications of predication. What these theories have in common is that they offer a unified account of predication in terms of exemplifiables (though they differ over whether exemplifiables are to be conceived of as abstract Platonic entities, Aristotelian universals, concrete immanent universals, the tropes familiar from certain forms of contemporary nominalism, or the divine concepts of which Augustine speaks). We may state the thesis that is common to all these theories as follows:

> P: The truth of *all* true predications, or at least of all true predications of the form "*a* is *F*", is to be explained in terms of a subject and an exemplifiable (however exemplifiables are themselves to be conceived).[10]

Our argument will be that the conjunction of T and P results in a contradiction, and hence that T implies the falsity of P. Before mounting this argument, however, it will be useful to consider both what it is about T and P that appears to make them inconsistent and why so many traditional theists have thought that the Augustinian response mentioned above is sufficient to resolve the apparent inconsistency.

---

[9] For further defense of the claim that traditional theism includes the aseity-dependence doctrine, see Morris (1987). Cf. the discussion of the 'Sovereignty-Aseity Intuition' in Plantinga (1980: 28–37) and the discussion of the 'Ultimacy Assumption' in Leftow (1990b: 584–92).

[10] Again, we ignore complications arising from Russell's paradox. Cf. n. 2 above. Here again it's important to emphasize that when we speak of "the truth of all true predications" we have in mind the truth of the *truths* expressed by such predications (rather than the predications themselves).

The Apparent Inconsistency of T&P and the Response of Theistic Activism

In "Absolute Creation," a paper originally co-authored with Christopher Menzel, Thomas Morris identifies the source of the apparent tension between traditional theism and Platonism. According to traditional theism, which includes the aseity-dependence doctrine, God is the "absolute" creator of everything—that is to say, he is the creator of everything distinct from himself. According to Platonism, by contrast, the entities in terms of which predications are to be explained are necessarily existing beings—namely, abstract properties or universals—and hence not the sorts of thing that appear to be capable of being created.

In light of this tension, it is not surprising that many traditional theists have been attracted to the Augustinian view according to which Platonic universals are identical with divine concepts—that is, entities that, despite their necessary existence, are nonetheless dependent on God as thoughts are dependent on a thinker. Contemporary philosophers now typically refer to this Augustinian view as "theistic activism", since according to it, the existence of properties and propositions is due to the *activity* of the divine intellect: properties are divine concepts resulting from God's acts of conceptualizing and propositions are divine thoughts due to God's acts of thinking or considering.[11]

Now as Morris himself recognizes, traditional theism still presents a difficulty even for the Augustinian view:

Of course the whole project of theistic activism is to recognize some divine activity as responsible for the existence of absolutely everything distinct from God. But it would sound at least exceedingly odd to say that God creates the very properties which are logically necessary for, and distinctively exemplified within, his creative activity—properties such as his omniscience and omnipotence—to say that he creates his own nature. In fact, many people would find this suggestion incoherent or absurd.   (1987: 172)

Later, Morris refers to this problem as the "circularity of God's creating his own nature" (ibid. 173) and asks:

[I]f God creates his own haecceity [i.e. his individual essence or nature], and the existence of his haecceity is logically sufficient for his existence, as is the

---

[11] See Morris (1987). Morris reminds us that false propositions aren't beliefs God has. They are thoughts that are considered and denied, not ones that, like true propositions, are considered and affirmed.

case with any necessarily existent being, do we not have the result that on this view God creates himself? And of course, the very idea of self-causation or self-creation is almost universally characterized as absurd, incoherent, or worse. (ibid. 174)

Thus, as Morris recognizes, there is a tension *within* theistic activism—a tension that derives from the fact that it appears to include an objectionable sort of circularity. Unlike the tension between Platonism and traditional theism, however, Morris thinks that this tension can be resolved. For the circularity in question, he maintains, is ultimately benign.

In order to resolve the tension in question, Morris does two things. First, he presents an analogy of an eternally existing *materialization machine* (itself a material object about the size of a clock radio) that produces material objects *ex nihilo* and sustains them in existence, including its very own parts which it replaces from time to time with newly produced parts.[12] He intends this analogy to go some distance toward showing the coherence of a thing's essence depending on its own creative activity. Of course, he recognizes that the analogy is imperfect insofar as the machine doesn't produce the very properties it instantiates, but only some of its material parts. Nevertheless, he thinks it models "in central ways what the [theistic] activist alleges about God" (ibid. 176). To those who aren't persuaded by this response (and we count ourselves among them), he has the following to say:

But, strictly speaking, there is no need of any such analogy to defend the implication of activism now in view. The value of the analogy is mainly heuristic, or pedagogical. *It just seems to me* that there is nothing logically or metaphysically objectionable about God's creating his own nature in precisely the way indicated [by theistic activism]. (ibid. 176, emphasis added)

We suggest that the reason it *just seems to Morris* that there is no objectionable circularity is that he isn't clear enough about precisely what the objectionable circularity is. In fact, Morris never gets any more explicit than he is in the passages quoted above about the exact nature of the damaging circularity. In the next subsection, we will offer an argument that provides a better target for defenders of theistic activism. Indeed, we will say precisely what the objectionable circularity is and

[12] Morris (1987: 174–5).

provide a formal argument for the conclusion that such circularity infects not only views such as theistic activism, but *any* view that combines traditional theism with a unified account of predication in terms of exemplifiables (however the exemplifiables are themselves understood). Thus, we will be providing theistic activists, along with anyone else who endorses a unified account of predication in terms of exemplifiables, the opportunity to respond to our objection by pinpointing where our argument goes wrong, and thus remove the need for them to rely instead on imperfect analogies or the apparent absence of anything objectionable about their view.

Morris's second response to the circularity problem is to point out that, from the fact that God's nature is *causally* dependent on God and God is *logically* dependent on his nature (in the sense that the existence of his nature entails his existing[13]), it doesn't follow that there is any objectionable circularity. For logical dependence, like logical entailment, can be mutual. There is nothing objectionable about each necessary truth entailing every other such truth; nor is there anything objectionable about the existence of each necessary being entailing the existence of every other such being. Hence there is no difficulty with the suggestion that logical dependence (as Morris understands it) is *not* an asymmetrical relation. As for causal dependence, although it may be an asymmetrical relation, there is no reason to think that God is causally dependent on his nature (though of course the theistic activist is committed to saying that God's nature causally depends upon God). For the fact that God is *logically* dependent on his nature (in the sense noted above) doesn't imply that God is *causally* dependent on anything, much less his nature. Indeed, on any view according to which, say, the numbers two and nine are necessary beings, it will follow that each is logically dependent (in Morris's sense) on the other. But such a view needn't add that the numbers two and nine are causally dependent on each other.

We agree wholeheartedly with Morris's points summarized in the previous paragraph. From them we take the following lesson: in order to establish that there is an objectionable circularity in such a view as theistic activism, we must establish not only that (*a*) there is a dependence relation of some sort running in both directions between a pair of things (such as God and his nature), but also that (*b*) it is the *same*

---

[13] As Morris points out (ibid. 176), this is a trivial consequence of the fact that both God and his nature are necessary beings.

relation that holds in both directions, and (c) the relation in question is *asymmetrical*. With this lesson in mind, we shall now attempt to establish that there is a form of circularity that both meets conditions (a)–(c) and infects the conjunction of traditional theism with any unified account of predication in terms of exemplifiables.

A Theistic Argument against P

Although our argument for the inconsistency of T and P is somewhat complicated, the basic idea behind it is fairly intuitive. If a view such as theistic activism is true, then every property (or exemplifiable) will be a product of God's creative activity. But this implies the general principle that, for any property F, God's creating F is a prerequisite for, and hence logically prior to, F.[14] Notice, however, that in order to create F, God must have the property of *being able to create a property*. Here is where the trouble begins. For on the one hand, it would seem that this property (i.e. *being able to create a property*) must be logically prior to God's creating it, since God's having it is a prerequisite for the creation of *any* property. On the other hand, however, it would also seem that this property must be logically posterior to God's creating it, since insofar as it is a property (or exemplifiable), it must fall under the general principle articulated in AD, and hence be a product of God's creative activity. Evidently, therefore, in order for it to be true that God is the creator of all properties, there must be a property—namely, *being able to create a property*—that is both logically prior and logically posterior to God's creating properties. Assuming that logical priority is an asymmetrical relation, however, this conclusion is obviously absurd.[15]

With this intuitive statement in hand, we can now turn to a more precise statement of the argument, extending its scope so that it applies not just to theistic activism, but to any unified account of predication in terms of exemplifiables. To begin, let us note that our argument will establish the inconsistency of T and P by showing that their conjunction entails the following two claims, which give rise to an objectionable circularity:

---

[14] We discuss the notion of logical priority below.
[15] Brian Leftow has drawn our attention to his own intuitive statement of a similar argument (though his argument is for a less general conclusion). See Leftow (1990a: 201).

C1: God's creating an exemplifiable is logically prior to the exemplifiable *being able to create an exemplifiable*.

C2: The exemplifiable *being able to create an exemplifiable* is logically prior to God's creating an exemplifiable.

Notice that C1 and C2 together entail a claim of the form "*a* is logically prior to *b* and *b* is logically prior to *a*". Assuming once again that the relation of logical priority is asymmetrical, the conjunction of C1 and C2 is impossible, for it involves circularity of the sort described in conditions (a)–(c) mentioned at the end of the previous subsection. But since T and P together entail the conjunction of C1 and C2, the conjunction of T and P is also impossible, which is what we are aiming to show.

Before stating the argument proper, we need to set out the assumptions on which it relies:

A1. For any exemplifiable F, if F depends on God's creative activity for its existing, then God's creating an exemplifiable is logically prior to F.

A2. For any x and any action A, x's being able to do A is logically prior to x's doing A.[16]

A3. For any x, any y, and any exemplifiable F, if x's exemplifying F is logically prior to y, then F is logically prior to y.

A4. x's being able to create an F = x's exemplifying *being able to create an* F.

A5. For any x and any y, if x is logically prior to y, then y is not logically prior to x.

Since the notion of logical priority plays a crucial role in these assumptions and, hence, in our argument as a whole, it requires some comment. Perhaps the best way to clarify the notion is by way of example. Consider, therefore, a whole consisting of several parts—say, an ordinary pocket watch. Its parts, we say, are *logically prior to* the whole of which they are the parts. Or consider a thinker and its thoughts. The thinker, we say, is *logically prior to* its thoughts. As these examples

---

[16] Notice that A2 says that abilities are logically prior to their being exercised (i.e. to doings). This should not be confused with the claim that potentialities are logically prior to actualities (i.e. that x's *being possibly* F is logically prior to x's *being* F). Our point here is not that the latter claim is false (we aren't taking a stand on that), but rather that A2 (on which we *are* taking a stand) should be distinguished from that latter claim.

serve to indicate, logical priority is associated with a special type of dependence. If an object *a* is logically prior to an object *b*, then *b* depends for its existing on *a* (in a way that *a* doesn't depend on *b*)—in fact, it depends on *a* in the way a whole depends on its parts or a thought depends on its thinker. This type of dependence, however, must be sharply distinguished from several other types of dependence.

First of all, logical priority must be distinguished from the type of dependence associated with being a mere *necessary condition*. The existence of a part is a necessary condition for the existence of the whole of which it is a part; likewise, the existence of a thinker is a necessary condition for the existence of its thoughts. Nonetheless, the logical priority of parts to wholes, or of thinkers to their thoughts, cannot be reduced to their being necessary conditions. For the relation of dependence that holds between parts and wholes and between thinkers and their thoughts is asymmetric, whereas the relation of *being a necessary condition of* isn't (e.g. any pair of necessary truths is such that each member of it is a necessary condition of the other).

Secondly, logical priority must be distinguished from *temporal* priority. Parts are necessarily logically prior to their wholes, but not necessarily temporally prior to them. Suppose that there existed an *eternal* pocket watch with parts as eternally existent as the watch itself; or suppose that both the watch and its parts had come into existence simultaneously. In either case, the parts of the watch would be logically prior to the whole watch even though they wouldn't be temporally prior to it. Indeed, the parts of the watch would be logically prior to the whole watch even if both existed necessarily. The same is true for thinkers and their thoughts. According to traditional theism, God not only exists necessarily but is also essentially omniscient. Thus, he not only exists in all possible worlds, but also knows—and hence has the thought—in all possible worlds that $2 + 2 = 4$. Nonetheless, he must still be regarded as logically prior to this (or any other such) thought of his.

Finally, logical priority must be distinguished from entailment (or what Morris calls 'logical dependence'). Although the existence of any necessary being *entails* the existence of any other, not every necessary being is logically prior to every other. Indeed, as the examples just given are intended to make clear, logical priority is unlike entailment in that it cannot be mutual. Although God is logically prior to his thoughts, his thoughts are not logically prior to him. On the contrary, they are *logically posterior* to him. And this is so despite the fact that both God and certain of his thoughts (such as that $2 + 2 = 4$) are necessary beings and, hence, mutually *entailing*.

Is there anything more we can say about logical priority, apart from the fact that it is associated with a special type of dependence? Perhaps the most illuminating thing to say is that if a is logically prior to b, then b depends on a in such a way that a at least *partially* explains b whereas b is not even a partial explanation of a. Thus, the existence of the parts of a watch explain (at least partially) the existence of the watch itself, whereas the watch does nothing to explain the existence of the parts.[17] Likewise, the existence of God is at least a partial explanation of the existence of his thoughts, but not vice versa.[18]

In light of all this, it should be clear that the relation of logical priority is asymmetric, and, hence, that assumption A5 above is true. Also, given P (whose conjunction with T will be assumed for *reductio* in our argument), the equivalence stated in A4 seems to be uncontroversial. Furthermore, assumptions A1 and A2 are extremely plausible. The act of creating seems to be logically prior to the creature (and not vice versa); and, the having of an ability seems to explain (at least partially), and hence to be logically prior to, the exercise of that ability (and not vice versa).[19] It is difficult to see, therefore, how one could plausibly deny either A1–A2 or A4–A5. Thus, the only assumption that requires any extended comment is A3.

---

[17] It might be objected that our claim that parts are logically prior to wholes does not hold for Morris's materialization machine, which creates its own parts. After all, doesn't it present us with a case of a whole explaining the existence of its parts? Not in the relevant sense. To see why not, we need to employ time indices. Using them, the more careful way to state our claim in the text is this: the existence *at t* of the parts of a watch partially explains the existence *at t* of the watch itself, whereas the existence *at t* of the watch does nothing to explain the existence *at t* of the parts. Here is the parallel claim with respect to the materialization machine: the existence *at t* of the parts of the materialization machine partially explain the existence *at t* of the machine but the existence *at t* of the materialization machine doesn't even partially explain the existence *at t* of its parts. As we understand the example of the materialization machine, the claims in the previous sentence are true because the machine's creating and sustaining activities are temporally prior to the created or sustained existence they produce. If we are mistaken about this, and the example is, instead, to be understood as lacking such temporal priority, then the example seems to us to be incoherent—as incoherent as the suggestion that something can cause itself to come into existence from nothing.

[18] God's existence doesn't itself produce the thoughts. That's why we say God's existence is only a *partial* explanation of the existence of his thoughts.

[19] Of course the having of an ability isn't sufficient by itself to explain its exercise. Here again, therefore, we speak of only a *partial* explanation.

Assumption A3 strikes us as intuitively plausible. In order to see why, we need to focus on the relationship between a property and its exemplification. In particular, we need to consider which, if either, is logically prior to the other. In our view, a property is logically prior to its exemplification. This position can be stated as follows:

> A3*: For any x and any exemplifiable F, F is logically prior to x's exemplifying F.

In defense of A3*, we note, first, that an exemplifiable, F, seems to be related to the state of affairs *something's exemplifying F* in roughly the way in which a constituent is related to that of which it is a constituent or the way in which a proper part is related to the whole of which it is a part. Furthermore, it seems that constituents are logically prior to the things of which they are constituents (and not vice versa), in much the same way that proper parts are logically prior to the wholes of which they are parts (and not vice versa). By parity of reasoning, therefore, it seems that F is logically prior to *something's exemplifying F* (and not vice versa).

Given A3*, A3 seems to follow. For consider these three things: a, F, and b's exemplifying F (where F is an exemplifiable and a and b are anything at all). Given that we know (by A3*) that F is logically prior to b's exemplifying F, we may conclude the following: if b's exemplifying F is logically prior to a, then F is also logically prior to a. And A3 is just that conclusion generalized.

We turn now from our assumptions to our argument. As we noted above, we will be arguing that the conjunction of T and P entails both C1 and C2. Since the relation of logical priority is asymmetrical (by assumption A5), the conjunction of C1 and C2 is impossible. Hence T and P are inconsistent. For convenience, we'll begin by restating AD, T, P, and our five assumptions:

> AD: (i) God does not depend on anything distinct from himself for his existing and (ii) everything distinct from God depends on God's creative activity for its existing.
> T: Traditional theism (which includes AD) is true.
> P: *All* true predications, or at least all true predications of the form "*a* is F", are to be explained in terms of a subject and an exemplifiable (however exemplifiables are themselves to be conceived).

A Theistic Argument against Platonism | 371

A1. For any exemplifiable F, if F depends on God's creative activity for its existing, then God's creating an exemplifiable is logically prior to F.

A2. For any x and any action A, x's being able to do A is logically prior to x's doing A.

A3. For any x, any y, and any exemplifiable F, if x's exemplifying F is logically prior to y, then F is logically prior to y.

A4. x's being able to create an $F = x$'s exemplifying *being able to create an F*.

A5. For any x and any y, if x is logically prior to y, then y is not logically prior to x.

We will break our argument into two parts: the first part argues that the conjunction of T and P gives us C1; the second part derives C2 from our assumptions.

Here is the first part of the argument:

1. T&P. [Assume for *reductio*.]
2. All exemplifiables depend on God's creative activity for their existing. [From T.][20]
3. For any exemplifiable F, God's creating an exemplifiable is logically prior to F. [From 2 and A1.]
4. C1: God's creating an exemplifiable is logically prior to the exemplifiable *being able to create an exemplifiable*. [From 3.]

Our argument so far depends only on A1.

Consider next the second part of our argument, which derives C2 from assumptions A2–A4:

5. God's being able to create an exemplifiable is logically prior to God's creating an exemplifiable. [From A2.]
6. God's exemplifying *being able to create an exemplifiable* is logically prior to God's creating an exemplifiable. [From 5 and A4.]
7. C2: The exemplifiable *being able to create an exemplifiable* is logically prior to God's creating an exemplifiable. [From 6 and A3.]

To complete our argument, we need only appeal to A5:

8. $\sim$(4&7). [From A5.]

---

[20] We take for granted here that God isn't an exemplifiable, from which it follows that all exemplifiables are distinct from God. Cf. Brower (Unpublished) for discussion of this topic.

9. ∼(T&P). [From 1–8 by *reductio*.]

In short, traditional theism implies the falsity of all unified accounts of predication in terms of exemplifiables. The challenge, therefore, both for theistic activists and for all other supporters of T and P, is to identify a problem with our argument.[21]

Weakening the Aseity-Dependence Doctrine

One response to our argument is to try to maintain traditional theism without endorsing the aseity-dependence doctrine as defined in AD. For example, one might suggest that that doctrine need not be understood in the strong way we define it—i.e. in terms of the dependence of things on God's *creative activity*—but may be understood more weakly as follows:

AD*: (i) God does not depend on anything distinct from himself for his existing and (ii) everything distinct from God depends on God (though *not*, in every case, on God's creative activity) for its existing.

Those who favor this weaker version of the aseity-dependence doctrine, AD*, can then insist that traditional theism should be understood, not in terms of T, but rather in terms of T*:

---

[21] Although we shall not dwell on the point here, it is worth noting that arguments parallel to the one just given might be constructed for the conclusion that traditional theism is also incompatible with abstract objects of other kinds (such as certain propositions and certain states of affairs). Our argument draws attention to the fact that a certain exemplifiable—namely, *being able to create an exemplifiable*—has to be both logically prior and logically posterior to God's exemplifying it. It has to be logically posterior to God's exemplifying it because God's exemplifying it is a prerequisite for God's creating any exemplifiable (and, hence, for any exemplifiable). But it also has to be logically prior to God's exemplifying it because, as A3* makes clear, every exemplifiable is logically prior to (because it is a constituent of) its exemplification. It seems that something similar can be said with respect to propositions. Consider the proposition *God is able to create a proposition*. Apparently, this proposition must be both logically prior and logically posterior to its being true. It has to be logically posterior to its being true because its being true that God is able to create a proposition is a prerequisite for God's creating any proposition (and, hence, for any proposition). But it also has to be logically prior to its being true because of a general principle, much like A3*, according to which every proposition is logically prior to (because it's a constituent of) its being true. A similar sort of argument could be constructed in connection with the relationship between the abstract state of affairs *God's being able to create a state of affairs* and its obtaining.

T*: Traditional theism (which includes AD*) is true.

Once traditional theism is understood in this way, however, the proponent of the weaker aseity-dependence doctrine can ignore our argument above on the grounds that it fails to show that T* and P are incompatible, even if it succeeds at showing that T and P are incompatible.[22]

We think there is some precedent (e.g. the Nicene creed) for understanding traditional theism as favoring the stronger version of the aseity-dependence doctrine, AD, over the weaker AD*.[23] Nevertheless, we think an argument similar to the one given in the previous subsection can be given for the incompatibility of T* and P. Except for A5, according to which logical priority is an asymmetrical relation, this argument relies on only three assumptions (two of which are modified versions of earlier assumptions, and another of which we have already encountered):

A1*. For any x, if x depends on God for its existing, then God's being who he is is logically prior to x.

A3*. For any x and any exemplifiable F, F is logically prior to x's exemplifying F.

A4*. God's being who he is = God's exemplifying his nature.

Assumption A3* was employed and defended earlier in accounting for the plausibility of A3. And A4* is similar to A4 insofar as it says that a gerundial phrase of the form 'x's being F', which includes no explicit mention of exemplification, can be restated in terms of the exemplification of a property—i.e. in terms of a phrase of the form 'x's exemplifying F'. In light of P, which is being assumed for *reductio* in this argument as well, we take A4* to be as uncontroversial as A4.

As for assumption A1*, it too is a modified version of its ancestor, A1. The idea behind A1* is this: it must be in virtue of *something* about God that everything distinct from him depends on him for its existing. But in virtue of what? According to theistic activism, it is in virtue of God's *creative activity* that all things depend on him. But not according to AD*. Nevertheless, even those who endorse AD* will, if they endorse P, agree that God necessarily exemplifies the divine nature. And, since it is in virtue of *something* about God that all (other) things depend on him for their existing, it seems that we can say, at the very least, that it is in

---

[22] This sort of response was brought to our attention in discussions with Jan Cover and Michael Rea.
[23] Cf. also the references cited in n. 9 above.

374 | Michael Bergmann and Jeffrey Brower

virtue of God's being who he is—i.e. that it is in virtue of his *being divine* or his *exemplifying the divine nature*—that all things distinct from him depend on him for their existing.

In our previous argument, we showed that a problematic conjunction (in that case, T and P) resulted in an objectionably circular statement of the form "*a* is logically prior to *b* and *b* is logically prior to *a*". Our new argument will show the same thing, only this time the problematic conjunction will be "T* & P" and the resulting objectionable circularity will arise from the following two claims:

C1*: God's exemplifying his nature is logically prior to the exemplifiable *God's nature* (or *being divine*).

C2*: The exemplifiable *God's nature* is logically prior to God's exemplifying his nature.

Here, then, is our new argument:

1. T*&P. [Assume for *reductio*.]
2. All exemplifiables depend on God for their existing. [From T*.]
3. For any exemplifiable F, God's being who he is is logically prior to F. [From 2 and A1*.]
4. God's being who he is is logically prior to the exemplifiable *God's nature*. [From 3.]
5. C1*: God's exemplifying his nature is logically prior to the exemplifiable *God's nature*. [From 4 and A4*.]
6. C2*: The exemplifiable *God's nature* is logically prior to God's exemplifying his nature. [From A3*.]
7. ~(5&6). [From A5.]
8. ~(T*&P). [From 1–7 by *reductio*.]

Thus, by slightly altering two of our original assumptions, A1 and A4, and by appealing to A3* (used earlier to explain the plausibility of our original A3), we've shown that P is incompatible not only with T but also with T*, which includes only the weaker aseity-dependence doctrine, AD*.

II. IN SUPPORT OF TRUTHMAKERS AND DIVINE SIMPLICITY

Assuming the arguments in the first part of the chapter are sound—an assumption hereafter taken for granted—traditional theists (of either the T- or T*-variety) have no choice but to reject P, and with it any unified account of predication in terms of exemplifiables. The reason is that, as our earlier arguments make clear, there are at least some *divine* predications that cannot be explained in terms of exemplifiables. Our first argument showed that traditional theists (of the T-variety) cannot ascribe to God the property (or exemplifiable) of *being able to create an exemplifiable*. But, of course, if this is right, then divine predications such as "God is able to create an exemplifiable" cannot be explained by traditional theists in terms of exemplifiables. Our second argument established a similar conclusion, showing that traditional theists (of the weaker T*-variety) cannot ascribe to God the property (or exemplifiable) of *being divine*. Once again, however, this just goes to show that predications such as "God is divine" cannot be explained by them in terms of exemplifiables. And perhaps there are other such properties (or exemplifiables) that cannot be ascribed to God, and hence other divine predications that provide exceptions to P.

All this presents traditional theists with a challenge—in fact, it presents them with two challenges. The first and most immediate challenge is that of providing an account of divine predications—or at least of those divine predications that are problematic. But assuming such theists are also interested in preserving a unified or systematic general theory of predication, there is also the second challenge of explaining how divine predication relates to predication generally. In what follows, we present what we take to be the best responses to these challenges available to traditional theists. In doing so, we not only defend a truthmaker theory of predication, but also show that such a theory yields an understanding of the doctrine of divine simplicity that rescues that doctrine from the standard contemporary objection leveled against it.

The Truthmaker Theory of Predication

As we've indicated, the immediate challenge facing traditional theists is that of providing an account of the truth of predications such as "God is able to create an exemplifiable" and "God is divine." In order to meet this challenge successfully, however, they must appeal to something *other* than properties or exemplifiables. But to what else can they plausibly appeal? The answer, we suggest, is truthmakers. In order to see why, we need to consider each of the two divine predications in question.

Consider first "God is divine." Like any statement involving the predication of a thing's nature, "God is divine" is a case of essential predication: in all possible worlds in which God exists, he is divine. It follows, therefore, that God is such that, necessarily, if he exists, he is divine—that is to say, God himself necessitates the truth of "God is divine." Some philosophers take this as evidence that God by himself, apart from any exemplifiables, can *explain* the truth of "God is divine" and they commonly express this view by saying that God is what *makes* the predication in question true, that he alone is its *truthmaker*. Indeed, as John Bigelow (1988: 128) points out, it is natural for such philosophers to generalize their view to all essential predications, so that individuals are always taken to be the truthmakers for predications of things which are (part of) their essence.[24]

The notion of a truthmaker is, no doubt, familiar from the contemporary literature. Nonetheless, a few words about it are perhaps in order. Despite the misleading connotations of its name, the notion is *not* to be understood in causal terms (i.e. literally in terms of *making*). On the contrary, it is to be understood in terms of broadly logical entailment— as is evident from the fact that contemporary philosophers habitually speak of truthmakers as *entailing* the truth of certain statements or predications (or better, the truths expressed by them).[25] Although this way of speaking seems perfectly acceptable to us, we realize that it may strike some as misleading on the grounds that only truths (or truth-bearers) can entail one another.[26] To remove any possibility for misunderstanding, therefore, we offer the following (partial) analysis in its place:

TM: If an entity E is a truthmaker for a predication P, then 'E exists' entails the truth expressed by P.[27]

In what follows, we will need to speak of the relationship between a particular truthmaker and the predication it makes true. In order to

---

[24] Such philosophers standardly assume that distinct predications can be made true by the same truthmaker—so that, for example, "Socrates is human," "Socrates is an animal," and "Socrates is human or the moon is made of green cheese" can all have the same truthmaker (namely, Socrates), despite the fact they differ in meaning and logical form. For discussion and defense of this assumption, see Armstrong (1978: ii. 7–18, 52–9), and Mulligan, Simons, and Smith (1984: 295–304).

[25] See e.g. Armstrong (1997: 13).

[26] Bigelow (1988: 126).

[27] Cf. Rodriguez-Pereyra (2000: 260); Bigelow (1988: 126); Fox (1987: 188); and Oliver (1996: 69).

avoid using the potentially misleading notion of entailment, we will speak instead of truthmakers as *necessitating* the truth of the predications they make true. Here again, however, the form of necessitation we have in mind is not causal but broadly logical.

One final observation about TM: it is intended to provide only a *partial* analysis of the notion of truthmaking. This is important because a complete analysis of truthmaking in terms of entailment would lead to obvious absurdities, including the claim that necessary truths—such as $2 + 2 = 4$—have any existing thing whatsoever as their truthmakers. But if TM does not provide a complete analysis of the notion of truthmaking, then what, in addition to entailment or necessitation, is required for something to qualify as a truthmaker? This is a difficult question, and one that we shall not attempt to answer here.[28] For present purposes, it will suffice to note that even if the fact that an entity E necessitates the truth expressed by a predication P does not *guarantee* that E is P's truthmaker, it does make E a candidate—perhaps even a prima facie good candidate—for playing this role.

With these clarifications in mind, it should now be possible to appreciate the point of our suggestion, on behalf of traditional theists, about how best to meet the basic challenge facing their view—at least with respect to the predication "God is divine." If traditional theists want to explain the truth of this predication in terms of something other than properties or exemplifiables, they can do so in terms of truthmakers. For given that "God is divine" is a case of essential predication, and hence that God necessitates its truth, God is already a plausible candidate for its truthmaker. Notice, moreover, that the same account can be given of the other problematic divine predication discussed above, namely, "God is able to create exemplifiables." For like "God is divine," it too appears to be a case of essential predication (assuming that exemplifiables are capable of being created). But, then, as in the case of "God is divine," God will be a plausible candidate for its truthmaker as well. And presumably, if there are any other divine predications that present a difficulty for traditional theists, they can be explained in the same way.

In the end, therefore, it appears that traditional theists can answer the most immediate challenge facing their view. Even so, there is still a question concerning the nature of predication in general—and in

---

[28] Cf. Restall (1996) for an attempt to answer this question by appeal to "relevant" entailment, and Smith (2002, 1999) for an attempt to answer it without such an appeal.

particular how to reconcile it with the account of divine predication just given. This is the second main challenge facing traditional theists. Here again, however, the challenge appears to admit of a straightforward resolution.

As we have seen, what raises trouble for traditional theists is not just Platonism, but any of a group of theories that take for granted the following thesis about predication:

> P: The truth of *all* true predications, or at least of all true predications of the form "*a* is *F*", is to be explained in terms of a subject and an exemplifiable.

To this point, we have suggested that, if traditional theists want to avoid the circularity problem associated with P, they ought to adopt a truthmaker account of certain divine predications (namely, "God is divine" and "God is able to create exemplifiables"). However, it seems natural to go further and to suggest that, if traditional theists want a theory to replace P, they ought to adopt a truthmaker theory of predication generally—that is a theory that, instead of P, takes for granted the following alternative thesis about predication:

> P*: The truth of *all* true predications, or at least of all true predications of the form "*a* is *F*", is to be explained in terms of truthmakers.[29]

By taking this extra step, and endorsing P*, traditional theists are able not only to resolve the circularity problem associated with P, but also to present this resolution as falling out of a general account of predication

---

[29] It might seem objectionable that we contrast P* with P (which is endorsed by Platonism and other theories of predication) by calling the former 'a truthmaker theory of predication'. For P might itself seem to be a form of truthmaker theory in that, like P*, it aims to explain *why* certain predications are true by saying what makes them true (namely, a subject and an exemplifiable).

It is important to recognize, however, that in addition to explaining the truth of certain predications (or the truths expressed by them), P* invokes the notion of a truthmaker in another more fundamental way. The suggestion made by P* is that the most important feature common to all truthmakers for claims of the form 'The truth expressed by predication X is true' is just that they are *truthmakers*. But according to P, there is another more important feature that all such truthmakers have in common, namely, that they involve a subject and an exemplifiable. It is only because P* invokes the notion of a truthmaker in this second way that we call it (but not P) a 'truthmaker theory of predication'.

A Theistic Argument against Platonism | 379

that is every bit as unified or systematic as P itself. In short, by taking this step, they are able to meet each of the challenges facing their view.[30]

It is important to emphasize that the truthmaker theory of predication, as we've stated it at P*, is an ontologically *neutral* theory of predication. According to this theory, if a predication of the form "*a* is F" is true, then its truth must be explained in terms of its truthmaker—that is, in terms of an entity (or a group of entities) whose existence necessitates the truth of the predication in question. But in principle, there is no restriction on the nature or ontological category to which such an entity belongs. Hence this theory does not require us to say that the truthmaker for "*a* is F" either is or involves an exemplifiable. Indeed, for all the theory itself says, the truthmaker for this predication may be nothing but the single individual, *a*. Even so, this theory doesn't rule out the possibility of explaining at least some predications in terms of properties or exemplifiables. On the contrary, it actually invites such an explanation in certain cases.

We have already indicated that, in the case of essential predications, it is possible to take the subject of predication itself to be the truthmaker.

---

[30] Since we are primarily concerned in what follows only with affirmative (atomic) predications of the form "*a* is F", our statement of P* ignores the difficulty associated with claims such as "*a* is not F" and "there are no Fs". These sorts of claim are often thought to be the undoing of truthmaker theory, since the only candidate truthmakers for them appear to be negative facts such as a's *not being* F and *there not being any Fs*. Appealing to negative facts, however, strikes many as extremely implausible. As David Lewis (1999: 204) points out: "It seems, offhand, that [such claims] are true not because things of some kind *do* exist, but rather because counterexamples *don't* exist." It is important to note, however, that we could take account of these and other related difficulties in a way that is, at least in the spirit of truthmaker theory, by modifying our account of predication. First, we could divide all (atomic) predications into two sorts: (A) those (like 'there are no Fs') whose candidate truthmakers are negative facts (e.g. *there not being any Fs*) but whose denials ('there are Fs') are such that the candidate truthmakers for them are not negative facts but entities of some kind (namely, one or more Fs); and (B) those (like '*a* is F') whose candidate truthmakers are entities of some kind (say, the individual *a*, or a non-transferable trope of F-ness, or the fact that *a* is F) but whose denials ('*a* is not F') are such that the only candidate truthmakers for them are negative facts (a's *not being* F). With this division in mind, we could then say that (A)-type predications will be true just in case there is no truthmaker for their negation and that (B)-type predications will be true just in case they have a truthmaker. In line with this, P* could then be revised as follows:

P** *All* true predications are such that either their truth can be explained in terms of truthmakers or the falsity of their negations can be explained in terms of the absence of truthmakers.

For further development and defense of this sort of truthmaker theory, see Bigelow (1988: 128–34) and especially Lewis (2001).

Thus, Socrates may be regarded as the truthmaker of "Socrates is human", just as God may be regarded as the truthmaker for "God is divine"—since in each case the subject is such that it necessitates the truth expressed by the corresponding predication. Notice, however, that the same cannot be said for accidental or contingent predications. Socrates, for example, cannot be regarded as the truthmaker for "Socrates is wise," since Socrates does not necessitate its truth. But then what is the truthmaker in such cases? There is more than one way to answer this question, but the two most common ways appeal directly to properties or exemplifiables. First of all, one can say, as David Armstrong does, that the truthmaker for contingent predications are facts (or concrete states of affairs) that include properties as constituents.[31] In that case, the truthmaker for "Socrates is wise" will be the *fact that Socrates is wise*, which includes the property *wisdom* as a constituent. Alternatively, one can say, as C. B. Martin does, that the truthmaker for contingent predications are non-transferable tropes (or concrete individual properties that are essentially dependent on the subjects of which they are the properties).[32] In that case, the truthmaker for "Socrates is wise" will not be the *fact that Socrates is wise*, but *Socrates's wisdom*—an entity such that, in all possible worlds in which it exists, Socrates exists and is wise.

It might be thought that the ontological neutrality of the truthmaker theory compromises our claim that it is every bit as unified or systematic as the alternative stated at P. After all, if the truthmaker theory of predication can allow some predications (e.g. "Socrates is wise"), but not others (e.g. "God is divine"), to be explained in terms of exemplifiables, then it might not seem to be a *unified* theory of predication after all.

In fact, however, the ontological neutrality of the truthmaker theory merely calls attention to the distinctiveness of the principle of unity underlying it. To characterize an entity as a truthmaker is to characterize it in terms of a certain function or role—that of necessitating the truth of the predications it makes true. In this respect, 'truthmaker' is similar to other sorts of functional characterization one finds in philosophy—ones that prescind, to some extent, from the intrinsic nature of the entity being characterized. Thus, just as functionalists in philosophy of mind claim that we can make progress in understanding mental states (such as pain) only if we abandon the attempt to characterize them in

---

[31] See Armstrong (1997, 1989).
[32] See Armstrong (1989: esp. 116–19). For a more complete development and defense of this view, see Mulligan, Simons, and Smith (1989).

terms of a single ontological category (namely, physical or non-physical), so too, we have been suggesting, traditional theists can make progress in understanding predication in general, and divine predication in particular, if they adopt the same sort of strategy. We call the truthmaker theory of predication a 'unified theory', therefore, *not* because it explains all predications in terms of entities from a single ontological category, but rather because it explains all predications in terms of entities of one familiar functional kind.

We have been emphasizing the ontological neutrality of the truthmaker theory, not only because it is what enables traditional theists to meet the main challenges facing their view, but also because, as we now want to show, it is what enables them to go a considerable distance toward rehabilitating the doctrine of divine simplicity. Since this doctrine remains one of the most historically important and theologically influential expressions of the thesis at the core of traditional theism (namely, the aseity-dependence doctrine), this result ought to be of significant interest.

Truthmakers, Divine Simplicity, and the Category Problem

According to the traditional doctrine of divine simplicity, God is an absolutely simple being devoid of any form of metaphysical complexity whatsoever. Although this doctrine has its roots in antiquity, it received its most elaborate development and careful defense at the hands of philosophers and theologians during the Middle Ages. According to the medievals, this doctrine entails not only that God lacks the sort of complexity associated with the possession of material or temporal parts, but also that he lacks even the minimal form of complexity associated with the possession of properties. Thus, from the fact that God is simple, the medievals infer that God lacks any (intrinsic) accidental or contingent properties, and hence that all true predications of the form "God is (intrinsically) F" are cases of essential predication. And even in the case of essential predications, the medievals take the doctrine to have fairly radical consequences. Hence, from the truth of "God is divine," they infer that God is identical with his nature or divinity; from the truth of "God is good" they infer that he is identical with his goodness; and so on for every other such predication. And, of course, from the fact that God is identical with each of these things, they infer that each of these things is identical to each of the others.

Ever since the publication of Alvin Plantinga's (1980) *Does God Have a Nature?*, the literature on divine simplicity has been dominated by the discussion of a particular objection to its coherence. The alleged difficulty arises from the fact that the doctrine appears to entail the absurdity that God is identical with a property or exemplifiable. Predications such as "Socrates is wise" are widely assumed (and rightly in our opinion) to require the existence of such things as *Socrates's wisdom* or *wisdom* in general—that is, some entity that can serve as the referent for a so-called abstract singular term, such as 'wisdom'. (Terms such as 'wisdom' are called abstract singular terms because they are grammatically singular in number and function as the abstract counterparts of concrete terms such as 'wise'.) But what sort of entities could serve as the referents of abstract singular terms besides properties or exemplifiables? Without an answer to this challenge, we would appear to have no choice but to assume that endorsement of a predication such as "God is divine" commits defenders of divine simplicity (which requires that God is identical with his divinity) to the view that God is identical with the property of *being divine*. For the same reason, endorsement of divine predications such as "God is good", "God is powerful", and "God is wise" will commit such theists to the view that God is identical with the properties of *being good, being powerful,* and *being wise*—and indeed, by transitivity of identity, that each of these properties is identical with each of the others. And so on for every other such divine predication.

Now why does this identification of God with his properties seem so objectionable? Because one of the most *obvious* things about God is that he isn't an exemplifiable. Unlike universals, tropes, or property-instances, God is a person and persons aren't the sorts of thing that can be exemplified. The doctrine of divine simplicity, therefore, seems to be guilty of making a category mistake: it places a non-exemplifiable thing, a person, into the category of exemplifiables. Let's call this familiar objection to the doctrine of divine simplicity, 'the category problem'.

Now if the doctrine of divine simplicity could be stated in such a way that it avoided this problem, that would be a significant result for contemporary discussion of the doctrine. For, as we've just noted, worries about that problem have been the main focus of the recent literature on the topic. In what follows, we will explain how the truthmaker theory of predication presented at P*, and to which we were led by the arguments in Section I, enables proponents of the doctrine to avoid the category problem. As will emerge, the solution is to recognize that although defenders of divine simplicity must agree that God is identical with the referent of abstract singular terms such as 'God's goodness' or 'God's divinity', they need not construe the referents of such terms as exemplifiables.

From the perspective of the truthmaker theory of predication, there is nothing problematic about saying that God is identical with his nature, goodness, power, wisdom, or any other such things. To put the point more carefully, there is nothing problematic about saying that God is identical with the *referents of abstract singular terms* corresponding to each of the true intrinsic predications that can be made about him. For in light of the truthmaker theory developed above, there is a straightforward answer to the challenge raised earlier: "What could the referents of abstract singular terms be if not exemplifiables?" Just as the defenders of Platonism (or, more generally, P) typically assume that properties (or exemplifiables) are what serve as the referents of abstract singular terms, so too the defenders of the truthmaker theory (or P*) can maintain that truthmakers play this role. Thus, it is open to the defender of divine simplicity to say that the truthmaker for predications such as "God is divine" is also the referent for the abstract singular term 'God's divinity' or 'God's nature'. Indeed, if we reflect on the fact that expressions such as 'God's divinity' are the abstract nominalizations of predications such as "God is divine," we might expect them to refer to the truthmakers corresponding to such predications. For abstract nominalizations are typically introduced precisely for the sake of referring to the entities corresponding to their concrete counterparts. But if an expression such as 'God's divinity' is understood in this way, then to say that God is identical with his divinity will just be another way of saying that God is identical with the truthmaker for "God is divine." Likewise, to say that God is identical with his goodness, power, wisdom, and so on—and that each of these is identical with each of the others—will be the same as saying that there is only one truthmaker for each of the true intrinsic predications that can be made of God. Now suppose that the truthmaker in each case is God himself. Then to say that God is identical with his goodness is just to say that God is identical with God. Unlike the claim that God is identical with a property or exemplifiable, however, this claim is perfectly coherent.

The claim that God is the truthmaker for every true intrinsic predication of the form "God is F" not only provides a response to the category problem, but also seems to make the doctrine of divine simplicity attractive in certain ways. In order to see why, consider the sorts of intrinsic predication that can be made about God, beginning with "God is divine." Like any other statement involving the predication of a thing's nature, "God is divine" is a case of essential predication. But since God is essentially divine, his existing necessitates the truth expressed by "God is divine" (since if God is essentially divine, he will be divine in all possible worlds in which he exists). But, then, for the very same reason, God himself will be a plausible candidate for the role of the truthmaker of "God is divine."

Now as it turns out, similar remarks apply to other such divine predications. For as traditional theists conceive of him, God is not only good, but essentially good (or omnibenevolent); likewise, he is not only powerful, but also essentially powerful (or omnipotent). Indeed, *if* we accept that aspect of the traditional doctrine of divine simplicity that requires that all intrinsic predications of the form "God is F" are cases of essential predication,[33] then the same remarks will apply to each of the intrinsic or non-relational predications that can be made about God. This aspect of the doctrine is, of course, controversial and difficult to square with other aspects of traditional theism, which appear to imply that God has intrinsic accidental properties (say, in virtue of freely choosing to do certain things, including responding to human free choices). Our purpose here, however, is not to provide a complete defense of divine simplicity, but only to show that the truthmaker theory of predication (to which one is naturally led by the conclusions of our arguments in Section I) enables proponents of that doctrine to avoid the problem that has dominated contemporary discussion of it—namely, the category problem.

In the end, therefore, it seems to us that, whatever *other* difficulties the doctrine of divine simplicity might have, it can at least be defended against the standard charge of incoherence leveled by contemporary philosophers. Indeed, as we have attempted to show, if one grants to the defenders of this doctrine the (admittedly controversial) claim that all true divine intrinsic predications are cases of essential predication, the doctrine actually becomes somewhat appealing—at least when interpreted within the context of P*. Obviously this by itself does not give us reason to accept the doctrine. But we do hope it goes some distance toward showing that the doctrine deserves further consideration than it has yet received by contemporary philosophers. At the

---

[33] See e.g. Aquinas's remarks in *Summa Theologiae* Ia q. 3 a. 6 for a defense of this aspect of the doctrine.

very least, it shows that critical reflection on the doctrine needn't be focused entirely on the category problem.

Conclusion

We have now completed the two projects we set out to accomplish in the chapter: first, to provide a theistic argument against Platonism (as well as any other theory of predication that accepts P), and second, to show how this argument provides support for a certain theory of predication and, to a lesser extent, the doctrine of divine simplicity. We developed our theistic argument against Platonism in two stages. In the first stage, we argued for the inconsistency of Platonism with what we take to be the proper understanding of traditional theism. In the second stage, we argued that even if we are wrong about the proper understanding of traditional theism, and it can be understood in some weaker way, this is irrelevant from the point of view of its consistency with Platonism.

Although our theistic argument against Platonism proceeded fairly straightforwardly, the support we offered for truthmaker theory and divine simplicity is more indirect. As we suggested, the denial of Platonism seems to lead in the direction of a unified theory of predication, one that does *not* appeal to exemplifiables. Indeed, it seems to us that once traditional theists have jettisoned P (as they must if they are to remain traditional theists), a very attractive strategy—one that enables us to preserve a *unified account of predication*—is to accept P* in its place, and with it the view that truthmakers are required to explain the truth of predications. By itself, of course, the truthmaker theory of predication does not support the doctrine of divine simplicity. Nonetheless, it does enable us to make some progress toward understanding it—and more importantly, to remove what has been, at least in recent years, the greatest obstacle to this doctrine's being taken seriously by contemporary theists.

REFERENCES

Aquinas, Thomas (1980). *S. Thomae Aquinatis Opera Omnia*, 7 vols., ed. R. Busa (Stuttgart-Bad Canstatt: Friedrich Frommann Holzboog).
Armstrong, David (1978). *Universals and Scientific Realism*, 2 vols. (Cambridge: Cambridge University Press).
—— (1989). *Universals: An Opinionated Introduction* (Boulder, Colo.: Westview).

Armstrong, David (1997). *A World of States of Affairs* (Cambridge: Cambridge University Press).
Bigelow, John (1988). *The Reality of Numbers: A Physicalist's Philosophy of Mathematics* (Oxford: Clarendon).
Brower, Jeffrey (Unpublished). "Making Sense of Divine Simplicity".
Campbell, Keith (1980). "The Metaphysic of Abstract Particulars", in Peter A. French et al. (eds.), *Midwest Studies in Philosophy Volume VI: The Foundations of Analytic Philosophy* (Minneapolis: University of Minnesota Press), 477–88.
—— (1990). *Abstract Particulars* (Oxford: Basil Blackwell).
Fox, John (1987). "Truthmaker," *Australasian Journal of Philosophy* 65: 188–207.
Leftow, Brian (1990a). "God and Abstract Objects", *Faith and Philosophy* 7: 193–217.
—— (1990b). "Is God an Abstract Object", *Noûs* 24: 581–98.
Lewis, David (1999). *Papers in Metaphysics and Epistemology* (Cambridge: Cambridge University Press).
—— (2001). "Truthmaking and Difference-Making", *Noûs* 35: 602–15.
Loux, Michael J. (1978). *Substance and Attribute* (Dordrecht: D. Reidel).
—— (1998). *Metaphysics: A Contemporary Introduction* (London: Routledge).
Mann, William (1982). "Divine Simplicity", *Religious Studies* 18: 451–71.
—— (1983). "Simplicity and Immutability in God", *International Philosophical Quarterly* 23: 267–76.
Morris, Thomas V. (1987). "Absolute Creation", in Thomas V. Morris, *Anselmian Explorations* (Notre Dame, ind.: University of Notre Dame Press), 161–78. [Originally co-authored with Christopher Manzel and published in *American Philosophy Quarterly* 23(1986): 353–362.]
Mulligan, Kevin, Simons, Peter, and Smith, Barry (1984). "Truth-Makers", *Philosophy and Phenomenological Research* 44: 287–321.
Oliver, Alex (1996). "The Metaphysics of Properties", *Mind* 105: 1–80.
Plantinga, Alvin (1980). *Does God Have a Nature?* (Milwaukee: Marquette University Press).
Restall, Greg (1996). "Truthmakers, Entailment and Necessity", *Australasian Journal of Philosophy* 74: 331–40.
Rodriguez-Pereyra, Gonzalo (2000). "What is the Problem of Universals?", *Mind* 109: 255–73.
Smith, Barry (1999). "Truthmaker Realism", *Australasian Journal of Philosophy* 77: 274–91.
—— (2002). "Truthmaker Realism: Response to Gregory", *Australasian Journal of Philosophy* 80: 231–4.
van Inwagen, Peter (2004). "A Theory of Properties", *Oxford Studies in Metaphysics* 1: 107–138.
Wolterstorff, Nicholas (1970). *On Universals* (Chicago: University of Chicago Press).

13. Beautiful Evils

Hud Hudson

A FAMILIAR PROBLEM

Let 'E' be a proposition that precisely describes the amount, the intensity, and the distribution of all the so-called 'natural evil' consisting in the suffering of non-person animals that has ever occurred in the history of our universe.

Let 'G' be a proposition that asserts the necessary existence of an essentially omnipotent, essentially omniscient, essentially perfectly good being.

In the well-established tradition of those who believe that proper reflection on the problem of mere animal suffering can lead to a denial of the existence of God, let us put an initial question to a philosopher who affirms G: "Do you agree that there is such a proposition as E and that some of the conjuncts of E assert the existence of and describe genuinely horrific evils?" And let him not hide behind some grossly implausible claim that our mistaken impression that the world contains evil is simply due to our limited powers of insight into the real value of things. In other words, let him answer with a simple and straightforward, "Yes."

Further, let us ask our theist to endorse a conditional: "Do you agree that the conjunction of E and G is true only if there exists a compensating good for the evils described by E?—i.e. only if some state of affairs, S, obtains and is such that (1) for any state of affairs, S*, if S*'s obtaining is equivalent in value to or better than the obtaining of S, then it is metaphysically necessary that S* obtains only if some state of affairs equivalent in value to or worse than that described by E obtains, and (2) the obtaining of S is so valuable that it sufficiently compensates for the disvalue of the obtaining of the state of affairs described by E?"

I would like to thank Dean Zimmerman, Kris McDaniel, and Shieva Kleinschmidt for helpful criticisms and comments on an earlier draft of this chapter.

And once again (although the pressure to give an affirmative answer here is less severe than before—owing to such demanding constraints on 'compensating good'), let him reply with a simple and straightforward, "Yes."

Finally, in attempt to get him to relinquish his endorsement of G, let us ask our theist: "Do you agree that some of the conjuncts of E describe genuinely inscrutable evils?—i.e. evils for which we can identify no such compensating good?" And once again (although the pressure to answer in the affirmative continues to decline), let him present himself as a target with another simple and straightforward, "Yes."

Despite his willingness to give so much ground, any claim of victory over our theist would be premature at this juncture.[1] After all, conceding an inability to identify a compensating good for some acknowledged evil is not itself a concession of the non-existence of such a compensating good, and it is the latter not the former concession that would spell trouble for our unusually agreeable theist. In order to move so directly from our inability to identify a compensating good to its non-existence, we would need a bridging principle:

> (A) If there were a compensating good for the evils described by E, then we would be aware of it and would identify it as such.

Demonstrating (A) is a daunting task. But perhaps our theist's opponent can reasonably proceed with something seemingly easier to defend:

> (B) It is very probable that if there were a compensating good for the evils described by E, then we would be aware of it and would identify it as such.

And perhaps the most tempting route to a defense of (B) comes by way of backing an anti-skeptical premise:

> (C) We have good reason for thinking that the possible goods we know of are representative of the possible goods there are.

As an alternative to defending either (A) or else (B) and (C) and then making use of our theist's confessed inability in order to drive him

---

[1] Of course, the theist *need not* have given so much ground. For instance, a free will theorist who makes use of genuine risk or recalcitrant counterfactuals of freedom would countenance possible worlds having more good and less evil than ours owing to features of the world outside God's control. But the theist I have in mind is in a giving mood, and I am interested in just how expensive his gift really turns out to be.

either to inconsistency or unreasonableness, the theist's opponent might instead simply make a direct case for the non-existence of a compensating good for the evils described by E, and then infer the negation of G from E together with the need for (but lack of) a relevant compensating good.

In this chapter, I propose to assist the theist who is willing to give so much ground. In fact, the generosity of our theist (let us imagine) need not stop here. He is also willing to relinquish the thesis that (causal) incompatibilism is true, and thus (according to many of his cohorts) is reckless enough to jeopardize even the so-called free will defense as well. (Although appeals to natural evil are often designed so as to sidestep worries about the free will defense, those worries reappear as soon as one entertains the epistemic possibility that the suffering in question may be the result of the misuse of freedom by creaturely, non-human persons. Just to be on the safe side, then, let's explicitly close this route of retreat as well.)

My strategy for assisting the theist willing to give so much ground consists in presenting a metaphysically possible state of affairs whose obtaining could serve as a compensating good for the evils described by E. Moreover, I will provide good reasons to think (1) that (for all anyone knows) this state of affairs does obtain and serves as a compensating good—thus blocking the claim that we *know* there is no such compensating good, (2) that it is not very probable that if it were such a compensating good, then we would be aware of it and would identify it as such—thus *diminishing* (if not eliminating) any threat to the theist from (B), and (3) that one prominent reason to endorse the claim that we have good reason for thinking that the possible goods we know of are representative of the possible goods there are (i.e. the we've-looked-long- and-hard-defense) is inadequate—thus *diminishing* (if not eliminating) the prospects for a defense of (B) by way of establishing (C). I have no further ambitions for this chapter; it certainly contains nothing so grand as a theodicy or a defense of G.[2]

---

[2] The volume of literature on the so-called 'Problem of Evil' is staggering, and representative-citations are becoming unmanageable. Still, excellent work has been done and should be acknowledged. I think the strongest atheistic case that falls under this many-colored heading is what is known as the evidential argument from evil, superb discussions of which can be found by authors such as Rowe, Draper, Swinburne, Stump, Plantinga, Alston, Wykstra, van Inwagen, Russell, Gale, and Howard-Snyder—in Daniel Howard-Snyder's recent anthology, *The Evidential Argument from Evil* (Bloomington: Indiana University Press, 1996). The present essay is in the tradition of those just cited and

THE MUSEUM CURATOR STORY

A warm-up exercise will prove helpful: suppose you are to visit the Museum of Wondrous Things. Rumor has it that the museum's west wing is under the watchful eye of the ever-vigilant supreme artist. The supreme artist (if he exists at all) has total power over the existence and properties of any and all material objects in the west wing, knows all there is to know about how to bring it about that a given material object inhabiting the west wing exemplifies the finest aesthetically valuable properties that it is possible for that object to exemplify, and is motivated by his very nature to prevent or eradicate aesthetic disvalue as well as to create or maintain aesthetic value.

The problem is that the supreme artist (if he exists at all) seems to keep himself well-hidden (or at least many visitors profess not to see him), and thus doubts about his reality surface from time to time.

The day of your special visit arrives, and upon entering the Museum of Wondrous Things, you make straight for the west wing. But as you walk down the corridor you are startled to pass what appear to be a series of rather nondescript paper-like cut-outs wholly devoid of any aesthetic interest. Worse yet, as you move further into the interior of the west wing, you begin to wince at the rather ungainly and ridiculous flat figures you encounter at every turn. And finally (after some real investigating) you find yourself thoroughly repulsed by what you clearly recognize as some of the ugliest silhouettes you could have imagined—horrific uglinesses.

Sorely disappointed by your experience, you nevertheless take some satisfaction in thinking you learned one thing that made the visit worthwhile—there's no supreme artist who cares for the west wing! If he did exist (as described), what in the world could explain his permitting *this* aesthetic monstrosity or *that* one?

Before you can storm out of the west wing with your newly acquired opinions, however, your companions confess that they have played a practical joke on you. It turns out that they fitted your glasses with

presupposes a modest background, but then veers off sharply in an unexplored direction. Of course, theses (A), (B), and (C) have come under heavy scrutiny in these debates—with variants on (B) and (C) often taking center stage. For a careful and penetrating exchange on (C) in particular, see Michael Bergmann's paper, "Skeptical Theism and Rowe's New Evidential Argument from Evil", and William Rowe's reply, "Skeptical Theism: A Response to Bergmann", in *Noûs* 35/2 (2001), 278–96, 297–303.

special lenses, lenses that show only a two-dimensional cross-section of any three-dimensional artifact that happens to be lit by the kind of lights found only in the west wing. After finding your reserve pair of glasses you are able to see a collection of beautiful—stunningly beautiful—three-dimensional statues. In your new condition, it takes some concentrated exercise of imagination to remember the two-dimensional cross-sections you so recently took for the whole of the artistic pieces, but their presence (safely embedded in marble) seems of small consequence now. Moreover, (although the supreme artist who is in fact watching over your shoulder doesn't bother to explain this to you) it turns out that it is metaphysically necessary that aesthetic value of the sort had by the statue in front of you is realized in the world only if there is something aesthetically equivalent to or worse than the two-dimensional cross-section you viewed with your modified glasses. In other words, the horrific and inscrutable ugliness you saw moments ago was not a pointless ugliness—for it had a compensating beauty.

After some reflection, you come to realize that not every $n-1$-dimensional cross-section of an n-dimensional object need have the same aesthetic status as its host. A plurality of uglinesses may have a beautiful fusion.

A reminder—the goal I earlier set for myself was to present a metaphysically possible state of affairs whose obtaining could serve as a compensating good for the evils described by E. I have no desire to show that we have reason to think the state of affairs to be presented actually obtains—or even that it is probable that it obtains, given G. A generalized version of the lesson just extracted from The Museum Curator Story will soon play a central role in my attempt to accomplish my primary goal.

THE HERMIT FLATLANDER STORY

Another useful warm-up exercise: Imagine a hermit triangle in Flatland. Flatland is a two-dimensional plane space (i.e. a tile-shaped space, not a sphereshell-shaped space). The two-dimensional inhabitants of Flatland may move right and left or forth and back, but not up and down (at least not on their own power). The hermit prides himself on keeping at least eight inches away from any other polygon. But alas, our hermit doesn't realize that the plane on which he lives and moves is but one of an uncountably infinite stack of such planes. Our unfortunate hermit triangle is embedded in 3-space and has no idea that he is (at this very moment) only an inch from another triangle similarly confined to her plane (i.e. confined to a plane parallel to and an inch from the hermit's). Our hermit can acquire no evidence of this proximity through any investigation of his own, however, and so never becomes anxious about his condition. Still, even though our hermit cannot point or move in the direction of the offending triangle, he is in fact at a distance from her which is measured in the same units used to mark his distance from his own fellow Flatlanders.

Now suppose you and I are embedded in 4-space, and yet live and move about in our own 3-space cross-section. This supposition, I maintain, is metaphysically possible. By analogy with our hermit triangle's predicament, there is a direction in which neither you nor I can point or move, and along that direction are stacked uncountably many, non-overlapping 3-spaces. Here's the surprising bit: Choose some object in your visual field that lies only eight inches away from your eyes. In that mysterious direction you can neither point to nor move in, there are uncountably many, non-overlapping, big-as-you-please, three-dimensional regions—each of which has some subregions (and each of which may sport some inhabitants) that are closer to you than is whichever object you chose from your visual field. *Closer* in exactly the same units of measure, too—just inches away. Such recreational opportunities so close at hand! Of course, you might not be able to get to them (despite their proximity) without the help of some good natured 4-spacer—but don't ask for help. Unless he has truly miraculous powers, he'll never get you back home. Note that you or I could move our hermit triangle out of Flatland and into another space, but we'd have an awful time getting him back in his original plane. There are uncountably many targets, after all.

A FIRST ATTEMPT TO APPLY THE LESSONS: THE GOOD, THE BAD, THE BEAUTIFUL, AND THE UGLY

In reverse order from the section heading: first recall the metaphysically possible 4-space which consists of uncountably many, non-overlapping, big-as-you-please, 3-spaces. Suppose one of the 4-space subregions of this 4-space (a subregion that extends only a few feet in that direction in which neither you nor I can point or move) contains 3-space cross-sections each of which confines several inhabitants. Further suppose that among the prisoners of these 3-spaces, there are some fantastically ugly ones, some aesthetically indifferent ones, and no beautiful ones. Yet it is perfectly possible for some 4-space artist to position one such prisoner from each such 3-space so that although each prisoner remains confined to his own 3-space (perhaps light years away from any who share his prison), he is unknowingly just feet away from uncountably many strangers for whose existence and doings he can acquire no evidence whatsoever. Moreover, our 4-space artist might further arrange the strangers so that despite an ugly three-dimensional part here and there, he creates a stunningly beautiful four-dimensional statue. In fact, The Museum Curator Story could now be told one dimension up. Imagine the 4-spacers playing a similar trick on their friend who visits the 4-spacers' museum only to see aesthetically unimpressive three-dimensional cross-sections of four-dimensional aesthetic marvels.

That was the ugly and the beautiful. Now for the bad and the good.

Perhaps it is harder to see how there might be a two-dimensional evil than it is to see how there might be a two-dimensional ugliness. Hence, in the warm-up exercises, I concentrated on aesthetics. The general lesson of The Museum Curator Story, though, seems to transfer to other kinds of value as we move from a context of two-and three-dimensional objects to a context of three-and four-dimensional objects. That is to say, just as not every $n-1$-dimensional cross-section of an n-dimensional object need have the same aesthetic status as its host, so too, not every $n-1$-dimensional cross-section of an n-dimensional object need have the same value as its host. Just as a plurality of uglinesses may have a beautiful fusion, so too, a plurality of evils may have a valuable fusion.

Of course, there is no need to insist on literal fusions here (although I am happy to do so). We might have said that a plurality of material objects each of which is *non-F*, may be arranged in such a way that *F-ness* supervenes on certain features of the plurality (whether or not they compose anything). Or that a plurality of events each of which is *non-F*, may be so structured that *F-ness* supervenes on certain features of that plurality. Moreover, one obstacle to the suggestion that a property such as being beautiful may supervene on properties had by a plurality of objects—namely, that the objects might fail to have a certain crucial proximity to one another—is simply removed in the above discussion. The relevant objects or events can be arbitrarily close to one another.

A COMPENSATING GOOD FOR THE EVILS DESCRIBED BY E (FOR ALL ANYONE KNOWS)

No one (save our theist's God) even entertains proposition E, much less *knows* E to be true. Still, we take ourselves to be painfully aware of some of the outstanding conjuncts of E—propositions that describe horrors usually regarded as sufficiently well qualified to drive an argument against the theist all on their own. Consider as an example, then, some long-ago mammal who had the misfortune to tumble and fall into a ravine where its flesh was torn from its body by predators as it went to its death in agony.

What might we identify as a compensating good for this apparently inscrutable evil? Let us not retry the prospects of any familiar appeals to the value of freedom, or to the significance of various lessons free creatures might learn from reflecting on such misfortunes, or to the advantage of culling the herds and preventing worse pains, or to avoiding the harms of an irregular natural order in which such things don't occur. Instead let us look to The Museum Curator Story and to The Hermit Flatlander Story for strategy.

Suppose that our unfortunate mammal is embedded in 4-space, and yet lives and moves about in his own 3-space cross-section (a home he shares with us). This supposition, I maintain, is metaphysically possible. Accordingly (as before) there is a direction in which neither you nor I nor he can point or move, and along that direction are stacked uncountably many, non-overlapping 3-spaces. And (as before) we may further suppose that he is unknowingly just feet away from uncountably many strangers (each confined to its own 3-space cross-section and each just inches away). Finally (as before) we may further suppose that the event of our mammal's horrific death together with the events happening to and with and through various of his neighbors are so configured that certain value properties supervene on the plurality in question.

Which value properties? Aesthetic properties. I predict such a proposal will seem appalling to many, but here's why it might be worth a second thought. Most of us will grant that enduring a small amount of pain (acknowledged as an intrinsic evil) might yet be compensated for solely by aesthetic gain or by aesthetic gain together with assorted pleasures arising from the aesthetic gain when, for example, one experiences backache from standing stock still in a piece of performance art or when one returns home sore from a long day of walking the exhibit at the gallery. Significantly, many of us are not likely to retract this claim of sufficient compensation even if someone were to note that the dog who accompanied us (enjoying none of the artistic treasures) is likewise a bit sore.[3] Moreover, many of us will grant that the disvalue of this small amount of pain is commensurable with the disvalue of the great suffering of our mammal in the ravine—e.g. that it is—say—1/1,000,000th as bad. This pair of admissions, however, suggests that we should take the following supposition seriously. There exists some state of affairs the obtaining of which is so aesthetically valuable that it could sufficiently compensate for the disvalue of the great suffering of our mammal in the ravine. Of course, not everyone will see promising prospects for a comprehensive strategy here. Regardless of the popular intuition about the disvalue of the dog's soreness being commensurable with the disvalue of the suffering of the mammal in the ravine, one might well hold that there is some type of disvalue, K, such that some amount of K could not be compensated for by any amount of aesthetic value. Perhaps this strategy will be blunted a bit by the reminder that the evils currently in question are not moral evils, but instead the sufferings of non-person animals. Just to be clear—I am *not* suggesting that such suffering is insignificant; rather I am merely noting that there is a better case to be made for commensurability here than elsewhere. Still, let us record this as a worry and press on.

Prior to The Hermit Flatlander Story, we might have assented to this possibility but thought it of little interest, since it is so obvious that there is no such collection of objects or events anywhere in the vicinity of the event of our mammal's death. But after internalizing the lesson of The Hermit Flatlander Story, we might be a bit more cautious. Just as our hermit could have been unknowingly only inches away from uncountably many strangers for whose existence and doings he could acquire no evidence whatsoever, so too, you and I and the mammal in the ravine could also be so surrounded—without the slightest hope of detecting our neighbors in that direction in which we can neither point nor move. Moreover, prior to The Museum Curator Story, we might

---

[3] Don't balk yet. This is an *exceedingly* popular view, variants of which we encounter daily. The literature on the ethical treatment of non-person animals, for example, is overflowing with evidence that this position is the standard one—although (to be fair) such evidence is also regularly accompanied by lamentations about how eager we are not just to endorse this thesis but to exaggerate and exploit it.

have assented to this latter point too, but thought it of little interest, since it is just so hard to see what could be so valuable about a swarm of invisible things in the vicinity of this horrific death. But after internalizing the lesson of The Museum Curator Story, we might be a bit more cautious. Just as a stunningly beautiful three-dimensional statue may have a horrifically ugly two-dimensional cross-section, so too, a stunningly beautiful four-dimensional (plurality of) object(s) or array of events may have a horrifically natural-evil, three-dimensional cross-section. Furthermore, since there may be vastly many different fusions (or different pluralities) all of which overlap (or include) the death of our mammal in the ravine, we leave open the possibility that there are a sufficiently large number of overlapping but distinct objects or pluralities to exemplify the aesthetic value that will serve as a compensating good for this apparently inscrutable evil.

Do I believe that we have any good reason to think that certain evils of our world are always enveloped in such loveliness? No. Do I believe that their being so is probable, given G? No. Do I believe that such a story is metaphysically possible? Yes. Do I believe that anyone can acquire a justified belief that it is metaphysically possible to secure the value in question (or something equivalent in value or better) without permitting the evils in question (or something equivalent in value or worse)? No. Is it very probable that if this were, in fact, a compensating good for the evil of the death of our mammal in the ravine, then we would be aware of it and would identify it as such? No—for as with the hermit triangle, whether we are alone or in the midst of an uncountable horde of creatures is a question for whose answer we can acquire no evidence whatsoever. Should we think that we can establish that we have good reason for thinking that the possible goods we know of are representative of the possible goods there are by appealing to the fact that we have made an extensive and careful search of the territory available to us? No—for as with the hermit triangle, the territory available to us might be (at least) one dimension less than the total territory there is, and there is no reason to suppose that the goods realizable in n-dimensional space are representative of the goods realizable in $n+1$-dimensional space.

INDEX

Ackrill, J. L. 112 n. 1; 115 n. 6
Acquinas, T. 325; 346; 357; 359 nn. 4–5; 384 n. 33
Adams, M. 133 n. 25
Agustine 362
Albert, D. 129 n. 20
Allaire, E. 211 n. 14; 216 n. 21; 228n. 38
Alston, W. 389 n. 2
Anaxagoras 241 n. 55
Aristotle 112–117; 127; 135 n. 26; 207–214; 216–220; 222–227; 229–236; 238–240; 243–249; 330
Armstrong, D. M. 39; 137; 145–146; 148; 149; 151; 185 n. 19; 210–211; 215n. 19; 216 nn. 21–22; 221 n. 29; 227 n. 34; 233 n. 45; 235 n. 48; 236 n. 51; 238–239; 241 n. 56; 246 n. 65; 251; 252 nn. 4, 6–7; 253; 254–255 n. 11; 256 n. 14; 267; 273 n. 38; 277; 279–281; 283; 335 nn. 14–15; 338 n. 21; 339–340; 343–344; 360 n. 6; 376 nn. 24–25; 380
Arnauld 4
Austin, D. F. 26–27 n. 16; 36 n. 22
Ayer, A. J. 215 n. 29; 228 n. 36

Bach, K. 167 n. 6
Balog, K. 8 n. 5; 48 n. 31
Barnes, J. 207 n. 2
Barwise, J. 177 n. 13
Bell, J. S. 128 n. 19; 128–129
ben Yitzchack, S. 111–117; 124; 127; 130–135; 135 n. 26

Bergmann, G. 208 n. 4; 210–211; 216 nn. 21–22; 221 n. 29; 225 n. 32; 233 n. 44
Bergmann, M. 352 n. 37; 354 n. 38; 389–390 n. 2
Berkeley, G. 48 n. 31
Bigelow, J. 103–104 n. 1; 149–150; 264 n. 29; 274–275 n. 42; 280 n. 48; 376; 379 n. 30
Black, M. 3; 5–6; 13–18; 20–21; 228 n. 37
Block, N. 8 n. 5; 22 n. 13; 23 n. 14; 30; 34; 37 n. 23; 39; 40 n. 27; 57; 58; 66; 72; 74; 79–80; 82 n. 3; 83 n. 4; 85–89; 91–92; 94–96; 97–100
Bohm, D. 129
Bohr, N. 128
Boyd, R. 31–32
Boynton, R. 48 n. 31
Braddon-Mitchell, D. 105
Bradley, F. H. 345
Bricker, P. 260 n. 20; 274 n. 41; 282 n. 53
Broad, C. D. 103–104 n. 1; 104; 106–107
Brogaard, B. 138–139
Brower, J. E. 371 n. 20
Burge, T. 4 n. 2; 19; 23; 51; 62 n. 36; 63
Byrne, A. 19; 23; 33; 51

Campbell, K. 360 n. 6
Carey, S. 30
Carnap, R. 166
Casteñeda, H.-N. 215 n. 20; 238 n. 53

Casullo, A. 221 nn. 28–29
Chalmers, D. 3 n. 1; 8 n. 5; 12–13 n. 9; 17–18; 22 n. 13; 24; 28–30; 32n. 20; 35 n. 21; 35; 37; 57; 67 n. 38; 70–72; 88; 269–270 n. 35
Chisholm, R. 326 n. 3; 327
Chomsky, N. 39 n. 26
Code, A. 231n. 42
Cover, J. A. 373 n. 22

Davidson, D. 138 n. 2; 267 n. 3; 273 n. 38
Davies, M. 70
Descartes, R. 4; 145; 301
Devitt, M. 20
Dorr, C. 318 n. 32
Draper, P. 389 n. 2
Duns Scotus, J. 325
Dworkin, G. 30

Einstein, A. 127–128; 129
Evans, G. 96; 119–120 n. 9

Feigel, H. 40 n. 27
Field, H. 37 n. 23; 195–196; 309 n. 19; 314
Fine, G. 236 n. 51
Fine, K. 123 n. 13; 302 n. 14
Fischer, J. M. 133 n. 25
Fodor, J. 62 n. 36
Forrest, P. 137; 138 n. 3; 142; 151
Fox, J. 376 n. 27
Frege, G. 83–84; 96; 97–98

Gale, R. M. 389 n. 2
Goldbach, C. 310
Grelling, K. 187 n. 20

Hare, R. M. 267 n. 34
Hawthorne, J. 32 n. 20; 68
Hazen, A. P. 256 n. 14

Heisenberg, W. 128
Hempel, C. 39 n. 26
Hill, C. 3 n. 1
Hirsch, E. 120 n. 10
Hochberg, H. 228 n. 35
Hofweber, T. 163–165; 193 n. 25
Horgan, T. 9 n. 6; 269–270 n. 35
Horwich, P. 37 n. 23; 195–196
Howard-Snyder, D. 389 n. 2
Humberstone, L. 70
Hume, D. 141; 253; 273; 276–277; 283

Jackson, F. 3; 3 n. 1; 5; 10 n. 8; 11; 12–13 n. 9; 15–16; 35 n. 21; 43; 67–68; 79
Johnston, M. 300 n. 10

Kaplan, D. 296
Katz, J. 73
Keisler, H. J. 177 n. 13
Khlentzos, D. 137
Kim, J. 267n. 34; 269–270 nn. 35–36; 271 n. 37; 349 n. 34
King, J. 167 n. 6
Kneale, M. 115 n. 5
Kneale, W. 115 n. 5
Kosso, P. 128 n. 19
Kripke, S. 17–18; 22 n. 13; 24; 29; 31–32; 67–68; 71; 314; 317

Langton, R. 342
Leftow, B. 349 n. 33; 362 n. 9; 366 n. 15
Leibniz, G. 261; 282
Levine, J. 3 n. 1
Lewis, C. I. 73
Lewis, D. K. 39; 39 n. 25; 65; 84 n. 6; 103–104 n. 1; 119–120 n. 9; 138; 145; 151; 234 n. 47; 246 n. 65; 248 n. 66; 251 n. 1; 252 nn. 5–6; 253; 258 n. 15;

264 nn. 28–29; 273; 274–275 n.
42; 314–318; 342; 355–356;
379 n. 30
Lewis, F. A. 213 n. 18; 219 n. 26
Loar, B. 3 n. 1; 8 n. 5; 9 n. 6; 26;
32 n. 20; 44 n. 29; 45–46;
48 n. 31; 67–68
Lockwood, M. 129 n. 21; 130 n. 22
Loewer, B. 129 n. 20
Loux, M. 207 n. 2; 209 n. 5;
213 nn. 17–18; 217 n. 24;
225 n. 33; 228 n. 36; 230 n. 40;
236 n. 51; 326 n. 3; 337 n. 18;
338 n. 21; 360 n. 6
Ludlow, P. 332 n. 12
Ludwig, K. 47
Lycan, W. 9 n. 6

Mann, W. 360 n. 7
Markosian, N. 103–104 n. 1
Martin, C. B. 380
Martin, N. 332 n. 12
McCall, S. 142 n. 6
McGee, V. 118 n. 8; 125 n. 17
McGinn, C. 3 n. 1; 31; 32–33;
32 n. 20
McKinsey, M. 59
McLaughlin, B. 118 n. 8; 125 n.
17; 269–270 n. 35
McTaggart, J. M. E. 117
Menzel, C. 331 n. 11; 359; 363
Merman, N. D. 128 n. 19
Merricks, T. 103–104 n. 1;
122–124
Montero, B. 40 n. 27
Morris, T. 359; 360 n. 6; 362 n. 9;
363–366; 368; 369 n. 17
Mulligan, K. 137; 376 n. 24; 380
n. 32

Nagel, T. 58
Newton, I. 83

Nilda-Rümelin, M. 32 n. 20

Ockham, W. 133–134; 135 n. 26;
140; 277 n. 44; 325; 355
Oliver, A. 360 n. 7; 376 n. 27

Papinau, D. 8 n. 5; 23 n. 14;
40 n. 27
Parmenides 137; 141; 150–151
Pelletier, J. 193 n. 25
Perry, J. 3; 6 n. 4; 8–9; 12–13 n. 9;
13–18; 20–21; 29 n. 18; 31; 44;
79; 80; 84 n. 5
Plantinga, A. 209–210; 362 n. 9;
380; 389 n. 2
Plato 209–210; 337 n. 18;
338–339; 345; 357
Prior, A. N. 140
Pryor, J. 19; 23; 33; 51
Putnam, H. 62–64; 70; 72; 74; 339
Pythagoras 210

Quine, W. V. O. 73; 103–104 n. 1;
157; 211 n. 15; 255 n. 13; 314;
317; 350; 355

Ramsey, F. 256 n. 14
Rashi *see* ben Yitzchack, S.
Ratzsch, D. 328 n. 8
Rea, M. 235 n. 49; 373 n. 22
Restall, G. 274 n. 40; 278 n. 47;
377 n. 28
Rodriguez-Pereyra, G. 355 n. 39;
376 n. 27
Rowe, W. 389–390 n. 2
Rozemond, M. 4
Russell, B. (Bertrand) 96; 97; 139;
142; 148; 150–151; 209–210;
221 n. 28; 253; 256; 348;
357–358 n. 2; 362 n. 10
Russell, B. (Bruce) 389 n. 2
Ryle, G. 14

Scaltas, D. 246 n. 64
Schaffer, J. 3 n. 1; 5
Schiffer, S. 26 n. 16; 52; 159 n. 4; 303
Schmitt, F. F. 195–196
Searle, J. 199 n. 28
Sider, T. 103–104 n. 1; 106; 300 n. 10
Silins, N. 311 n. 22
Simons, P. 137; 215 n. 19; 376 n. 24; 380 n. 32
Skyrms, B. 253 n. 8
Smart, J. J. C. 3; 3 n. 1; 4–5; 6 n. 4; 7; 10; 31; 32 n. 20; 39; 41
Smith, B. 137; 138 n. 2; 138–139; 376 n. 24; 377 n. 28; 380 n. 32
Speusippus 209
Stalnaker, R. 72; 74; 84 n. 6
Stoljar, D. 39 n. 26
Strawson, P. 208 n. 4
Stump, E. 389 n. 2
Sturgeon, S. 9 n. 6
Swinburne, R. 348 n. 32; 389 n. 2

Tarski, A. 194
Thomason, R. 115 n. 5
Tooley, M. 103–104 n. 1; 106; 107; 327–328
Tye, M. 100 n. 3

van Fraassen, B. 115 n. 5
van Gulick, R. 9 n. 6; 10
van Inwagen, P. 357–358 n. 2; 389 n. 2

Wedin, M. 209 n. 5
White, S. 3; 5 n. 3; 19 n. 12; 28–30; 31; 32 n. 20; 38; 39; 41 n. 28; 42–43; 52; 56; 67 n. 38; 68–69; 99 n. 2
Whitehead, A. N. 147
Williams, D. C. 211 n. 13; 215 n. 20
Williamson, T. 113–114; 115 n. 4; 115 n. 5; 117; 118 n. 8; 120 n. 10; 123 n. 13; 124 n. 15; 124–126; 125 n. 17; 127; 130; 130 n. 22; 134; 289–290; 300 n. 10; 302; 303–307; 309–312; 318–320
Wiser, M. 30
Wittgenstein, L. 251
Wolterstorff, N. 207–210; 212; 214; 361 n. 8
Wykstra, S. 389 n. 2

Yablo, S. 156 n. 1; 342
Yourgrau, P. 112 n. 1

Zimmerman, D. 103–104 n. 1; 146; 149; 342 n. 25; 354 n. 38